Architects of Fortune

MIES VAN DER ROHE

Architects of Fortune

AND THE THIRD REICH

ELAINE S. HOCHMAN

WN

WEIDENFELD & NICOLSON
NEW YORK

Published by Weidenfeld & Nicolson, New York
A Division of Wheatland Corporation
841 Broadway
New York, New York 10003-4793

Published in Canada by General Publishing Company, Ltd.

Portions of this book in an early version were published in *Oppositions*
and *Sites*.
Grateful acknowledgment is made to *The Architectural Review* for
permission to quote from "Mies Speaks" which appeared in the December
1968 issue; the M.I.T. Visual Arts Center for permission to quote from *The
Bauhaus* by Hans M. Wingler; and to the University of Chicago Press for
permission to quote from *Mies van der Rohe: A Critical Biography* by
Franz Schulze, © 1985 by Franz Schulze. All rights reserved.

Library of Congress Cataloging-in-Publication Data

Hochman, Elaine S.
    Architects of fortune: Mies van der Rohe and the Third Reich
       p.   cm.
    Bibliography: p.
    Includes index.
    ISBN 1-55584-182-1
    1. Mies van der Rohe, Ludwig, 1886–1969—Criticism and
interpretation.   2. National socialism and architecture.
3. Architecture, Modern—20th century—Germany. I. Title.
NA1088.M65H6   1989   88-29409
720'.92'4—dc19   CIP

Manufactured in the United States of America

This book is printed on acid-free paper

Designed by Irving Perkins Associates

First Edition

10 9 8 7 6 5 4 3 2 1

EXPERIENCE HAS SHOWN THAT TO BE TRUE WHICH APPIUS SAYS IN HIS VERSES, THAT EVERY MAN IS THE ARCHITECT OF HIS OWN FORTUNE.

—**Sallust** (86–35 BC), Speech to Caesar on the State

For my father, in loving memory

ACKNOWLEDGMENTS

This book is primarily indebted to Professor Dore Ashton, who not only suggested its subject, but whose advice, encouragement, and support sustained me over its fifteen-year course. I am also grateful to Mr. Albert Speer, who, for nearly a decade, kindly shared with me his intimate acquaintance with Hitler, the leading figures of the Third Reich, and the regime's architectural practices; reviewed all phases of the book for historical accuracy; and suggested the names of individuals and institutions who could offer additional assistance. This book would not have been possible without his help. As always, Mr. Philip Johnson was endlessly generous and illuminating in his commentaries on Mies, which took place over the course of several years. I was also the fortunate recipient of the assistance of Ms. Stephanie Golden, whose collaboration was critical to the book's present form; and to the probing critique of Mr. John Herman of Weidenfeld & Nicolson, and my editor, Mr. William B. Strachan, who further refined the substance and kept me from straying too far afield.

I am indebted to the following individuals for their suggestions and responses to my queries: Mr. Howard Dearstyne, Mrs. Anni Albers, Mr. Herbert Bayer, Mrs. Ise Gropius, Mrs. Nina Kandinsky, Mr. Hans Weidemann, Mr. Otto Andreas-Schreiber, Professor Herbert Hirche, Mr. Egon Hüttmann, Mr. Herbert Rimpl, Mr. Sergius Ruegenberg, Mr. Marcel Orphuls, Mr. John B. Rodgers, Mr. Stanley W. Resor, Jr., Mr. Bertrand Goldberg, Dr. Doris Schmidt, Professor Erich Fromm, Professor and Mrs. Ludwig Grote, Mr. Hans Keszler, Professor Peter Selz, Mrs. Margaret Nissan, Dr. Martin Urban, Professor Peter Gay, Professor Hans Gatzke, Mr. Gerhard Weber, Professor Henry-Russell Hitchcock, Mrs. Margaret Scolari-Barr, Mr. Edward D. Stone, Mrs. Marianne Lohan, Dr. Paul Esters, Professor Reyner Banham, Mr. Erich Holthoff, and members of the Verseidag Executive Board, Dr. Hans Wingler and Dr. Christian Wolsdorff.

Many institutions made their invaluable resources and staff available to me, for which I am most grateful: The New York Public Library, the Library of Congress, the Bundesarchiv, the Aachen Stadtarchiv, the Akademie der Künste (successor to the Prussian Academy of Arts), the Institut für Zeitgeschichte, the Berlin Document Center, the Library and Mies van der Rohe Archive of the Museum of Modern Art, and the Avery Architectural Library of Columbia University.

I am indebted to Mrs. Lily DiStefano for her patient typing of the manuscript. To my children, Elizabeth, Andrew, and Russell, goes my deepest appreciation for all the sacrifices they were called on to make. And to my husband, Ray, I can only express my profoundest gratitude for his endless patience, support, and understanding, without which this book would never have been written.

CONTENTS

PREFACE

SO LANG NOCH "UNTER'N LINDEN"
DIE ALTEN BÄUME BLÜHN,
KANN NICHTS UNS ÜBERWINDEN,
BERLIN BLEIBT DOCH BERLIN.

SO LONG AS THE OLD TREES STILL
BLOOM ON UNTER DEN LINDEN,
NOTHING CAN VANQUISH US—
BERLIN REMAINS BERLIN.

(**Walter Kolo,** Popular Berlin song written for the revue *Drunter und Drüber*)

In the 1930s, the place where I stood had been known as Potsdamer Platz. Now, in 1980, it lay quiet and barren, a weed-filled wasteland, without pavement, cobblestones, street signs, or any mark to bear witness to the activity that had once surged along its stony course. Only the shell of a building—"Hotel Bellevue" marked in fading black letters down its side—served notice that things had once been different.

I had come to Berlin in search of the enigmatic Mies van der Rohe, the great German architect, who had called this city his home for over three decades. Although a great deal had been written about him, much about Mies and his art remained a mystery. He was a bulky man, of awesome physical presence, who preached that "less is more"; a man of humble and unlearned background who spoke of grave profundities; the creator of an architectural style of extraordinary luxury and finesse of detail that was born out of the simple factory shed; and a professed rationalist who elevated his art to a form of visual poetry. What especially interested me were the years he spent under Hitler—1933 until Mies's departure in 1937—four years during which, despite all that has been written about him, he remains essentially unknown. Was Mies's own silence about this difficult period simply a manifestation of his generally uncommunicative nature ... or was there something he was trying to hide? Did he try to work for the Nazis? Did his efforts to remain in Germany practicing his profession differ from what others were doing or attempting to do? This book is an inquiry into those forgotten years, and the events and incidents that led him, with overwhelming sadness, to decide to leave his homeland.

Rumors of efforts by Mies to gain architectural commissions from the Nazi government began even before his death in Chicago in 1969. In May 1964, at a session of the Symposium of Modern Architecture held at Columbia University, Sibyl Moholy-Nagy spoke of Mies's "desperate attempts to play up to National Socialism. . . . When he accepted in July 1933, after the coming to power of Hitler, the commission for the Reichbank he was a traitor to all of us and a traitor to everything we had fought for." She also spoke of Mies's signing "a patriotic appeal . . . to the artists, writers, and architects of Germany to put their forces behind National Socialism. I would say," she continued, "that, of the leading group of Bauhaus people, Mies was the only one who signed. This was a terrible stab in the back for us."[1]

Ten years after Mies's death, Ise Gropius, widow of Walter Gropius, the founder of the Bauhaus, also spoke of Mies's signing a published statement urging the support of Hitler.[2] Ascribing these accusations to the protestations of embittered, cantankerous women, jealous over the American success of their husbands' rival, the architectural community virtually ignored their comments.

Mies himself, never prone to excess in prose or construction, rarely spoke about himself or his German past. "It is not possible to move forward and look backwards," he had written in 1924; "he who lives in the past cannot advance."[3] This credo became the virtual hallmark of his American life. As with so many German refugees, the truth was far more complex than he or they cared to admit.

Most Americans prefer to believe that those who fled Nazi Germany were moral heroes who sacrificed life and limb in the pursuit of freedom. In fact, it is difficult to find Germans who left their homeland purely out of a sense of moral indignation. One has to search far and wide to find someone—anyone— who did not leave under threats, real or implied, or for reasons of race, religion, political beliefs, inability to find a job, or to practice one's profession. Some of those forced into exile admired Hitler; some were even among his most ardent supporters. This falsely idealistic framework within which most Americans have viewed the German émigrés, combined with Mies's reticent nature, has tended to distort the perception of the reason for his departure from Nazi Germany. He left not because he opposed Hitler, but because Hitler had very strong architectural views. Mies left, in fact, because Hitler fancied himself an architect.

Few architects have engendered so much praise during their lifetime and so much censure after their death as Mies van der Rohe. Although he is universally regarded as one of the creators of modern architecture—his "skyscraper" style straddles the globe—opinions regarding the aesthetic and moral implications of this style are less unanimous. While the refinement of his architectural vision, his sensitivity toward materials, and urge for perfection have been lauded, his authoritarian instincts, single-mindedness, and refusal to acknowledge the validity and diversity of human claims have been vigorously criticized and have triggered, to a great extent, much of the disrepute into which modernism has fallen since his death.[4]

It is not enough simply to admire the grandeur and beauty of Mies's architectural vision: we must also understand the moral principles upon which it is based. If we wish to share the glories of his architectural ideals, we must also bear the burden of their moral imperatives. We all live in Mies's glass houses. Universal acceptance of the "Miesian" style bears witness to our complicity, however secret and unacknowledged, in its moral principles. By examining the nature of the relationship between Mies and the Nazis, we gain insight not only into his architecture, but into our own moral assumptions.

Mies built as he lived: the principles that underlay his architecture were also the cornerstones of his life. Thus the events that took place during the four years that he spent in Nazi Germany offer possible insight into his art. The question is not whether or not Mies was a Nazi sympathizer, "a traitor to us all" as Mrs. Moholy-Nagy proposed, or an aesthetic innocent struggling vainly to pursue his noble craft, as Philip Johnson suggested. Instead, we should ask what it was in Mies's outlook that permitted him, encouraged him perhaps, to ignore the moral degeneracy around him, and examine the relevance of such obliviousness to both the praise and criticism his architecture has generated. In doing so, we must work against our abhorrence of the Nazis and reprobation of the vast majority of Germans, who, like Mies, chose to "go along," while taking care that our admiration of Mies's genius does not impel us to forgive too much.

I do not wish to malign Mies, but to understand him, his architecture, and his times; and through this understanding, perhaps to grasp an attitude that he shared with so many of his fellow countrymen. Mies has earned his place in history as a great architect, and it is as an architect that he must be judged. His stature as a creator of our time remains undiminished. In the mirror of history, we search not only for Mies and his Berlin, but for ourselves as well.

PART I

CHAPTER 1

PRELUDE: HITLER'S WEATHER

FOR CONTEMPORARIES ENTANGLED . . . IN THE INEXORABLE
DEMANDS OF DAILY LIFE, THE DIVIDING LINE BETWEEN ERAS
MAY BE HARDLY VISIBLE WHEN THEY ARE CROSSED; ONLY
AFTER PEOPLE HAVE STUMBLED OVER THEM DO THE LINES
GROW INTO WALLS WHICH IRRETRIEVABLY SHUT UP THE PAST.

(**Hannah Arendt**, "Home to Roost: A Bicentennial Address")

The springlike warmth that descended on Berlin shortly after
the March 1933 elections was known as "Hitler's weather."
Usually, the months that lay between the snow-glittering, crisp
winter days and the first green of May were most disagreeable;
this year was different. Already in the second week in April the
sidewalks in front of the small cafés were crowded with tables.
"We can thank van der Lubbe," went the joke making the
rounds in the Berlin cafés that week. "His Reichstag fire
melted all the snow."[1] Real Berlin humor . . . enjoy, savor, but
take nothing seriously. Nice weather in April and the promises
of politicians: they were all the same.

Along the Grosse Frankfurter Strasse, one of the seemingly
endless boulevards that linked the sprawling city of Berlin,
a tram clanged noisily. Ocher-stuccoed housing, now grime-

covered and peeling, lined both sides of the street; pots of geraniums on the balconies provided the single touch of cheer. Behind the dark entryways, past the rows of rusted mailboxes, lay steep and narrow courtyards into whose depths the noon-day sun never penetrated. Inside these *Mietskasernen*, packed from cellar to attic, lived the workers of Berlin. Tall and straight these buildings presented themselves to the world, yet inside they bowed and leaned toward each other like tired tin soldiers. Buried in this labyrinth of courtyards, with their sour smell of cabbage and urine, children played or sat on the stoops trying to catch a glimpse of the narrow strip of blue sky high above. An occasional black, white, and red flag hung motion-less from a window.

Gone for the past month were the red flags of the hammer and sickle—the companions of the swastikas, which had so long accompanied their neighbors in these windows. Now they lay hidden under mattresses, or—if their owners were smart—in the garbage bins. Gone also were the badges of the nonna-tionalist parties that had been worn so proudly only the month before. It was as if an entire segment of convictions no longer existed. On the blistering sooty courtyard walls, fading chalk marks of the hammer and sickle and, occasionally, scrawled fragments of the slogan *"Erst Essen—dann Miete"* ("First food, then rent!") bore mute testimony of the winter's trials.

At Alexanderplatz, one of the working-class centers of Ber-lin, poverty and unemployment had made the vast square even more bustling than usual: with little else to do, great numbers of idle and aimless people gave themselves up to every impres-sion that offered itself, imbuing this Nordic vista with a lan-guid, almost Mediterranean air. The shop windows; street vendors; kiosks; troops of uniformed men on horseback, foot, or automobile were all excuses to stop and watch. Here the unemployed and forgotten men of Berlin came to lounge, fight, go to the urinals, pick up cigarette stubs from the gutters, listlessly look for work, or play checkers at the Labor Exchange. Not only were there fewer peddlers and street singers than in the old days, but their more imaginative activ-ities had ceased. The singing of folk songs or opening of car doors for a few *Groschen* no longer paid: no one had any change to spare.[2]

"Hoek van Holland" and "Oświęcim" proclaimed the signs on the sides of the S-Bahn that roared overhead. The recently completed U-Bahn disgorged more crowds from its canyons below the street. At least, mused the world-weary Berliners, one's life was now endangered only by the traffic and not by the nightly street fights that had taken place here last winter between the Nazis and the communists, to which the pitmarks in the tall yellow and green buildings and kiosks under the shadows of the elevated railway bore grim and silent testimony.

Two of Berlin's most democratic institutions were located on Alexanderplatz, both catering—without discrimination—to rich and poor alike: Aschinger's, the *"Restaurant-Konditorei aller Berlin,"* and "Big Alex," the sprawling red-brick building that served as headquarters for the Berlin police and, now, the newly established gestapo.

Aschinger's had made its name during the socialist Weimar government's takeover from the Kaiser after World War I with its offer of "all the free bread you can eat," a tradition that had continued and was, at the moment, much appreciated. Consumption of its beer sausages was considered a veritable barometer of bourgeois stability. In 1925, when Hindenburg had become president, consumption had increased from 40,000 to 65,000 pairs. At the moment, the total was dropping.

Since 1886, "Big Alex" had served as headquarters for the Berlin police, its grim, sprawling structure an appropriately gloomy symbol of its pervasive presence in the lives of the city's residents. From determining the proper angle of crossing the street to the identification of ladies' hat pins as a public hazard, few aspects of life escaped police scrutiny. Surviving the zealotry of their police was a source of gleeful pride to Berliners of all castes. Among the comics on Friedrichstrasse, a well-turned comment about the latest police regulation was always good for a few laughs.

No ugly tracks or unnerving noises jarred the sensibilities of those imbibing at Kranzler's or Bauer's, Berlin's most fashionable cafés on the Unter den Linden. Here, and along the surrounding streets, were located the smart shops, elegant hotels, cafés, and ponderous buildings—a parliament house, an opera, museums, a domed cathedral, embassies, churches, and a triumphal arch—that stamped Berlin as a true *Weltstadt.* Now, under the warm April sun, the worries of the winter—the political chaos, the roving bands of hoodlums, and ceaseless gun battles—seemed but a distant memory. Faced with the apparent choice of anarchy or communist revolution, many of the well-off people sitting at these cafés had backed Hitler, confident that President Hindenburg would keep him and his band in their place. Basking on the sunny terrace of the Linden and enjoying the music, flowers, and ice cream, they seemed reconciled to sharing their favorite haunts with the upper echelons of a party that still reeked of the beer halls of Munich. Even the swank Adlon Hotel considered itself fortunate to claim the patronage of the new chancellor, Herr Hitler, who visited periodically to indulge his passion for whipped cream and chocolate.

Along Leipzigerstrasse, one of the great retail business streets of the city, the sparkling window displays alternated with coarsely drawn stars of David. *"Kauft nicht bei Juden!"* ("Don't shop at Jewish stores!") read the signs, tattering now at the edges. *"Deutsche! Wehrt Euch!"* ("Germans! Defend yourselves!") The smashed windows, dating from the April 1 boycott of Jewish stores, had been cleaned up by now: but many shops were still boarded up, their proprietors in jail or the hospital or, perhaps, out of the country.

Brown-shirted storm troopers were everywhere, their faces serious and set, distributing pamphlets, soliciting funds, or merely striding purposefully along the street. Several of them stationed themselves prominently in front of stores, evidently intending to hinder any customers who might be inclined to enter. Most people paid them no heed.

At Potsdamer Platz, the pavement of the sidewalks was dirty and uneven, the asphalt worn out and mended with paving stones. The storefronts mirrored the dilapidation of the streets; there was no money to repair anything. Berlin was in rags and tatters. One could see its poor, sandy Brandenburg soil through the holes in the pavement and, when the gusts blew, as they frequently did, feel its sting in one's eyes.

It was here that Mies waited for a tram. A mountain of a man, the son and grandson of stonemasons, he stood nearly two meters tall and half that in breadth. "If you see two men coming towards you, and it turns out to be one, it's Mies," joked his students.[3] He moved slowly, with deliberation, yet he did not lack grace. His presence dominated, overpowered the space around him: he seemed totally withdrawn into the depths of himself, unconcerned with the intensity of this personal radiating force. Now forty-seven years old, his enormous body and sharply chiseled features, seemingly carved out of some primeval block of granite, were going fleshy. Germany's foremost architect, he was on his way to its foremost school of art, the Bauhaus, which he headed.

The tram clattered along Potsdamer Strasse, where the posters on the kiosks lining the sidewalks screamed *"Deutschland erwacht!"* ("Germany awake!"); *"Wahlt Kommunisten!"* ("Vote Communist!") answered their fading neighbors. The tram veered southward now toward Nollendorfplatz. Mies's eyes, sharp behind their heavy, fleshy lids, took in the scene, his artistic preoccupations shielding him from the disarray on the street. The swastikas that hung from some of the windows were but a decorative device to him, like climbing ivy that covered up architects' mistakes.

The tram stopped at Nollendorfplatz; beyond lay Kleiststrasse. Honeycombed with countless decrepit and run-down bars, dance halls, cabarets, and movie houses in dreary imitation of Montmartre and Manhattan, the neighborhood displayed Berliners' preference for culture by osmosis ... for pseudo-French, fake American, neo-everything and nothing. Basking in the reflected glory, refinement, and accomplishments of others, the area bespoke a persistent and undeniable cultural insecurity.

At Birkbuschstrasse, Mies got off the tram; there he waited for another to take him over the canal. He was in the Berlin suburb of Steglitz which, despite the numerous factories that lined the canal banks, still retained the languor and leafy freshness of the countryside.

Mies always enjoyed this particular segment of his daily trip. "The working atmosphere which surrounds us suits us completely," he had said, ". . . especially because the path from the building into nature is not far."[4]

Haussuchung im „Bauhaus Steglitz"
Kommunistisches Material gefunden.

Auf Veranlassung der Dessauer Staatsanwaltschaft wurde gestern nachmittag eine größere Aktion im „Bauhaus Steglitz", dem früheren Dessauer Bauhaus, in der Birkbuschstraße in Steglitz durchgeführt. Von einem Aufgebot Schutz-

war jedoch verschwunden, und man vermutete, daß sie von der Bauhausleitung mit nach Berlin genommen worden waren. Die Dessauer Staatsanwaltschaft setzte sich jetzt mit der Berliner Polizei in Verbindung und bat um Durch-

Alle Anwesenden, die sich nicht ausweisen konnten, wurden zur Feststellung ihrer Personalien ins Polizeipräsidium gebracht.

polizei und Hilfspolizisten wurde das Grundstück besetzt und systematisch durchsucht. Mehrere Kisten mit illegalen Druckschriften wurden beschlagnahmt. Die Aktion stand unter Leitung von Polizeimajor Schmahel.

Das „Bauhaus Dessau" war vor etwa Jahresfrist nach Berlin übergesiedelt. Damals waren bereits von der Dessauer Polizei zahlreiche verbotene Schriften beschlagnahmt worden. Ein Teil der von der Polizei versiegelten Kisten

suchung des Gebäudes. Das Bauhaus, das früher unter Leitung von Professor Gropius stand, der sich jetzt in Rußland aufhält, hat in einer leerstehenden Fabrikbaracke in der Birkbuschstraße in Steglitz Quartier genommen. Der augenblickliche Leiter hat es aber vor wenigen Tagen vorgezogen, nach Paris überzusiedeln. Bei der gestrigen Haussuchung wurde zahlreiches illegales Propagandamaterial der KPD. gefunden und beschlagnahmt.

Newspaper article concerning the police search and closing of the Berlin Bauhaus on April 11, 1933, appearing in the *Lokal-Anzeiger* (Berlin) on April 12, 1933 (Bauhaus-Archiv)

Although he had not yet reached Siemensstrasse, his final destination, he decided to disembark from the tram and walk across the bridge, enjoying the tranquillity of the softly flowing canal, with its *Kanalforellen* (canal trout) that occasionally swam by. Here, in the refreshing silence of nature, he could think.

Like so many of his friends, Mies did not take the Nazis too seriously. *"Ver-führer"* (mis-leader, seducer) was how his friend, the painter Max Beckmann, referred to Hitler.[5] Like many, Mies was convinced that the Nazi government would not last. After all, Hitler's predecessor, the far more experienced Kurt von Schleicher, had spent a scant fifty-seven days in office.

As he turned left on Siemensstrasse, the peaked roof of the Bauhaus came into view. The grimy, red-brick building and the gravelly lot that served as the school's athletic field lay hidden behind a dilapidated wooden fence. The faculty had decided to keep the ugly fence for the moment—better to keep their activities from prying and unfriendly eyes. In better days, they would tear it down: the Bauhaus had nothing to hide.

It was noon now and the students would be sprawled, eating lunch or enjoying the spring sun, beneath the scraggly trees. Others might be kicking a soccer ball, and a few would have wandered over to the canal that ran behind the school building.

But today—April 11, 1933—there was no laughter, no heckling, no clever taunts. Surrounding the building were hundreds of black-uniformed gestapo troops, their bayonets bared and glistening in the sun. Mies stopped dead in his tracks.

CHAPTER 2

A STRANGE DUALITY

THE MIND IS ITS OWN PLACE, AND
IN ITSELF
CAN MAKE A HEAV'N OF HELL, A
HELL OF HEAV'N.

(**John Milton,** *Paradise Lost*)

By 1933 Mies van der Rohe was recognized, both at home and abroad, as Germany's greatest architect. In the space of a few years—fewer, according to Philip Johnson, than any other architect—Mies literally invented a new architecture.[1] His 1921 Friedrichstrasse skyscraper design—the technology to build it not yet in existence—pointed the way toward the modern skyscraper that has come to define the very essence of the twentieth-century city around the world, and his villa designs of 1923–24, with their freely floating, planar space, irrevocably altered the notion of architecture as space-defining and enclosing masses. These revolutionary concepts pushed Mies to the forefront among his architectural peers—a position secured by his leadership roles in the respected Deutsche Werkbund and the Weissenhofsiedlungen of 1927,

10

ies van der Rohe, perspective of the Friedrichstrasse Office Building project,
Berlin, 1921 (Collection, Mies van der Rohe Archive, the Museum of Modern Art,
New York. Gift of Ludwig Mies van der Rohe)

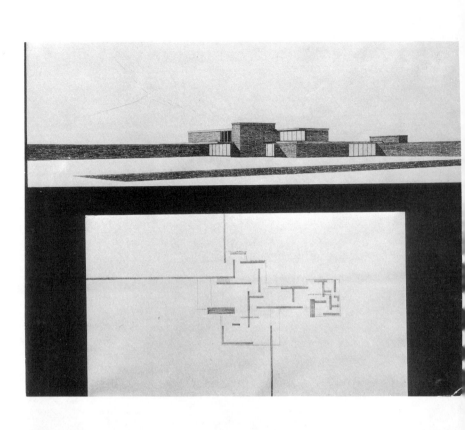

Mies van der Rohe: top, perspective and plan of the Brick Country House, 1924; below model of the Concrete Country House from the garden side, 1923 (Photo courtesy Mies van der Rohe Archive, the Museum of Modern Art, New York)

the Werkbund's major exposition of modern community design. His Reich Pavilion, built for the International Exposition in Barcelona in 1929, brought to dazzling realization the concepts he had earlier articulated in his villa drawings. Universally hailed as the most lyrical and successful demonstration of the new "modernist" architectural style, it brought him international recognition, a preeminence reaffirmed with his appointment as director of the famed Bauhaus in 1930 and the completion, that same year, of the Tugendhat House in Brno, Czechoslovakia. The Museum of Modern Art's landmark architectural exhibition of 1932, where the new architecture first received its name—"the International Style"—and was hailed as being "as original, as consistent, as logical, and as widely distributed as any in the past," brought Mies's name before the world.[2]

But nothing about Mies, neither his person nor his architecture, was quite as it seemed. He cut an elegant, finely tailored figure, yet he was of humble, peasant stock: a Brueghelian peasant (his build and massive, well-padded hands told that) turned out as a Renaissance prince. An advocate of an architectural style born of the simple frugalities of the factory, his architecture was synonymous with "luxe"—marbles, onyx, stainless steel, and impeccable (and costly) craftsmanship. His fame rested on a scant handful of projects—few of which had been built and his most renowned, the Barcelona Pavilion, no longer existed.[3] Yet, his actual buildings—exceeding in number those for which he became known but not publicized by him—were villas for the wealthy that did nothing to advance the state of the art and were almost indistinguishable from what had been built in Berlin since the turn of the century. He was not above saying one thing and building another.

He prided himself on his ability to concentrate, to remove himself in thought from the distractions of this world. Yet, his fleshy, ample, well-fed, and well-wined frame bespoke little abstinence from the delights of the senses. He appeared before the world as an intellectual, a profound thinker, a man of few, but salient, words. And yet, according to Philip Johnson, Mies's highest words of praise for any building were "This building is really built!"—an affirmation of the senses, not the intellect.[4] Despite his remarks regarding "truthfulness . . . to the spirit of the age" and statements of apparent philosophical profundity, what mattered to him finally came down to that sense, felt in the hands falling lovingly across the stones and immediately apparent to the eye, of a building well put together.

Even his name was not his own. He was born Maria Ludwig Michael Mies. "Mies" has many meanings in German—none of them positive—from "mussel" to "seedy," "miserable," "awkward," "awful," or "bad." In the early 1920s, when it appeared clear that such a name was unequal to his ambition, he adopted his mother's name "Rohe," to which he added "van der" (its Dutch "van" bearing not unpleasant intimations of the aristocratic German "von"), as well as an umlaut over the "e" in "Mies," transforming it into the un-Germanic "Mi-es," two syllables instead of one. As Ludwig Miës van der Rohe, he presented himself to the world. He was, as he proudly confided to his daughter Georgia, not simply a self-made man, but a "self-created one."[5] But like the peasant core of his aristocratic bearing, the factory that lay at the base of his elegant architectural style, or the explosive temper that lay beneath the visage of cerebral distance, simple "Mies" lay behind the mellifluous nomenclature by which he wished to be known to history.

Mies was born in Aachen on March 27, 1886, the fifth and last child (an earlier son had died in infancy; two daughters and an older son, Ewald, survived) of Michael and Amalie Mies. Whatever Mies was, or would become, lay here in this birthplace of the Reich, the frontier between the Latin and Germanic worlds. "Aachen has given me much," Mies once said.[6]

His father was a master stonemason charged with the restoration and maintenance of the stonework on Aachen's architectural masterwork, the Great Dom, built by Charlemagne around 800. Of humble circumstances and ambition, it was a family whose sons automatically followed in the stonemason tradition; the home fostered simple tastes, was devoid of books and worldly aspirations.[7]

As a young child, Mies accompanied his mother on her daily trips to the Dom, where she brought his father his midday meal. From the dark, mean spaces of the family home on Steinkaulstrasse, where he was born, with its gloomy, narrow staircase; plain, cobblestoned courtyard; and laundry flutter-

Mies's birthplace, Steinkaulstrasse 29, Aachen (*Aachener Volkszeitung*)

ing from the windows, they would turn down Adelbertstrasse,
past the signs pointing to Liège, Maestricht, Brussels, and Lux-
embourg and the neat displays of Bauern Holländer, Echte
Gouda, and Holländischer Edamer. Suddenly, the vast bulk of
the city's cathedral, Charlemagne's *Wunderbau*, as the Dom
had always been called in Aachen, loomed ahead, its towering
spires, huge dome, and tall peaked roof dominating the horizon. At the intersection of Ursulinerstrasse, it disappeared
from sight, only to reappear again, as magically and as unexpectedly, at Münsterplatz, where one could touch its mighty

Cathedral and Münsterplatz, Aachen, about 1910 (Stadtarchiv Aachen)

flanks. In later years, Mies often spoke of searching the walls, counting the stones, and tracing the joints.[8]

Intended by Charlemagne to inaugurate a new era, a new moment in the history of man, when ideals of reason, stability, faith, and order once again reasserted themselves in the history of the West, the great ninth-century chapel was now almost hidden by later additions—any stylistic coherence it may have once possessed, lost. It was now an astonishing mélange of soaring pinnacles and round arches; rough, Roman-style brick-work, with its thick, grainy mortar of the earliest years, next to ogival arches; and elegantly cut stone blocks of the Gothic era. Inside was a similar array of styles: the soaring, glass-walled Gothic choir, known since 1414 as the "Glass House of Aachen," its colored-glass transforming the light of day into the light of God, contrasted strikingly with the somber, thickly walled and marble-veneered severity of Charlemagne's octagonal chapel, modeled after ancient Roman imperial mausolea.

It was here, in the compelling shadows of Charlemagne's awesome structure, and other buildings of similar antiquity that dotted Aachen, that Mies learned of architecture.

> I was impressed by the strength of these old buildings . . . because they didn't even belong to any epoch. But they were there for 1000 years and still there and still impressive and nothing could change it. . . . And all the styles, the great styles, passed, but they were still there—didn't lose anything . . . and still [as] good as they were [on] the first day they were built.[9]

The city's name, like Mies's own, partook of a strange duality. "Mies" and "Rohe," like "Aachen" and "Aix-la-Chapelle" . . . the one harsh, Teutonic, compressed; the other mellifluous, inviting, Gallic. Aachen, like its famed son, was a perverse confluence of passion posing as intellect, of unswerving faith cloaked in the righteous mantle of reasonability. Created as a city of faith, a "city of God," a "new Jerusalem," it was hailed as a cradle of reason, a "new Athens." But, while dedicated to God and to peace, it has borne witness to much of history's carnage.

The city was primarily the creation of a single man—Charlemagne. Praised by contemporaries and history alike as a bringer of peace and order, a voice of reason in a world of barbarism, he was not above imposing his beliefs wholesale and by force. An innovator, committed to leaving nothing as it was before and certain that God was on his side, he had himself crowned by the pope. Under the banner of justice, he instituted harsh and repressive laws—reducing some he opposed to second-class citizens. Seeking to bring order to a dislocated and fragmented world, he adopted policies of mass deportations and resettlement, occasionally invoking the death penalty for those who refused to take an oath of loyalty to himself or broke it once taken.[10] His rages were legendary. According to a poet of the day, fear of Charlemagne's personal severity made all men as gentle as lambs in his presence.

Charlemagne perceived himself as "surely and permanently in possession of the power and grace to guide the course of civilized life" and justified his ambition in terms of a special, divinely endowed favor.[11] He began as a local ruler and lived to see his reign extend over much of Europe. Viewing his people as the chosen instrument of God, he sought the collective renewal of his nation. War campaigns were crucial to his reign, making possible whatever achievements he anticipated.[12] Architecture was to crown Charlemagne's ambitions. He sought to build a capital city worthy of his vision of a new golden age and, taking personal command of the vast enterprises, consciously attempted to recreate the splendor of ancient, imperial Rome. However, this dream of creating a second Rome under a German master crumbled with his death.

From Charlemagne, the creator of the first Reich, derived the peculiarly Teutonic notion of the autocratic ruler, who, inspired by his vision of what a civilized world ought to be, justified unlimited power by the desire for peace and order—a dream of European unification under a German banner that was ultimately stymied by "barbarian" outsiders. Charlemagne was a German hero—one of his particular admirers was Hitler—and for Mies, as for many of his fellow countrymen, Hitler was, in many ways, nothing new.[13]

But Mies learned more from Aachen than the lesson of its buildings. From his father and his own early childhood experiences in the family stonecutting shop ("We always had some-

thing to do with buildings . . . [as children] we were allowed to
join in everything right from the start") came a profound
respect for craft and for the possibilities, as well as the limitations, of materials.[14] "Architecture begins when two bricks are
put carefully together," Mies was fond of saying.[15]

He was proud that his father was more the craftsman than
the businessman. "About the economics of capitalist speculation," Mies related to his grandson, the architect Dirk Lohan,
"he understood nothing."[16] When his elder brother Ewald
argued with his father over the value of putting much effort
into an ornament that was going high up on a building, Mies
recalled, "My father wanted no part of that. 'You're none of you
stonemasons anymore!' he would say. 'You know the finial at
the top of the spire of the cathedral at Cologne? Well, you can't
crawl up there and get a good look at it, but it is carved as if you
could. It was made for God.' "[17] For the rest of his life, to the
distress of his clients (and their budgets), Mies built "for God."

Although Mies's formal education ceased when he was fifteen, it played a critical role in his life and the development of
his art. Between 1896 and 1899, he attended the Domschule, a
Catholic institution attached to the cathedral. Because the
school's records were destroyed during World War II, it is not
possible to know what subjects he studied and how well he did.
It seems clear that he received a thorough grounding in traditional Latin and Catholic subjects, although it is unlikely,
according to the current cathedral archivist, that he studied, as
he later claimed, either St. Augustine or St. Thomas, whom he
was fond of quoting in his efforts to justify his architectural
philosophy.[18]

Mies's first steps toward an "independent profession" ("einen
freien Beruf"),[19] by which he would emancipate himself from
his father's workshop and the family tradition of stonemasonry, came with his attendance, between 1899 and 1901, at
the Gewerbeschule, a local trade school. Here, in 1901, at the
age of fifteen, Mies's drawing talent seems to have received its
initial recognition. His daughter Georgia vaguely recalls her
father speaking of receiving a one-man show within the group
show in the exhibition of school work required for gradua-
tion.[20] For the next few years, as Franz Schulze puts it, Mies
"earned his calluses," working first as an apprentice for local

building contractors and then as a draftsman in various local offices.[21] His confidence in his "eye" and hands, combined with his early training with his father, embued in him the most profound respect for materials and the basic, gritty stuff of building—mortar and bricks, the problem of corners—and, as Schulze puts it, "the consolation . . . in the cup that cheers" that seems especially appealing after a bone-wearying day of hard labor.[22] How confident and touching are Mies's words on the craft of building:

> [L]et us guide [our students] into the healthy world of primitive building methods, where there was meaning in every stroke of an axe, expression in every bite of a chisel.
> Where can we find greater structural clarity than in the wooden buildings of old? . . .
> Here the wisdom of whole generations is stored . . .
> What warmth and beauty they have! They seem to be echoes of old songs.
> And buildings of stone as well: what natural feeling they express!
> What a clear understanding of the material! How surely it is joined! . . .
> Where do we find such wealth of structure? Where more natural and healthy beauty?
> . . . What better examples could there be for young architects? Where else could they learn such simple and true crafts than from these unknown masters?
> We can also learn from brick.
> How sensible is this small handy shape, so useful for every purpose! What logic in its bonding, pattern and texture!
> What richness in the simplest wall surface! But what discipline this material imposes![23]

Mies's confidence in his drawing abilities was further confirmed by his experiences after school. For two years he worked in the local stucco shop of Max Fischer, starting in the time-honored tradition as office boy and moving up to draftsman when a member of the firm was drafted into the army. It was here, Mies later claimed, that he learned to draw. He was required to make full-scale drawings for plaster ornamentation in all styles, "Louis XIV . . . in the morning and Renaissance . . .

in the afternoon. . . . [O]r Gothic . . . [a]nd every now and then a new ornament was invented." After that, he said, "I could draw anything free-hand, no matter what it was . . . without so much as looking."[24]

His confidence was occasionally misplaced. One day, while drawing elaborate cartouches (perhaps looking in the opposite direction, as he was wont to brag he did), he made a mistake.[25] Taking him to task, his boss made a threatening gesture. "Don't try that again," said Mies, infuriated.[26] Packing his things, he stormed out of his office: an illegal act for someone his boss considered an apprentice. The police were sent to Mies's home, where Ewald saved him by explaining that Mies was no apprentice, but "a novice draftsman." This was apparently a significant enough difference to keep Mies out of jail, but the job was finished for him.[27]

It was not the last time that Mies would leave a mentor under strained, if not stormy, conditions, nor was it the last time he would turn to Ewald for help. Born in 1877, Ewald Philip Mies was nine years older than Ludwig. As eldest son, he was the inheritor of the family stonemasonry tradition, calling himself—in the manner of the day—both sculptor and architect. Of all the members of the family, Mies was closest to Ewald, who never married and who shared with his brother ambidexterity and a locally renowned "eye."[28] Throughout his life, Mies turned to Ewald for counsel.

Between 1901 and 1905, Mies worked as a draftsman for several local architects. If his initiation into drawing began in Fischer's studio, his initiation into the broader area of aesthetic speculation—which would eventually become a lifelong preoccupation—began in the office of his new employer Albert Schneider, a local architect, with his accidental discovery of a copy of *Die Zukunft*, an avant-garde cultural journal that he found in the drawer of his drafting table. Noting the books mentioned in the footnotes, Mies went to the library and read them all. Years later, when asked how his speculative pursuits had begun, he replied, not without a touch of pride, "From footnotes!"[29]

Schneider's office had received a commission to design a local branch of Tietz, the great Berlin department store. Eventually, Tietz decided to engage a large Berlin architectural firm, demoting Schneider's office to that of associate. Berlin architects, engineers, and office assistants soon descended upon the office and Mies found himself amidst people from the sophisticated capital. An architect from Königsberg, by the name of Dülow, took a liking to the young man and invited him one evening for dinner, Mies later told Dirk Lohan. "Listen," Dülow said, "why do you want to hang around here, in this tank town? Go to Berlin; that's where things are happening."[30]

But Mies could not just take off: he needed a job. Dülow took an architectural journal from his drawer and found two openings available for a draftsman, one in the city building office in Rixdorf, a Berlin suburb, and the other at a large firm. Mies was accepted by both, but Dülow knew someone who worked in the Rixdorf office—"Martens, a fine man, from the Baltic, painstaking architect . . . above all, an artist"—so Mies went there.[31]

In 1905, at nineteen, Mies left for Berlin, his personality—strong, stubborn, brimming with confidence—and his way of thinking already defined. His early Thomistic education had exposed him to the postulation of a transcendental world where phenomena of the experiential world were perceived as mere symbols of a greater reality. Known as the philosophy of idealism, it was the classical philosophical attempt to reconcile the disparity between man's ability to postulate order, reason, and the notion of "meaningfulness" with the existence of an empirical world notable for the absence of these virtues.[32] This world view was based on a hierarchy of values. To the higher realm of the spirit belonged God, Perfection, Order, Meaning, Truth, Reason, and the Good. The mundane world of everyday experience—the world of family cares, politics, and daily affairs; of chaos, misery, and diversity—belonged to the lower realm. "Questions concerning the essence of things," said Mies in later years, "are the only significant questions."[33]

Whatever was "significant" partook of the "higher" realm. Since it included order and reason, what was "significant" had necessarily to partake of logic. Throughout his life and in his art, Mies understood the world of order and rationality to be higher (more "perfect and more significant") than the "real" world.

In his later years, as he struggled to define the nature of

architecture, and despite the multitude of experiences, influences, and ideas to which he was exposed, he returned, almost instinctively, to the idealistic conceptualizations of his youth. It was, quite literally, the only way he could think. For Mies, these notions were self-evident, beyond debate or the need for confirmation. "He who has once learned to think correctly can no longer change his thinking," he declared.[34] It was this assuredness and absolutism that so awed and frightened those who knew him. "It was the final word," remarked the architect Kevin Roche, one of his students. "Whatever it was, it was the final word. You wouldn't even dream of questioning him."[35]

"Do you ask God where He got the Commandments?" asked Philip Johnson, undoubtedly recalling an incident of the late 1950s, when he had dared to question Mies.[36] The two were sitting in Johnson's famed Connecticut glass house, a building that forever annoyed Mies because of its obvious indebtedness to his own concepts, later realized in the Farnsworth House in Plano, Illinois.[37] Late in a "liquor-logged" evening,[38] Johnson questioned Mies's well-known admiration for H. P. Berlage and his Amsterdam Stock Exchange.[39] In fact, Johnson continued, he could hardly imagine Mies in that building. Mies's response was to explode in anger and without bothering to answer, stormed out of the house. "He never returned," Johnson recalled.[40]

Further education might possibly have softened the edges of such intransigence and perhaps refined Mies's thought, but whatever he picked up after age fifteen was acquired not in school but on his own. His later absorption of the classicist principles of order, clarity, and logic from Karl Friedrich Schinkel and Peter Behrens was kindled by the early rationalistic bent of his schooling. "The senses," wrote Thomas Aquinas, "delight in things duly proportioned."

With his initial introduction to architecture (which he always preferred to call "Baukunst," the art of building) coming out of his early exposure to the construction crafts and his minimal academic background, Mies never felt comfortable with the more formal, Beaux-Arts approach to architecture and always deprecated it. His basic constructivist, from-the-ground-up approach to architecture formed the core of the curricula he developed for the Bauhaus in 1930 and later at the

Armour Institute in Chicago. He proudly admitted to being an autodidact, and spoke frequently of his ongoing readings in difficult and obscure subjects, such as physics, philosophy, and astronomy.[41] His library in Germany, he claimed, contained three thousand books, three hundred of which he brought with him to America.[42] Philip Johnson, however, remains skeptical.

> Mies! He wouldn't admit it, but he was a violent anti-intellectual. He said, "I've been reading," so I looked at his library, and he hadn't—only three books, anyhow. Not one of them had left the shelf for years.[43]

Mies's propensity for philosophical pronouncements of grave profundity but dubious meaning and faulty logic—"Truth is the significance of facts"[44]—the particular need he had and obvious satisfaction he seemed to take in being perceived as a deep thinker (virtually alone among the great twentieth-century architects); his inability to tolerate debate or even questioning; and the inordinate pride he took in receiving academic honors, whether membership in the Prussian Academy of Arts, Germany's most prestigious honorary institution, or the honorary doctorates he received in later years, can only lead one to believe that Mies sustained a deep, pervasive, and life-long insecurity about his intellectual qualifications—something not unusual in individuals of great ambition and limited background. With respect to his designing talent, his innate "eye," he was on firmer ground. Here, he had no such doubts.

Mies's education pushed him toward rationality and conceptualization—"[I am convinced] of the need for clarity in thoughts and action. Without clarity, there can be no understanding. And without understanding, there can be no direction—only confusion."[45] But his natural, full-blooded instinct asserted the subjective and irrational. The latter offered no justification; the former demanded it. This duality set up an irresolvable dialectic, a constant struggle between reason and intuition that would inform his life and his art. An unmitigated sensualist, he appeared before the world as an intellectual, a deep thinker, reserved, austere, unemotional, ignorant of self-doubt, and serene: "I am very skeptical about emotional expressions. I don't trust them."[46] But his core lay, finally, in a simplicity, an unshakable bedrock of certainty, derived not from the higher regions of the intellect that he professed ("I would look for more profound principles") but from the sureness of the hand and eye.[47] This schism informed not only Mies, but his entire age; nowhere was it more apparent than in architecture—and nowhere more vivid than in Berlin.

The Industrial Revolution had set in motion a profound upheaval of society. Amidst new notions of personal freedom, liberty, and rights previously undreamed of by common men, a new class was created, the bourgeoisie. Neither peasant nor prince, it needed utilitarian buildings: housing, schools, and other middle-class accoutrements previously unknown. Unconstrained by the burdens of tradition, class, or propriety, simple practicality became the new standard. This powerful new class demanded railroads, engines, bridges, stores, office buildings, all built cheaply and quickly in a manner previously unimagined, with new materials, such as steel (after the mid-1850s) and plate glass.

How could art and architecture, with their indebtedness to tradition, be accommodated to these new needs, materials, and values? Making art "relevant" became the byword of the nineteenth century: bringing art to the masses unfamiliar with the great classical myths, depicting *la vie moderne* without betraying the cherished values of the past. Nowhere was this dilemma more acute than in architecture, where the great traditions of Greece and Rome, the power of cathedrals, the glory of marbles seemed to offer little guidance for the new world of turbines, trains, and housing for the working class. The demands of art—its uniqueness, its handicraft, its indebtedness to tradition—had to be reconciled with the demands of commerce and its concern with utility, cost efficiency, innovation, and mass production.

For most of the nineteenth century, art and the machine seemed irreconcilable opponents. Construction meant for commerce—office buildings, workers' housing, railroad stations, factories, bridges, docks, department stores, exhibition halls—was free to utilize the new materials, iron, steel, and later, reinforced concrete; and new means, such as prefabrication. Builders, such as James Bogardus in New York, Sir Joseph

Paxton and Thomas Telford in England, and Gustave Eiffel in France, did not fancy themselves architects. They were engineers, and their constructions—Paxton's Crystal Palace of 1850–51 and Eiffel's Tower of 1887–89, the wonders of the nineteenth century—were not considered "architecture."

By the end of the century, from Chicago to Vienna, it had become clear that architects could no longer ignore these powerful new forms and materials, and great efforts were made to synthesize what appeared to be conflicting elements, to somehow free architecture from the constraints of tradition and open it to the realities of the day. In Chicago, Louis Sullivan struggled to articulate the new office building; in Europe, Victor Horta in Brussels, Antonio Gaudi in Spain, C. F. A. Voysey in England, Charles Rennie Mackintosh in Scotland, and Otto Wagner in Vienna sought to free themselves from historicism and come to terms with the new conditions. The dawn of the new century brought a special urgency to this quest, for the twentieth century was generally seen as the century of technological triumphs without precedent in human history. The conditions of life in the dawning age appeared on the verge of unheard-of improvement. The wonders of technology thrilled the hearts and minds of those, like Mies, attaining their maturity. Anything and everything having to do with technology, from its techniques of production, its emphasis on efficiency and mass production, the availability of vast new products and materials, to the simple unadorned shed—the factory building itself that housed these wonders of engineering—assumed teleological significance in their minds.[48]

Not everyone, however, was seduced by the wonders of the machine age. From the very beginning, doubts about the machine had accompanied the glorious revolution. Concerns about the severing of families from their rural roots, the human abuses of the factory and housing, the fumes, the desecration of the landscape all formed a persistent counterpoint to the growth of industry. This was the dialogue of the age and nowhere was it more apparent than in Berlin at the turn of the century.

Berlin, in 1905, was a capital in search of itself. Only thirty-four years earlier, in 1871, Bismarck had unified the German princely states into a single country under Prussian leadership, and Berlin found itself not merely one capital among many, but the first city in a new Reich. Lagging culturally and artistically behind other German cities, it now strove to vie with such worldly centers as Paris and London. A city of swirling spires and domes of all sizes and shapes, Berlin's desperate search for identity, authenticity, and pedigree was apparent everywhere.

Gargoyles burst forth, not from cathedrals, but from sausage shops, their "antiquity" supplied by highly paid craftsmen wielding iron spikes. Artificially eroded gods decorated new stucco fronts of marzipan stores. "Antique" lamp reflectors sported a patina made of green porcelain and affixed in patches. Plaster angels blew apocalyptic trumpets on the walls of soldiers' barracks and flaming swords menaced many a porch and spectator. Patches of stucco stones, complete with fake fossils—lizards, ferns, and pterodactyls—embellished the walls of one house in the west of Berlin. Simplicity seemed something to be avoided at all costs.

The kaiser, like his Hohenzollern predecessors, provided little in the way of artistic leadership. He fired Dr. Hugo von Tschudi from his post as director of Berlin's National Gallery for favoring modern artists and refused to present to the artist Käthe Kollwitz a gold medal awarded her by the prestigious Prussian Academy of Arts. His patronage leaned toward military art and a severe, Prussian monumentality noticeable as early as 1797 in Friedrich Gilly's project for a monument to Friedrich the Great. With a marked preference for ponderous stone constructions of Assyrian proportions and heaviness, the kaiser seemed bent on transforming Berlin into a reflection of the *Glanz und Gloria* of the new Reich. The Sieges Allée in the Tiergarten, opposite the Brandenburger Tor, reflected the Hohenzollern artistic taste. This Prussian via triumphalis, with its stern marble images of the Hohenzollern line from Albert the Bear to Emperor William I, offered Berliners more of a history lesson than intimations of aesthetic delight.

Nevertheless, Berliners—indeed the entire German nation— owed a tremendous debt to the kaiser's jealousy of the preeminent position enjoyed by his English uncle, King Edward VII. Recognizing that Edward's status rested on England's economic supremacy, he determined to challenge it. It became clear to Wilhelm that if Germany was ever to attain the status of a world power, it had to be transformed into an industrial power whose products could successfully compete with those of the British in the world's markets. To this goal, the kaiser dedicated his personal prestige and the resources of the government.

The thrust toward industrialization that marked Germany and, most notably, Berlin at this time, bore the imprint not only of official government policy at the highest levels, but also of the special urgency felt by a newly aroused and vigorous country straining to achieve as quickly as possible what it had taken England more than a century to accomplish. In architecture, Germany had been little more than a backwater of the currents that had flowed through Europe since the Renaissance, but the dialogue that had earlier taken place in England and more recently, in Vienna, now reached the capital with a special, if belated, impact.

The year Mies came to Berlin was an epochal one in architecture. In 1905 Frank Lloyd Wright was completing the Larkin office building in Buffalo, New York; Otto Wagner's Postal Savings Bank in Vienna, begun in 1904, was a year from completion; Auguste Perret's apartment building on rue Franklin in Paris (utilizing reinforced concrete) was two years old; and Hector Guimard's Paris metro stations, five. All attempted to somehow come to terms with the implications of the machine age, and in all, the voice of Germany was conspicuously missing. The publication, in 1904–05, of Hermann Muthesius's *Das Englische Haus*, an examination of the English efforts to invigorate ordinary housing by breaking away from historicist traditions, further enlivened the Berlin architectural scene.

Given the Germans' inclination to support their views with a complete Hegelian Weltanschauung, the architectural dialogue in Berlin began to assume ponderous philosophical overtones. Berlin architects, driven by the feverish pace of industrialization, passionately debated the issues that had long preoccupied their brethren. In 1907 the Deutsche Werkbund was established to promote the integration of art and industry. Down came the photographs of Greek temples and Ruskinian-Gothic cathedrals; in their place went photographs of American grain silos and factories. Humble shed structures offered visions of a new architectural aesthetic: notions of efficiency and simplicity replaced those of historical association. Steel and plate glass, materials created in the factory, now were thought of as having the glittering beauty that previously was seen in granite and marble.

However, not all reflections of the kaiser's anglophilia were so profound. Almost overnight, everything English (and by consanguinity, American) became a source of blind devotion and aspiration. Berlin twinkled with "West-End Clubs" and "Grill Rooms." Shops advertised "Real English Trousers-Cuts" and "Cravats as worn by King George." "Smartheit" was desired by one and all. In an "amerikanische Bar," the newly clean-shaven Berliner ordered his "Rie High-bowle" or "Silver Juleppe with Rom," as he nuzzled the neck of his tempting Prussianized Gibson girl companion. Young men spent hours poring over *Der Gentlemen: A Guide to Dress and Manners,* where they learned, in a chapter entitled "Der Shawl," that the *englische* gentleman in evening dress wears a shawl to keep his collar clean. *The Elegant World,* a weekly journal, was read enthusiastically in certain aspiring quarters. America's "moving picture" soon became Berlin's passion. English words such as "Dogge," "Nervenschoc," "Punsch," and "Scheck" (for "check") invaded German. A century earlier, German lexicographers had counted a mere 150 English words in common usage; now there were 700. Those most worldly-wise spoke of a "struggle for lifetum."[49]

To see their city become a *Weltstadt* before their eyes was a source of almost unbearable pleasure to Berliners. Everyone, from the lowliest worker to the nouveau-riche industrialist, strove to be *weltstadtisch.* Every event, no matter how calamitous, how outrageous, was an indication of Berlin's new status—the burgeoning traffic, the increased level of noise, the new *Flimmerkisten* (movie houses),[50] the erection of a new sport palace, the increase in accidents . . . even the increase in pickpockets. Berlin, which Mark Twain had called the "Chicago of Germany," that shapeless, stony heap of spires, domes, and gargoyles, was becoming a world city.

Lured by the city's promise and vigor, as well as its rapid growth and seemingly countless employment opportunities, individuals like Mies poured into the metropolis from all over

Germany. Workers, artists, architects, literary figures, and scientists rushed to Berlin, so that the city achieved a heterogeneity unknown elsewhere in Germany. Fresh from the farms and small towns of the countryside, these new Berliners found themselves confronted by new ideas, new people, and newly discovered vices. Affecting sophistication and worldly wisdom, these new Berliners came to look down on their country relatives as provincial hicks or *kleinbürgerlich*. How could their relatives back home understand "Smartheit" or "Rie High-bowles"?

To call oneself a Berliner came to mean more than simply living in the city: it implied a certain toughness; detachment; an impudent contempt for authority; an ability to spot what was phony, pretentious, hollow, or ridiculous; a propensity to view with bemused cynicism calamitous events that elsewhere drove people to revolution, suicide, or the mental asylum. Leading Berliners to accept their woes with a wry, caustic humor and embrace their pleasures with a frenzied abandon that startled, as much as it embarrassed, foreign observers, this attitude also made them occasionally forget that the drama being enacted before their eyes—however appalling, however absurd—was real and being played for keeps.

In time, Berlin came to seem like a land apart from Germany and Berliners a breed apart from their countrymen. There was an intensity, a vigor, an air of belligerence almost, about Berliners that invigorated debate as it did life in general; and what in other countries had evolved as a vociferous but gentlemanly dialogue between pro- and antimachine age forces blossomed in Germany into a philosophical, and ultimately political, confrontation. So vituperous would this particular aesthetic battle become, that only the intrusion of the war of 1914 prevented the total collapse of the newly founded Deutsche Werkbund.

The innovations that elsewhere evoked generalized fears of industrialization, in Germany came to be seen as specific threats to the fatherland, to the traditional German values of family cohesiveness and attachment to the soil; and Berlin became the focus of these fears. A resented symbol of cosmopolitanism, Berlin came to symbolize the danger of "foreign" ideas, first English, then American—and finally Russian, when Berlin became the center of postrevolutionary activities.

To many, Berlin seemed irrevocably linked with the devil. Few aspects of the city did not frighten or alienate much of the German population—from the threat that mass production posed to the traditional craftsmen, to the veneer of toughness and cynicism that became the Berliner's hallmark.

Just as adulation of technology came to assume metaphysical proportions in Berlin, so too did hostility to it. What some, such as Mies, saw as the clarion call of modernity, the very definition of the age, others saw as the enemy of nature, of *Kinde, Küche, und Kirche,* the death-knell of God. To many Germans, any Berlin manifestation—literary, musical, artistic, architectural, or political—appeared threatening, radical, cause for grave suspicions, and worst of all, "un-German." Berlin and the radical ideas it would spawn in the arts and architecture—in which Mies was to play a leading role—began a long and ultimately catastrophic divorce from the rest of Germany.

This was the Berlin to which Mies came in 1905, a young man from a "tank town," uncultured, unread, unlettered, armed solely with talent, driving ambition, pride, and "a will of titanic proportions."[51] Arriving in Rixdorf, alone, attempting what no one else in his family before had done, Mies—momentarily overcome by the difficulties of the course he had chosen—sat down on the curb and vomited.[52]

CHAPTER 3

A BLIND AND FATEFUL COURSE

[I]T IS NOT NECESSARY . . . TO ARGUE WHETHER THE OTHER-
WORLDLY OR THE HUMANISTIC IDEAL IS "HIGHER." THE
POINT IS THAT THEY ARE INCOMPATIBLE. ONE MUST CHOOSE
BETWEEN GOD AND MAN.

(**George Orwell,** "Reflections on Gandhi")

However exposed Mies's anxieties were by his less-than-trium-
phant entry into Berlin, they were soon forgotten in the tedium
of his initial assignment, the detailing of ornament for wooden
paneling to decorate the council chamber of the Rixdorf Town
Hall. Although his drawing experience in Aachen had prepared
him well for this task, he was uncomfortable in working with
wood, a material that he tended to avoid—except for a brief
period—throughout his career and for which he was unsuited
by temperament and training. Fortunately, his involvement
with the Rixdorf firm was short-lived, for within a few months
he was drafted into the army. His army career was equally
brief. He contracted a lung infection during a particularly gru-
eling drilling session in the rain and was discharged as "unfit
for service," his relief—"The army . . . didn't really need us
cripples"—revealing a certain disinterest in patriotism.[1]

Mies never returned to the Rixdorf job. He enrolled instead as a student in two technical schools, the Academy of Arts and the School of Berlin Arts and Crafts Museum,[2] where he was assigned to the atelier of Bruno Paul, who, in 1907, was the newly appointed head of both institutions; a leading designer of furniture and interiors in the "Jugendstil" (the German variant of Art Nouveau, an essentially European effort to find in organic, curvilinear forms an alternative to the traditional historicist design vocabulary); a well-known member of the avant-garde; and Mies's next employer. Paul had continued to maintain his private practice, branching now into architecture. Because no one in his office, including himself, was particularly experienced in building practice, Mies, thanks to his construction experience in Aachen, found himself the firm's resident "architect."[3] It was in Paul's office and later in that of Peter Behrens—another of Germany's most influential designers—that Mies learned more than architecture: he found not only his style of building, but a way of speaking and presenting himself and a clientele—and wife—willing and wealthy enough to support his aspirations. It was also in Paul's office that Mies received his first architectural commission, from Alois Riehl, a philosophy professor at Humboldt University, and his wife, who were looking for a talented newcomer to design their home in the upper-class Berlin suburb of Neubabelsberg. Paul's office, to which they came for advice, recommended Mies. Twenty years old, and having built nothing, Mies was a bit more of a newcomer than the Riehls had counted on.

> "I *can* build a house," he said to Frau Riehl. "I've done it. I just haven't done it all by myself. What would life be like if everybody insisted you must have actually built such and such a thing by yourself? I'd be an old man and have nothing to show for the aging."[4]

Anxious to assuage the Riehls' concerns, Bruno Paul offered to supervise Mies in his design of their house. Mies, however, refused! Taken aback, at first, by such arrogance, Paul eventually gave in, graciously commenting later that his only regret was not being able to claim its design himself.[5]

Although the house was praised by a contemporary critic as

being "so faultless that no one would guess that it is the first independent work of a young architect"[6] and was certainly distinguished in detailing and finesse of proportion, its stucco-covered brick surface with steep roof, dormer windows, and gables strongly allied it not only with Paul's work of the period, but with the traditional eighteenth-century manner then so popular in Germany, especially in the Potsdam-Neubabelsberg area. It did not fit easily with Mies's later classicizing bent, nor apparently with how he wished to be perceived, for although it was mentioned by Philip Johnson in a monograph of 1947, Mies suppressed publication of its photograph.[7]

To the Riehls, Mies owed not only his first commission, but his entry into Berlin society. His own recollection of Frau Riehl's invitation to a formal dinner reveals his initial awkwardness and awestruck admiration of this milieu. "You'll have to wear a dinner jacket, of course," said Joseph Popp, an assistant in Paul's office who had recommended Mies to the Riehls.

> "A dinner jacket?" I said. "I have no idea what that is."
> "You can buy one anywhere. Or rent one."
> I remember rushing around to all the desks in Paul's office, borrowing money from anyone I could find so that I might buy a frock coat. And once I had it, I didn't know what kind of cravat to wear with it. I ended up with some wild yellow thing, totally out of place.
> The evening came all too soon. I proceeded to the Riehls' apartment in Berlin, where a splendid-looking couple rode up the elevator with me, very fancily dressed, the man in tails and covered all over with medals. I figured they must be going where I was, so I let them get off first and followed them.
> The door opened and they glided, zummm zummm zummm, across the slick parquet, like a pair of expert figure skaters. For my own part, I was afraid I would break my neck.[8]

With a circle of acquaintances that consisted of many of Berlin's leading intellectual and financial figures—such as the philosopher Eduard Spranger; the art historians Adolf Goldschmidt and Heinrich Wöfflin; and Walther Rathenau, the industrialist and financier (several of whom would later become Mies's clients)—it is difficult to imagine a milieu farther removed from Mies's simple background than that of Professor and Mrs. Riehl.[9] Here Mies came to know a new level of philosophical discourse and to appreciate the German admiration of philosophical profundities. Here he came in touch with the image of the stern, patriarchal *Kraftmensch* beloved of German males since Bismarck, whose powerful, larger-than-life persona and autocratic image inspired fear in the hearts of lesser folk. It was an image that Germany demanded of its men of power—political leaders, revered professors, intellectuals, and artists.

Thanks to the Riehls, Mies could now call himself an architect and learn the demands of such a calling. He seems to have learned his lessons well. He apparently made a good impression on the Riehls, both as an architect and guest, and became a frequent visitor and welcomed member of their social set. A photograph of Mies sitting on the porch of their house in 1912 shows the twenty-six-year-old confident and at ease in his impeccably tailored frock coat and cravat. Seven years after he had arrived in the city Mies had become a real Berliner.

Mies's rationalistic inclinations were further strengthened by the influence of his next employer, the architect Peter Behrens, and through him, that of Karl Friedrich Schinkel, the great nineteenth-century German architect whose buildings dotted Berlin. Here, within a decade, the neoclassical formulations of Behrens and his predecessor Schinkel would lay the foundations of twentieth-century German architecture, from Mies to the Third Reich. By the early years of the twentieth century, the sinuous organic convolutions of the Art Nouveau were appearing less convincing as a viable alternative to historicism, and interest was turning toward a more sober and "objective" (*sachlich*) style more in harmony with the needs of a rapidly industrializing society. More and more, Berlin architects were turning toward the precise, stern forms of a stripped-down neoclassicism, whose restraint and disposition of simple, geometrical forms offered—with adjustments of scale and pitch of roof—as much to private clientele as to the state, and appeared as responsive to the hallowed claims of

Mies at Riehl House, about 1912 (Private collection)

tradition as to the demands of the machine age. Disguised in rhetoric, it would later flourish from Moscow to Washington, D.C., from Paris to Berlin.

Peter Behrens, a founder of the Deutsche Werkbund, whose atelier, between 1908 and 1911, included Walter Gropius, the founder of the Bauhaus; Le Corbusier, who would become the leading architect of France; and Mies, stood at the very forefront of the struggle to evolve a "relevant," modern architecture that responded to the needs of both industry and art. Although this struggle had been going on elsewhere for many years, it was taking a unique turn in Berlin, owing to the government's intense involvement in German industry and the nature of the monumental Prussian architectural tradition, which, while classical in style, ranged from the somber late eighteenth-century severity of Gilly to the megalomaniacal excesses of the Wilhelminian age, the latter so expressive of the expansionistic aspirations of the Second Reich. Backed by the prestige of the German crown, German industrial complexes, especially in Berlin, often demanded a monumentality normally associated with buildings of state.

Nowhere is this idiosyncratic nature of "official" German factories more apparent than in the AEG Turbine Factory building designed by Behrens in 1909, which attempts to fuse industrial needs and materials with the heroically scaled monumentality of Prussian public architecture. While one might assume that the influence of utility and the simple factory shed would push architectural development away from the monumental—which in fact it did in the buildings of Gropius and the Bauhaus (their factory aesthetic evolving, to a great extent, in reaction to the overblown qualities of the Wilhelminian style)—in these early buildings of Behrens, it was proceeding in the opposite direction. That this antipathy between simple utility and the symbolic demands of monumentality might lead to difficulties is apparent from the variability in Behrens's building production and in the range of his admirers, which included, for varying and equally compelling reasons, Albert Speer, Mies, and Adolf Hitler.

Perhaps no building was more identified with the so-called "Prussian" style in the early decades of the twentieth century than Behrens's stolid and ponderously classical German

Peter Behrens, AEG Turbine Factory, Berlin, 1909 (Photo courtesy of AEG Aktiengesellschaft)

Embassy of 1912 in St. Petersburg, for which Mies worked as the supervising architect. Mies referred to this building, with its heavy, overscaled classical forms, as "very Berlin . . . something like the Brandenburger Tor."[10] The "Prussian" style had many lessons to teach. For Mies, it was "the grand form," and the affirmation of his rationalistic bent through the classicist principles of order, clarity, and logic. "To me, structure is something like logic. It is the best way to do things and to express them," he wrote.[11] But Mies learned more than rationalism from "the grand form"; in it he also saw an expression of the "spirit of the age"—"the only way by which we can have a communion with the essentials of our civilization."[12] Mies appears to have recognized the narrow line that separates the neoclassical copyist from one who distills its principles. "The old architects . . . copy this sort of thing," said Mies, commenting about an engraving of an Ionic column that hung in his living room. "We appreciate it."[13] Through Behrens, Mies came to perceive architectural form as a kind of geometrical essence distilled from neoclassical principles, and to realize the need to control scale through refined proportionality. He also came to appreciate Schinkel. "I studied him carefully," Mies said, "and came under his influence. . . . I think Schinkel had wonderful construction, excellent proportions and good detailing."[14] While Mies spoke often and generously of his debt to Schinkel, he spoke only of his formal influence. Left unsaid were the particular circumstances of Schinkel's success, his historic collaboration with the Prussian ruler, Friedrich Wilhelm III. It was a lesson that few Berlin architects ignored.

Mies van der Rohe, Bismarck Monument project, Bingen am Rhein, 1910: TOP, exterior and elevation (Collection, Mies van der Rohe Archive, the Museum of Modern Art, New York. Gift of Ludwig Mies van der Rohe) BOTTOM, perspective from the festival field (Photo courtesy of Mies van der Rohe Archive, the Museum of Modern Art, New York)

Walter Gropius, date unknown (Bauhaus-Archiv)

Mies's amazingly assured, if derivative, Bismarck Monument project of 1910, sited assertively atop the imposing heights overlooking the Rhine at Bingen, confidently disposing well-proportioned and harmonious forms and stern monumentality, showed that Mies had absorbed the neoclassical lessons of Behrens and Schinkel. Planned to commemorate the centennial in 1915 of the late chancellor's birth, its stripped-down geometrical style was unabashedly nationalistic in inspiration and expression. "[A] Bismarck monument," declared the program, "must stand in those oft-embattled, much threatened yet faithfully defended borderlands of Germany."[15] Located in the Rhineland, and ostensibly a memorial to German unification, it was in fact a stern warning to France. A superfluous gesture by 1914, it was never built.

The greater Mies's confidence grew, the more his patience and ability to work with others diminished: his tenure with Behrens, between 1908 and 1912, was marked by personality conflicts and stormy departures.[16] His participation in the Bismarck Monument competition, and his building of the Hugo Perls House in 1910–11, indicate that Mies's confidence in his ability to pursue an independent architectural practice was not misplaced. The fact that Walter Gropius, only three years his senior, was his superior, did not make Behrens's atelier any more appealing to the talented, proud, and ambitious Mies.

Gropius had been born in 1883 to a distinguished family long involved in the Berlin building community. His father was a city building councillor, a position of considerable prestige, and his great-uncle, Martin Gropius, a follower of Schinkel, was a well-known and admired architect of the mid to late nineteenth century, as well as the designer of the School of the Berlin Arts and Crafts Museum, which Mies had earlier attended. In contrast to Mies, Gropius had all the benefits and distinctions that birth and education could grant in a country where such things mattered greatly. He had attended not one, but four Gymnasia, studied at a prestigious Technische Hochschule and graduated from another, and volunteered for a distinguished cavalry regiment, whose membership was denied to draftees of Mies's background.

Other than his invention of the name of the Bauhaus, however, there was little about Gropius that Mies admired. His reminiscences of their Behrens years fairly reek with envy over Gropius's financial independence. Gropius, said Mies, did not need a salary. He was the "gentleman's chief," there "just to learn."[17] Mies, of course, was striving to emulate what Gropius *was*, a member of the haute bourgeoisie, and pursued its manner as he decried its limitations. While Gropius may have claimed class, Mies claimed genius. Gropius welcomed diversity; Mies deplored it. As early as 1910, when he prepared a paper for the AEG (the Allgemeine Elektricitätsgesellschaft) on the merits of low-cost workers' housing,[18] Gropius (who was personally kind and generous) saw architecture as serving peo-

Ada Bruhn, 1907 (Private collection)

ple; Mies saw it as serving art. Their rivalry, sometimes subdued, other times sharp, would extend throughout their lives
and across two continents. In any event, by the time Mies
returned to Behrens's office in late 1910 (having left for a time
to design the Perls House and the Bismarck Monument), the
"gentleman" architect had been commissioned to design the
Faguswerke shoe factory and was gone.[19]

Gropius, however, was not the only fly in the Behrens oint-
ment. Mies encountered difficulties with other employees,
even with Behrens himself. The two men almost came to
blows when Mies expressed his admiration of H. P. Berlage, the

Dutch architect, whom Behrens considered old-fashioned. "[H]e would have liked nothing better than to give me one in the face," said Mies years later.[20] Mies's tenure in Behrens's office came to an unhappy end when Frau Kröller-Müller, the wealthy German wife of a Dutch industrialist, dissatisfied with the villa that Behrens had designed for her in Wassenaar, Holland, withdrew the commission from him and gave it instead to his assistant Mies, whom Behrens had suspected of "coveting" it.[21]

Mies's design, however, was never built, and in either late 1912 or early 1913, he returned from Holland to Berlin. He apparently was not interested in becoming a member of the artistic avant-garde, for he had not joined the Deutsche Werkbund, nor did he visit its major exhibition in Cologne in 1914.[22] Instead, he seemed concerned about securing his position among Berlin's wealthy bourgeoisie, where—for much of the next twenty years—he would find his clientele. He set up his atelier in Steglitz, and in April 1913 married Ada Bruhn, a tall, imposing, and handsome woman a year older than himself, whom he had met some years before through the Riehls.

It seemed a perfect marriage: a wealthy young woman—her family manufactured small motors—with artistic inclinations marrying a talented and ambitious young man who needed her wealth and social standing, as well as her devotion, to attain his goals. Mies, by now, had become quite a dazzling personality, a real *Kraftmensch*. "You could feel his eyes on you from across the room," said Doris Schmidt, art critic for the *Sud-Deutsche Zeitung*.[23] "He was the most impressive human being that I have ever met." Egon Rakette, one of Mies's Bauhaus students, was moved, in describing Mies, to quote *Hamlet*—"[T]ake him for all in all, I shall not look upon his like again."[24] With a commanding presence and air of mysterious brooding, he was as compelling to men as to women, suave, assured, at once sensuous and profound. When moved, by either convivial company or sufficient spirits, he displayed an earthy, often profane humor. The Bruhns were, at first, unenthusiastic about him. They did not care for his Catholic background (they were Lutherans), his limited education, his unprepossessing family, and his name, with its unpleasant connotations. But Ada was resolute, and having already seen

Mies, about 1912 (Private collection)

her through one broken engagement (to Heinrich Wölfflin, the renowned art historian), they eventually consented.

Although Mies enjoyed the benefits of the haute bourgeoisie, assumed its habits, and culled its patronage, he was unable (and unwilling) to submit to its limitations. Arrogant, exceedingly critical, quick-tempered, as demanding of others as he was of himself, uncommunicative, and totally committed to his art, he was difficult to get along with. He cringed from Ada's demands for a normal family life. "There was something about him," remarked Mary Wigman, a pioneer in German modern dance and a close friend of both, "that thrived on freedom, required exemption from convention. It was his way. . . . As a married man, he was a caricature."[25] Signs of stress appeared early in their marriage; weekends spent away from Ada, suicidal threats from her. "I lived through some pretty terrible times with the two of them, early in their marriage," said Wigman. "I recall Ada, sometimes in the middle of the night, threatening to jump out of the window of their house, to get away from him, to leave him."[26]

The initial rupture came during the war. Stationed at first in Frankfurt and then in Berlin, Mies left in 1917 for Romania, where he served with the army corps of engineers. Despite moments of domestic felicity and the birth of three daughters during this time, the marriage, already strained, began to unravel. He would never resume his role as a family man.

With the war's end in 1918, the debate over the nature of the relationship between industry and art resumed, even more contentiously than before. That the forms of architecture should be ahistorical and reflect the uncluttered geometric simplicity of the factory and machine production, that they should utilize the new materials of the machine age—steel, concrete, and plate glass—seemed clear. What was less apparent was the nature of architecture's relation to the worker, without whom there could be no industry. Should the goals of this new architecture be the betterment of workers' lives? To many, an architecture predicated on the industrial age had a moral obligation toward the worker. Another question was to what degree this architecture was obligated to utilize mass production and prefabrication, with the resulting sacrifice of uniqueness and refinement of finish. And how? Was it right for a "modernist" to build costly buildings beyond the reach of the working class—or any building that did not serve a socially beneficial function?

The convergence of German modernism with the interests of the working class took place in November 1918—a month that witnessed the armistice, the abdication and clandestine departure of the kaiser, a revolution, and the proclamation of the German Republic. To a generation pitched to millennial expectations, this radical alteration of German society seemed the incarnation of the long-awaited "new era." The almost completely socialist government that was provisionally established under the leadership of Friedrich Ebert, the vice president of the Social Democratic party, appeared to many of Germany's avant-garde as the political realization of the new industrial age. "A world has come to an end," said Walter Gropius, of the events of this month. The broadly diverse goals of the party's competing factions, which ranged from the conservative wing of Ebert and Philip Scheidemann to the radicalism of the Spartacists headed by Rosa Luxemburg and Karl Liebknecht on the left, severely hampered the government.

Formed after the October 1917 Soviet upheaval, the Spartacists, a group of Marxist revolutionaries, envisioned a radical reform of Germany's political and educational systems. Their rejection of Ebert's and Scheidemann's conciliatory, patchwork approach was shared by many moderates as well. Their dissatisfaction with the provisional government came to a head toward the end of December, when Rosa Luxemburg declared that the government had betrayed their ideals. The Spartacists thereupon split from the social democrats and established the German Communist party, the KPD, setting the party inexorably on a revolutionary course: the left was now effectively and permanently crippled.

The fervent idealism of the communist revolutionaries and their goal of a utopian, classless society, provided the perfect political and social expression of the avant-garde's artistic aspirations, conditioned as they were by a nineteenth-century Hegelian mentality that assumed the existence of a vital connection between life and art, between society and its artistic output. "Don't let them tell you it was a revolt of armchair

Abb. 1

Max Pechstein, poster, "Call to Socialism": original title "Aufruf zum Sozialismus" (*Wasmuths Kunsthefte,* v. 5)

soldiers who were sick of going hungry and going without," wrote Karl Jakob Hirsche. "It was more than that. It was really the dawn of a new age; the war was over, absolutely over, and it had to be the last war ever. That was the will of most of the enlightened people. In those days we all believed in a new and better future."[27] The radical art movements that emerged in the winter of 1918 saw themselves as an integral part of the communist revolution, although many of their interests, such as reform of art education, had already been prewar preoccupations. What was new was the "revolutionary" context into which these issues were placed. For the most part, the goals of these radical movements were far more conservative than what was suggested by their names and their impassioned manifestos. The inexorable and ultimately fatal intertwining of the avant-garde with politics had begun, and although this political connection actually grew more tenuous during the Weimar years, its origins were never forgotten, especially by the political right.

The November Group was created during the month of the revolution and named in its honor. Founded by the expressionist artists Max Pechstein and César Klein, the organization was described as "a union of radical artists wishing to establish close alliance between mainly Expressionist artists and the socialist state." Its circular, printed in November 1918, demanded public interest and collaboration in all architectural projects, the reorganization of art schools and their curricula, the transformation of museums into repositories of folk art, as well as the allocation of exhibition space and legislation concerning art—hardly the rhetoric of hell-bent revolutionaries.

In December 1918, Walter Gropius founded the "Workers' Council [Soviet] for Art," largely inspired by the "soviets" that

"The Workers' Council for Art": original title "Arbeitsrat für Kunst," manifesto cover (Photo courtesy of the Archiv der Preussischen Akademie der Künste, Akademie der Künste, Berlin)

had arisen after the Revolution of 1917. The purpose of this organization, which merged with the November Group a year later, was ostensibly to reunite art and the masses. Many of its leading figures, such as Bruno Taut and Max Pechstein, belonged to the November Group as well.[28] Most of the involved artists perceived the communist revolution in utopian terms, as symbolizing the breakdown of national divisions. Such a doctrine was bound to appeal to artists who had long sought inspiration in what they perceived as universal ideals. It was utopia they were after, rather than any particular political or social fabric. Thus their artistic-social aspirations fit in easily with the aspirations of the Marxist revolutionaries.[29] Walter Gropius believed that the new art (and ultimately, the new man) could only be attained through social reform. His establishment of the Bauhaus in Weimar in 1919 attempted to connect the long-standing desire for educational reform with the new utopian aspirations.

"Political revolution must be used to liberate art from decades of regimentation," wrote Gropius in March 1919, a month before the establishment of the Bauhaus, in a circular printed for the Workers' Council for Art, in which many of the school's principles were initially articulated. In its founding manifesto he wrote, "Together let us desire, conceive, and create the new structure of the future, which will embrace architecture and sculpture and painting in one unity which will one day rise toward heaven from the hands of a million workers like the crystal symbol of a new faith."[30] As a reflection of the hoped-for classless society, there would be no "Herr Professors" at the Bauhaus.

Not everyone, however, was delighted by this intermingling of art and politics. "Intellectual matters are being identified and confused with political matters in a most stupid fashion," lamented the painter Oskar Schlemmer.[31] Even Mies, whose numerous writings, speeches, and architectural projects of the Weimar years would be marked by a persistent and often lonely struggle to sever modernism from what he saw as its fatal involvement in politics—from what his critics, and most of his peers, saw as its central task—appears to have been briefly touched by the moral fervor of the times. That the improvement of the human lot was a valid architectural concern—an issue almost unique within Mies's oeuvre—may be seen in his entry in a competition sponsored by the Prussian Building Academy (see page 11), the Friedrichstrasse skyscraper drawing of 1921, a startling design that established his reputation and placed him at the very forefront of modernism. Although the technology to build it did not yet exist, his design offered a prototype for the modern skyscraper that would become the hallmark of the century.

Mies's vision—a glass tower of startling crystalline simplicity—rises in the far horizon of a realistically rendered Friedrichstrasse, in vivid contrast with the existing buildings. Where these buildings are horizontal, Mies's soars in an uninterrupted vertical thrust. Where their masonry surfaces are highly decorated and sculptural, his is sleek and unadorned. The earlier structures recall an assortment of historical styles; his rests only on the beauty of the glass and the purity of its geometrical form. Dark and foreboding shadows surround the older buildings, while the crystal tower shines forth in radiant brilliance. This beacon of light, soaring upward to the heavens, dispels, by its luminescent glory, the way of the past, of old buildings, old ideas, and old forms that huddle close to the dark, earthbound soil. The turbulence and heterogeneity, the chaos of conflict that marked the real Friedrichstrasse are nowhere to be seen. The mountain of the gods has triumphed over the dusky and chaotic valley of man.

Like Paul Scheerbart before him,[32] Mies seems to suggest that architecture, specifically the new glass environment, could transform mankind by offering itself as a moral beacon.[33] Yet, beyond this, the moral implications of this dazzling design are as vague and unspecified as the technology needed to build it. They are merely one element among many of the varied, often contradictory, artistic interests that Mies had so piercingly and cohesively brought together: the emotive, visionary, and empathetic ideals of expressionism; the faceted, crisp, fragmented cubes of the French cubists; and the searing dynamism of the Italian futurists, whose poetic evocations of vertically soaring cities of the future had captured the thrilling power and dynamic energy of the new technology.

Of all the possibilities suggested by this design, that of moral concern (or the improvement of the human condition) would be abandoned. As the expressionistic fervor waned, the qualities of simplicity, quietude, clarity, and order—elements all apparent in the Friedrichstrasse design—would come to dominate Mies's concerns. "The long path . . . to creative work has only a single goal," he would later say, "to create order out of the desperate confusion of our time."[34]

In addition to being a year of artistic innovation, 1921 also marked a major turning point in Mies's life. About this time he added "van der Rohe" to his name and, in keeping with an arrangement that had informally existed since the early years of his marriage, permanently separated from Ada and his daughters. Thus, the "finding" of his architectural voice was accompanied by a similar "finding" of himself as a man and as an artist; and the otherworldly instincts, which had brought him to disclaim the demands of family life, came to characterize his architecture as well.

Demanding solitude and introspection—"One cannot climb into a perception," he once said, "as one does into a streetcar"—Mies created an architecture and theoretical principles on which it was based that were equally remote from the constraints of practical reality.[35] His aesthetic philosophy, fully developed by the mid-1920s, sought to provide theoretical justification for an architecture that was both relevant and timeless, an apparent disparity seemingly mediated by Mies's broad definition of "relevance" as partaking of "the essence of the epoch," the "sustaining and driving forces of civilization." In Mies's view, his architecture was at once timeless and timely, existing both *within* its cultural context and above it. "Architecture," wrote Mies, is "the will of the epoch translated into space."[36] The essence of the twentieth century—"the only thing worth expressing," according to Mies—was technology and industrialization. The materials of technology, such as steel, concrete, and plate glass, as well as its techniques, such as prefabrication and standardization, utilized in a manner that stressed structural honesty, as well as refinement of detail, proportional relationships, and expression of material, were the means by which the essence of a building was brought into existence and the building could be said to express the essence of its time (zeitgeist). "Architecture," said Mies, "is not a martini. . . . It is like a chess game—there are certain rules."[37]

Mies persistently championed the separation of architecture from nonarchitectural concerns. Apparent in his writings and villa designs of the early 1920s, it was a view that frequently brought him into conflict with his more socially involved colleagues. In 1927, while his contemporaries were struggling to resolve the very pressing issue of workers' housing, Mies wrote that "the problem of the modern dwelling is primarily architectural."[38] That same year, when the debate occurring in architectural circles over the relative virtues of the flat versus the pointed roof had reached vitriolic levels, Mies published an article on March 19 in the *Berliner Tageblatt* that urged a return to architectural fundamentals, undiverted by "petty concerns. This battle," he wrote, "is being carried out . . . as if it were a matter of . . . architectural life and death. But it is only a battle for external matters. It has nothing to do with the wrestling for the *foundations* of a new architecture . . . which is taking place on quite a different level." Mies, his opponents claimed, aestheticized architecture; he accused them of politicizing art. "What do you think the youth were saying?" commented Philip Johnson. "That Mies was the invention of the devil and should be put in jail for using silk and matching marble slabs. . . . Mies was terribly hurt by it. He couldn't understand why all the people hated him."[39]

As might be expected from a proselytizer of architectural "purity," Mies fervently opposed the intrusion of political considerations into architecture. His most powerful plea for the separation of politics and architecture—for an end to the identification of modernism with "cultural bolshevism"—came in an address before the Deutsche Werkbund in Vienna in June 1930, as the Nazis were making their initial mark as a major, national political force. "The new era is a fact," he declared.

> It exists, irrespective of our "yes" or "no." Yet it is neither better nor worse than any other era. It is pure datum, in itself without value content. . . . Let us accept changed economic and social conditions as a fact. . . . All these take their blind and fateful course.[40]

Mies, Liebknecht-Luxemburg Monument, Berlin, 1926 (Photo courtesy of Mies van der Rohe Archive, the Museum of Modern Art, New York)

In later years, too, he strenuously urged the independence of architecture from its political and social milieu. "I don't construct sociological systems. . . . I believe that you have to accept reality. . . . I would accept it and then do something with it. . . . I don't think we can change [civilization] fundamentally."[41] "The present has to be accepted," he stated, on another occasion.[42] Concerned, as he believed it should be, with universal principles, and forgetting that the podium upon which he so frequently placed his buildings connected as well as separated them from the earth, Mies saw his architecture as available anywhere, anytime, and for anyone. He could design a chair for the king of Spain in his Barcelona Pavilion (the "Barcelona" chair), a home for the editor of *The Red Flag*, and in 1930, purge the Bauhaus of its communist students. "How apolitical can you get?" asked Philip Johnson. "If the devil himself offered Mies a job he would take it."[43] For Mies, as he once said, "Architecture is the real battleground of the spirit."[44] It was an attitude that would often—to his dismay—get him into difficulties with both left and right; none more so than the monument he designed for the martyred communist leaders,

Rosa Luxemburg and Karl Liebknecht, in 1926, a commission that seemed to attest to his political sympathies. According to Mies, however, it did no such thing, and his version of how he became involved—apocryphal though it may be—demonstrates this.

Learning that an addition was being planned by the current owner of a home that he had earlier designed, Mies, anxious to gain the commission, wangled an invitation to a dinner party that the owner was giving.[45] The host and current occupant of the house was Eduard Fuchs, a broadly educated Berlin Jew and a director of the Society of German Friends of the New Russia.[46] Delighted to have the famed architect at his table, Herr Fuchs, during the dinner, asked Mies his opinion of a proposed monument to Liebknecht and Luxemburg that the Society of German Friends was planning. Mies, forgetting his manners for the moment, could not refrain from laughing at the banality of its sodden design. "The somber stone columns and medallions seem more appropriate for a banker than for fallen revolutionary leaders," he declared to his startled and embarrassed host. The offending photographs were quickly removed and the subject changed. By dinner's end, the communist memorial appeared forgotten. The next morning, however, Mies received a phone call from Fuchs who expressed interest in seeing what he would propose. "[S]ince you found the monument so amusing," he added drolly.

Mies casually suggested a brick wall, "since most of these people were shot in front of a wall." Unable to imagine a brick wall as a monument, Fuchs asked Mies to prepare a design.

"A few days later I showed him my sketch of the monument, which in the end was built," said Mies.[47]

On January 12, 1926, undoubtedly intending to further ingratiate himself with Herr Fuchs, Mies joined the Society of German Friends of the New Russia. However much his membership might later return to haunt him, it was undoubtedly an effective gesture. Two years later, Mies completed the renovation of the Fuchs' home.[48]

Another manifestation of Mies's attitude of aesthetic disdain maintained throughout his career was his persistent disregard for practical considerations, such as restrictions of program and budget. This disposition may be seen as early as his design for the Bismarck Monument. "[T]he indispensable terraced area alone would necessitate a significant excess over the cost allowances," claimed the judges in disqualifying Mies's entry.[49] The budgetary constraints of workers' housing—a major priority of the Weimar government and source of most commissions for the German modernists, as well as being of central urgency to an industrial age—seemed to bore Mies. To the complaint that workers could not afford the housing he designed for them on Afrikanischestrasse in Berlin, Mies replied, "Pay them more money!"[50] His buildings were notorious for coming in over budget.

Given his disinterest in practical concerns, it is understandable that exhibitions—projects that imposed the least constraints—numbered among his most successful accomplishments, and more than any other major twentieth-century architect they claimed as much of his genius as building. His numerous exhibition designs displayed the same concern with spatial demands; impeccable craftsmanship; interest in texture, material, and proportion; and the special balance of "logic . . . rational clarity . . . [and] intellectual order [with] . . . spirit . . . beauty and sensitive feeling" that marked his most notable architectural achievements.[51] When Mies spoke of "abstract elements of contrast, rhythm, balance, proportion and scale becom[ing] real only when distilled through the character of materials,"[52] he referred as much to his exhibitions as to his buildings. Freed from the constraints of necessity and clients' bothersome demands, Mies could experiment with materials and, most notably in his 1927 Exposition de la Mode, initiate his revolutionary concept of freely flowing space. According to Mies, the Barcelona Pavilion, considered one of his most exquisite inspirations, "was to be just a representational room, without any specific purpose. No objects were to be exhibited in it—nothing."[53] It was demolished eight months after its completion.

Perhaps no aspect of Mies's disdain for practical constraints caused more difficulties than his persistent disregard of his clients' wishes. "[W]e should treat our clients as children," he once declared.[54] If there was any yielding, commented Bertram Goldberg, the Chicago architect and one of his students, it was the people who had to submit to the buildings. "I will teach

Mies, German Pavilion at the International Exposition, Barcelona, Spain, 1929 (Photo courtesy of Mies van der Rohe Archive, the Museum of Modern Art, New York)

people to live in my buildings," Mies once said to him.[55] In his belief that "[a]nything less than perfection is unacceptable," he allowed no deviation from his stern guidance.[56] In his renowned Esters House in Krefeld, the family roasted in a southern-facing room, owing to Mies's refusal to ruin the lines of a large plate glass window by permitting an opening pane. The immensely complicated—and costly—electric device that was supposed to lower the massive pane into the ground never worked. For the Tugendhat House, which has been described as "less a home than an architectural ideal,"[57] the family received furniture they did not want, but—as Mies proudly declared—later learned to love.[58] The Seagram employees were not allowed to close the venetian blinds in their offices in his skyscraper in New York, lest the resulting disorder mar the appearance of the facade from the street. Only Mies's death released them from this constraint. And the Farnsworth House of 1952, perhaps Mies's most beautiful

American building, was uninhabitable much of the year due to the architect's refusal to allow for the particular circumstances of the site. Located on the bank of a river that was heavily infested with mosquitoes on summer evenings, Mies would not allow a screened porch, arguing—not without merit—that to do so would have ruined the jewellike design.

But the brunt of his dedicated pursuit of the sublime fell not on his clients, but on those individuals closest to him. For whatever reasons, he never formally divorced Ada. His wife and daughters would continue to carry his name, but not his notice; his hardships, but not his peace. "[O]ne thing is sure. I am not a sentimentalist," he said.[59] He never spoke about his wife and daughters: many of his closest friends were surprised to learn of their existence. He barely acknowledged their presence on those rare occasions when his daughters came to visit him. A distracted "Hello," without looking up from the newspaper, is how Georgia recalled these moments. "He really didn't know what to say to us," she recalled, her pride and pain still apparent after forty years.[60] "Everyone has feelings," Mies once said. "Everyone has emotions and this is the hell of our time."[61] His emotional distance did not moderate with time. In 1953 Mies looked forward to meeting his fifteen-year-old grandson, Dirk, for the first time, but had nothing to say to him when he did.[62] Ada continued to remind her daughters to be proud and accepting of their father's need to be free. She herself, however, became a lifelong semi-invalid, subject to bouts of depression. In light of their history of emotional deprivation, Schulze's description of one of Mies's daughters physically blocking the hospital door to prevent resuscitation of her dying father in 1969 is particularly harrowing and may reflect a lingering resentment, as well as the desire to protect him from further pain. "Let nature take its course," she said to the nurse who had come to help.[63]

Along with Ada, no one better understood Mies's single-minded determination, his need for withdrawal and self-absorption than Lilly Reich. A year older than Mies, and a brilliant designer in her own right—she had studied with Josef Hoffmann at the Wiener Werkstätte—Lilly Reich became his confidante, his business manager, the organizer of his life, and perhaps the only person, other than his brother Ewald, from

Lilly Reich, spring, 1933 (Bauhaus-Archiv)

whom Mies took advice. Their relationship began around 1925 as a love affair, settling down, after a while, into an intimacy profoundly beyond sexual liaison. She introduced him to Hermann Lange, founder of the Verseidag, whose wife frequented her couturier shop in Frankfurt-am-Main.[64] A fellow Rhinelander, amiable drinking partner, and faithful and generous client of rare and discerning eye—he was a notable collector of modern German art—Lange would prove Mies's most important and constant patron. To speak of Mies's achievements without the Langes would be like speaking of Michelangelo without the Medicis. Thanks to the Langes, Mies received a commission to design the Silk Exposition—the Exposition de la Môde—in Berlin in 1927; and it was Hermann Lange who brought Mies's name to the attention of Freiherr von

Schnitzler, a director of the I. G. Farben concern, when they were looking for an architect to design the German Pavilion at Barcelona in 1929.[65]

Lilly Reich's sensitivity to materials and brilliant sense of color heightened Mies's own natural elegance; the commissions they worked on jointly are notable for their dynamic use of color and the curvilinear forms that now entered his architectural vocabulary.[66] She was his supporter, his nurturer, his sustainer, and his defender from the onslaught of daily life. She answered his letters, paid his bills, settled his arguments, reminded him of his fatherly obligations, and looked after the needs of Ada and the girls while offering him guidance, solace, occasional financial support, and companionship. Her apartment near the Potsdamer Platz was available to him at any time to accommodate his frequent and unpredictable need for total withdrawal. She was too plain to hold on to him as a lover, and too smart to let this interfere with their relationship. Like Ada, she felt privileged simply to share his life; and like Ada, she too would be abandoned.

CHAPTER 4

"THE IRON FIST"

SO LET'S NOT BE SO FANCY PANTS ABOUT WHO RUNS THE
COUNTRY. LET'S TALK ABOUT WHETHER IT'S GOOD OR NOT.

(**Philip Johnson,** *Conversations with Architects*)

By 1930, Mies had every reason to anticipate continuing success. His Barcelona Pavilion and Tugendhat House had brought
him worldwide recognition: he had become Germany's most
acclaimed architect. Instead, at the age of forty-four and at the
height of his artistic energies, he witnessed the collapse of his
architectural practice through economic and political forces
that he both disparaged and depended on.

Like most architects, Mies's practice was tied to economic
conditions: good times meant work, bad meant none. Although
he had begun his independent practice prior to the war, it was
only in 1921, with his path-breaking Friedrichstrasse design,
followed in 1923–24 with his equally visionary brick and concrete villas, that his name became well known. The chaotic
postwar economic and political conditions, unfavorable as they

were to building commissions, had pushed the young architect inward, and one might argue that but for the lack of actual commissions coercing Mies into reflection, his visionary breakthroughs might not have occurred. Eight years later and riding the crest of Germany's economic recovery, Mies was able to realize, in the Barcelona Pavilion and the Tugendhat House, what he had only imagined earlier. In less than a decade, Mies had changed the face of architecture. He had done so not only through his genius, but through his ability to creatively harness his artistic process to—as he put it—"the spirit of the age"; or as others might say—less poetically—economic and political realities.

In 1930 Mies, like his fellow countrymen, began to suffer the effects of the worldwide economic depression. Aside from some inconsequential work, commissions vanished.[1] One of his jobs was the renovation of Philip Johnson's New York apartment. "In 1930, he had only my apartment to do," recalled Johnson, then twenty-four years old and newly appointed director of the Department of Architecture at The Museum of Modern Art. "He did it as if it were six skyscrapers—the amount of work he put into that apartment was incredible."[2] Mies's need for funds was undoubtedly a factor in his agreeing to take over the directorship of the Bauhaus in June of that year. But, as surmised from his address delivered before the Deutsche Werkbund in Vienna that June,[3] neither the critical demands of the Bauhaus, his intense involvement in the design of Johnson's apartment, nor his disclaiming of interest appeared to blind him to the political realities of the day, as the Nazis—in the words of Albert Einstein—"living on the empty stomach of Germany" gained in power and prestige.

Considering his aloof demeanor and aesthetic stance, Mies's political astuteness was remarkable. Three months after his speech, the Nazis achieved an astonishing victory in the elections of September 1930. Catapulted to national prominence, they had become Germany's second largest political party. Given modernism's early leftist associations, Mies's concern was not unreasonable. It was not politics per se that interested Mies, but rather the survival of modernism—and his own career—in a potentially hostile milieu. Like others, Mies, refusing to take the Nazis seriously, viewed them only as a temporary threat. He undoubtedly would have agreed with Einstein's assessment. "As soon as economic conditions in Germany improve," declared the renowned physicist in 1930, "[Hitler] will cease to be important."[4]

But in the fall of 1931, Germany plunged fully into the social and economic catastrophe of the depression and Mies, but for his directorship of the Bauhaus and his involvement in the German Building Exposition earlier in the year, would have joined the over 500,000 people in the building trades who were without work.[5] Economic activity in Germany virtually ceased: violence engulfed the country. Left and right met daily in bitter confrontations, and the streets became stained with the blood of German youth. Challenged by open revolt, the government was unable to halt the civil disorder. As in wartime, the newspapers reported daily figures of the dead and wounded. A civil war seemed imminent. Faced with the unpleasant choice of a Reichswehr dictatorship or a Nazi government, many Germans, who were neither anti-Semitic nor nationalistic nor espoused the Nazi cause in any manner, believed that Nazi participation in the government offered the only solution to the apparent anarchy into which their country had fallen. Even to liberals, such as Count Harry Kessler, the Nazis seemed the lesser of two evils. "The Nazis are not nearly so bad as their programs . . . make them appear," he wrote in his diary on December 9, 1931.

Nineteen thirty-two offered little economic improvement for either Germany or Mies. He designed two small homes in Berlin, the Lemcke House, which was built, and the Gericke House, which was not. The worsening economic situation may help to explain the flexible and aggressive behavior that Mies displayed with regard to the Gericke House. On June 9, he received an invitation to participate in a competition to design a small country house in the Berlin suburb of Wannsee for Herbert Gericke, the director of the German Academy in Rome. Not only did he respond with uncharacteristic haste (that same day!), but when informed four weeks later, on July 17, that his design had not been chosen, he offered to rework his proposal "without obligation"—an offer that was ignored.[6] In the July elections the Nazis scored an impressive victory.

Claiming 13,745,000 votes and 230 seats in the Reichstag, they more than doubled their constituency.[7] Although they still fell far short of a majority in the 608-member House, they had become the country's largest single political party.

Backed by this undeniably strong showing, as well as the increasingly belligerent activities of the Nazi militia, the SA and the SS (the black-shirted "Schutzstaffel")[8]—whose combined membership now surpassed that of the Reichswehr— Hitler demanded inclusion in the cabinet as chancellor with full powers to rule by decree and thus override the parliament.[9] While recognizing the legitimacy of Hitler's claims to representation in the cabinet, many in the government, headed by the ailing, eighty-five-year-old president, Field Marshal Paul von Hindenburg, harbored grave doubts as to Hitler's suitability, not to mention an understandable reluctance to relinquish their own power.[10]

What Hitler could not obtain by demand, he attempted to gain by intimidation. "Assaults, bomb-throwings, and murders continue in East Prussia, Bavaria, and Holstein," wrote Harry Kessler in his diary on August 5, 1932. "It has now been officially established that the cases of arson and bomb-throwing at Königsberg were committed by Nazis."[11] On July 17, the day that Mies learned that his design for the Gericke House was turned down, an especially violent confrontation occurred between the Nazis and the communists in the Hamburg suburb of Altona, where 19 died and 285 were wounded. Seizing upon the apparent inability of the police to maintain order, Chancellor Papen unilaterally dissolved the Prussian government by presidential decree and himself assumed the office of interior minister of Prussia, which also made him head of the Prussian police,[12] his joint holding of federal and state offices not without precedent in German history.[13] By mid-August, Berlin was an armed camp, with the storm troopers ringing the city and the Reichswehr surrounding the storm troopers.

The Nazis' insolent and outrageous behavior only strengthened Hindenburg's resolve to deny Hitler's demands. Long distrustful of the "Bohemian Corporal," as he had called him some years before, Hindenburg also hesitated to transfer power to a "new" party that did not even command a majority and was so intolerant, noisy, and undisciplined. Hindenburg was far from alone in his doubts about the respectability, even legitimacy, of a party that not only included such criminal elements as the storm troopers, but praised their barbarous activities, and whose leader, in August, sent a telegram pledging his "unconditional fidelity" to convicted Nazi murderers, and despite his recent air of respectability, had bragged that "heads will roll!"[14] Meeting with Hitler on August 13, Hindenburg informed him that he was turning down his demands. The negotiations were over.

Rumors of Hitler's imminent arrest and the establishment of a Reichswehr dictatorship under Papen and Schleicher flooded Berlin. "What now?" wrote Harry Kessler on August 14. "Civil war or the inglorious crumbling of the Nazi movement? The one thing that is certain is that we are heading for the darkest reaction. It is difficult to say which of the two competing parties, the Nazis or the Schleicher clique, is the more reactionary. The only hope is for these two lots of bigots to exterminate each other, now that they have fallen out."[15] Hitler's refusal to cooperate with Hindenburg, as well as the increasingly repugnant behavior of the SA troops, raised uneasy questions about the Nazis in the minds of many citizens. For the first time since 1930, support for the Nazis began to wane. In the elections of November 1932, they lost 34 seats in the Reichstag. Although their 196 seats made them still the largest party, they were further away from the needed majority, and Hitler's quest for control of the government seemed to be failing. The swelling Nazi tide had abated: the myth of their invincibility, that sense of a national force unalterably coming to the fore, which Joseph Goebbels had so brilliantly orchestrated, was in danger of collapse.

Schleicher, who became chancellor in early December, succeeding Papen, was convinced that the moment had come to exclude the Nazis from the cabinet. To achieve this, however, he had to broaden his base of support within the Reichstag. He decided to try to reach out to previously ignored groups, most notably the trade unions. In a nationally broadcast speech on December 15, he advocated a plan known as *Osthilfe* that would take away 800,000 acres from bankrupt Junker families and distribute them instead to 25,000 peasant families. This vaguely socialistic-sounding proposal shocked not only the industrialists, but also President Hindenburg, himself a Prussian Junker.[16] Suspicious of Schleicher's sudden change of heart, the trade unions refused to accept his overtures. By the end of December, Schleicher had managed to lose the support of the landowners, the trade unions, *and* the industrialists. With his government hovering on the brink of collapse, he abruptly switched his strategy, deciding instead to splinter the opposition by offering the vice-chancellorship to Gregor Strasser, the Nazi leader of Berlin, who claimed a greater loyalty than even Hitler among the more left-leaning party members. Schleicher's maneuver infuriated Hitler, who never forgot what he called this act of "treachery." While Schleicher was wooing Strasser, Papen—Schleicher's one-time protégé and now his rival—was wooing Hitler, with whom he met in the home of a Cologne industrialist. Disenchanted with Schleicher since his recent overtures to the unions and his apparent "softness" toward socialism, the industrialists were once again ready to swing behind Hitler, whose "responsibility" was now vouched for by Papen. They opened their purses to Hitler and his failing party was saved once more. The major worry of the Nazis at this moment—financial insolvency—had been overcome.

By the end of January 1933, it became clear that Schleicher's machinations were accomplishing nothing. Strasser turned him down; he was unable to command a majority in the Reichstag; and Hindenburg had refused to grant him his wish to "temporarily eliminate" the Reichstag. On January 28, after fifty-seven days in office, Schleicher was forced to resign. That noon, Hindenburg entrusted Papen with exploring the possibilities of forming a new government under Hitler "within the terms of the constitution."

By this time Berlin was like a city under siege. The government had virtually ceased to exist: civil war was threatening to engulf the Second Reich. The English writer Christopher Isherwood, living in Berlin during these painful months, describes the scene:

> Hate exploded suddenly, without warning, out of nowhere; at street corners, in restaurants, cinemas, dance halls,

swimming-baths; at midnight, after breakfast, in the middle of the afternoon. Knives were whipped out, blows were dealt with spiked rings, beer-mugs, chair-legs or leaded clubs; bullets slashed the advertisements on the poster-columns, rebounded from the iron roofs of latrines. In the middle of a crowded street a young man would be attacked, stripped, thrashed and left bleeding on the pavement; in fifteen seconds it was all over and the assailants had disappeared.[17]

Sirens blared constantly; police were everywhere—walking among the shopping crowds or waiting silently in the police vans that lined the side streets. Berliners—never prone to take even the police seriously—ignored them, believing them to be more for show than anything else. Since Papen (no longer chancellor, he remained as Prussian minister of the interior and thus head of the Berlin police) was now their ally, the SA and SS roamed the streets unimpeded, save for their frequent and bloody confrontations with the "Red Front," the Communist party's fighting arm and their match in arms as well as brutality.[18] No one—whether participant in the drama or dazed observer—knew exactly what was going on. The entourage surrounding Hitler in the Kaiserhof Hotel was as frantic as the occupants of the Presidential Palace. Frightful rumors spread like wildfire. "The Reichstag is being dissolved. . . . Hitler is about to be arrested. . . . The army is to set up a dictatorship. . . . The Reichswehr is about to stage a coup d'état. . . . Hindenburg is about to be abducted. . . . The Potsdam garrison of the Reichswehr has been put on alert. . . . The SA is on alert." For a country that not unreasonably imagined itself as the cornerstone of European culture, the situation was a disgrace.

Dazed and miserable, the citizens of Berlin sought only an end to the chaos; there, as throughout Germany, the desire for order could forgive much. In this, Mies would agree. His orderly architecture postulated an orderly world—and order, more than anything else, was what Hitler appeared to offer. "There is a time for the iron fist," said Mies, speaking later about the "new" Germany.[19]

* * *

On January 30, 1933, Hindenburg named Hitler chancellor of
the Reich. However, Hindenburg had refused Hitler's request
for a presidential cabinet, insisting that he rule by the parliamentary majority prescribed by the constitution, a majority
that still eluded the Nazis. Of the eleven cabinet posts, only
three went to the Nazis, and these, outside of the chancellorship, were minor positions: Wilhelm Frick was made minister
of the interior and Hermann Göring minister without portfo-
lio. Little noticed in the general concern over the federal posts
was Göring's appointment as Prussian minister of the interior,
formerly held by Papen, a position that controlled the Prussian
police.[20] Papen's conservative colleagues filled the eight
remaining posts: Papen himself was named vice-chancellor
and premier of Prussia, the highest authority of the Prussian
state and—in this capacity—Göring's superior. Furthermore,
Hindenburg promised that he would never receive Hitler
unless the vice-chancellor, Papen, was present. Surely, with
such restrictions, even the most unruly elements among the
Nazis could be controlled.

Under the banner of "law and order" the Nazis began their
reign. The "Red terror," they claimed, was responsible for the
civil disturbances; eliminate this threat and tranquillity
would return. On February 4, four days after he assumed the
chancellorship, Hitler persuaded Hindenburg to promulgate a
decree "for the protection of the German people," forbidding
any criticism of the regime in the press and authorizing appropriate "actions" if such occurred. Communist newspapers and
publishing houses were closed, their editors imprisoned or
worse; there appeared to be no limits to the arrests, prohibi-
tions, and house searches. "I am living in a situation at present
which seems to be the beginning of a war," wrote Eric Mendelsohn to his wife on February 11. "[E]very day . . . another
shading of the same cloudy furor, of uncontrolled promises and
the incitement of hatred. These are the prison bars of a free
mind, a thousand trips to the guillotine, every second a barbed
wire entanglement for the creative passion."[21] Outside Berlin,
things were much the same. "Left for Weimar by evening
train," wrote Harry Kessler on February 28. "Things are terri-

ble [there] ... with 'auxiliary' police [SA] everywhere and nobody daring to speak a word."[22]

Göring, since his appointment on January 30 as Prussian minister of the interior, moved quickly to make the Prussian police force a tool of the federal government, issuing a series of decrees in early February that granted him almost total control over Prussia. Papen offered little resistance. One of Göring's first decrees was to the Prussian police, informing them that they were expected to stand in with the "constructive forces of the nation" and act ruthlessly against the Reds. On February 22, he created an "auxiliary" police force of 50,000 troops, 40,000 of whom came from the SA and SS, and 10,000 from the Stahlhelm, the right-wing veterans' private army, further tightening Nazi control over the police.

Reports of terrible ordeals filled the foreign press. The Vienna *Montag-Zeitung* wrote about Herr Otto Lehmann-Rüssbuldt, an elderly gentleman whose "offense" seems to have been that he was president of the League for Human Rights and had made pacifist speeches on its behalf. For these "crimes," he was purportedly "kept in chains for days" and subsequently beaten when unable to stand at attention before the police prefect.[23] But German media could only print the reassurances of the Nazi leaders. "Throughout all Germany," declared Minister Göring, "there has not been one person from whom even one fingernail was chopped off."[24]

Along with suspected members of the left, the major thrust of Nazi harassment was directed against the Jews. No profession was immune. Jews were expelled from all musical organizations, from the lowliest percussionist to Bruno Walter of the Berlin Philharmonic; from the theater; from journalism; from law and medicine; from all chambers of commerce and exchanges. Jewish banks were forced to discharge their Jewish employees; publishers were afraid to publish books by Jews and booksellers refused to display them. Municipalities discharged their Jewish officials, cancelled all orders placed with Jewish firms, and withdrew all official notices from newspapers wholly or partly under Jewish ownership. Jewish stores were molested, Jewish bank accounts impounded, and Jewish judges removed from criminal cases. Many Jews had already fled the country—among them, Eric Mendelsohn, Albert Einstein, Lion Feuchtwanger, and Bruno Walter. Nazi storm troopers marched down the Potsdamer Strasse singing viciously anti-Semitic songs—"When Jewish blood spurts from the knife, things will be even better!"—while Minister Göring piously denied anti-Jewish bias. "I will never stand for persecuting a man," he declared, "simply because he is a Jew!"[25] On April 1, the Nazis ordered a Jewish boycott in retaliation for the "false" reports of Nazi brutality that had appeared in the foreign press: "*Volkswut,*" they called it, a spontaneous expression of "the people's anger." The excessive enthusiasm with which the SA troops carried out this task provoked protests not only by outraged Europeans and Americans, but by many Germans as well, even those who had furtively, with a deep secret pleasure, looked forward to less competition from their Jewish rivals. Not yet secure in its power and still sensitive to foreign opinion, the Nazi leadership was stunned by the protests and quickly forbade such overt actions.

No institution seemed immune from Nazi persecution, even the Prussian Academy of Arts, Germany's most prestigious artistic society of which Mies, since 1931, was a proud member. On April 2, a poster urging a boycott of "destructive Marxist-Judaic elements" appeared in the academy's austere hallways. Several of the names that appeared on the list, such as Oskar Schlemmer and Hans Poelzig, were neither Jewish nor Bolshevik.

Stand, fight, run, protest . . . what should one do? "[I]n the end," wrote Schlemmer, "we shall probably be fired. I just wonder what form it will take. . . . Where to? What then?"[26] Such questions were posed often and answers were few. It seemed best to keep silent, to ignore the widening chasm between fact and fiction, between the reality one saw (or chose not to see) and the perfidy of the press and politicians. Five times the Germans had gone to the polls in 1932; once again in 1933. And what had they to show for it? Hunger, no work, and parades. The deceptions, impotence, and outright lies of politicians were accepted by almost everyone, which was not surprising in a society that demanded so little of the political realm.

Lulling much of Germany's population into silent complacency was the fact that the Nazis lacked the two-thirds majority in the Reichstag needed to enact constitutional changes. What was reassuring for many Germans, however, was for Hitler intolerable. Having literally to beg Hindenburg every time he wished a decree was cumbersome, awkward, and demeaning. Hitler resolved to overcome this final impediment to unencumbered executive rule; and at the cabinet meeting of March 15, Göring offered him a solution that was as ingenious as it was simple. He would arrest as many of the opposition deputies as necessary in order to ensure a two-thirds majority! According to a decree of February 28, opposition to the regime was now a punishable crime, and the fact that members of the Reichstag were constitutionally immune from arrest was of little significance. On March 23, denuded of Nazi opponents, the Reichstag voted for the "Enabling Act" (*Ermächtigungsgesetz*), a law which granted Hitler the right to rule by decree for four years. The Reichstag had literally voted itself out of existence.

Outside of Prussia (which, through Göring, was already controlled by the Nazis) the German states retained their traditional control over all city and state offices, schools, universities, museums, orchestras, theaters, and libraries. Given the Nazis' insistence on *Gleichschaltung*, the bringing into line of all spheres of political, cultural, and social activities, the continued retention by the states of powers more extensive than their national government was intolerable, and beginning in March, a series of decrees was imposed to systematically dismantle the governmental structure of the states and bring them under federal, and hence party, control. When these maneuvers proved awkward, "The Law for the Restoration of the Civil Service" was passed on April 7, authorizing the federal government (i.e., the Nazis) to appoint the state governors, who, in turn, were empowered to "appoint and remove local governments, dissolve the diets, and appoint and dismiss state officials and judges." With this act, the continued independence of the German states from federal sovereignty—a tradition as proud and as long as German history itself—was abrogated and a serious impediment to Hitler's quest for total power removed. Under the provisions of the law, any individual employed by the state (which meant virtually every teacher, musician, actor, director, museum curator, and city official) who was considered politically or racially undesirable was subject to immediate dismissal. Those of non-Aryan descent (namely, Jews) and real and imagined opponents of the regime were no longer acceptable to the state. Affected by this law were such people as Mies's close friend, the painter Max Beckmann (who was dismissed from his teaching post at the Frankfurt Kunstgewerbschule), Paul Klee, Otto Dix, Bruno Taut, Martin Wagner, Hans Scharoun, Richard Döcker, Bruno Paul, Oskar Schlemmer, Hans Poelzig, Georg Muche, Max Reinhardt, Karl von Ossietzky, Kurt Tucholsky, Erwin Panofsky, Fritz Busch, Ernst Cassirer, Edmond Husserl, and such politically independent city officials as Konrad Adenauer of Cologne, Fritz Hesse of Dessau, and countless others. Imperiled also were the Prussian Academy of Arts and the Bauhaus. No other single legislative act of the Nazis had such a devastating effect on Germany's cultural community.

With barely a whimper, democracy in Germany had appeared to collapse. But democracy had never really flourished there; its demise, hardly noticed by its citizens, took place long before Hitler came to power.[27] His programs and decrees differed little from many of those proposed by his predecessors: Hitler was simply more successful than they had been in carrying out what many in Germany believed had to be done to get things in order once more. There were many proponents of "the iron fist"!

For Mies, as for the great majority of German citizens, life was not much different after January 30, 1933 than before. Neither the torchlight parades with their thundering beats, nor the glorious appeals to the fatherland could dispel the disheartening awareness that there was still no work, barely enough food, and little money. The trams broke down as regularly as ever, *Pfennigs* enough for a *Schultheiss* brew were still hard to come by, and politics was still garbage . . . something better off discarded. Like his fellow Berliners, Mies dismissed politics as readily as ever. Looking out the window from his apartment on Am Karlsbad, he watched the goose-stepping Nazi troops marching below. "They have nothing to do with me," he said and turned away.[28]

CHAPTER 5

SO DEADLY A BATTLE

HELL IS EMPTY,
AND ALL THE DEVILS ARE HERE!

(**William Shakespeare,** *The Tempest*)

Lilly Reich, however, viewed things differently. If many found her outspoken and often unpleasantly assertive—"pushy" was a term frequently used in speaking of her—few would dispute her ability to face up to things as they were, without sentiment or ideological bias.[1] In her view, Mies could plead all he wished for a depoliticized architecture, yet she felt that his position as Germany's foremost modernist architect and director of the Bauhaus—the country's most politicized symbol of modernism—placed him in a particularly vulnerable position in 1933.[2] A candid review of the facts, unfortunately, bore out her view. For more than a decade, modernism and the Bauhaus had been represented by the Nazis as a foreign virus from which Germany had to be purged. There was nothing in their battles, past or present, to indicate a change of heart.

While antagonism toward modernism had always been a

part of the Nazi posture and references to "Bolshevik art" appear in Hitler's speeches and writings during the 1920s, this antipathy was sporadic, haphazard, and vague. The definitive association of the Nazi party with overt antimodernism occurred in 1929, with the establishment of The Fighting League for German Culture (Kampfbund für Deutsche Kultur) under the leadership of Alfred Rosenberg. Editor since 1923 of the Munich-based Nazi newspaper *Völkischer Beobachter,* Rosenberg was chosen to lead the party's first cultural division, The NS Society for Culture and Learning, two months after it was organized during the party's first great Nuremberg rally in August 1927. When it became clear in 1929 that such an organization would be more effective if removed from overt partisan affiliation, it was renamed The Fighting League for German Culture.

The program of the KDK, as it became known, was twofold: first to repudiate all manifestations of modernism in German culture, and second to foster the development of so-called "native" and "characteristic" German art in order to enhance "total cultural Germanness without regard to political borders."[3] Socially critical and pacifist literature, new music (including jazz, which was labeled a "footstep stamped upon the German essence"), futurist and cubist painting, and modernist architecture were ostracized and ridiculed as examples of *Nigger-kultur* that was infecting the "national culture."

Local chapters of the KDK were set up throughout Germany. To their highly publicized meetings flocked Nazis and proto-Nazis, as well as those who would later lay down their lives in opposition to them. Traditionalists or racists, ignorant or esteemed, they shared only their bewilderment and distrust before the new art. In the KDK, these diverse and scattered groups gained a single, powerful political voice; while the Nazis, ostensibly defending "German" culture, gained much-welcomed publicity and prestige in a country that during the 1920s had come more and more to associate "foreignness" with the ruin of Germany, thanks to the harsh reparations policies of the Allies and subsequent disastrous inflation, the French and Belgian occupation of the Ruhr, and finally, in 1929, the catastrophic economic depression. To the eager embrace of the KDK came those who merely longed for the peace and order of the *Kaiserzeit,* the racists for whom modernism was "a dan-

gerous, . . . death-dealing spirit [that] will murder . . . the German soul,"[4] and craftsmen for whom industrialization presented a very real threat to their livelihood. Indeed, the
aggressive statements of some of the modernists contributed
to the growth of the building trades membership in the KDK.
Mies, for example, in 1924, had written, "It is quite clear to me
that [the new trends in architecture] will lead to the total
destruction of the building trade in the form in which it has
existed up to now."[5]

Chronologically, and by virtue of its leftist origin, much of
Germany's avant-garde culture was associated with the
Weimar years. In 1930, the Weimar government began to falter;
and as the Weimar era came to symbolize failure, frustration,
and disappointment, so too did its culture. Modernism came to
be seen not only as the symbol of a disintegrating and failed
society, but—especially by the far right—as its very cause, that
is, the harbinger and carrier of amorality, internationalism, and
hedonism, some sort of bubonic flea carried by a doomed and
misbegotten rat. Few manifestations of the new art—painting,
buildings, plays, and literature—escaped the scurrilous barbs
of the KDK as trumpeted by Rosenberg's *Völkischer Beobachter.* The painter Emil Nolde, himself a member of the Nazi
party (to its eternal embarrassment), was referred to as a "technical bungler," while the paintings of Dix, Hofer, and Grosz
were said to be grinning concoctions of "ethical nihilism."
Foreign acclaim was but an index of political suspectability.
The works of Thomas Mann, Bertolt Brecht, Kurt Tucholsky,
Erich Kästner, Paul Klee, members of the Bauhaus, and countless others were dismissed as "subversive and disintegrating,"
their very persons said to be unworthy of the name "German."
Museum directors who patronized modern art, such as Dr.
Hildebrand Gurlitt, the director of the Zwickauer Museum,
were ridiculed—Dr. Gurlitt was decried as a promotor of the
"smears of Kokoschka, the childish scribbling of Klee, [and] the
subhumanity of Kollwitz [and] . . . Barlach"—and where possible, as in the case of Gurlitt, expelled from their posts.[6] (Dr.
Gurlitt was dismissed in April 1930.)

Nazi attacks on architecture were equally pernicious. Mies's
house at the Berlin Building Exposition of 1931 was labeled a
"horse stable." The brunt of Nazi antagonism, however, was

borne by the municipally sponsored workers' housing. These constituted the most prominent group of modernist buildings in Germany and also provided the only encounter most Germans had with the style. Because of limited funds, as well as the acute need for quickly built housing, these developments, which dotted the suburbs of the country, were often poorly built. As a result, modernism came to be associated with shoddy construction—an identification fostered and encouraged by the KDK, as well as conservative architectural groups. In 1929, the conservative architectural journal *Deutsche Bauhütte* devoted an entire issue to photographs of construction defects in the Törten Siedlung, a small housing project in a suburb of Dessau designed by Gropius and members of the Bauhaus, with graphic photos of cracks, peeling paint, and streaks caused by dampness and rusted fittings.[7]

Germany's introduction to the Nazi meaning of "cultural renewal" took place in January 1930, when the Nazis won their first electoral victory in Thuringia and transformed what had been simply malicious verbiage into action. Thanks to their large plurality, Dr. Wilhelm Frick, the suave and efficient local party leader, was able to demand two ministries for the Nazis, occupying them both himself. As minister of the interior, he could control the Thuringian police; while as minister of education, he saw an opportunity "from which the forces of moral and spiritual renewal could reach out into the Reich."[8] Frick introduced racist prayers into the schools and brought the architect Paul Schultze-Naumburg into the state administration. Schultze-Naumburg would become one of the Nazis' most indefatigable supporters and the most effective popularizer of their charges against modernism.

In the years before the war, Schultze-Naumburg had been one of Germany's most respected architects. The simple, uncluttered lines of the neo-Biedermeier country mansions that constituted the bulk of his architectural practice made him a leader of the more progressive wing of prewar German architecture. From 1902 to 1905, he had been professor at the Kunsthochschule in Weimar, where he edited the prestigious nine volume *Kulturarbeiten*. In 1918, at the age of forty-nine, he had witnessed the collapse of his architectural practice and reputation, as commissions for large country residences

Paul Schultze-Naumburg, 1939 (*Deutsche Bauzeitung*, 1939, v. 24. Photo from Avery Architectural and Fine Arts Library, Columbia University, New York)

became increasingly scarce and his architectural style came under vociferous attack by modernists attempting to discredit historicism. In 1926, the year that he met Adolf Hitler in the Wagner House in Bayreuth, he published his *ABC of Building*, in which he criticized the building techniques associated with the modernists as being untried, impermanent, and shoddy.[9] That same year, racist theories (namely the notion that certain races, most notably the Aryans, are superior to others by virtue of their degree of purity) came under broad discussion,[10] and his use of racial innuendos in architectural criticism (he was one of the first to do so; in an article published in a conservative architectural journal, he described the flat roof, one of modernism's most prominent features, as "a child of other skies and other blood"[11]) brought Schultze-Naumburg to the Nazis' attention. His full-fledged racial doctrine appeared in his 1928 book *Art and Race,* where he argued that the decadence reflected in modern art and architecture was of biological and racial origin. Modernism, according to this view, was no longer simply bad, it was un-German. Around 1929, his arguments began to appear in the right-wing press. Mies was described as a "two-raced foreigner,"[12] perhaps because of his name; and the Weissenhofsiedlungen, which he directed, was called a "Jerusalem suburb." Prominent members of the avant-garde were portrayed as agents of a threatening "oriental invasion." To Schultze-Naumburg's racial epithets, the right-wing press added its own accusation of "bolshevism." Rosenberg referred to the theatrical productions of Max Reinhardt as "Mongolian waves of Bolshevism";[13] Leopold Jessner's avant-garde productions were attacked for their "Spartacist manner" and "absolutely non-German staging."[14] By the time of his appointment by Frick, in 1930, as head of the Weimar Kunsthochschule, the successor institution to the original Bauhaus, Schultze-Naumburg had become one of the most prominent opponents of the new art.

On April 1, 1930, Frick introduced an "Ordinance Against Negro Culture," by means of which he proposed to rid Thuringia of all "immoral and foreign racial elements in the arts." Under the aegis of this law, Schultze-Naumburg ordered the painting over of Oskar Schlemmer's famed Bauhaus wall frescoes in the building that had originally housed the school. Several days later, acting as advisor to Frick, he ordered the removal of seventy works of modern art—including pieces by Dix, Feininger, Marcks, Nolde, Heckel, Barlach, Kandinsky, Klee, Schlemmer, Schmidt-Rottluff, and Lehmbruck—from public view in Weimar, claiming that they had "nothing in common with the Nordic-German essence, but rather limited themselves to depicting the eastern or otherwise racially inferior sub-humanity."[15]

Frick and Schultze-Naumburg's actions soon caught the attention of Rosenberg, whose *Völkischer Beobachter* had been providing broad coverage of the developments in

Thuringia. In Schultze-Naumburg, Rosenberg recognized an individual of great potential value to the party, and in 1931, the KDK sponsored Schultze-Naumburg in a highly publicized lecture tour around Germany. Widely reported throughout the German press, these lectures, in which Schultze-Naumburg revealed purported similarities between depictions by such modern artists as Nolde, Barlach, and Kirchner and the more hideous deformities of human disease, contributed more than any other event to the notoriety of the KDK. Schultze-Naumburg was soon recognized as the party's leading spokesman on art.

As might be expected, Frick's policies brought him into conflict with other state and federal officials, and his tenure was mercifully brief. Ignoring this setback, the Nazis continued to lavish praise on his cultural programs. In recognition of his efforts, the first big convention of the KDK was held in Weimar in June 1930. The KDK issued a resolution calling for undiminished actions against "all native-destructive influences" in the arts, as well as architecture "which is foreign to our essence." Sharing the podium, Frick and Rosenberg heaped lavish praise on the racial theories of Schultze-Naumburg, whose future within the party seemed brilliant.

Despite the Thuringian experience, the swiftness and virulence of the Nazi cultural actions in March and April 1933 caught almost everyone in the art world by surprise. With no warning, exhibitions were closed and paintings physically stripped from the walls of public museums as well as private galleries. As in Thuringia, works of modern art were the Nazis' special targets. Boycotted by the press and radio, artists found themselves suddenly unable to earn a living; avant-garde journals were confiscated and prohibited. The absence of any apparent logic in the Nazi actions kept many people off their guard. Some cities were left free to pursue their normal cultural activities, while others were subjected to extensive police harassment. An artist respected and praised in one city often found his works banned and politically suspect in another. With no clear directions coming from the central government in Berlin, cultural policy was determined by the whims of the local party leaders of state cultural ministers. Even those, such

as Schlemmer, who had already borne the brunt of Nazi persecution in Thuringia were startled and undone. "I wanted to
close up shop entirely and have no more exhibitions for the
present," wrote Schlemmer to F. C. Valentien on March 18,
when advised of the closing of an exhibition of his paintings in
Düsseldorf,

> my feeling being that one should ride out this storm and
> keep calm. What weapons does one have against passions?
> . . . On the other hand, I cannot ignore your suggestion that
> this business should be blown up into a "case" while there
> is still time. . . . We should enter the lists and fight the
> good fight. For the worst has not yet come! . . . The best
> question remains whether one should react to the Nazi
> provocations or hold one's peace.[16]

Four days later, on March 22, the situation seemed no less
chaotic. "How are things down your way?" Schlemmer
inquired of Willi Baumeister in Frankfurt. "Events are coming
so thick and fast. Who has taken over the government in your
city, and what is he like? That will probably determine
whether you hang or go free." Schlemmer then described the
scene in Stuttgart, where he lived:

> Speaking of hanging: I "did" and was taken down. In the
> Stuttgart Art Guild. Then mounted in two back rooms,
> accessible only to insiders of unquestionable character.
> Count Baudissin, a longtime devoted National Socialist,
> apparently wrote to Hitler immediately, but couching his
> letter in terms of principles instead of exposing himself on
> my behalf.
>   Valentien in Stuttgart had wanted to show my paintings
> at his gallery even before they went to the Art Guild. Still
> wants them. I am wavering between "closed until future
> notice" . . . and standing to fight. At the moment, so much
> tension is in the air that the latter course seems very risky,
> although it would certainly force a decision on principles
> and future policies.
>   Hofer tells me that there are apparently some decent
> people among the Nazis, but the ruling clique consists of
> petty-minded characters who know no tolerance.

> Nothing has happened here yet. Just rumors. . . . Bad
> times are coming. What course should one take?
> Cultivate art only within one's four walls, on Sundays?
> Find some practical second profession? But what?[17]

Deprived of meaningful discourse in the press, members of the
cultural community eagerly combed Hitler's public statements for some indication of party policy toward art. They
found nothing but platitudes expressing sentiments with
which few Germans could have disagreed. "Art will always
remain the expression and reflection of the longings and the
realities of an era," said Hitler on March 23, in a nationally
broadcast speech before the Reichstag. "It is the task of art to
be the expression of this determining spirit of the age."[18] But
no one knew precisely what the Nazis preferred, although certain directions were evident. They appeared to oppose any art
whose principles did not arise out of a racial or biological
connection with "Germanness." Such art was labeled "Bolshevik." The "International Style," as the modernist architectural style had come to be called, with its debt to the postwar
leftist political movements and commitment to universal
principles, appeared to be a prime target.

Surprisingly enough, the most outspoken denunciations of
the Rosenberg-KDK faction's racist interpretations of artistic
nationalism came from within the Nazi party itself—specifically from a group of artists, art historians, and critics centered
around the National Socialist Students' Association in Berlin,
who tended to be younger, better educated, and more accustomed to artistic experimentation than their KDK counter-
parts. German expressionism had been their own formative
aesthetic experience,[19] and they were generally unfamiliar
with the long history of Nazi antipathy for modernism, which
had occurred mostly outside Berlin.[20] For them, Kirchner,
Schmidt-Rottluff, Barlach, Nolde, and Heckel were not subver-
sives, but bearers of the same "Germanic" truth that they
believed Nazism represented in the political realm.

That such diversity of opinion existed within the Nazi party
was a tribute to Hitler's political skill. Since power, not doc-
trinal purity, was his main preoccupation, Hitler's first priority
was to make his program as broadly appealing as possible, with

little regard for consistency or logic. The resulting broad and heterogeneous constituency, whose perceptions of the Nazis were diverse and often contradictory, precluded any strict programmatic unity, despite the monumental efforts of Nazi propaganda to assert otherwise. More often than not, as Albert Speer's recollections indicate, ideology was sacrificed to political expediency. In 1931, Speer who was to become Hitler's architect and was still working as an assistant to Professor Heinrich Tessenow at the Institute of Technology in Berlin-Charlottenburg, received his first party commission, to redecorate a villa for use as a local party headquarters. Timidly—for he was concerned lest his choice be considered "communistic"—Speer suggested the use of Bauhaus-designed wallpapers. He was astonished by the district leader's casual approval. "We will take the best of everything, even from the Communists," the young man said.[21] For years, the prestigious Nazi cultural publication *Art of the Third Reich*, headed by Speer, carried advertisements for the Bauhaus wallpapers.

Speer's concerns were well founded: the Bauhaus, headed since 1930 by Mies, had long been the focus of Nazi assault. There were few German groups that had been locked in so deadly a battle, as irrevocably and for as long, or had left so profound an impact on their time, as the Bauhaus and the Nazis. Their antagonism extended back to their formative years: Gropius was its progenitor, and, fourteen years later, Mies would be its heir.

Until late July 1930, when Gropius suddenly appeared in his Berlin office and implored him to take over the directorship— "Unless you take over," Gropius had said, "the Bauhaus will collapse!"[22]—Mies had had little to do with the Bauhaus. Other than offering his name in public support during particularly difficult moments, or participating infrequently in its architectural exhibitions, Mies had had no association nor any particular interest in the school. In later years, he persistently downplayed his association with the Bauhaus. "I owe the Bauhaus nothing," he angrily declared in 1964, when asked to participate in a worldwide Bauhaus exhibition. "[N]othing before I came, nothing during and nothing afterwards!" said Mies, turning down the request for his participation, while nearly throwing Alfred Hoppe, the organizer of the exhibition,

out of his room.[23] Aloof, uncommunicative, reticent, intro-
spective, possessing neither pedagogical experience nor even a
university degree, petulant, intolerant of debate, Mies seemed
ill-suited by temperament, background, and inclination to be
head of any school. His teaching style can only be described as
painful. Egon Hüttmann, one of Mies's Bauhaus students,
recalls an aspect of Mies's teaching style that must evoke agonized memories on both sides of the Atlantic.

> Let's speak of a correction during a lesson. Mies was very
> silent. He looks at it, says nothing, bends over it, says
> nothing. He's sunk deep in thought. One hour, two hours,
> you can't imagine the time ... maybe three hours. And
> then he himself begins to sketch. Once he got started, then
> it was wonderful. He was a deep, inward person. But then
> his thoughts worked all the more.[24]

Teaching sessions seemed equally nerve-wracking during
Mies's more extroverted moments. Howard Dearstyne, an
American architectural student at the Bauhaus, recalls Mies
running so "roughshod" over some students' designs—"marking them up with a soft pencil to indicate how they should have
been done"—that the students, "so hurt by Mies's ruthlessness
... stayed away from class for a full month."[25]

Aside from his personality traits, Mies's rigorous artistic
discipline and unbending philosophical principles made him
an unlikely choice to head the notoriously contentious, politically and artistically divided Bauhaus. And yet, surprisingly
enough, Mies accepted Gropius's offer. Searching for a plaus-
ible answer, Philip Johnson, disdaining altruistic motives, suggested that only Mies's poor financial situation in 1930 could
explain his acceptance of a position to which he was so temper-
amentally and philosophically unsuited.[26] With little work on
his drawing board and no major projects on the horizon, Mies
needed the money. One might conjecture, however, that something else lay in the back of his mind. It was very clear by late
July 1930, as it had been in June of that year when he had given
his Vienna address, that the Nazis were looming as an important political force in Germany. What better forum to convince
them of modernism's apoliticism than the Bauhaus, its most

prominent and politicized symbol? Eliminate politics from the Bauhaus and the centerpiece of Nazi opposition to modernism would collapse. The Bauhaus, in this perspective, offered the key to modernism's—and his own—survival under a Nazi government. There was no way he could build in a Nazi-dominated Germany unless modernism was decisively and permanently severed from its crippling, and in Mies's mind, irrelevant political associations. The Bauhaus would be the laboratory where Mies would prove his case.

On August 5, 1930, Mies, with a contract that ran to March 1935, was named as the new director of the Bauhaus. Anxious to make the proposal as attractive as possible, Gropius assured Mies that he could retain his Berlin practice and appear in Dessau—only two hours from Berlin—just two or three days a week. In view of what lay ahead, along with his essential unsuitability for the position, one must wonder if Mies ever regretted his decision. His fury at Hoppe in 1964 suggests that he did!

To both admirers and detractors, the Bauhaus had come to symbolize the essence of modern design. Its undeniable accomplishments—the teaching of arts and crafts, the nature of good design, the shaping of our environment and its effect on people—altered the very "look" of its time; its equally undeniable flaws, attacked relentlessly by its enemies, led not only to its own demise, but to the discrediting of the entire modern movement. What is more, its early identification with "cultural bolshevism" did much to undermine modernism in the Germany of the 1920s.

The Bauhaus was established by Gropius in Weimar in 1919. Like so much else in Germany during this time, its roots lay in the prewar years—specifically in the urgent quest for reform of art education. Not realized until after the war, the original idea became altered—like the country itself—almost beyond recognition. What had begun in 1915 as an effort to reform the art education of the Grand Ducal School of Arts and Crafts in Weimar, ended in 1919 in an institution vastly different from anything either Gropius, the Weimar authorities, the artists, students, faculty, or local citizens could possibly have envisioned in the earlier years.

Its difficulties began with its location in Weimar, a leafy, peaceful city of 40,000 inhabitants and little industry, which, although located about 140 miles from Berlin, was far removed from the prewar cosmopolitanism or postwar revolutionary chaos of the capital. The former capital of the Grand Duchy of Saxe-Weimar, associated with Goethe, Schiller, Johann Sebastian Bach, the Cranach brothers, Liszt, and Nietzsche, Weimar understandably viewed itself as the center of hallowed German values. Chosen for this very reason as the home of the new socialist republic, Weimar was as little prepared to assume this role as to harbor so innovative an institution as the Bauhaus. From the beginning, the Bauhaus, as conceived and organized by the thirty-six-year-old Gropius, was simply the wrong institution for the wrong city.

A benevolent and kindly man, who saw others as he was himself, and without any teaching or administrative experience, Gropius was ill-prepared to deal with the problems he encountered in Weimar: the demands of the conservative professors of the original art school, who, by the terms of the agreement with the state (for the Bauhaus, like most German academic institutions, was state supported), remained on the faculty of the Bauhaus in the same building; the conflicts that were inevitable in any community of diverse and strong-willed artistic personalities; the fears of the local tradespeople in the face of so radical a crafts institution and of a traditional conservative community that did not take kindly to the nude sunbathing, promiscuity, and propensity to painting over, in bright, loud colors, the city's beloved statuary by a student population described by Schlemmer as "an insolent band of young people, . . . a mad assemblage of today's youth."[27] There were also fears that "strange, alien elements" (a German euphemism for Jews) were taking over not only German art and values, but the country as well. The conflict between "town and gown" that plagued the Bauhaus from the very beginning reflected the schism that was developing throughout the country in the arts and in politics.

By the end of World War I, Gropius's long-standing compassion for workers' welfare had been transformed into a fervent leftist political commitment.[28] This was clearly evident in his founding in December 1918 and directorship of the Workers' Council for Art, whose program declared "that the political revolution must be used to liberate art from decades of regimentation."[29] Begun amidst his involvement in the Workers' Council, the Bauhaus was meant by Gropius to realize many of its ideals, most notably the direct involvement of "creative people ... in the forging of a new social order."[30] However utopian it may have been (and it became more utopian in retrospect than it ever was in fact), the Bauhaus was perceived from the start—as indicated in its program—as a "cathedral of Socialism."[31] For years Gropius belonged to the pro-Soviet circles in Berlin. Like much else about the school, however, Gropius's Marxist inclinations expressed themselves in a strangely ambivalent manner. Despite his leftist sentiments, he seemed to recognize the need for political neutrality in an institution dependent on public support and funding. His vacillation between what he wanted to do and what he was able to do helps explain the school's strangely eccentric, almost schizophrenic, political character.

Gropius's elimination of the title "professor" proclaimed the school's opposition to the usual ivory tower of German academicism, while his use of the term "masters" for the faculty, and "apprentices" and "journeymen" for the students announced its craft orientation and desire to participate in the real, everyday world not normally associated with traditional German art schools.[32] In an effort to build "a world of beauty ... completely anew," as Gropius wrote for the Workers' Council in 1919, and to bridge the gap between craft and fine arts, workshops in bookbinding, weaving, carpentry, printing, and metalwork joined those of color theory, painting, and the fundamentals of aesthetics. But Gropius's idealistic expectations were dampened by outside political pressures that intruded from the start. In December 1919 the Bauhaus, then only a few months old, was publicly accused of being "un-German." That this meant "too many Jews" is evident from Gropius's response that there were "only 17 students ... of Jewish extraction, of whom none has a grant and most have been baptised. All others are Aryans."[33] The accusations continued, however, and by June 1920, Gropius, obviously exasperated, complained in a letter, "We must destroy parties. ... I want to found an unpolitical community here."[34] With this idea apparently in mind, Gropius admonished some Bauhaus students for participating in a funeral of a group of strikers who had been shot in Weimar in 1920. Yet, the following year, he designed a prominent concrete monument in Weimar's main cemetery commemorating their death.[35]

Despite his awareness of the need for at least the appearance of political neutrality, Gropius's equivocating actions continued. In 1922 he appointed two controversial artists to the faculty, Wassily Kandinsky and László Moholy-Nagy. An abstract painter with strong Russian affiliations, Kandinsky, inspired by Gropius and the Bauhaus, had set up the Moscow Institute of Art and Culture in 1920;[36] while Moholy-Nagy had been a supporter of Bela Kun's Hungarian Soviet. Although Mies claimed that it was Gropius's first wife, Alma Mahler, who encouraged him to engage celebrities to teach at the Bauhaus as the only way to assure the school's success, the presence of these two individuals contributed substantially to the criticism of the Bauhaus by the far right.[37]

In 1928, exhausted by the endless crises, and complaining that 90 percent of his efforts were spent in defending the school against its critics, Gropius resigned.[38] But to head the Bauhaus, by now "one of the most hated institutions of the 'new Germany' ... [and] a first-class target in election campaigns,"[39] Gropius appointed the Swiss architect and dedicated Marxist Hannes Meyer. Under Meyer's aegis, a vociferous communist cell was formed, classes in political theory introduced, formalistic art ridiculed (to the disgust of such faculty members as Albers, Kandinsky, Klee, and Schlemmer), and Russian revolutionary songs sung. Although Meyer denied the charge that he was involved in a collection made by leftist students on behalf of striking miners, the accusation led to his abrupt dismissal in 1930 by Mayor Hesse of Dessau (where the school had moved in 1925). In his passionately aggrieved response to his forced resignation, Meyer accused the Bauhaus of "flirting" with cultural bolshevism while forbidding its students to be Marxists, a not entirely inaccurate assessment.[40]

Ambivalence was not limited to the school's political identity; it also marked its artistic character. The Bauhaus's pronounced artistic vacillation produced an internal tension that characterized its history as much as the ever-present political pressures. "[A] wasp's nest," was how Lyonel Feininger

Members of the Red Bauhaus Brigade (Photographer unknown, courtesy of the Hochschule für Architektur und Bauwesen, Weimar, Bauhaus-Bildarchiv)

Hannes Meyer

René Mensch

Klaus Meumann

Konrad Püschel

Bela Scheffler

Philipp Tolziner

Anton Urban

Tibor Weiner

described the school in May 1919 in a letter to his wife in Berlin;[41] while Schlemmer, writing to his friend Otto Meyer in March 1922, spoke of "a thousand clashing ideas."[42] Nothing better illustrates the astonishing artistic diversity of the Bauhaus than the list of artists who served on the school's faculty at varying moments in Weimar: this collection ranged from the bizarre and mystical Swiss painter Johannes Itten, whose cultish antics included flowing robes, meditation, garlic-laced diet, and breathing exercises, to Moholy-Nagy, the "image of sobriety and calculation"[43] in his worker's overalls and nickel-

Bauhaus members in KPD demonstration, Dessau, 1930 (Photographer unknown, courtesy of the Hochschule für Architektur und Bauwesen, Weimar, Bauhaus-Bildarchiv)

rimmed spectacles. Although its name eventually became synonymous with artistic functionalism, the Bauhaus began as an arts-and-crafts institution, reflecting the pervasive rejection of technology by many in Germany. Engendered by technology's role in creating the tremendous destruction in World War I, it was felt especially keenly by Gropius.[44] If anything, the initial program of the Bauhaus deprecated the functionalistic priorities of technology, lauded only a few years before. "Things shaped by utility and need cannot still the longing for . . . the rebirth of . . . spiritual unity," Gropius wrote in 1919.[45] By 1923 it was clear that Gropius's intention of creating a new art for a new society (at taxpayers' expense) was degenerating into little more than a romanticized arts-and-crafts school with expressionistic longings "for a revolutionary 'breakthrough' to a better world."[46] Taking its cue from an outraged and conservative populace—whose mothers admonished their children to behave lest they be sent to the Bauhaus![47]—the state successively reduced the school's allotment of operating funds, which had been parsimonious to begin with.[48] In 1923, sensitive to increasing criticism of the school as well as the renewal of interest in technology, and realizing that the survival of the Bauhaus depended on securing some degree of financial independence from the state, Gropius, in a radical artistic "about-face," shifted the school away from its arts-and-crafts orientation toward technology and functionalism, hoping—in offering a partnership arrangement with private industry—to secure their support. The idea was to induce industry to partially finance the workshops, which would now be geared toward designing quality products that could be cheaply mass produced, in exchange for which the Bauhaus would receive royalties—thus freeing them from total dependence on state support. Sobriety, practicality, and discipline replaced idealistic fervor, and the workshops now turned their attention to the design of electric-light fixtures, teapots, furniture, textiles, tiles, radiators, ceramic food containers, and toys, with an eye toward commercial production and sale. Faculty and students who had come to one Bauhaus now found themselves in a profoundly different—and divided—institution. "The reality of our century is technology: the invention, construction and maintenance of machines," declared Moholy-Nagy.[49] To which the painter Paul Klee, committed to art's basic connection with life, replied, "The machine's way of functioning is not bad. . . . [But] [w]hen will a . . . machine have babies?"[50]

Mies, whose voice in the affairs of the Bauhaus had been notably absent, joined in the carping among the European intellectual community about what was going on at the Bauhaus. Never kindly disposed to Gropius's activities, Mies was critical of the new orientation, complaining in a letter to Theo van Doesburg, the founder of the internationally famed Dutch De Stijl art movement and stern critic of the romanticization of the Bauhaus, that Gropius's reform did not constitute an "authentically constructive approach." It will lead, he predicted, to an "arty formalism," a "juggling of constructivistic [that is pseudo-constructivist] form."[51] Despite his reproach, Mies accepted Gropius's invitation to participate in an international exhibition of postwar European architecture that the Bauhaus was sponsoring in 1923, as part of the huge series of festivities honoring—and publicizing—its new direction. The exhibition—which ran from August 15 to September 30, 1923, and filled the hallways, entrances, and stairways of the school, as well as the city museum—was an enormous success, attracting 15,000 people and such international celebrities as Stravinsky, Busoni, and the famed Dutch architect J. J. P. Oud.

Gropius opened the occasion with a lecture, the title of which, "Art and Technology: a New Unity," became the hallmark of the "new" Bauhaus.

Despite these changes, the Bauhaus continued to be harassed by the community and state. Local businesses were understandably upset that their tax money was going to an institution that felt free to engage in business deals with possible competitors. By 1924, with the difficulties of the Bauhaus contributing largely to the gains made by the far right in the Thuringian parliament (Weimar had been named the capital of Thuringia in 1920), it was clear that the school's days in Weimar were numbered. Toward the end of 1924, ostensibly after an investigation revealed that only seven out of eighty-two students came from Thuringia, the Thuringian ministry of education served warning that state funds could be committed only through the following March, and Gropius was forced to announce the school's closing.[52]

During the final, confusing months, Gropius and the faculty pondered their course of action: should they change, move, or simply close up? Although they received offers from several cities, such as Breslau and Darmstadt, they decided to accept the offer from Dessau, extended to them by Fritz Hesse, the city's liberal mayor. Dessau was a far different community than Weimar. An industrial city (it housed the Junkers airplane factory as well as a number of other industries); closer to Berlin; with a larger, more heterogeneous population, it was in 1925 the only German province to have socialist rule. Given the school's background, it seemed very natural for it to find refuge in such a politically sympathetic milieu, and the Bauhaus's association with Dessau was perceived by some as very much "a Party matter," as Kurt Schwitters commented in a letter to Theo and Nelly van Doesburg.[53] In addition to covering faculty and student stipends, additional funds were made available by the city for an extensive building program, and Gropius was able to design a large complex that included facilities such as workshops, administration offices, a cafeteria and an auditorium, and housing for the students and faculty—buildings that became world famous and synonymous with the new architecture. Most of the students and faculty joined in the move. Yet, despite this expression of support, the new

Gropius, Bauhaus Building, Dessau, 1925–1926 (Bauhaus-Archiv)

location and impressive facilities, the addition and elimination of some workshops, and the creation of a department of architecture (to which Gropius appointed Hannes Meyer as head), the move to Dessau in 1925 changed nothing.

The Bauhaus's problems were, by now, intrinsic and due, to a great extent, to the nature of Gropius's personality and leadership. Gropius took great pride in encouraging the members of the Bauhaus to "find their own way" and, as he put it, "take nothing from me on authority,"[54] a generous, idealistic intention that invigorated the school, but also led to fragmentation and the creation of an atmosphere described as "a mad-house" by Lyonel Feininger.[55] What held the school together was Gropius himself—his strong personality, the high regard in which he was held by everyone, and the fact that he never took sides. His conciliating manner is evident in Feininger's description of a scene in a letter written to his wife in June 1919. With several students threatening to petition for his dismissal, Gropius invited the rebels in for, as Feininger put it, "a heart-to-heart talk. He listened to everybody's complaints," wrote Feininger. "That eased their minds and helped to clear the situation."[56] Given its factious tradition, it is no wonder that Gropius's departure in 1928 precipitated a major crisis—one, many claimed, from which the school never recovered. Disbelief and dismay greeted Gropius's decision, while the news that the controversial and less highly regarded Meyer had been appointed the new director provoked—in the words of

Gropius's wife, Ise—a near "general revolt" and sense of "catas-trophe."[57] Schlemmer, Klee, and Moholy-Nagy left, while Kan-dinsky remained, working behind the scenes to undermine Meyer, who he believed—correctly—to be uninterested in sup-porting the painting workshop, in which he saw little social value. Indeed, Meyer set out to destroy what he mockingly referred to as the Bauhaus's "ivory tower." Art, he declared, was anchored in life; building was a "collective . . . biological and not an esthetic process."[58] While his emphasis on the social mission of art may be seen as an extreme expression of the antiformalist trait that had existed from the start at the Bau-haus, his insistence that the creative artist play a social role outraged those Bauhäusler with more formalistic priorities. As might be expected, Mies thought little of Meyer,[59] who recipro-cated the feeling, referring reproachfully to Mies as "the arm of the Muses."[60] To Meyer's motto that "all life is a striving after oxygen + carbon + sugar + starch + protein" and that there-fore "all design must be anchored in this life," Mies, according to Gropius, replied, "Try stirring all that together; it stinks!"[61]

Preoccupied by its own inner crisis, and confident in Mayor Hesse's ability to keep its foes in check, the Bauhaus paid remarkably little heed to Dessau's growing antagonism. By 1930, with political and economical conditions deteriorating there as in the rest of Germany, Hesse found himself less and less able to protect the Bauhaus, which was mystifyingly insensitive to community relations, from rightist attack. Meyer's appointment had rekindled the taint of Marxism that had never entirely left the school, and in Dessau, as in the country at large, the Bauhaus was generally regarded as a Marxist institution.[62] Dessau citizens understood the avant-garde Bauhaus art as little as had their Weimar compatriots, and the Bauhaus did as little as before to help them. As in Weimar days, the Nazis found the Bauhaus to be an easy vote-getting issue. They had little difficulty in arousing the hostil-ity of the financially strained community against an "alien" institution whose highly visible and costly housing and tech-nical facilities seemed like a provocation to people who were unemployed, ill-fed, and poorly housed. The Bauhaus had become modernism's most prominent symbol and its identi-fication as a Marxist institution served to confirm modernism's link with "cultural bolshevism" in the public mind. Support of the Bauhaus, and, by extension, avant-garde art, was made by the Nazis to appear not merely unpatriotic, but treasonous.

Pushed to the brink, Gropius—who had continued to keep an eye on the school—and Hesse moved quickly to rectify the rapidly deteriorating situation.[63] The opportunity presented itself in mid-July 1930, when Hesse was able to fire Meyer for his alleged participation in the International Worker's Relief Fund. A new director had to be found at once—someone who understood the need for an "unpolitical community." Gropius turned to Mies, who, only the month before, in his Vienna Deutsche Werkbund address, had argued so persuasively for the severance of art and politics.[64]

"[P]eace and quiet will reign," observed Schlemmer, who, although gone since 1929, still kept abreast of Bauhaus affairs, when he learned of Mies's appointment, "for this was the idea behind summoning Mies van der Rohe to Dessau. You will be bedded in roses . . . not a political creature will be stirring, even to leave the sinking ship. That is about the way I picture such a regime, first left, now right."[65]

But "peace and quiet" did not reign at the Bauhaus. Learning the astonishing news upon their return from summer recess, the Bauhäusler reacted with shock and outrage, as much by the circumstances of Meyer's departure, as by the appointment of Mies. Criticism focused on Mies's Vienna speech, where he had spoken out against the suitability of a single artistic style for a particular epoch—most notably modernism's responsiveness "to the great struggle for the new way of life"—a position that he himself had advocated only three years before.[66] Espousing a position of aesthetic purity and strict political neutrality, Mies urged the cessation of modernism's strident identification with a style of living which seemed to alarm many people (such as the Nazis and their supporters). The justification of modernism, Mies declared, as with any style, must be purely aesthetic and functional. This applied equally to the Nazis. If the new era was without value-content, as Mies stated, then appeals to such qualities as "Germanness" or "technology" were irrelevant in evaluating its art. The quality of a building was independent of elements extrinsic to itself, such as social usefulness or racial suitability. Artistic value came only from artistic means applied toward artistic goals. With one society as good as another, an architect could, and should, build for anyone—a strange hypothesis coming from an architect who justified his art by appealing to "the spirit of the age." To speak of such a "spirit" implies belief in the existence of a single characteristic that others may neither agree with nor even perceive and contradicts the espousal of social, artistic, and political diversity. Either Mies did not see the conflict, or—more likely—he did, but realized that desperate days demanded desperate measures. For him the important thing was to build. "One thing will be decisive: the way we assert ourselves in the face of circumstance," he said.[67]

Already incensed over Meyer's abrupt firing, many Bauhäusler—not all of them communists—felt great sympathy for his social priorities and were repelled by their absence in Mies, who seemed to them unconscionably devoid of compassion and social responsibility. How could one speak of "Beauty" in a land where seven million were unemployed? How could one claim that "the new era was without value-content" in the midst of turmoil, hunger, and injustice everywhere? And where, they wondered, could they store their hearts while working on the ideal displacement of space? While Mies's meticulous avoidance of political polemics had brought Gropius to his door, it was precisely this quality that angered many at the Bauhaus.

"Only a self-centered person who has lost all contact with the rest of the world would be able to view the world this way," complained one student, with regard to Mies's sentiments. "Every Bauhaus student knows enough not to believe such nonsense any longer. This statement would not be worth mentioning if it were not that the director of the Bauhaus made it."[68] While Mies's involvement with the Liebknecht-Luxemburg monument sat well with the students, many remained appalled by the social irresponsibility implied by his formalistic style and the fact that he "built mansions for the wealthy when," as they put it, "he should have provided dwellings for the poor."[69]

It is unlikely that Mies realized what he was stepping into: his first taste of Bauhaus life began immediately upon his arrival in Dessau, where a large group of students, "egged on by a handful of militant communists," according to Dearstyne, had gathered in the cafeteria to argue their course of action.[70] Impassioned argument raged round the clock; classes had to be canceled. At first, Mies ignored them, hoping that the students would eventually tire and return to class.[71] Instead, they "demanded" he speak with them: he refused. When they further "demanded" that he exhibit his work so that they could "judge whether or not he was qualified to be the director of their beloved school," Mies exploded in rage.[72] He did not deny that the students were entitled to their political opinions, but he felt that the Dessau taxpayers were supporting an art school, not a political forum, and that politics had no place at such an institution. He ordered political discussion to cease, and the cafeteria to be emptied at once. "Either you stop, or I will be forced to take strong action," Mies declared, according to Ludwig Grote, the curator of the Dessau Museum, who had been instrumental in convincing Hesse to invite the Bauhaus to Dessau. When the group didn't stop, Mies called in the Dessau police.[73]

Accustomed to Gropius's patient mediation and, from repute at least, anticipating the same on the part of their new director, the students were outraged by Mies's act. Grote, however, insisted that Mies called the police merely to frighten the recalcitrant students, and sent them away as soon as they arrived. "I have always looked upon this drastic action of Mies as an error in judgment," wrote Dearstyne.[74] Almost half a century later, when asked to comment on their Bauhaus years, many former students specifically mentioned this incident and refused to speak of Mies, other than in the most abusive terms.

After the police incident, Mies closed the school for about six weeks to let things simmer down, expelling several of the ringleaders during this lull. When the school reopened, Mies personally interviewed each remaining student—the left called these sessions "inquisitions"—each of whom was required to sign an affidavit agreeing to refrain from discussing politics on the school's premises or holding political meetings of any sort. Those who refused to sign had to leave. Despite Mies's actions, the communist faction—known as kostufra (kommunistische Studentenfraktion)—never entirely disappeared. Going underground, they continued to direct their activities against the rising national socialists, as well as the school's leadership and such faculty members as Kandinsky and Albers. Mies countered by refusing to issue travel permits to those who wanted to attend a lecture by Hannes Meyer in Leipzig; he also had removed a "socio-critical" painting from a school exhibit.[75] In the eyes of the left, Mies's willingness to use force, his annulment of students' "rights," his repeal of their "freedom" to form coalitions—which many Bauhäusler considered indigenous to their school—amounted to nothing less than "fascization" of the school. "Always obedient, bübchen!" wrote Egon Rakette, in his fictionalized account of his Bauhaus years. "Don't make Poppa van der Rohe angry!"[76] It is ironic how often Mies's single-minded pursuit of the apolitical politicized him in the eyes of his opponents: to the left, he seemed nothing less than a "fascist," while to the right, he remained a "cultural bolshevist."

No matter what the students felt about Mies's methods or principles, it was difficult not to harbor respect, however grudging, before so reluctant, but determined, a fighter. At the Christmas party that year, appreciative of Mies's efforts, the remaining Bauhaus students presented him with a medal that read, "For bravery in the face of the Bauhaus."[77] Many, however, wondered whether what remained deserved to be called the "Bauhaus." Encouraged by Gropius, contentiousness and the broadest possible artistic and political expression had always characterized the Bauhaus community. If so many of the school's problems had stemmed from this free and untrammeled expression, so too had much of its legendary vitality. Seemingly dedicated to its singular artistic pursuits and devoid of political harping, Mies's Bauhaus, to many, was transformed beyond recognition.

Mies's efforts at depoliticization proved of no avail; in the fall 1931 election campaigns, the Nazis once again made the school a major local issue. Blanketing the city with campaign posters, they urged immediate cessation of all funding for the Bauhaus and demolition of the Bauhaus buildings. The inflammatory posters also urged the firing "without notice" of all foreign teachers, "because it is inconsistent with the responsibility which good community leadership bears to its citizens, that German comrades hunger while foreigners are paid more than sufficiently from the taxes of the needy people."

The Nazi efforts were eminently successful: they gained control of the Dessau city legislature. To the surprise of many within the Bauhaus and Dessau community at large, who had dismissed the Nazi prose as mere campaign rhetoric, Nazi harassment of the school continued even after their victory.[78] Despite Nazi opposition on the city council, Mayor Hesse, with the help of the communists, was able to pass a budget—although severely reduced—for the Bauhaus. This dependence on the communists strengthened the position of kostufra, and undercut Mies's efforts to effectively depoliticize the school.[79] On January 21, 1932, Senator Hofmann, a member of the NSDAP—the National Socialist German Workers' (Nazi) Party—proposed the dissolution and demolition of the "un-German buildings" and the cancellation of the school's appropriation, which he suggested be channeled instead to the recipients of social welfare, assistance for the unemployed, and the creation of jobs.[80] Although the Nazis and their allies controlled twenty of the thirty-six votes in the city council, they were unable to carry out this proposal. Financial support for the Bauhaus was controlled by the state of Anhalt, whose senate (Landtag) was as yet free of Nazi domination.

Virtually incapacitated by the meager budget, the Bauhaus situation got progressively worse during the winter semester of 1931–32. By the following spring and summer, the school was barely able to function: survival became a hand-to-mouth battle. The old political clashes reemerged. As Mies focused his attention on disbanding the leftist faction at the Bauhaus, the nationalistically oriented group grew more aggressive and outspoken. Whether or not Mies worked as diligently to diminish their voices as he did with those on the left is unknown. What is known is that the far right grew increasingly influential at this point. In July 1932 they helped draft an appeal to President Hindenburg, urging his intervention in the embattled Bauhaus situation; this appeal ultimately proved futile.[81] Despite Mies's orders, the Bauhaus students found it difficult to disengage themselves from the political strife that was enveloping their country, as may be seen in the correspondence of a Swiss architectural student in June 1932. "[T]wo factions at the Bauhaus," he wrote,

> ... are fighting each other like cat and dog. The communists and leftists on the one side and the rightist representatives, all shades, beginning with those of the "youth" movement and right up to the Nazis, on the other. ... Later when we were all assembled at the canteen ... the old student representatives (who had been suspended by the director a few days earlier) appeared at the ... meeting and attempted to defend themselves before all the students. Thereupon, the Director banned them from the premises and they had to leave the canteen. Today the Bauhaus is a school in which cliques prevail as hardly anywhere.[82]

So factious had the situation become, that when the students ignored his order for them to disband, Mies, once again, called in the police to break up their meeting and expelled the ringleaders.[83] Despite Mies's efforts, the Bauhaus, both within and without, was as politicized as ever.

Internal dissension was far from Mies's only problem that summer, as the Nazis on the city council intensified their attacks on the school. To support their contention that the Bauhaus produced useless and bad art, and, by inference, to prove that their opposition was not based on political motivation at all, the city council decided to invite a panel of "experts" to judge the exhibition traditionally put on by the Bauhaus at the end of each term. Depending on its report, the city council would make its recommendations to the Landtag, which, by then, seemed assured of having a nationalist majority. Named to head this panel was Professor Paul Schultze-Naumburg.

At sixty-three, Schultze-Naumburg not unreasonably anticipated more than gold medals and approbation from the Nazis; he had served them faithfully and well. What is more, having suffered the collapse and subsequent discredit of his architectural career by the postwar modernism, he surely felt more than an ideological triumph in his appearance as "judge" over Mies van der Rohe. It must have been a moment of ineffable personal jubilation.

The implication of Schultze-Naumburg's participation was

lost on no one. The event was clearly a sham. To save Mies from inevitable embarrassment, Hesse offered to excuse him from participation in what could only be viewed as an insult. "I know you'd like a two-week vacation. I'm delighted to give it to you," Mies recalled his saying. Mies refused. "I'd like to stay here," he said. "I'd like to see these people."[84] One can only speculate as to why he insisted on participating in so fruitless and potentially humiliating an event; the first of several that would mark his Bauhaus years. Perhaps his reasons for doing so lay at the very heart of his association with the Bauhaus; that is, his singular crusade to assure the continuing existence of modernism (not to mention his own career) under the very real possibility of a Nazi national government. Behind Mies's willingness—one even detects a certain pugnacious eagerness—to participate in this artistic "trial" seem to lie two intentions: first, to convince the Nazis that issues of "un-Germanness" were irrelevant to modernism, as much as to any other artistic style; and second, to discredit the perception that art is related to society—that judgmental attitude which associated an artistic style with a political system and permitted the linkage of the term "cultural bolshevism" with modernism. Face to face with Schultze-Naumburg, the very individual responsible for propagating what had come to be the Nazi "line" on art, Mies could tangibly demonstrate his contention that modernism was neither more nor less "German" than anything else and show that modernism (and the German avant-garde) could flourish as well under a Nazi regime as under any other political system. Thus, it was for more than the Bauhaus that Mies was fighting: as one of its most prominent spokesmen, he was fighting for the future of modernism in a Nazi-dominated Germany. Convinced of the correctness of his position and with complete confidence in his commanding personal persuasiveness, Mies believed that no opportunity should be lost to convince the authorities that political issues were irrelevant to the Bauhaus as well as to modernism, which the school had come to symbolize. Whatever modernism and the Bauhaus had been in the past, both now had to be scrupulously apolitical to survive—and Mies was determined to demonstrate this. Whatever fate might hold in store for his country, modernism—the truth and "correctness" of which Mies never doubted—must survive. In his view, art was irrelevant to politics and politics irrelevant to art. This so-called "trial" struck at the very heart of Mies's association with the Bauhaus. "It was a political movement," Mies said in later years, speaking of this event. "It had nothing to do with reality and nothing to do with art. I had nothing to lose, nothing to win, you know."[85]

As usual, Mies had his problems with the Bauhäusler, as well as with the Nazis. The communist students, refusing to participate in what they saw as a farce, attempted to sabotage the pointless exhibition and convinced others to go along with their boycott. One student placed a piece of ham under glass on the display table: Mies, "whom the circumstances had made more than usually exacting," according to Dearstyne, immediately expelled the student and her ham.[86] Kandinsky insisted on displaying some old geometric abstractions that Mies knew would antagonize the jurors. Nevertheless, Mies went ahead with the exhibition; it was smaller than planned, but no less fine. Kandinsky's controversial works were placed on a table in the center of the room that Mies carefully avoided as he escorted the rapidly moving visitors through the exhibition hall. The maneuver, of course, was meaningless, since the decision was preordained.

On August 22, 1932, assured of support in the Anhalt Landtag by the newly elected nationalist majority, the Dessau City Council voted 20 to 5 to close the Bauhaus. The "somber glass palace of oriental taste," the so-called "aquarium"—the Dessau Bauhaus, that incubus of "Jewish-Marxist" art—was finished: round one of a confrontation that would continue for the next five years was over.

Mies was determined to prevent the Bauhaus from closing under such a political cloud: to do so would legitimize and confirm the Nazi antimodernist claims. "One should not be intimidated, coerced by fear to remain passive," said Mies in a speech that he gave at the anniversary celebration of the Deutsche Werkbund in Berlin in October. "Now more than ever, it is important to stand up for one's principles, to remain steadfast and upright; to stick to the true essentials."[87] Thanks to the efforts of Mayor Hesse, the Bauhaus was able to partially salvage its finances, along with some supplies and heavy equipment, such as looms and kilns. In its haste to force the closing of the school, the city of Dessau had prematurely terminated its contract, permitting Mies and the faculty to claim the monies still legally due them. In addition to these funds, the school was allowed to retain the royalties it received for its various designs, the most notable being those for wallpaper. The Bauhaus thus found itself in a surprisingly good financial position. What was painfully clear, however, was that it could no longer survive on public support. For this reason, Mies turned down invitations from other cities, such as Leipzig and Magdeburg. In a Nazi-governed Germany, the only hope for the Bauhaus lay in its transformation into a private institution, free of state subsidy—and control—in a cosmopolitan environment that would not condone the Nazi antics to which it had been subjected in the past. Berlin was obviously where the Bauhaus belonged. Set up as a private school, it would be beholden to none but its aesthetic conscience. Despite the unceasing personal defamation that continued in the rightist press—an article in the *Deutsche Bauhütte* described his Weissenhofsiedlungen apartment building as being "in the collective style of barracks for Russian workers detained by the Soviets"[88]—Mies continued to vigorously assert the Bauhaus's apoliticism. "Mies van der Rohe *emphatically* added that he conducts the institute beyond the realm of all political tendencies," reported the *Steglitzer Anzeiger* in an interview with the director on the occasion of the move to Steglitz. In a similar interview published in the *Montag Morgen*, Mies declared, "We hope for nothing and fear nothing." He anticipates, the article went on to say, the Bauhaus functioning in Berlin "quietly, unnoticed, and undisturbed."

However favorable the financial settlement with Dessau may have been, it was insufficient to permit the Bauhaus to operate with complete financial freedom. To enable it to rent a "terribly black," old, deserted telephone factory in Steglitz, Mies put up 27,000 marks, a considerable sum of money, of his own. The decrepit building lay hidden behind a wooden fence, so ugly and broken-down that more than a few, upon seeing it, withdrew from the school. But over one hundred students— more than four fifths of the Dessau enrollment—stayed, as did most of the faculty.[89] All joined in scraping, cleaning, laying

Bauhaus Berlin, Birkbuschstrasse, Steglitz, 1932–1933 (Photo by Hans Keszler, courtesy of the Bauhaus-Archiv)

mortar and brick, and whitewashing the interior walls until the decrepit old building was transformed into a glittering schoolhouse hardly smaller or less equipped than what they had left behind and "a good deal less pretentious," as Mies declared, as critical as ever of Gropius's architectural achievements. The school's quarreling days seemed over. By October 25, 1932, less than a month after they began their renovation, the Bauhäusler were able to return to their lessons in a new-found spirit of brotherhood and common purpose that seemed to have repressed their old enmities. For the first time in its torturous history, the spirit of the Bauhaus seemed united.

Habits, however, die hard; by the winter, with the hardships fading into memory, the petty bickering and political quarreling soon resumed. Located now in what was popularly known as "Red" Berlin, the leftist elements at the Bauhaus reemerged. They decried Mies's move to Berlin and privatization as a "flight into the desert" and demanded the right to form a coalition, receive scholarships, and free food.[90] "Mies took over the Bauhaus for egotistical reasons," they claimed.[91] "[I]n yielding to the Fascist pressure and adapting the house to the demands of the 'Third Reich,'" wrote the *Weltbuhne,* a left-wing intellectual journal, "[the Bauhaus administration is] in reality supporting Fascism."[92] So deteriorated had the situation become by early December, that Mies was forced to expel several students, an act immediately condemned by sympathetic students and press as authoritarian and a violation of Bauhaus principles.[93] The nationalist groups also continued to have their say. When the Nazis gained their first majority in the Reichstag in March 1933, student enthusiasts ran up the swastika in front of the school.

In mid-March 1933, the first concentration camps opened.[94] Those who had been merely deprived of their means of livelihood by the April 7 law considered themselves fortunate in comparison to those placed under arrest or, as it was called, "protective detention." While not much was known about the camps, judging from the number of individuals reported as "shot in flight," life in them appeared to be neither pleasant nor safe. Germany's intellectuals, most of whom—like Mies—had considered themselves "above politics" in the "noblest" German tradition, or had even harbored sympathies with many Nazi tenets, now found themselves plunged into the sickening maelstrom that they had so diligently attempted to ignore. Frightened and confused, they remained, for the most part, notably and painfully silent. Only a few voices were raised expressing muted concern. One of these was Mies. In March, in an obscure article on the significance of glass in architecture, he called for "a measure of freedom of design which we must never relinquish."[95] Attracting far more attention was the voice of Wilhelm Furtwängler, the renowned director of the Berlin Philharmonic, whose incisive questioning of Nazi artistic goals, directed to Joseph Goebbels, the newly appointed minister for people's enlightenment and propaganda, appeared, along with Goebbels's response, in the *Deutsche Allgemeine Zeitung* and various other Berlin newspapers in mid-April.[96] Their dialogue was avidly followed by Mies and the entire cultural community.[97]

Like Mies, Furtwängler was concerned about the intrusion of ideology into art with the passage of the Nazi-sponsored April 7 law, which threatened such notables as Bruno Walter and Walter Klemperer in the musical world and Max Reinhardt, among countless others, in the theater. Like Mies, Furtwängler recognized only "good" and "bad" art: other issues—specifically, the Jewish question—were irrelevant. "The question of *quality*," argued Furtwängler, "is not just an ideal for music, but a matter of *life and death.*" The dismissal of Jewish artists, he claimed, was justifiable only if they were bad artists, not merely because they were Jews. "[A]rtists . . . are much too rare for any country to be able to afford to be rid of them without cultural forfeit. . . . I call to you, in the name of German art, so that things do not happen which perhaps cannot be set right again," he concluded.

"True artists are rare . . . [and] . . . must be encouraged and supported," Goebbels replied, assuring Furtwängler that the Nazi policymakers "consider ourselves to be artistic people. . . . [T]rue artists . . . will be able to make their artistic statements in Germany, now and in the future as well." In a classic demonstration of Nazi double-talk, Goebbels assured Furtwängler that "every real artist should be given a field for unhindered work," providing that he was a "constructive, creative person . . . and not on the side of [the] rootless [and] seditious"—qualities that since April 7 encompassed a frighteningly broad constituency. "Please be convinced that a call in the name of German art will always be heard in our hearts," Goebbels declared. "Artists of real ability, whose work outside the field of art does not offend the elementary norms of state, politics, and society will continue to find in the future, as they have always had in the past, the warmest encouragement and support."[98]

Their correspondence was published on April 11, the day of the Bauhaus raid.

CHAPTER 6

BLACK LEATHER BOOTS AND BAYONETS

I WOULD THROW OUT EVERYTHING THAT IS NOT REASON-
ABLE.

(**Mies,** *Print*)

"I nearly died," Mies said, when speaking twenty years later of his first sight of the bayonet-armed gestapo troops surrounding the school. "It was so wrong!"[1] Never once during his tenure as director had he been able to forget the school's perilous situation; yet, in all that time, it had not seemed possible that things would come to this. However fragile or flawed was Gropius's utopian vision of a new art for a new world, surely it had nothing to do with black leather boots and bayonets.

Recovering his composure, Mies ran toward the cordon of troops that surrounded the building.

"What's the idea?" he said to the armed sentry. "This is my school; it belongs to me."[2]

"Stop here," said the sentry.

"What?" replied Mies. "This is my factory. I rented it. I have a right to see it."

"You are the owner?" responded the sentry. "Come in."[3]

Under normal circumstances, one does not hesitate to enter one's own quarters; an invitation by the gestapo was quite a different matter. Mies's disinterest in politics did not make him impervious to its perils, as his recollection makes clear; "He knew I would never come out if they didn't want me to."[4] Inside, he was informed by the officer-in-charge that they were looking for incriminating evidence of communist activity to be used against Mayor Hesse, whose long-standing opposition to the Nazis and well-known commitment to the "bolshevik" Bauhaus were now, under the April 7 Civil Service Law, grounds for "protective detention" and possible prosecution. Technically, they were not interested in the Bauhaus. "They regarded us as perfectly harmless," recalled Mies, "and so we were."[5]

By now, nearly two years into his directorship and painfully aware of Nazi hostility toward the Bauhaus, Mies had taken the precaution of shipping all possibly incriminating documents to Switzerland.[6] Whether this was done on his own initiative, or at the suggestion of the politically savvy Lilly Reich, remains unknown. Certain that nothing remained on the school's premises that could be "misinterpreted," Mies grandly ordered everything to be made available to the police. "Open everything for inspection," he said. "[O]pen everything."[7] Having already searched the building the night before, the gestapo knew this, too. Other than a few old copies of *Die Weltbühne* and the slightly less radical, but equally left-wing periodical *Das Tagebuch*, they found nothing. After several hours, the men began to complain.

"What shall we do?" asked the officer-in-charge, speaking to his superior at headquarters on the telephone. "We must go and eat!"

"All right," responded his superior, "seal up the whole place and come back!"[8]

Before leaving, the gestapo examined everyone's identity cards. Fifteen individuals were unable to produce proper credentials; they were loaded into police vans, taken to headquarters for further questioning, and released later that day. According to Dearstyne, the grim situation was not without its moments of humor. Some students were amused by the apprehension of Alcar Rudelt, a member of the faculty[9] and suspected Nazi sympathizer; and by the "flabbergasted" expression on the face of the interrogator of Ivo Panaggi, an Italian journalist-artist enrolled at the Bauhaus chiefly to report on the school's activities to the Italian press, when he produced "an invitation signed by Joseph Goebbels to some Nazi soirée or other."[10] Those not present at the school that day were later privately interrogated, the gestapo having confiscated the entire student register.[11] The building was then sealed and sentries posted at the door.

"And we were on the outside unable to get in," said Mies.[12]

That afternoon, the Bauhaus faculty gathered in Mies's apartment. While they had long experienced Nazi harassment, never before had it been backed by the power and prestige of the national government. What had previously been dismissed as the irresponsible rantings of far-right fanatics, as a "delirium of the German lower middle class," had now become the sovereign law of the land.[13] The faculty, divided over how best to handle the situation, remained locked in argument for hours. Since important personal items, such as passports of several foreign students, remained locked inside the premises, their immediate recovery seemed urgent. A student was dispatched to gestapo headquarters to arrange a temporary reopening of the building. What immediate actions needed to be taken seemed obvious; longer-term strategy aroused more controversy. Was the police action the final "coup de grâce" to the Bauhaus—or simply as Mies believed—a minor element in the prosecution of Hesse and of little consequence to the affairs of the school itself? Were there steps the school should be taking to ensure its continued existence; and if so, what should they be? Would expressions of support suffice or would more substantive steps be necessary? In fact, the dialogue that took place in Mies's apartment that afternoon differed little from those going on elsewhere, privately and in the corridors of power, both inside Germany and beyond, as to the proper response to the Nazi outrages. Should they be treated as expeditiously as possible, ignored or appeased in the hope they were but a passing phenomenon? Or should they be challenged, sternly, relentlessly, and publicly?

Once the initial shock of the incident passed, Mies's tendency toward procrastination reasserted itself. As politically disinclined as ever and prone by nature toward simplification ("I want things to be simple. . . . Mind you, a simple person is not a simpleton," he once said[14]), Mies was convinced that the Nazis needed only to be reassured about the "harmlessness" of the Bauhaus in order to convince them to reopen the school. Normally impassive and excessively rationalistic, Mies—to the dismay of students and faculty alike—was inclined to laugh away the whole affair, viewing it as a perverse mistake that reasonable men would soon correct.[15] Further affecting Mies's usual passivity, was the fact that he had recently been invited to participate in the most important architectural event of 1933—his first major project in years—the competition to design a new building for the Reichsbank, the national bank of Germany; and he appeared determined to do nothing that might jeopardize his chances of success.

The Reichsbank competition had been announced at the beginning of February 1933, coinciding by chance with the Nazi assumption of power.[16] Thirty of Germany's best architects were invited to participate, their styles encompassing virtually the entire spectrum of current architectural practice. Among those invited were Heinrich Tessenow, Hans Poelzig, German Bestelmeyer, Gropius, and Mies. The jury, which consisted of Peter Behrens, Paul Bonatz, Heinrich Wolff, the head of the Reichsbank's building department, and another representative of the bank, was equally distinguished. Pointedly missing from the list of invited architects was the prominent Jewish modernist architect and friend of Mies, Eric Mendelsohn. Although, like most German Jews, he was well acquainted with anti-Semitism—he had mockingly referred to himself as an "East Prussian Oriental" in more serene days—he was despondent over his omission from so prestigious an architectural event. However, the architectural community, excited over the possibilities of this competition, seemed little concerned over the plight of their Jewish colleagues. Instead, they preferred to view the contest's stunning scope, particular timing—coming at a moment, as it was put, of "national renewal"—and inclusion of several noted modernists as cause for hope. Did this signal a modification of the Nazis' attitude? Were the modernists—at least those "unblemished" by racial or political stigma—now going to be tolerated, perhaps even honored? Was it possible that they *could* play a significant role in the government's future building plans?

Nurtured on the successful collaboration between the great Schinkel and his ruler, Friedrich Wilhelm IV, German architects everywhere harbored visions of a similar artistic partnership. Whoever won this competition would gain immeasurable status with the infant regime, whose leader was rumored to be "interested" in architecture. For Mies, then, far more lay at stake than the future of the Bauhaus, and simply dissociating himself and the present-day institution from its Red-tainted past no longer seemed enough. If he entertained any hope of participating in the government's building plans, he had to convince the regime, once and for all, that neither he, the Bauhaus, nor modernism represented a threat to its ideology. The current Bauhaus crisis thus presented Mies with a particularly difficult dilemma: too impassioned a defense of the school could threaten his goal as much as none at all. Yet, the Bauhaus's predicament did offer him an opportunity to convince the Nazis that modernism—and himself as well—could exist in the Third Reich. As he himself had said in his 1930 Vienna address, it was pointless to make judgments about any period in time. "[W]hat is right and significant for any era," he had said, "including the new era, is . . . to give its spirit the opportunity to exist."

But to whom should he present his case? At the moment, no one claimed cultural leadership of the regime. Recent events, however, offered a clue. The closings of exhibitions of modernist art; the removal of paintings from public museums; the racist campaigns; the threats, arrests, and persecutions; the April 7 Civil Service Law; and the police action against the Bauhaus all bore the unhappy imprint of the Thuringian "experiment"—an impression reinforced by the prominence of Wilhelm Frick in the new Nazi government. (Along with Hitler and Göring, he was one of the three party members in the cabinet.) It appeared that the KDK faction was running the cultural scene. Within that group, certain cultural leadership belonged to only one man. Late that same evening, Mies made his decision to call Alfred Rosenberg.

*   *   *

Alfred Rosenberg, 1933 (Ullstein Bilderdienst)

However scorned and ridiculed Rosenberg may have been among his Nazi peers, few would have denied the contribution of the haughty and acerbic Balt to the Weltanschauung of their party. Even those who personally despised him were forced to concede his influence on Hitler in the early years of the NSDAP: both Hitler's *Mein Kampf* and the daily propaganda outpourings of the party bore evidence of Rosenberg's racist theories. "[Hitler] was deeply under the spell of Rosenberg," wrote Ernst "Putzi" Hanfstaengel, scion of a wealthy and cultivated Munich family of art publishers who were early supporters of Hitler. "Hitler seemed to have a very high opinion of his abilities as a philosopher and a writer."[17]

When Göring declared, "A true German thinks with his blood!"[18] he was expressing in a vulgar, but succinct, way Rosenberg's view that the essential core of the German community lay in the mystical bond that existed between one's own blood and the land of one's forebears.[19] "Germanness" was perceived as a distinctive racial entity, discernible everywhere, in painting, architecture, politics, and theater, as well as facial features. Reduced to matters of biology and race, everything—including art and politics—became inextricably linked, although the specific operation of this linkage was never explained. "Art is not an aesthetic affair," wrote the art historian Wilhelm Rüdiger, "but a biological one."[20] Any creed that preached universality, that expressed attachment to ideals beyond nationalistic precepts, was declared "un-German." Communism, pacifism, Judaism, and modernism were all seen as threats to the *corpore sane* of the fatherland—viruses that had to be obliterated in order for Germany to express its divine and true nature. The destruction of believers in such creeds—whether Jews or modernists—became, therefore, the highest patriotic act. Within such a frame of reference, modernism was synonymous with treason.

Alfred Rosenberg was born in 1893 in Reval, Estonia, which, since 1721, had been a province of ethnic Germans who lived among the predominantly Slavic population. These Balten, as they were known, fiercely maintained their separateness from the surrounding Slavic culture by retaining their language, schools, religion (Protestantism), and traditions, fortifying themselves with the idea of their "superior" culture and romantic glorifications of their distant "homeland." Rosenberg, who received his degree in architecture in Moscow in the midst of the Bolshevik revolution, in 1918 wrote to Peter Behrens requesting employment.[21] Behrens apparently agreed to meet with him, for on the basis of his reply, Rosenberg left for Berlin, arriving in time to witness the Kaiser's defeated troops marching down the Unter den Linden. Despite his claims of consanguinity, he found himself just another Russian refugee among the desperate thousands seeking asylum from the October Revolution in the teeming, distracted city. Realizing that it was not the best time to begin an architectural career, Rosenberg abandoned his intentions and left for Munich, where he allied himself with nationalistic groups whose notions of "blood Germans" and hatred of the Jews reinforced his own feelings of superiority. In 1919 he joined the German Workers' Party (the DAP, or Deutsche Arbeiter Partei, to which National Socialist was added the following year) and met Hitler at about the same time.

Rosenberg's hodge-podge of mystical, heroic, and biological theories, reinforced by his meditative demeanor, seemed evidence to Hitler of his intellectual gifts. Still smarting from his own failure to enroll in architectural school in Vienna, Hitler was impressed by the young Balt, who had succeeded where he had failed. Rosenberg provided not only a philosophical framework of sorts for Hitler's doctrine of discontent but also lent a much-needed element of respectability to his coterie. For his part Rosenberg was deeply flattered to be looked upon as the party "intellectual" and not merely another impecunious Russian refugee.

Like the Austrian-born Hitler, Rosenberg was an "outsider," a foreigner on German soil seeking affiliation through consanguinity with a supposedly "superior" people. Rosenberg was never able to relinquish the burden of his birth. His name, common in the Baltic region, bore a Semitic ring in the south; while his dour, taciturn personality, again characteristic of his people, always distanced him from his Nazi colleagues. His Baltic accent and difficulty in clearly expressing himself laid him further open to derision among his party peers. Despite the general acceptance of his racial theories in the Nazi dogma, Rosenberg himself remained an outsider everywhere.

The apparent unanimity with regard to artistic policy within the Nazi government—an impression reinforced by the broadly publicized activities of the KDK and the recent actions in the art world—was largely illusory.[22] Since March 5, when a national referendum had confirmed the legitimacy of the Nazi government, dissent began to be heard within party circles and beyond. Whether from motives of self-interest, intraparty rivalry, serious attempts at programmatic consistency, or as among the nationalist groups within the Bauhaus, opposition to perceived *retardataire* views of the KDK, the earnest, often frantic, debate centered around the definition of "nationalism" in art and architecture.

Wishing to ensure the widest range of art in the future, the bourgeois-liberal press—or what remained of it—argued for the broadest possible definition of nationalism. Concerned that nonartistic criteria, such as racial origin of the artist, were wrongly being applied, writers argued that endangered works of art be certified as "national" and "Nordic" by virtue of aesthetic criteria alone, such as their indigenous characteristics of subject matter, color, and manner of composition. Similar arguments were applied to architecture. In an article published in the *Deutsche Allgemeine Zeitung* on March 26, 1933, Wassily Luckhardt, one of the most prominent modernist architects and an acquaintance of Mies, argued that radical architecture should be given "an essential place in the political refashioning of the *Volk*" because its artistic style was supported by "Prussian" principles.[23] The Berlin National Socialist (NS) Students' Association also questioned Rosenberg's doctrines. Why, they asked, was Rosenberg's rabid, exclusionary racism more "nationalist" than the art of Emil Nolde, the renowned expressionist painter and dedicated Nazi party member? In Nolde's eyes, as well as in those of his advocates, his paintings represented the incarnation of the "blood and soil" ideology he so wholeheartedly endorsed. Furthermore, if modernism and nationalism were truly as incompatible as the KDK claimed, how could one explain the successful liaison between the Italian modernists and the fascists—an alliance of

which the Nazis, as well as Germany's avant-garde community, including Mies himself, were keenly aware?[24]

With many members of the NS Students' Association coming to the NSDAP from leftist origins, like those of the party's
Berlin membership in general, the "revolutionary" aspect of
Nazism was as significant to them as its appeal to nationalism.
Why not, they argued, look within modern Germany for an art
that represented the "new" and "revolutionary" Reich, rather
than backward to some mythical and highly dubious relationship between the Hellenes and the Nibelungen? As the effective relationship between Italian futurists and Mussolini had
clearly shown, nothing in fascism (or in any other "ism" for
that matter) was inherently inconsistent or incompatible with
the principles or forms of modern art and architecture. To
argue otherwise was to allow passion and prejudice to override
common sense. Did not the Führer himself assert upon countless occasions, "To be German is to be clear!" In a series of
student conferences and meetings, Otto Andreas-Schreiber, a
painter and deputy leader of the NS Students' Association,[25]
scathingly attacked the KDK as "an organization of bad-
humored mudslingers."[26] He spoke of artistic "black lists" and
the threat that loomed for art in Germany. He condemned the
KDK for refusing to admit Nolde, and spoke of the planned
defamation of him and such other German artists as Barlach,
Heckel, Kirchner, Mueller, and Schmidt-Rottluff as a "lapse in
German culture."[27]

Mies, like most members of Berlin's bewildered and appre-
hensive artistic community, keenly followed the activities of
this exuberant, youthful party wing,[28] whose artistically "liberal" views were shared by many within the far-right circles of
the Bauhaus.[29] Bolstering the optimism that these "liberal"
artistic views were not confined merely to a noisy but insignificant wing of the party, was the appointment in March 1933
of Hans Weidemann—a twenty-nine-year-old expressionist
painter, holder of the coveted gold badge, one of the party's
highest honors, and known avant-garde supporter—as associate and close advisor to Joseph Goebbels, newly appointed
minister of propaganda and people's enlightenment, and deadly
rival of Alfred Rosenberg.

*   *   *

Hans Weidemann, 1935 (Ullstein Bilderdienst)

Joseph Goebbels, 1939 (Photo from UPI/Bettmann Newsphotos)

Within the Nazi inner circle, Goebbels bore a double stigma. Not only was he one of the few—perhaps the only one—who had not joined the party of his own volition, having been recruited in 1925 to edit the "National Socialist Letters," a series of guidelines for party officials, but he was the *last* among these leading figures to come into the party, facts which among the back-biting leadership served as ceaseless fodder for rumors questioning the depth of Goebbels's commitment. If Rosenberg felt the need to prove his "Germanness," Goebbels felt compelled to prove over and over again his loyalty to Hitler. His mental agility and literary talents had been quickly recognized by Hitler, and in November 1926, barely a year and a half after he had come into the party, he was made district leader (Gauleiter) of Berlin. As holder of a doctorate, he was a bona fide intellectual, while his quick tongue and personal charm was assuredly more winning than the dour and tight-lipped personality of Rosenberg, who with Goebbels's ascension, found himself more and more removed from Hitler's inner circle.

Goebbels challenged Rosenberg's preeminence in the field of press and propaganda in 1927 with the establishment of the Berlin-based Nazi newspaper, *Der Angriff,* whose more sophisticated tone and ability to reach the newsstands earlier in the day than the Munich-based *Völkischer Beobachter* seriously undermined Rosenberg's readership. With his assumption of the leadership of the KDK in 1927 and the diversion of his attention to cultural affairs, Rosenberg virtually conceded Goebbels's domination of press and propaganda; his apparent unwillingness to confront his rival opened him to accusations of personal cowardice. He continued, however, to predominate in Nazi cultural matters. Having anticipated that the KDK would serve as a model of artistic policy formulation and implementation that would eventually be transformed into a government department with, of course, himself as its head, Rosenberg had urged Hitler to include cultural affairs within the party's drive toward "synchronization" (*Gleichschaltung*). In January 1933, just before the Nazis achieved power, Rosenberg moved the headquarters of the KDK to Berlin and awaited his Führer's call. Hitler was apparently impressed by Rosenberg's proposal to integrate culture and party goals, and on March 13, in an initial step toward bringing the entire cultural apparatus of the nation under party control, he established the Ministry of Propaganda and People's Enlightenment. However, at its head, Hitler placed not Rosenberg, but Goebbels. Nevertheless, despite this setback for Rosenberg, the KDK remained the party's major cultural organization, its most powerful cultural voice, and most impressive cultural administrative organization. And this time Rosenberg had no intention of willingly relinquishing his dominance in party cultural affairs to Goebbels. Not only did he claim many powerful and loyal allies, but his group had worked too long and hard, and was too firmly entrenched to be easily removed from positions of cultural leadership. In addition, Rosenberg was deeply committed to the dogma he preached.

No two opponents in the same arena appeared more at odds. Where Rosenberg was tall, handsome, and impressive-looking, Goebbels was small, ugly, and misshapen. If Rosenberg's emotional remoteness and air of superiority made everyone uncomfortable in his presence, Goebbels was fearsomely articulate, constantly striving to divert attention from his physical infirmities with his charm and brilliance. Where Rosenberg kept his frustrations and resentments to himself, Goebbels did not hesitate to attack where he detected the slightest sign of weakness. But, most important, Rosenberg deeply believed in principles, however nebulous and ill-conceived; Goebbels— like Hitler—believed only in power. With little experience and scant interest in cultural affairs, Goebbels brought few aesthetic principles or any specific programs to his new task, other than propagating what he believed to be the interests of the party and, of course, pleasing the Führer, who, at this time, was preoccupied with consolidating Nazi power in the government.

Since his student days in Heidelberg, where he had been vaguely associated with the Stefan George circle, and his subsequent brief, unsuccessful fling as an expressionist writer, Goebbels had always fancied himself as belonging to the avant-garde. Thanks to his relatively late entrance into the party and his having lived in Berlin since 1927, Goebbels had been both geographically and intellectually distant from the cultural machinations of Schultze-Naumburg and the KDK that had preceded the party's coming to power. The liberal cultural stance he projected did not arise out of any particular aesthetic convictions, but rather from his Berlin orientation, his self-esteem, and personal commitment to undermine his hated Baltic rival.[30] Whatever critical discernment Goebbels did possess lay in the areas of film, theater, and opera. According to Albert Speer, he had no feeling for art and architecture and depended for artistic advice on his close aide, Hans Weidemann.[31] At Weidemann's prompting, Goebbels sent a congratulatory telegram to Edvard Munch on his sixtieth birthday and purchased a Barlach sculpture of a beggar woman.[32] In the midst of this maneuvering, Weidemann was preparing an exhibition of German religious art that the Propaganda Ministry was going to send to the Chicago "Century of Progress" exposition in mid-1933. It included several works of Ernst Barlach and Emil Nolde.[33]

When members of Berlin's avant-garde community—Mies, as well as the nationalists within the Bauhaus—spoke of "having friends in high party circles," they almost invariably referred to individuals associated with Goebbels's new ministry.[34] Yet, for the moment, the earnest and impassioned discourse of the Berlin students, along with the optimistic plans of Goebbels's associates, remained simply vague slivers of hope that could not block out the unpleasant realities of the day, which bore the unmistakable mark of the recent masters of Thuringia. While hope for modernism apparently lay with Weidemann and Goebbels, power was undeniably in the hands of Rosenberg and the KDK.

Only so prodigious a goal as Nazi acceptance of modernism makes comprehensible Mies's approach to Rosenberg, the Nazi leader most associated with its persecution. It was an act that stunned his contemporaries as it has posterity. Even the politically canny Lilly Reich was appalled. "Who visits the Nazis voluntarily?" she asked.[35] Forty years after the event, Philip Johnson remained incredulous. "Can you *imagine* Mies's meeting with Rosenberg?" he exclaimed.[36] Even Rosenberg was resistant. "I'm busy," he replied curtly to Mies over the telephone.

But Rosenberg, his curiosity probably whetted by the oddity of the call and the urgency in the famed architect's voice, finally agreed to meet with him at eleven o'clock that evening. Ludwig Hilbersheimer, a member of the Bauhaus faculty, and Lilly Reich did not want Mies to go. But he insisted, and they had to settle on accompanying him. It was not that Mies was unafraid. If his inferences were correct and Rosenberg's cultural policies were allowed to continue unchallenged, he could forget about winning the Reichsbank competition. There would be no possibility for him—or any other modernist—to build. "I'm not afraid," he reassured his friends. "I have nothing. I'd like to talk with this man."[37]

And so, settling themselves into wooden seats in the café window across from Rosenberg's building, Hilbersheimer and Lilly Reich awaited Mies's return.[38]

Mies and Rosenberg were more similar than either might have imagined or have been willing to admit. Imperious and imperiled men, enmeshed in shadowy cocoons of silence and indisputability, each was struggling to maintain his position in a world in which his eminence was imperceptibly ebbing away. Like ghosts of Hegel, both justified their philosophical beliefs on flimsy webs of metaphysics and apparent irrefutability, seeking the assurance of truth in certainty and simplification; and both would have denied the assertion of Jakob Burckhardt, the Swiss historian, that in the denial of complexity lay the essence of tyranny. For years now they had sparred: Rosenberg, the soldier of sectarianism, the educated architect who had never built, and Mies, the prophet of righteous idealism, the uneducated builder. They were unseen opponents whose ideals left no room for the other.

Mies wasted no time in getting to the issue. "Where do you, as the cultural leader of the new Germany, stand on the aesthetic problems which have emerged as the result of technical and industrial development?" he asked Rosenberg.[39] It was the central issue of modernism, as Mies saw it. Rosenberg seemed genuinely stunned by the question. "Why do you ask?" he replied, unable to perceive the issue of modernism or the Bauhaus outside a political frame of reference. Mies assured him that aesthetic issues were central to modernism, as well as to the Bauhaus, at least now under his directorship.

Again, Rosenberg seemed unable to deal with Mies's perspective, and rephrasing the issue in political terms, asked, "Why do you want the backing of political power? We are not thinking of stifling individual initiative," he continued. "If you are so sure of what you are doing, your ideas will succeed anyway." Rosenberg believed Mies to be seeking political support; Mies saw himself as seeking peace.

"For any cultural effort one needs peace," Mies replied. "I would like to know whether we will have that peace."

"Are you hampered in your work?" asked Rosenberg, apparently unaware of the Bauhaus raid.

"Hampered is not the correct term," replied Mies, undoubtedly surprised by Rosenberg's ignorance of the affair, and described the gestapo's actions. At this, Rosenberg revealed that he had received a degree in architecture, and their conversation took on a franker and less formal tone; in rank-conscious Germany, they could now speak to each other as equals.

"Then we certainly will understand each other," responded Mies.

"Never," said Rosenberg. "What do you expect me to do? You know the Bauhaus is supported by forces that are fighting our forces. It is one army against another, only in the spiritual field," he went on, apparently referring to the school's communist reputation.

"No," answered Mies. "I really don't think it is like that."

"Why didn't you change the name, for heaven's sake, when you moved the Bauhaus from Dessau to Berlin?"

"Don't you think the 'Bauhaus' is a wonderful name?" asked Mies. "The best thing Gropius ever did was to invent that name. I wouldn't change it for anything."

The conversation was clearly going nowhere. Speaking to Mies as a fellow professional, Rosenberg relaxed enough to drop the party rhetoric and turned to what ultimately lay at the core of Nazi hostility to modernism—personal distaste.

"I don't like what the Bauhaus is doing," he said. "I know you can cantilever something, but my feeling demands a support."

"Even if it is cantilevered?" asked Mies.

"Yes," answered Rosenberg.

"Listen," said Mies. "You are sitting here in an important position. And look at your lousy writing table. Do you like it? I would throw it out the window. That is what we want to do. We want to have good objects that we do not have to throw out the window."[40]

Rosenberg's manner hardened abruptly: Mies had apparently gone too far. "I will see what I can do for you," he said, rising suddenly from behind his desk.

Mies stood up too. "Don't wait too long," he answered, his tranquillity, as well as his beliefs, unruffled by this abrupt dismissal.

* * *

It was clear that Rosenberg neither knew nor cared about the Bauhaus situation. Although this meeting did not accomplish what Mies had intended—the reopening of the Bauhaus and Nazi recognition of modernism's aesthetic basis (at least as perceived by Mies)—it did expose him to the Nazis' rigid political mentality. It was obvious that simply proving to them that the Bauhaus, under his direction, was a nonpolitical institution devoted solely to artistic matters would no longer suffice. Seizing upon the apparent schism that existed between the more artistically moderate Berlin faction of the party and its conservative wing, Lilly Reich—in an effort to arouse public support—came up with the idea of publicly announcing a "mass enlistment" of the Bauhaus community into the KDK.[41] On April 15, a letter addressed to the director of architecture and technology of the KDK and signed by some Bauhaus students appeared in the *Deutsche Allgemeine Zeitung*, its contents going far beyond protestations of political neutrality. Although Mies was not a signatory, the letter could hardly have been written without his knowledge and consent; while initiated by another, his permission to allow its publication—and implied approval—reveals his disposition toward political expediency.

> The students of the Bauhaus are most aware of the new situation created by the national revolution. They thus considered it their duty to clarify the present conditions at the Bauhaus, in order to facilitate an objective judgment by the KDK.
>
> It is probably not known that widely differing and opposite currents have alternately existed at the Bauhaus. Thus, it is a fact, for example, that under Hannes Meyer, the Bauhaus strongly sympathized with the communist party. Mies van der Rohe, who was called to Dessau to succeed Hannes Meyer, tried to make the Bauhaus nonpolitical. . . . As a result of more careful analysis of new applicants and also of the removal of a series of Marxist students . . . it was gradually possible to take a new direction. Just as Marxism was expelled from the Reich, so too did this happen at the Bauhaus . . . .
>
> Thanks to the removal of politics from the Bauhaus, the undersigned students believe that the basic foundation

necessary for positive cooperation in the new Germany has been laid.

Of course, only the future will tell which direction art turns in the new Germany. To help determine its course is the task of The Fighting League for German Culture [the KDK]. To cooperate is the duty of every German artist, every school, and every student.

The Bauhaus does not intend to flee this duty; on the contrary, it is willing to honestly cooperate and to place all its forces at the service of this task.

The German students mentioned in the following list have decided to apply for acceptance in the Fighting League.

With respect,
The students of the Bauhaus[42]

In light of the KDK's long and vigorous opposition to the Bauhaus and German modernism in general, the appeal —which today seems little short of absurd—must be seen in the context of the confused and contentious atmosphere that existed within Berlin Nazi circles at the time. The letter represented a desperate temporizing effort to keep the Bauhaus alive, while the Nazi government moved to secure its power. Like many of his fellow countrymen, Mies was uncertain about the Nazis, and questioned their durability as well as their potential benefit to the country.[43] Absorbed by the Reichsbank project and as distant as ever from the political machinations of the day, Mies was undoubtedly delighted to turn over to Lilly Reich responsibility for dealing with such political unpleasantries. Prone to elevate aesthetic priorities, Mies—like so many of his generation—saw himself as concerned with "things that really mattered." "I don't care whether the man who mixes cement is a Nazi or a communist," Mies was fond of saying. "I'm just interested in whether or not he makes good cement!"[44]

Not for Mies was George Orwell's observation on the pointlessness of hierarchical values, of arguing over which is "higher," things of the spirit or things of life. "[T]hey are incompatible," Orwell wrote. "One must choose between God and Man."[45] What to Mies and those of his ilk appeared as the pursuit of the noblest and highest claims to others seemed simple opportunism.

CHAPTER 7

A FEARSOME SILENCE

THEY THAT GIVE UP ESSENTIAL LIBERTY TO OBTAIN A LITTLE
TEMPORARY SAFETY DESERVE NEITHER LIBERTY NOR SAFETY.

(Benjamin Franklin)

The bench that ran along the walls of the waiting room of gestapo headquarters was hard and narrow, barely four inches wide. It reminded Mies of the bench that Friedrich the Great had installed at Sansouci to keep his pages from falling asleep.[1] It was mid-May now; Mies was waiting to speak to the director of the Berlin gestapo, so far to no avail.

Despite the impression of his comments of twenty years later—"from [the time of the Rosenberg meeting] I went every second day for three months to the headquarters of the Gestapo"—Mies had come neither voluntarily nor on his own initiative.[2] In fact, since his approach to Rosenberg—and to the disgust of many at the Bauhaus—he had done nothing.[3] Fed up by Mies's persistent ignoring of the problems of the Bauhaus, a group of rightist students had made their own inquiries.

125

When it became apparent that these initiatives were going nowhere, Helmut Heide, an architectural student and one of the rightist leaders desperate to get things moving, organized a student meeting at the beginning of May. Only Ludwig Hilbersheimer among the faculty showed up. Frustrated by Mies's inactivity, Heide exploded in fury, attacking him—in his own words—"strenuously and passionately."[4] Hilbersheimer then telephoned Mies and urged him to come. Mies apparently was reluctant; it was only after a long conversation and the intervention of Lilly Reich, who, according to Heide, "stepped in and lit a fire under Mies," that he "condescended," in Heide's words, to come.[5] A student group—Heide among them—was then set up, charged with seeking to establish contact with the gestapo, and the propaganda and cultural ministries. Despite his evident frustration over Mies's distance and inaction, Heide does not seem insensitive to the difficulties of Mies's situation. "Thus Mies did something," commented Heide, in his usual sardonic tone, "and managed simultaneously to gain the time he needs to complete his project for the Reichsbank competition."[6]

Rosenberg's unawareness of the gestapo action, and—even more surprising considering his record—his evident disinterest, as well as the inquiries initiated by the student activists, had indicated that the closing of the school was not the result of some deliberately planned policy decision, but was probably due to some low-level bureaucratic bungling. Determined not to let the matter drag on and to reopen the school as quickly as possible, the rightist students set out vigorously, "marching constantly," according to Heide,[7] between gestapo headquarters, Goebbels's Ministry of Propaganda (to whom on May 3 they addressed a petition[8]), the Cultural Ministry, and Mies's apartment. Once they had "blazed the trail," in Heide's words, Mies followed, meeting with Hans Weidemann in the Propaganda Ministry and, at his suggestion, with Oberregierungsrat von Oppen, Weidemann's contact in the State Ministry of Culture.[9] "Our efforts with the political police," noted Heide, "have set things in motion."[10]

Lilly Reich, despite her influence in getting Mies moving, was worried over Mies's trips to the gestapo, their reputation—

even in these early months—already being well established.[11] "They abduct a man from his home," wrote Harry Kessler on April 25, from the safety of Paris, where he had recently fled, "keep him for a week to a fortnight, thrash him over and over again, and constantly threaten him with death. When he returns home, he is a physical and mental wreck."[12]

Although Mies himself remained confident that the gestapo had nothing on him, Lilly Reich was far less certain.[13] Not only was he director of the despised Bauhaus, and of the 1927 Weissenhofsiedlung exhibition (a model modernist community whose purported inappropriateness to the German landscape had been made the subject of an infamous collage depicting it as an Arab village), but he was a leader of a movement considered by the Nazis as anti-German and politically subversive, many of whose lesser known advocates were already crowding the concentration camps. Most damaging, was his design of the Liebknecht-Luxemburg monument, however "accidental" and "apolitical" Mies might wish it to appear. Nevertheless, Mies did not see himself as being either foolish or especially brave in his efforts to meet with the Nazi leadership, whom he barely took seriously. Insulated by his impenetrable shield of righteousness and despite his failings with Schultze-Naumburg and Rosenberg, Mies remained unswervingly confident of his ability to convince even fools of the reasonableness of his claims and, like his idol Thomas Aquinas, never doubted the virtue of rationality or its inevitable triumph. If his affirmation of rationalism could change the course of architecture in his time, surely, he believed, he could convince even the most recalcitrant of his fellow countrymen. Of far more pressing concern to him than his supposed vulnerability as a "cultural bolshevist" were his immediate difficulties with the Prussian Academy of Arts, a predicament over which he had ample time to mull in the gestapo waiting room.

The origin of this problem was the Nazi attack on the Prussian Academy of Arts through the activities of two of its members, Heinrich Mann and Käthe Kollwitz, both of whom had long been involved with the social and pacifist causes of their day. The Prussian Academy was Germany's most esteemed cultural institution: membership in it was the highest honor the nation could bestow on its leading cultural figures.[14] Essentially an honorific institution under the aegis of the Prussian Cultural Ministry, it was, in this sense, a public institution and its members were, broadly speaking, civil employees.

In return for the state's financial support, the academy was expected to offer its opinions on legislation that came before the city council in areas where it had special interest and expertise. Because it affected the outcome of so much cultural legislation, it became—in the words of painter and academy ex-president Max Liebermann—"a regulator of artistic life." Thus, even as most of its members considered themselves above politics, the academy itself was very politically involved. Dependent on public funding, as well as the support of the Prussian Ministry of Culture, the academy was well aware of its potential vulnerability to political harassment. As a result, its legislative recommendations tended to avoid the overly innovative or controversial and its influence on the country's cultural life was generally conservative—reflecting, as well, the outlook of its mature, if not elderly, constituency. Content to simply bask in the prestige of affiliation, most members avoided participating in the policy-making committees, and— like Mies—rarely even attended meetings.

Divided into two sections, fine arts and literature, the academy's membership constituted a virtual roster of artistic and literary achievement in Germany as well as abroad.[15] Given the age and conservatism of the majority of its members, the academy tended to view artistic as well as political radicalism (particularly of the left) with aloof displeasure. Only if his or her artistic achievements were especially outstanding (such as in the case of Kollwitz) could an individual with leftist leanings be considered for membership. Mies van der Rohe was a member; Walter Gropius was not.

Both sections of the academy reflected the deep-seated aesthetic schism that existed in the German cultural world between the avant-garde and the conservatives; those for whom art meant the free articulation of an artistic vision without regard to its source or value of its message, and those who linked the value of art to the worthiness of its ideology,

Meeting of the Literature Section of the Prussian Academy of Arts, 1929: seated at far right, Heinrich Mann; standing in center and leaning forward, Thomas Mann; standing left and next to T. Mann, Alfred Döblin (Photo courtesy of the Archiv der Preussischen Akademie der Künste, Akademie der Künste, Berlin)

especially its German *volkisch* content. This hostility was especially pronounced within the literature section. While writers such as Alfred Döblin, Heinrich Mann, and Ludwig Fulda—like Mies—were committed to preserving their prerogative of intellectual freedom or, as they phrased it, "the domain of reason," their nationalistic cohorts envisioned the task of art as protecting and serving the *Volk* and hence promulgating the "life force" of the nation. By 1931 this ideological antagonism threatened to paralyze the academy. In August of that year, Max Liebermann, one of Germany's most important impressionist painters and president of the academy since 1920, despairing of the situation and the apparent inability of the modernists to gain admittance by the normal route of admission upon the death of a member, convinced the new cultural minister Adolf Grimme, a liberal and social democrat, to invite thirteen of them, including Mies, into the academy in an unusual procedure known as *Pairschub*.[16] Labeled as "undemocratic" by Goebbels (of all people!), this controversial manner of admittance exacerbated the division within the academy and many of the nationalist writers left the academy to found their own "German Poets' Academy," which sup-posedly better represented the interests of the *Volk*.

Heinrich Mann and Ricarda Huch, a prominent representa-tive of *volkisch* literature who had remained in the Prussian Academy, now presided over the department of literature and, in an attempt to ensure a broader diversity of literary trends, brought in additional members to replace those who had left. Under the vigorous leadership of Mann and Döblin, a commit-tee was formed to contest cases of censorship and persecution of literary works (including films); to check for "nationalistic-inciting" trends; and to guard against what was referred to as instances of "cultural barbarism." A meeting scheduled for February 6, 1933 to discuss such instances was canceled after the Nazis entered the government.

Capitalizing on their loud defense of the *Volk* and anxious to realize the potential advantages of association with the coun-try's most prestigious cultural figures, the Nazis began to woo the nationalists who had remained at the academy, much as they had done in the cultural scene at large—most notably through Rosenberg's KDK. They soon found sympathetic sup-port among those members of the academy who had opposed those invited in 1931, most of whom had long been the target of Nazi opposition. The nationalist group waited impatiently for the opportunity to redress their long-simmering grievances. With the appointment on February 6, 1933, of Dr. Bernhard Rust as Prussian minister of culture and, hence, curator of the academy, their moment had finally arrived. The immediate objects of attack were Heinrich Mann and Käthe Kollwitz, whose recent actions provided a welcomed pretense for bring-ing the academy into the party's line.

Heinrich Mann, the sixty-two-year-old elder brother of Thomas, was himself the author of several books and an undis-puted leader of German *Kulturpolitik*. Outspokenly opposed to what he called "bellicose nationalism," he was an ardent advocate of pan-Europeanism and openly hostile to Hitler. Although Mann had been attracted to the Soviet Union between 1928 and 1932, he was as opposed to a dictatorship of the proletariat as he was to that of the right; and no political party claimed his allegiance. In 1932 his name had been pro-posed for nomination as president of the republic, in a futile

Bernhard Rust, 1933 (Photo by Carl Weinrother, courtesy of the Bildarchiv Preussischer Kulturbesitz)

Käthe Kollwitz (Bildarchiv Preussischer Kulturbesitz)

attempt to offer an alternative to the sad choice of Hitler or Hindenburg.

Käthe Kollwitz, famed graphic artist and head of the academy's graphic arts department, had been the first woman to be elected to full professorship there. Passionately opposed to war and social injustice, her entire oeuvre was pervaded by compassion for the poor and miserable of the world. She had long been identified with the interests of the working class, and although her sympathetic drawings of these people were greatly admired by the communists, she was not a member of the party.[17] Yet, most of her fellow academy members would have unhesitatingly called her a Marxist. So, too, apparently did the Soviets. In the spring of 1932, Russian artists commissioned her to create a poster opposing an imperialist war against the Soviet Union.[18]

Worried over the prospect of a fascist parliamentary majority in the referendum of March 5, 1933, Mann and Kollwitz had added their names to a petition urging a coalition of the long-split left, that is, of the KPD and the SPD. On February 13, three weeks before the referendum, the petition began to appear on kiosks throughout Berlin.

> Unless fascism can be warded off in the last moment by uniting the principal opposition, the imminent destruction of all personal and political freedom in Germany is at hand. . . . We address ourselves to everyone who shares our convictions to help in this urgent appeal. . . .
>
> . . . Let us take care that hesitation and cowardice of heart will not sink us into barbarism![19]

What to Mann and Kollwitz appeared as little more than the exercise of their rights as free citizens to freedom of political expression, as guaranteed by the still-existent Weimar constitution, was to the Nazis an insult, an unforgivable provocation, and an opportunity for long-sought revenge. The newly appointed Rust served as its instrument. Politically astute, Rust seemed determined not to allow his personal modernist sympathies—his admiration for the works of Barlach, Nolde, and Klee was well known—to interfere with his duties. Although he had already made ominous hints about his intentions with regard to the academy in numerous speeches before Nazi student groups in Hannover and Munich, he made his plans especially clear in a speech that he delivered before the NS Students' Association on February 13, barely one week after his appointment. "Let me give you an example of what I intend to do," said Rust.

> There is . . . an academy of literature, which . . . has a leader. . . . [Recently] we have seen the name of this man gloat down from the kiosks urging the social democrats and communists to form a "common front of defense." It seems to me that not only is the director guilty, but all those as well who elected this man, Herr Heinrich Mann. . . . Don't worry! I will put an end to the scandal at the academy!

Almost reluctantly and as an afterthought, Rust remembered that he was "bound by the law": the Weimar constitution, after all, still existed. "But," he warned, "wherever there is a legal possibility, wherever there is a way, I will undertake every step with maximum brutality to put an end to this destruction of German 'uniqueness.' "[20]

Rust meant what he said. The next day, February 14, he summoned Dr. Max von Schillings, the president of the Prussian Academy of Arts, to his office. Claiming that he was holding the entire academy responsible for the "misdeeds" of Mann and Kollwitz, Rust threatened to disband not only the literature department, but the entire academy.[21] Stunned, Schillings attempted to defend his institution. Arguing that neither the academy as a whole nor any single department should be held accountable for the action of two members, he offered his resignation instead. After bigger game, Rust refused his offer, insisting that a meeting of the membership be called "with the greatest of haste" to resolve the "issue" of Mann and Kollwitz, and implicitly, the fate of the academy.

The following day, February 15, an obviously intimidated Schillings called for an extraordinary meeting of the academy to be held that evening. Given the normal sparseness of attendance, not to mention the short notice for this one, it was not surprising that only fifty-three members showed up. No one was present from outside Berlin. Mies was not there. Nor was Heinrich Mann, who had not even been informed of the charges; Kollwitz first learned of the ultimatum from Schillings, into whose office she was summoned just before the meeting. Faced with the unbearable choice of resignation or the probable disbandment of the academy, she offered her immediate withdrawal. "It was all terribly unpleasant," she later wrote.[22]

With her resignation in hand, Schillings proceeded to the meeting hall.[23] Requesting confidentiality so that the minutes would not have to be sent to the minister of culture, he explained the painful purpose of the meeting. "Recognizing the error of her action, [Frau Kollwitz has] already declared her withdrawal today from the academy," he declared. Only the case of Mann remained.[24] Several members demanded that he be present to defend himself; and at nearly 10:00 in the evening he arrived, having learned from friends the purpose of the meeting and the charges against him.[25] Rather than subject himself to possible humiliation before his colleagues, he requested a private conference with Schillings in his office, where the president attempted to justify his position. "That is not necessary," replied Mann, a large and resolute-looking man with the frosty air of a retired admiral. "It is your duty to preserve the academy, and it is mine to support you in this undertaking. I am no communist. I signed this appeal as a republican."[26] Mann then offered his resignation, which Schillings accepted and announced immediately upon his return to the assembly.

Only three voices were raised in protest. Alfred Döblin, physician, writer, and Mann's personal friend, expressed outrage that not a single objection had been raised by the distinguished membership about the manner in which Mann was coerced into making such a decision and demanded that Mann—who was still in the president's office—be asked to come into the meeting to at least explain his side. Put to the vote by Schillings, his proposal was rejected by the membership. Martin Wagner, architect and head of Berlin's city planning—a position he would not hold much longer—joined Döblin in Mann's defense.[27] He too was outraged over the academy's "cool and calm response" to such an ultimatum and questioned even the legality of calling such a critical meeting within six hours. He affirmed Mann and Kollwitz's right to sign the petition and advised the assembly that he would reflect until the end of the meeting on whether or not he wished to continue as a member of such a group.[28]

"My only consideration," replied Schillings to Wagner, "was whether or not the entire academy should be sacrificed for the sake of two members. At the very least Mann and Kollwitz were guilty of tactlessness."

Wagner demanded that Schillings permit the assembly to vote on whether or not two members should be forced to resign because of "tactlessness."

"The issue is simply whether or not the president acted properly," responded Gottfried Benn, physician, one of Germany's major expressionist poets, and—for the moment—an avid Nazi supporter.

At this, Wagner declared his resignation and left the room.

The last defender of Mann was Ludwig Fulda, who, responding to Schillings's inquiry as to the opinion of the writers present, declared that, while the limited number of members of the literature division did not allow a proper consensus, those present "regretted" the withdrawal of Mann. "As for my own opinion," Fulda continued, "I believe that Mann only did that to which every citizen is entitled. In my opinion, Mann did not offend the academy."

But Mann and Kollwitz were out. Among Germany's most esteemed intellectuals present that evening, only a pitiful few had spoken out in their defense. Perhaps the others felt, like Oskar Schlemmer, that the Nazis would be placated by "feeding them" two "Marxists."[29] That even supposed Marxists should have the same constitutionally guaranteed rights as themselves seemed of no concern. Taking over the podium at the end of the meeting, Hans Poelzig, architect and vice president of the academy, praised the president's handling of the situation, noting that Wagner's proposal to put the issue before the academy membership was "totally impossible . . . since in this house we are only concerned with art, not politics."[30]

The Nazi press was euphoric: but not everyone shared their delight. On February 19, a meeting sponsored by the League for Human Rights was held to protest recent Nazi press restrictions. Although it had been planned before the events at the academy, the gathering took on deeper meaning in light of them. Organized by Heinrich and Thomas Mann, Ricarda Huch, and Martin Buber among others, more than sixty artistic, literary, and political organizations joined to declare before the world their desire for "free speech in a free land."[31] "The appeal goes forth to all Germans," declared a former police captain in the opening address, "regardless of their profession and class, to reinstate these rights, to support the fundamentals of intellectual life in Germany." One after another, they stood at the podium, former ministers, judges, distinguished professors, and lawyers. For three hours they spoke, none so naive as to believe that his name had not been carefully noted by the authorities.[32] What mattered was not the brevity of the event, but that it had occurred at all. "[F]or a long time to come," noted Harry Kessler, "[this might be the last occasion in Berlin] . . . when intellectuals would be able to publicly demonstrate on behalf of freedom."[33] For many, it was to be their final defiant gesture in their homeland. Two days later, on February

21, only moments before the SS, who had had him under close surveillance, entered his home, Heinrich Mann fled Germany.[34]

Unsettled by the Mann-Kollwitz affair, academy members pressured Schillings to call another meeting, to allow them an opportunity to express themselves confidentially with regard to the issue. At the second meeting on February 20, it was again argued that Mann was merely exercising his constitutionally guaranteed right of free expression. The legal basis on which the cultural minister was empowered to dissolve the academy was also questioned. Nazi supporters dismissed these issues as merely "formal," declaring that the "high inner task" of the academy as "the bearer of traditions took precedence over the basic rights of the Weimar constitution." Alfons Paquet, Ricarda Huch, and Ernst Barlach threatened to resign, unless strong measures were adopted to prevent further political interference by the Prussian minister of culture into the academy's affairs. A proposal made by Alfred Döblin that the academy publicly protest the forced resignation of Mann was adopted. However, Gottfried Benn altered the version that appeared in the press release, to a mere expression of regret at Mann's resignation and praise for his artistic merits. Despite unanimous approval of it, Schillings, bothered by its "indiscretions," forbade its publication.

Privately, the implications of the affair continued to unnerve some members. Does "remaining in the Academy of Arts carr[y] with it a certain politically oriented position?" inquired Ernst Barlach, in a letter of February 23 to Schillings. "Although I am not a member of any party at the moment, the differentiation of two rights, that of the free opinion of an artist and that of a citizen, is unacceptable to me."[35] On February 28, Schillings responded to Barlach, assuring him that no member of the academy would "be asked to join any particular political party nor will he be forbidden to join a political party."

> The right to free expression of opinion that he has as a citizen will not be denied him as an "artist" (as you wrote) by anyone. On the other hand, I am of the opinion that an

artist who has the honor of being a member of the academy
assumes not only the written sentences and paragraphs as
binding, but feels and recognizes higher discretions which
cannot be formulated into paragraphs. A certain amount of
restraint is part of this duty in the matter of exercising free
opinion, particularly during trying political times, where
the signing of an attacking socialist-communist call for
votes is offensive to the ruling government and therefore
gravely endangers the interests of the academy.[36]

Left unanswered was whether or not the notion of "higher
discretion" impinged upon or even refuted the notion of freedom of expression. Evidently, one was now free to be discreet!

The Nazis, however, were not long content with such temporizing actions. At a meeting on March 13, the members of the
literature department were asked to support a declaration recognizing the "changed historical situation" and agree to forgo
public political activity against the new government, dedi-
cating themselves instead to "loyal cooperation." As usual, the
Nazi supporters were well-organized; their opponents were
not. Oskar Loerke, the pronationalist secretary, arranged with
the Ministry of Culture to withhold the normal travel
allowances for non-Berlin members, preventing all but one
from showing up; Gottfried Benn ensured that only a written
yea or nay reply would be permitted. The few members present, however, agreed only to a voice vote. Three members
rejected the declaration, while four resigned—Alfred Döblin,
Thomas Mann, Alfons Paquet, and Ricarda Huch. Aside from
one who had become ill, all other members of the literature
department signed the "loyalty" agreement and elected the
Nazi sympathizer, Gottfried Benn, successor to the former
presiding officers, Heinrich Mann and Huch. The next day,
Ernst Barlach wrote his brother Karl, expressing sentiments
apparently shared by most of his fellow academy members:
"With regard to politics, one had best remain silent."[37]

Application of the April 7 Civil Service Law further deci-
mated the academy. Between May 5 and 8, many individuals—
Jews, as well as those with suspected leftist sympathies—were
informed that they could "no longer be counted as members of
the department of literature." Since the Nazis had long anticipated the "withdrawal" of these "undesirables," their replace-

ments were installed almost at once. Thus, fifteen of the thirty-one regular members of the literature department had either "withdrawn" or been "excluded." With the minister of culture now "releasing" and "appointing" members, all semblance of traditional democratic voting procedures disappeared.

Not everyone, however, waited passively for the Nazi ax to fall. Some, such as the eighty-six-year-old Max Liebermann, resigned of their own accord. On May 11, a letter explaining the resignation of this prominent Jew and Honorary Citizen of Berlin appeared in the *Zentral-vereins-Zeitung*.

> I have tried to serve German art during my long life with all my strength. According to my convictions, art is neither concerned with politics nor with origin.

When asked by an acquaintance his view of life under the Nazis, Liebermann—who, outlawed and solitary, would be dead two years later—replied, "I wish I could eat as much as I would like to vomit."[38]

The academy suffered abuse outside its serene facade as well. On the night of May 10, 5,000 swastika-bearing students marched past its building on Pariser Platz, down the Unter den Linden to a pile of logs beneath the statue of Alexander von Humboldt at the Opernplatz across from the old university. In a scene repeated in university towns throughout Germany and led by professors and rectors of the schools, they piled vast armloads of books and pamphlets atop the logs and set them aflame. "The soul of the German people can again express itself," proclaimed Goebbels to the 40,000 spectators, his raspy voice ringing out over the smoldering ashes. "These flames not only illuminate the final end of an old era; they also light up the new."

Within the academy, the Nazi offensive continued. Encouraged by their success in the literature department, the Nazis turned their attention to the fine arts division. Why, inquired Albert Gessner in a letter to Schillings on May 13, had nothing been done with the "Grimme appointees?" Undoubtedly taking his cue from the membership's timid behavior, Schillings acceded once again to Nazi pressure. On May 15, identical letters requesting them to resign—or, in the perverse language of the day, to "decline the nomination by Minister Grimme" of two years before—were sent to Paul Mebes, Eric Mendelsohn, Ludwig Gies, Renée Sintenis, Emil Nolde, Karl Schmidt-Rottluff, Otto Dix, Ernst Ludwig Kirchner, Edwin Scharff, and Mies van der Rohe.[39]

Mies—ungraced as he was by the privileges of high birth or formal education, the usual handmaidens of esteem in Germany—was terribly proud of his membership in the academy.[40] The request for his resignation must have hurt him a great deal: he seems never to have spoken about it to anyone. Mies's architectural triumphs spoke mostly to the "cognoscenti": his membership in the academy spoke to all. Not only was the request for his resignation a tremendous blow to his pride, but coming as it did a scant month after his difficulties with the Bauhaus, it appeared to indicate withdrawal of his country's recognition of his achievements. It was an index of honor that Mies did not intend to yield.

The issues involved in deciding whether or not to resign from the academy were complex and difficult, and confounded many of the country's best minds. To resign implied that one accepted the impropriety, at best, or the illegitimacy, at the worst, of one's membership—something most people neither believed nor wished to convey. Resignation also implied opposition to the academy's "new direction"—untenable for those, like Mies, engaged in delicate negotiations or with aspirations of working with the regime. In addition, opposition to one political direction or another, whether implied or direct, violated the principles of those who considered themselves apolitical or wished to project the image of political indifference.

The pervasive impression of Goebbels's artistic liberalism and its potential influence on the regime's future cultural direction was also not to be overlooked. In such dismal hours, for those struggling for rationality as well as survival it was both understandable and reassuring to focus on Goebbels's more positive side. The minister's choice of associates, his quiet alliance with the promodernist groups, and his propensity for using words dear to the hearts of the avant-garde, such as *"sachlich"* and "unsentimental," seemed very hopeful. His participation in such unsavory events as the May 10 book burnings and his occasionally harsh speeches tended to be dismissed as the usual political pandering to the masses. The transfer of any of Goebbels's associates to other high government posts was seen as an attempt by the minister to extend his liberalizing influence to a broader cultural area; the recent appointment of Hans Hinkel, Goebbels's longtime associate, to Rust's Cultural Ministry, was perceived in this light.

The impression of Goebbels's liberalism was further deepened by the countless inquiries, articles, and publicly printed letters addressed to him from all corners of German cultural life. "Only the new architecture ... fits your prescriptions, Herr Minister," noted *Die Neue Stadt,* a radical architectural journal "and can form the stone monument[s] of bold statesmanship over the centuries."[41] On March 29, in an article entitled "Art in the Third Reich" addressed to Goebbels, Rust, and Hinkel that appeared in the *Deutsche Allgemeine Zeitung,* Bruno Werner, the paper's eminent art and theater critic and longtime supporter of modern architecture, urged that " 'the fresh youthful strength of the Nazi movement conquer in the artistic field,' so that artists like Barlach, Marc and Nolde would no longer be attacked as Jews, nor architects like Poelzig or Mies van der Rohe as bolshevists."[42] Also reinforcing the perception of Goebbels's liberalism was Werner's appointment in mid-March as chairman of the Association of German Art Critics, a prestigious post that he never would have been allowed to gain—it was believed—if Goebbels opposed him. This implied support from Goebbels imbued Werner's writing with tremendous significance, and it was for this reason that an article of his—astonishing in this period of rigid press suppression—entitled "What's going on in German Art?" appearing in the *Deutsche Allgemeine Zeitung* on May 12, attracted so much attention.

Echoing a popular topic of conversation among the modernists, Werner referred to the sympathetic support and warm approval received by the Italian modernists, especially the futurists, from their fascist government, commenting especially on Mussolini's personal interest in the painter Marinetti. Werner derided the rampant misuse of the term "cultural bolshevism," claiming that it was used against artists who "indeed, in their own ways, were the forerunners of national sentiment in art." As for the harsh and haphazard persecution of the modernists taking place in Germany, Werner claimed that such actions were being initiated "from subordinate positions within the government" and had "nothing to do with Adolf Hitler's and other leaders' concepts of art."

> When an unknown artist is equipped with nothing other than nationalistic sentiment; when the director of the Dresden Gallery is forced to remove the greater part of the modern gallery from display; when such men as Director Sauerlandt in Hamburg and Director Schreiber-Weigand in Chemnitz are removed from their positions . . .; when the Bauhaus in Berlin, the Bauhaus which was even visited by national socialist students and which had such a national figure as Mies van der Rohe in the top position, is closed; this certainly is neither desired nor caused by the government.

On May 18, Mies turned down Schillings's request for his resignation.

> Dear Mr. von Schillings,
>
> I cannot decide to accept the mentioned suggestion in your letter dated the 15th of this month, particularly since such a step can give rise to misinterpretations in these times.
> Since I formerly had no influence on my nomination, I must now also leave it to the Ministry of Culture and to the academy to settle this matter.
>
> Yours truly,
> Mies van der Rohe[43]

Mies's response is curt and succinct. Unable to bring himself to even discuss "the mentioned suggestion," Mies goes out of his way to remove political connotation from the issue. He neither accedes to nor rejects the request: nor does his claim of possible "misinterpretation" denigrate the request for his resignation or admit to its implication that there was something wrong with his appointment in the first place. Given Mies's cautious nature, his rationalistic propensities, and current negotiations with the regime—not to mention his concern for the future—this was surely not accidental. There is no sense of anger or moral outrage, qualities apparently unknown to Mies outside his art.

Although there is no evidence that they discussed this among themselves, Mies's attitude was shared by most others in the academy: only three members, Karl Schmidt-Rottluff, Paul Mebes, and Otto Dix offered their resignations.[44] The confusing and fluctuating circumstances of the day; the belief that temporizing with today's demands would alleviate tomorrow's; the attitude that politics was rotten and political affairs unworthy of "great" minds; the willingness to throw others— especially if they were Marxists or Jews—to the wolves in order to save oneself; not to mention the long German tradition of deference toward authority—a propensity that had led a medieval pope to call Germany the "*terra obediantiae*"[45]—all contributed to the stunning inertia of Germany's intelligentsia. Instances abound of compromises made at this time by many of the country's most admired figures. Friedrich Meinecke offers but one example. Editor of the *Historische Zeitschrift* and the most respected historian of his time, described by Fritz Stern as "a humane, unimpassioned supporter of the Weimar Republic," liberal, tolerant, and trusted by his Jewish students, Meinecke removed Hedwig Hintze, the wife of his friend and colleague Otto Hintze and of Jewish background, from participation in the review section of the journal—a post she had held for years—in the hope of avoiding conflict with the regime.[46] Reflecting ingrained attitudes that in retrospect appear shameful, Mies, like the great majority of his cultural and academy peers, chose the path of least resistance. Given the insecurity and tenuousness of the regime at this time, one can only speculate on what might have happened had Mies and others of his prominence spoken out. The moment was now; but few saw it and fewer seized it. In this, Mies was hardly alone.

The reaction of the academy itself reflects the precariousness of the moment. Faced with such insubordination by so many members, it reacted by doing nothing. Mies and those others who had refused to resign remained as members; those who had opposed their inclusion in the academy continued to complain.

CHAPTER 8

TRIUMPH

ONE MORE SUCH VICTORY AND WE ARE LOST.

(**Plutarch,** *Pyrrhus*)

Familiar as he had become over the past few months with the evasive ways of bureaucracy, Mies had come to expect little from his meeting with the gestapo head, according to Hans Keszler, a Bauhaus student, who wrote of these events.[1] Prodded by Frau Reich and Heide, Mies had been going from one office to another—from the Dessau authorities to the police and various government agencies in Berlin—always with the same result: one office had no idea what another was doing and no one appeared willing to take responsibility for clearing matters up. Every official to whom Mies spoke assured him of his personal admiration for the institution. "If it were up to me," each would say, according to Keszler, "the school would be reopened." Understandably, perhaps, everyone was more concerned about their own situation than about the controversial Bauhaus. The climate of fear engulfed the party bureaucracy as

145

it did the country at large: even the gestapo was not immune. It was this disquietude that influenced the gestapo's uncharacteristically lethargic handling of the Bauhaus affair, in striking contrast to the aggressiveness they had exhibited at the school's closing in April.

For a government dependent on securing and maintaining control through fear and suppression, the establishment of a national political police was of critical importance. Immediately upon Hitler's assumption of power, Göring moved to strengthen and broaden the jurisdiction of the existing political division of the Prussian police, known as the gestapo.[2] A proud and entrenched force, the Prussian police did not view Göring's intentions lightly, and the success of his plans rested on the smooth transference of the established police bureaucracy into party hands. To accomplish this, he called upon the suave and able Rudolph Diels, placing him at the head of the political police shortly after the Nazi assumption of power.

Related to Göring through his second wife, the thirty-two-year-old Diels had established his reputation as a dedicated fighter of communists in the Prussian police bureaucracy, where, since 1930, he had headed the anti-communist section.[3] Not only did his presence satisfy the Prussian police that "one of their own" remained at the head of this sensitive unit, but, since Diels lacked any connection to the party other than through Göring—he was not a party member—the Reichsminister felt assured of his loyalty.

Diels's situation, however, was far from secure. Already various party factions were maneuvering for control of the potentially commanding force, in a manner not unlike the competition between Goebbels and Rosenberg in the cultural field. In May, Minister of the Interior Frick had circulated a plan claiming control for his department; while Heinrich Himmler, chief of the SS, and Reinhard Heydrich, the young and ambitious chief of the SD, the intelligence unit of the SS, pressed their claims as being the most logical. Realizing in this new force a potential competitor to his SA forces, Ernst Röhm was observing warily from the side. Also part of this malevolent brew was Göring, the Prussian minister of the interior and, hence, head of the entire Prussian police force, who viewed his appointment of Diels as an attempt to pacify the members of the police bureaucracy without giving them free rein and was understandably reluctant to relinquish control to any other clique of the Nazi party. Restless and suspicious, these competing groups worked ceaselessly to undermine each other. By May the battle lines were clearly drawn: the opposing groups quarreled over jurisdiction in political arrests, as well as control over the rapidly proliferating concentration camps. Diels's future—perhaps even his life—depended on his aligning himself with the right faction at the right time. With so intimidating a pack at his heels, it was certainly not the moment to involve himself in controversial issues—such as the Bauhaus, whose director persisted in mounting a one-man occupation of his waiting room. Adding to Diels's uncertainties was the increasingly open and vituperous battle between Goebbels and Rosenberg, which by June had brought the Nazi cultural offensive in Berlin to a virtual standstill. Party directives were only as effective as the bureaucrats who carried them out. Confronted by conflicting cultural directions, party officials—sensitive to the precariousness of their own careers—hesitated to take actions that might be used against them in the future. Simple prudence preached patience; and patience bred inaction. Within Berlin's perplexed artistic community, inaction bred hope.

For Diels, Mies and the Bauhaus were nothing more than a bother, a potential obstacle that might possibly topple his delicate high-wire act. Yet, Mies refused to go away, and the Bauhaus file lying on Diels's desk daily grew thicker with testimonials pouring in from the various ministries, under the prodding of Weidemann.[4] It was clear that if Diels wanted to resolve the irksome issue, he would have to meet with its persistent director. Twenty years later, Mies spoke of this meeting, which seems to have occurred sometime around the middle to end of May.[5]

"What is it you want?" Diels asked, extending his hand to the famed architect in a warm greeting.

Surprised by Diels's youth and apparent refinement, Mies replied, "I would like to talk to you about the Bauhaus. What exactly is going on? You have closed the Bauhaus. It is my private property and I want to know why it was closed. We didn't steal anything. We didn't make a revolution!"

"Oh," responded Diels, "I know all about the Bauhaus." Like most Berlin party officials, he did not seem notably antagonistic in speaking of the school. "I'm very interested in the Bauhaus movement. But," he went on, "we're uncertain about Kandinsky."

"Kandinsky?" replied Mies, startled. With Kandinsky's reputation as a stern theoretician and advocate for artistic objectivity now firmly established in Germany for the past decade, Mies had thought that controversy over the Russian artist's past involvement with the cultural politics of the young Soviet Union was long since dead.[6] *I will guarantee Kandinsky.*

"Be careful," said Diels. "We don't know anything about him, but if you want to keep him, it's okay with us. But if something happens, we pick you up. Do I make myself clear?"

"Absolutely," replied Mies. "That is fine with me."

Diels then promised to discuss the matter with Göring, and Mies, satisfied, took leave of the gestapo leader.[7] Diels too was pleased. Not only had he removed Mies from his office, but—in the time-honored tradition of the insecure and ambitious bureaucrat—he had deftly passed on a thorny and unpleasant issue to his superior.

Slowly, the Bauhaus story—a miasma of petty political ambitions and overlapping bureaucratic responsibilities between civic and party officials, between Dessau and Berlin—was emerging. It seemed that two Dessau party enthusiasts, one a minor bureaucrat by the name of Harms and the other, an editor of what Heide described as a "little yellow weekly"[8]—sensing an opportunity for self-advancement—had fabricated incriminating evidence against the Bauhaus, inducing some low-level official within the Dessau public prosecutor's office to press charges. The public prosecutor himself revealed to Mies—during one of his trips to Dessau—that he had no particular interest in the Bauhaus, and "had just gone along with it as an official bystander."[9] Before attempting to rectify the situation, the public prosecutor—anxious, like everyone else, to "cover" himself—sought permission from his superior, the new mayor of Dessau. Assured by the mayor—who, coincidentally, was an architect—of his disinterest in the persecution of the Bauhaus, the prosecutor proceeded to inform the Berlin gestapo in whose hands the suit now lay, that his office no longer wished to pursue charges against the school. With the realization that the closing of the school was simply a bureaucratic "error" and that it seemed only a question of time before it would reopen, spirits among the Bauhäusler remained high. "Our guess," wrote Heide to fellow student Carl Bauer on May 17, "is that [the reopening] will happen at the end of this, or beginning of next, week."[10] However, the anticipated opening was constantly postponed, as nervous bureaucrats—aware of the school's notoriety and anxious to protect themselves— kept the legal documentation crisscrossing back and forth between various offices in Dessau and Berlin. On May 31, Heide informed Bauer that "[t]he reopening . . . decreed by the responsible court authorities has not yet happened. But . . . we are counting the days, or, more correctly, the hours until the festive occasion."[11]

By mid-June, with the school still closed, new difficulties arose. On June 15, citing the fact that the Bauhaus had been a "germ-cell of bolshevism" (and hence engaged in "political activity" forbidden by the April 7 Civil Service Law) and that the faculty of such an institution could thus not offer the required "guarantees" of support for the National State "at all times and without reserve," the Dessau city council voted to cancel its continuing payments to the former masters of the school.[12] Deprived of these funds—its main source of income—the Bauhaus could no longer function, no matter what the outcome of the negotiations with the Nazis in Berlin—a single stroke that obliterated all their efforts of the past months. In what undoubtedly was a last-ditch effort to get Dessau to drop these charges, Mies—in a letter of June 17 addressed to the mayor of Dessau—attempted to refute their claims, going so far as to assert that under his direction "the leadership [of the school] gradually changed over to the national-minded students, who were supported by the faculty . . . [and that the closing of the Bauhaus in the fall of 1932] affected . . . national-minded young people almost exclusively."[13]

While Mies's earlier assertions of an apolitical Bauhaus were never entirely accurate—representing more his aspirations than actuality—the description of the school as an oasis of nationalism was flagrantly untrue. Like the appeal of the KDK of two months earlier—and all of Mies's actions but for the Rosenberg initiative—it bore the unmistakable imprint of Heide and the practical-minded Lilly Reich. "Mies did nothing without first speaking to Lilly Reich," declared Herbert Hirche, Mies's longtime associate.[14] But, whoever drafted the statement, Mies signed it and it is he who bears its responsibility. Forged as much by circumstance as by inclination, the attitude of political indifference it revealed was not unlike that exhibited within the Prussian Academy of Arts. Most everyone, it seemed, had "higher" priorities.

By the end of May, it had become quite clear that the Bauhaus could not continue as in the past, as long as the Nazi government remained in power. Certain "adjustments" would have to be made, and discussions among the faculty and students now centered around their nature and degree.[15] There was talk of a political "commissar" appointed by the party to oversee the school's political orientation (and hopefully ignore the curriculum); of alliance with the party's liberal cultural wing; of getting rid of certain "controversial" members of the faculty, such as Kandinsky and Hilbersheimer. There was even talk of replacing Mies, whose remoteness and extraordinarily passive behavior (he was described on June 20 by Alcar Rudelt as being "much too battle-weary"[16]) was coming to be seen as detrimental to the school's interests. By mid-June, the time of the new Dessau charges, some sort of accommodation to the regime had become generally accepted; and Mies's response— undoubtedly drafted by Heide and Reich—must be seen within that light. The source of the school's problems—as it had always been—was political, and any permanent resolution of their difficulties would likewise have to be political. The financial difficulties, while of grave importance, could possibly be resolved on their own; the political problems, surely not. Believing themselves close to political settlement, this group of Bauhaus leaders was anxious to claim whatever political support Dessau required. Mies, too, was desperate to get the Bauhaus situation behind him and resolved in a manner that would not impinge on the outcome of the Reichsbank project. Everyone felt that they had come to the end of the road. "I don't know, Carl," wrote Heide on May 31 to Bauer, "whether in fact this April 11 wasn't the day the Bauhaus died. One shouldn't be pessimistic, but all I can make out is the smell of corpses."[17]

As far as is known, Dessau ignored Mies's letter. There seems to have been no official response, nor were any further payments made to the faculty.[18] Now literally bankrupt—undone by the political and financial pressures that had plagued it from the start—the Bauhaus could not reopen even with the anticipated police permission. But Mies did not inform the police about the school's terminal financial state, indicating that it was not so much its survival in which he was interested, as the removal of the political stigmata from those associated with it—most notably himself. Events in June and early July had made this more critical than ever.

By the beginning of June, Minister Rust had come to realize that the "cleansing" of the Prussian Academy of Arts could not be left to the initiative of the membership. The decision was therefore made to apply the so-called "Aryan paragraph" of the April 7 Civil Service Law by sending questionnaires to the membership in order to determine their racial suitability. When Schillings expressed "reservations" over the dependability of such statements, Minister Rust suggested that the academy utilize the services of the Office of Racial Research (a division of the Ministry of the Interior) in addition to the questionnaires.[19] On June 16, Schillings made his first request to that office, asking for racial data on nine members of the academy, including the composer Alban Berg, Peter Behrens, and Oskar Kokoschka. On July 1, he requested information on nineteen additional members, including Max Pechstein, Renée Sintenis, Josef Hoffmann, Wilhelm Kreis, the composer Wolf-Ferrari, and Mies van der Rohe.[20] Since certain investigations had to be done in foreign countries, as in the cases of Berg and Kokoschka, expenses became higher than planned. Citing the insufficient "means put at [our] disposal by the Minister of the Interior," the Office of Racial Research requested on July 3 that the academy bear these additional costs. With the proviso that such costs remain "small, since our academy . . . does not have extensive means for such a purpose," Schillings agreed.[21] The Prussian Academy of Arts was now not only spying on its esteemed membership, but paying for it as well.

The questionnaires caused grave concern among the members. Although Mies never doubted his Aryan "purity," and asserted it on his questionnaire, he was troubled that the non-Germanic character of his family name—"Miës, with its perversely doubled syllables, and "van der Rohe," of Dutch (and Celtic) origin—might cause him difficulties with overly fastidious officials.[22] Having already been accused of being a "two-raced foreigner," and suspect because of his association with modernism (not to mention the Bauhaus), he worried that such racial innuendos—if they held—might make him, as he put it, a "second-class German"[23] and signal the end of his hopes for the Reichsbank commission and beyond.

In view of his dismal circumstances, it is understandable that Mies preferred to dwell on his hopes for the future, rather than on the joyless realities of the day. Heavily in debt over the Bauhaus, his financial state was precarious. He was living off the income he received from his Bauhaus contract (what remained of it), Ada's funds, and the 5,000 reichsmarks he had received from participating in the Reichsbank competition. At the most mundane level, the commissions involved with the Reichsbank project were substantial and desperately needed. On a more philosophic plane, if the Nazis should remain in power—and, at this point in light of recent short-lived national governments, their longevity seemed dubious—his securing of this important project would be of inestimable significance. Not only would it reaffirm the prestigious position he had so recently—and briefly—occupied, but it would go far toward ameliorating the difficulties he was currently encountering with regard to his political suspectability. But, most of all at the deepest core of his being, Mies needed to build.

Much had transpired in the two and a half months between the inception in February of the Reichsbank competition and the submission of entries in early May. The swift consolidation of Nazi power, the growth of rumors regarding Hitler's "interest" in architecture, and reports that the party planned large-scale building projects had radically transformed an important public commission into a likely presentiment of the architectural aspirations of the Third Reich. In February the political situation had barely merited mention in the program. By May it was the dominating consideration, and the program had been revised.

> [M]aking it of actual historical value is the fact that the
> contest falls into the months of our national rise, into a
> time with a deep sense of German culture in which the art
> of construction must also announce its goals.[24]

One major aspect of the commission, however, remained the
same: the need for a building of monumental and imposing
character.

> [A]n expansion of the state bank is unthinkable as merely a
> rational office building. It must have the character of a
> monument, it should be an ornament for the state capital
> and should represent the dignity of a world institution.[25]

Modernism, however, despite the fact that many of its roots lay
in the rationalism of the neoclassical tradition that resulted in
the monumental Prussian style, was, generally speaking, anti-
monumental. Not only was monumentality associated with
the *kaiserlich* days, but it was antithetical to the more socialistic modernists, concerned as they were with inexpensive,
quickly-built mass housing, and used to the priorities and budget restraints of the Weimar government, the main sponsor
of the modernist building projects of the 1920s. To a cost-
conscious government, committed to providing desperately
needed workers' housing on the broadest possible scale, monumentality seemed irrelevant, if not offensive.

In this regard, Mies remained somewhat distant from his
colleagues. In fact, his oft-expressed disdain for the budgetary
restrictions inherent in mass housing projects and his propensity for "luxe" in materials, finish, and decor, along with his
pronounced affinity for wealthy private clients, had earned
him frequent censure from his colleagues, who were affronted
by his lack of interest in what they perceived as the central
issue of modernism, that of improving the life of the working
classes and, ultimately, transforming society. Thus, perhaps
alone among the German modernists, Mies was suited to reconcile monumentality with the principles of modernism—an
ability that had become critical now, as the "new" Germany
sought to reaffirm its traditional values and identity in a technologically advanced world. And, indeed, without resorting to
the traditional devices of entablatures and classical orders, his

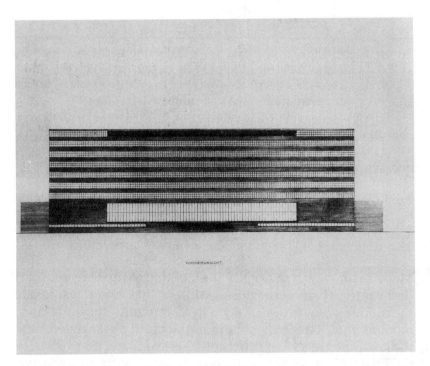

Mies van der Rohe, Reichsbank project, 1933:
TOP, elevation of main facade (Collection, Mies van der Rohe Archive, the
Museum of Modern Art, New York. Gift of Ludwig Mies van der Rohe)
BOTTOM, perspective drawing of river front facade (Photo courtesy of Mies
van der Rohe Archive, the Museum of Modern Art, New York)

Reichsbank design, by its notable monumentality, massive symmetry, regularity, use of geometrical shapes, and controlled proportionality, was a brilliant reinterpretation of the neoclassical tradition of Schinkel and Behrens. Yet its unembellished surfaces and broad, unbroken expanses of ribbon windows kept the design within the tenets of modernism and consistent with his work of the late 1920s.[26] Its vast and heroic scale—the public hall alone measured 350 feet in length— firmly laid to rest the myth that modernism was essentially incompatible with the Prussian tradition of monumentality. Like his Barcelona Pavilion of 1929, Mies's Reichsbank design proved that modernism—in his hands, at least—was entirely capable of producing buildings of elegant proportions and noble demeanor. Clearly Mies was capable of creating *une architecture civique* in the grand Prussian manner, and in accordance with the notions of Moeller van den Bruck, whom he had lately taken to reading,[27] and who saw in the austere monumentality of the Prussian style an expression of the state as hero, or—in his own words—"the steps of soldiers, the language of lawgivers, the contempt of the moment, [and] the reckoning with eternity."[28] Unfettered by the limitations of academicism, the coy references of *volkischness,* or the programmatic restraints of modernism, Mies had shown that he was indeed a worthy successor to Schinkel and Behrens, and his Reichsbank a striking ornament for the Prussian capital, whose loyal and talented architect sons had traditionally raised the architectural aspirations of their leaders to Olympian heights.

At the same time, while the antimodernist background of the Nazis could hardly be ignored, persuasive arguments were being sounded by the iconoclastic Nazi modernists in Berlin that favored a modern Reichsbank. A regime purporting to represent the radical renewal of society could hardly reject, out of hand, the world-renowned achievements of its modernist artists and architects. Philip Johnson, visiting Berlin that summer, summed up this reasoning:

> A good modern Reichsbank ... would prove to the German intellectuals and to foreign countries that the new Germany is not bent on destroying all the splendid modern arts which have been built up in recent years. ... Germany cannot deny her progress.[29]

Such arguments apparently had some effect, for on July 8, Mies was named one of the six finalists in the Reichsbank competition. The only winner of international repute, he suddenly appeared, in that summer of 1933, to be in an enviable position with regard to the building plans of the new regime.[30]

"Order champagne! I've got the letter," Mies said to Lilly Reich, his jubilation evident in his voice. "We can open the school again."[31]

"Order champagne?" Frau Reich replied, incredulously. She had known Mies for close to a decade and often his actions still mystified her. "What for?" she went on. "There are no students. There's no money. What good is their 'permission'? There's no way the Bauhaus can reopen." To the sturdily realistic Frau Reich, feeding a dead dog was an act of foolishness, not charity.

Her skepticism was shared by the remaining members of the Bauhaus faculty—Albers, Peterhans, Kandinsky, and Hilbersheimer—whom Mies had called to his apartment on July 20 to make known the letter's terms. As they had anticipated, Hilbersheimer and Kandinsky were to be removed from the faculty and replaced "by individuals who guarantee to support the principles of the National Socialist ideology"; the curriculum was to be revised "to satisfy the demands of the new State" and submitted for approval to the Prussian minister of culture. The remaining faculty were to satisfy the requirements of the civil service law.[32] However, it was neither the permission nor the terms of the reopening that interested Mies. "I went there for three months [sic] every other day just to get this letter," he said. "I was anxious to get this letter. I wanted permission to go ahead." Characteristically, he saw the Bauhaus issue as transcending the mere unlocking of the school's doors in Steglitz. The gestapo permission represented, for Mies, a very real admission by the regime that it no longer viewed the Bauhaus (and by implication, modernism) as a threat. With this letter, association with modernism was removed from the ranks of treasonous activities in the Third Reich.

His purpose having been achieved, Mies now offered to make his own proposal to the Nazis. "I hope you will agree with me," he said to his mystified friends. "I will write them a letter

ies van der Rohe, Lilly Reich, and Bauhaus students on board an excursion boat on
e Wannsee, a lake near Berlin, 1933 (Photo by Howard Dearstyne, courtesy of Mies
n der Rohe Archive, the Museum of Modern Art, New York)

back—'Thank you very much for the permission to open the school again, but the faculty has decided to close it!' "

Office of the State Secret
Police for the attention
of Ministerialrat Diels
Berlin, Prinz-Albrecht-Strasse

July 20, 1933

Dear Sir,

I beg to inform you that the faculty of the Bauhaus at a meeting yesterday saw itself compelled, in view of the economic difficulties which have arisen from the shutdown of the Institute, to dissolve the Bauhaus Berlin.

Your obedient servant,
Mies van der Rohe[33]

Mies was euphoric. He had triumphed where others had doubted. He had persisted where others had been afraid, and had reaffirmed the power of patience and reasonability. Adding to his sense of victory was the fact that his certification of "racial purity" had arrived from the Office of Racial Research at the end of July.

By now, Mies was exhausted, wearied as much by his exertions as by the precariousness of the times. Essentially a solitary man who preferred the lonely certainties of introspection to the capriciousness of daily life, he had become more involved with events during the past months than was his habit or inclination. When a Swiss architect offered him the use of his home on Lake Lugano for a working vacation, Mies gratefully accepted the offer. Shortly after August 10, accompanied by Lilly Reich and a small group of Bauhaus students who paid the equivalent of a semester's tuition to accompany him, Mies left Berlin jubilant over his astonishing success with the Nazis and confident of his place in the new order.[34]

CHAPTER 9

AN ASTONISHING TURN

THE REVOLUTION WHICH WE HAVE MADE IS A TOTAL REVOLU-
TION: IT DOMINATES EVERY AREA OF PUBLIC LIFE AND HAS
TRANSFORMED IT FROM TOP TO BOTTOM.

> (Joseph Goebbels, Opening Address of the Reich
> Cultural Chamber, November 15, 1933)

Events in Germany were not so easy to set aside, and in many ways, the benign tranquillity of Switzerland set them into sharper view. An assignment to his students to design a house on a selected site around Lugano seemed to evoke in Mies— who participated in the exercise by designing "an architect's house" in an Alpine setting—thoughts of staying in Switzerland. Similar ideas had already begun for others. Always painful, for some, such as Oskar Schlemmer, the thought of exile was paralyzing. "Hovering in the back- or foreground," he wrote on September 1 to Gunta Stölzl, another former member of the Bauhaus, "there is always the question: what does man live by? . . . [A]nd what about the . . . dependents?"[1] Many had already gone: Mendelsohn, the avant-garde playwrights Bertolt Brecht and Walter Mehring. Kandinsky, Klee, and Albers (whose wife was Jewish) were making plans to leave. Even for those, like Mies, who still were able to choose (and who were not yet, like Heinrich Mann, forced to flee one step ahead of the SS), the doubts had begun. An excursion to the Triennale, the big art and architecture exhibition in Milan, and a day trip from Lugano, collided with the long arm of the KDK. Along with Gropius and Mendelsohn, Mies had been included among the German architects invited to participate. Only Mies's work was on view; the others having been excluded as "undesirable to the German side" by pressure from the KDK.[2] The same group had pressured Milan to remove photographs of Gropius's works from an exhibition prepared for that city by the Deutsche Werkbund. Already hung for the exhibition, the Milanese authorities refused: but a lecture that Gropius had been invited to give was canceled. When Gropius demanded an explanation of this action, the Werkbund informed him that he was considered "too international": why Gropius was considered more "international" than Mies was never explained.[3] Perhaps Mies's having been named as one of the Reichsbank winners made him potentially "recognized" by the regime, or—at the very least—not inimical to them. Gropius had apparently become the "second-class German" that Mies so feared. What Mies thought of this is unknown.

Coming from Berlin, Switzerland seemed like a dream. One had almost forgot that there were still places where children threw balls instead of dummy hand grenades; where they carried balloons instead of wooden spears; where they ran helter-skelter, instead of marching—two by two—attempting to do the goose step; where streets were not deserted at night; where one's ears were not assaulted all hours of the day and night with military music, with "Siegreich werden wir Frankreich schlagen" ("Victoriously we will smash France") on the radio, beneath the windows, in the parks and cafés; where one slept soundly at night, not listening for the sound of the huge Nazi trucks doing their work at three o'clock in the morning; where the streets vibrated with the diverse cacophony of life, rather than the hammering tread of the goose step; and where the proud proclamation by a public official that his people had "left the path of Western civilization" was not greeted by hearty applause.[4]

Mies van der Rohe playing boccie, Lugano, 1933 (Bauhaus-Archiv)

Yet to most outsiders in Germany, such evidence of Nazi oppression remained invisible. For most travelers, whether the curious tourist lured by advertisements to "Visit the new Germany—less expensive, but otherwise unchanged," or the optimistic citizen, smug in the assurance of his Aryan stock and approved political creed—an excursion through Germany during the summer of 1933 appeared to confirm Hitler's success in restoring a sense of national pride to a divided and disheartened people. Everywhere, but most notably in the south, one sensed a feeling of confidence, euphoria even, conveyed by the pervasive appearance of the swastika: on buildings, private as well as public; on street cars; and on armbands. Acts of oppression—mentioned daily in the foreign press and labeled "libelous propaganda" or "atrocity fantasies" by the German media—were nowhere to be seen. Afraid of retribution, and with censorship so complete, those who had borne the brunt of Nazi persecution remained silent, hidden from view. By day, they kept to their homes, afraid to venture out in the streets; at night, trembling lest the Nazis return, they sat behind darkened windows and latched doors.

Who, among those traveling through the Reich, noticed the fresh mounds at the Jewish cemeteries or witnessed the burned hands and feet, the broken bones and abominable lacerations inflicted on those individuals deemed "unsuitable" by the government? Who, in the "*gemütlich*" city of Freiburg, visited the Jewish schoolboys who had been forced to run through a bonfire of burning books? And, while astute visitors to the famed university town of Heidelberg might note the return of the dueling ring and the resurgence of fresh facial scars among the student population, who noted the absence of Jewish professors from the gleaming new Robert Schurman Lecture Hall, built through the generosity of American Jews? Who saw the faces of those next of kin from whom payment of proper postage fees was requested, so that they might receive the ashes of their loved one? And who took heed of the quiet pleas for visas to America, to Switzerland, to anywhere? . . .

Snug in the comfort of their first-class hotels or preoccupied with their own private musings, scores of notable and responsible visitors denounced the apparently unjust accusation of the foreign press, expressing indignation at the "abominable atrocity lies." Mayor John P. Curley of Boston, waxing eloquent about the peace and sense of order that prevailed under the Nazis, paid public tribute to the "new spirit" engendered by Hitler. Even the dean of the Harvard Graduate School of Education, Henry Wyman Holmes, was impressed. "I think the reports of Hitler's oppression of the Jews have been exaggerated," he remarked.[5]

A clear understanding of what was happening was difficult even for those individuals most caught up by Nazi actions. In the cultural arena, where Nazi oppression was more open, its inconsistent application impeded many in the avant-garde community from seeing clearly what was going on. Events in Stuttgart—as witnessed and recorded by Alfred Barr, director of New York's Museum of Modern Art—typified what was taking place in cities throughout Germany.[6] With a population of almost 400,000 people; dozens of museums, theaters, and fine opera; a profusion of concerts and good modern architecture (one of its suburbs being the renowned Weissenhof), Stuttgart, the capital city of Württemberg, considered itself a cultural and intellectual center, its citizens priding themselves on knowing that Schiller, Hegel, and Kant were more than simply names of local streets. Its most famous living artist was Oskar Schlemmer. On March 1, Barr wrote, a retrospective exhibition of Schlemmer's works of art had opened at the Museum of Modern Württemberg Art, where it was scheduled to run a month. On March 12, after the appearance of a negative review in the local Nazi newspaper, the exhibition was closed. At about the same time, several of Schlemmer's paintings were removed from the museum's permanent collection and put in storage: "protection of the pictures following unfavorable press notices" was the explanation offered by embarrassed gallery officials, according to Barr. In early April, paintings by five of Germany's best-known modern artists—Schmidt-Rottluff, Kirchner, Otto Müller, Paul Klee, and Otto Dix—were removed from the large State Gallery of Art, while local newspapers hinted darkly of what would happen to curators who concerned themselves with modern art. Barr was present at a meeting on April 9 of the local chapter of the KDK, where the newly appointed minister of culture and education, Christian Mergenthaler, gave an address. "It is a mistake to think that the revolution is only political and economic. It is above all cultural," said the minister, adopting—according to Barr—Hitler's urgently aggressive, hoarse tones. "If anyone should ask," Mergenthaler went on,

> what is left of Freedom? he will be answered: there is no freedom for those who would weaken and destroy German art. Freedom is only for those who carry in themselves the German artistic spirit and a fanatical will to reform. . . . And come what may let this alone be our eternal watchword—*"Deutschland, nur Deutschland, ganz allein"!*[7]

In May, observed Barr, Stuttgart painters and sculptors were "invited" to attend a reception honoring Minister Mergenthaler (attendance was, in fact, mandatory). Lining the entryway to the museum were brown-shirted troops of the SA, rifles in hand, between whose ranks the artists were forced to walk.

By late spring of 1933, in towns and cities where the KDK reigned unchallenged, such stories had become commonplace. Modern artists and their supporters—curators, museum directors, and gallery owners—were intimidated, persecuted, dismissed, and subjected to public ridicule. ("For this 'Art' 2,500 marks were paid in 1924," stated a placard conspicuously placed next to a modernist work in the Nuremberg Civic Gallery.) Unable to teach or sell their art, these artists were often reduced to poverty.

Berlin, by comparison, was an oasis of artistic freedom. However repugnant the events taking place there—which by now included the dismissal of countless prominent artists and museum directors,[8] it was still possible, in June 1933, to find unmolested exhibitions of modernist works. On June 12, Schlemmer noted that his work, along with that of Klee, Feininger, and Kirchner, was being displayed at the Secession, although "causing violent controversy." He also observed that the Crown Prince's Palace, the section of the museum devoted to modern art, was still open; but that its distinguished director, Dr. Ludwig Justi, responsible for organizing the museum's collection of modern art, had been dismissed.[9]

By June, a pattern was clear. In areas where the KDK prevailed, cultural atrocities became the norm; where it lacked a following, or where it was challenged (as in Berlin), such events—although present—did not predominate. No wonder then that to Schlemmer, as well as his fellow modernists, the NS Students' Association seemed like "the good side,"[10] and a rally planned by them for June 29, to which Mies had been invited[11]—along with other leading Berlin cultural figures—evoked exhilarating anticipation. Even so, without the apparent backing of Minister Goebbels, the fevered activities of the Students' Association would have passed unheeded. Rumors regarding Goebbels's supposed liberal artistic interests appeared even in the foreign press. The propaganda minister was said to have had several works by Nolde removed from the National Gallery to be hung in his home and to have privately expressed regret for the rigorousness of the book burnings.[12] This impression was also fostered by his ambiguous public statements. "If the new Germany is to be represented," said the propaganda minister in a widely publicized speech he gave in Hamburg on June 17, "then it should be represented in a form that corresponds artistically and culturally to the magnitude of the movement." In a thinly veiled reference to the contention of Andreas-Schreiber that a revolutionary political movement demanded a revolutionary art (not without *its* reminiscence of the postwar liaison between the modernists and the left), Goebbels concluded, "We are convinced that the revolution is not yet over."[13]

"Youth fights for German Art!" proclaimed the red posters that appeared on the advertising kiosks throughout Berlin several days before the Students' Association rally. While anticipation had been running high among Berlin's cultural community, it is unlikely that either Mies or anyone else in the overflowing audience that gathered in the large auditorium of the Friedrich Wilhelm University was prepared for the announcement of what appeared to be a startlingly new Nazi artistic creed. Although Mies never appears to have commented on this event, one can imagine that he was no less disbelieving than others in the audience as one young Nazi after another strode to the podium to condemn Wilhelminian academicism, regimentation in the arts, and the abuse of the term "cultural bolshevism." He heard Barlach, Nolde, Heckel, and Schmidt-Rottluff hailed as the progenitors of the proposed "new German art"; and himself, along with Heinrich Tessenow, acclaimed in architecture.[14] "The formation of an art historical creed by uncreative people lies like a nightmare over all young artists of our movement," declared Otto Andreas-Schreiber, the last speaker. "The national socialist youth believes in nothing as strongly as in the victory of quality and truth." To resounding applause, Andreas-Schreiber proclaimed the dissolution of the KDK groups at the Berlin academies and art colleges and announced an exhibition of modern German artists to be held the end of July under the special protection of the Students' Association. "The living element of art is freedom," concluded the young leader, his words almost drowned out by prolonged cheers. With his person and art particularly suspect by the Nazis—neither the academy's racial inquiry, the Bauhaus, nor Reichsbank issues were as yet resolved—Mies must surely have been as delighted as other members of the cheering audience.

The revolt appeared to be an astonishing success: declarations of solidarity poured in from other university towns. "The Halle National Socialist Students' Association declares its enthused agreement with the announcement of the Berlin national socialist students against the art reaction. The struggle of the SA man on the street must not be betrayed in the cultural field."[15] What remained of the liberal press reacted with guarded optimism. Andreas-Schreiber's speech, comments by the prominent modernist painter Karl Hofer, and statements of solidarity from other university centers were published in the *Deutsche Allgemeine Zeitung*.

Bolstered by the overwhelming response to the June 29 rally, Andreas-Schreiber intensified his offensive against the KDK. Continuing with his plans for the forthcoming exhibition, he publicly attacked historicism in art and defended the tenets of expressionism. "The erection of historicism into dogma," he asserted, in a letter published in the *Deutsche Allgemeine Zeitung* on July 12, is the work of obscurantists who "don't even know enough to understand what they don't understand. . . . The national socialist student . . . demands a revolutionary view of art," a clear allusion to Goebbels's endorsement of the idea of an alliance of political and artistic revolutions. "Long live the complete national socialist revolution!" concluded Andreas-Schreiber,[16] either defying or ignoring a July 6 statement by Hitler implying that the national socialist revolution had ended, therefore depriving the party liberals of their political justification for modernism.[17]

Rosenberg's response was immediate and virulent: he counterattacked on both artistic and ideological grounds. While his derision of expressionism was nothing new, his political challenge raised far more dangerous issues. By cleverly identifying the progressives as defenders of the political and cultural "heroes of the old systems," as well as referring to Andreas-Schreiber as a "cultural Otto Strasser," Rosenberg brought into question not only their judgment, but their very allegiance to the party, thus playing on Hitler's well-known distrust of the Berlin party faction. The portrayal of the "Berlin" position as a political revolt in the guise of an artistic one was quickly seized upon by other KDK supporters. The *Zeitschrift für Nationalsozialistische Erziehung*, published by the Bavarian Ministry of Culture, pronounced the position of the Students' Association to be "openly aimed against the party sovereignty"; while Walter Hansen, one of the party's most zealous supporters, accused the June 29 rally of being "an act of sabotage."[18]

Other Nazi-oriented groups, opposed as much to the *volkisch* as to the progressive faction, added their voices to the fray. One of the most active, the Munich-based architectural group known as the "German Artists' League 33," one of whose members was Ludwig Troost, Hitler's favorite architect, issued press statements condemning the positions of both party wings. Practicing a simplified classicism (then popular for official buildings not only in Munich, where Troost had designed the Nazi party headquarters, but also in Paris, Washington, and Moscow), they saw the activities of Rosenberg's group, especially Schultze-Naumburg, as threatening to their own aspirations. They also condemned the "Berlin impudence" for daring to propose such "seditious personalities" as Nolde, Klee, Schmidt-Rottluff, Tessenow, and Mies van der Rohe as models for the art and architecture of the new German state.

Correctly assessing that some deep personal feud lay behind the bitter public wrangling, the Berlin cultural community watched this war of words with its usual wry detachment, a sentiment encouraged in this case by their cheery appraisal of its outcome. "Diametrically opposed trends exist among the Nazis," said Albert Flechtheim, the famous Berlin art dealer, to Harry Kessler, while visiting him in Paris in mid-July.

> One supports modern art . . . the other . . . wants to exterminate it. . . . [T]here is a bitter running fight between antagonistic trends and personalities inside the Party. . . . These internal quarrels and the inevitable dreadful economic emergency will destroy them. The crash . . . will come in the autumn.[19]

Indeed, the situation was rapidly becoming chaotic; the Nazis were the laughingstock of the cultural community. An assurance by Andreas-Schreiber, published in the *Deutsche Allgemeine Zeitung* on July 14, that "the student youth . . . was not polemicizing against [Rosenberg's] personal art philosophy" did little to squelch rumors of intraparty turmoil.[20] Accusing the participants of attempting "to split the front from the true, new German art," State Commissioner Hinkel threatened "the sharpest measures" against those party members who continued these discussions "aimed against each other."[21] On July 15, Minister Rust flatly prohibited further discussion of these issues.

Bewildered by the novelty of a Nazi-sponsored exhibition of modern art, and wary of provoking retribution, the critics reacted cautiously to the eagerly awaited Students' Association exhibition, which opened on July 22 at the Ferdinand Moeller Gallery in Berlin. "Refreshing," said one critic, "vividly filled with the desire for the new and the contemporary."[22] Entitled Thirty German Artists, the exhibition featured the works of Rohlfs, Pechstein, Marcks, Schmidt-Rottluff, Nolde, and Barlach—many of whom had been attacked as morally and aesthetically degenerate by Schultze-Naumburg and the KDK. The inclusion of several works by Andreas-Schreiber and Hans Weidemann revealed the vital continuity of the expressionist tradition in the younger generation and provided indisputable evidence of the compatibility between the ideals of national socialism and those of expressionism.

On July 25, three days after the opening of the exhibition, SS troops took up positions before the gallery entrance. In an action that recalled his tenure in Thuringia, Minister of the

Interior Frick ordered the exhibition closed. When it reopened a week later, Fritz Hippler, the leader of the Students' Association, and Andreas-Schreiber, organizers of the exhibition, had been expelled from the student group, which no longer appeared as sponsor of the show.[23]

Such were the cultural conditions as Mies, several weeks later, left for Switzerland: for himself and his fellow modernists, there was as much cause for elation as for despair. Although still a potent force, the KDK, with its claims to determine art policy, had been undermined and publicly repudiated by a clearly promodernist faction of the party leadership. Desiring only the freedom to pursue their art in peace, the modernists were now confronted by the alluring prospect that their art might not only be permitted to flourish, but in fact might be viewed as best representing the aspirations of the Third Reich. It was an astonishing turn of events that appeared to confirm the convictions of many individuals that the Nazis would "settle down" once they had achieved power. The old German proverb "one never eats porridge as hot as it's cooked!" was heard anew.

No one, however, could possibly claim that the Nazi cultural direction was firmly settled. On the contrary, to party officials and the public alike, the party's cultural "line" still appeared bewildering and capricious. It was thus with great eagerness that the general public and the party leadership—as well as Mies, from Lugano—turned their attention to Hitler's address on September 1, his first public statement on art since *Mein Kampf*.[24] Known as the Führer's Culture Day (*Kulturtag*) address, it opened the series of ceremonies honoring the Nazi party known as Party Day that came to be held each September in Nuremberg. Given the tenuousness of his government and his political preoccupations, however, Hitler seemed less interested in clarification than in conveying the appearance of party unity, along with pacifying two of his most visible and prominent deputies. Although it anticipated a clear signal of the Nazi cultural course, the public, no less than the factionalized and squabbling party leadership, was treated instead to a dazzling display of equivocation.

On one hand, Hitler made brutally clear his personal aversion to modernism, characterizing its manifestations as "conscious insanities" created by "debased" and "worthless" individuals.

> It is no accident that the age which was most blurred in world perception [i.e., the Weimar period], with its liberal . . . uncertainty . . . was also uncertain in the field of cultural creation. This uncertainty finally found its only suitable expression in the cubist, dadaistic cult of primitivity. Under the slogan "be new at any cost," any bungler could achieve something special.[25]

Yet, at the same time, his assertion that "today's tasks require new methods" and his demand for a "crystal-clear functionalism" for Nazi architecture appeared to ally his goals with those of modern, technologically oriented architecture, and—if taken literally—constituted an outright rejection of the KDK's position. He went on to condemn "those who think that the representatives of the cultural decade which now lies behind us [could] be the standard bearers of the future." Some took this statement as a clear repudiation of the Berlin faction's espousal of modern art and radical architecture, while others claimed it applied to the conservatives of the KDK. By means of this deliberate ambiguity, Hitler succeeded in preventing the alienation of any group of his supporters and in strengthening the party's image as a unified movement. If neither group was particularly pleased, neither were they angered, and each could continue the pursuit of its own policy, confident that it alone expressed "the will of the Führer." The paucity of his public statements on cultural matters led both the party and the general public to believe that the Führer, in the tradition of chancellors before him, was not particularly interested in the determination of artistic policy. What statements he made on art were regarded more as expressions of personal opinion than as definition of the party's cultural "line." "I must repeat it again and again," said Hans Weidemann in later years, "in 1933, we all held Hitler's artistic view to be his own personal opinion. Quite certainly, Mies thought so too."[26] And so, apparently did Goebbels and Rosenberg, each of whom felt encouraged to continue pursuing his own cultural direction.

*   *   *

But while Hitler "tolerated" Rosenberg—"He thought him not very able and complained about him," commented Speer. "He always said that the *Völkischer Beobachter* was the dullest paper"—he thought well of Goebbels.[27] And despite the equivocation of his Culture Day Address, his establishment of the Reich Cultural Chamber (Reichskulturkammer)—the RKK—on September 22, under the sole responsibility of Goebbels's Propaganda Ministry, seemed to clearly indicate not only the Führer's personal inclinations, but also the party's cultural direction. Divided into seven departments—film, theater, music, fine arts, radio, press, and literature, this new organization ensured that no cultural or intellectual area remained immune from party control. According to the ordinance of September 22, the Reich would now not only "lead and organize the professions," but "determine the lines of progress, mental and spiritual" of their membership. Germany's entire cultural sphere was now politicized. Any professional who wished to practice his chosen profession had to belong to the appropriate section of the RKK, which, in turn, passed judgment on his racial and political "suitability." Thanks to this "filter," Jews, pacifists, and those deemed less than enthusiastic about national socialism could be prevented from joining the RKK and hence from practicing their craft.[28] With Goebbels personally reviewing the file of any individual who was expelled or refused membership, his control over the entire cultural community was now virtually unlimited. To the beleaguered artistic community, however, the ascendancy of Goebbels over the dreaded KDK was seen as a step in the "right" direction. Their silence in the face of this threat to their artistic freedom is perhaps explained by their relief. Meanwhile, Rosenberg, who had originally suggested the idea to Hitler and undoubtedly envisioned himself being named as the party's cultural "czar," was bitterly disappointed. Now considerably diminished in authority and prestige, his KDK could no longer speak as the party's sole cultural voice. His reaction was to redouble its propaganda efforts. Thus the shift toward Goebbels, exemplified by his new appointment, exacerbated party discord.

Two months later, at the official opening of the RKK on November 15, an occasion at which Mies appears to have been present, Goebbels announced what appeared to be a radical new artistic course.[29] While his words were couched in vagueness—no modernists were named nor were the aims of the KDK specifically repudiated—he seemed to go further than any other major Nazi figure in support of modern art.

> German art needs fresh blood. We live in a young era. Its supporters are young, and their ideas are young. They have nothing more in common with the past, which we have left behind us. The artist who seeks to give expression to this age must also be young. He must create new forms.[30]

Encouraged by this apparent "victory" of the Berlin wing, tentative support for expressionism began to emerge. Private art galleries in Berlin and elsewhere began to exhibit the works of artists such as Barlach, Nolde, and Feininger to often heartening reviews. On January 7, 1934, Max Sauerlandt, whose impassioned advocacy of modern art had already cost him his directorships at Hamburg's Museum for Arts and Crafts and State School of Art, lauded the Students' Association for undertaking "the first attempt to open once again the path to these most genuine of artists of the recent past."[31]

Committed, more than ever, to undermining Goebbels's ascendancy, the KDK continued its relentless opposition. On December 16, in an article entitled "Cultural Bolshevism Again" that appeared in the *Völkischer Beobachter*, the international architects were attacked as "carriers of unculture, [purveyors of] charlatanism support[ing] itself . . . within dark international circles devoid of racial feelings." Angered by the KDK's insensitivity to the need for party unity and unwillingness to restrain its demands and accusations, Minister Hinkel, Goebbels's ex-associate now affiliated with the Cultural Ministry, publicly rebuked the group and incorporated it into the NS Association of Power Through Joy (NS Gemeinschaft Kraft durch Freude, known as the KdF), an organization concerned with workers' leisure-time activities.[32] The KDK, as molded and dominated by Rosenberg, was now effectively—and gravely—diminished.

Goebbels's appointment of Hans Weidemann to head several of the Propaganda Ministry's most important cultural events appeared to realize what his speech had merely implied. Weidemann was named director of an exhibition planned for the spring of 1934, entitled German People—German Work (*Deutsches Volk—Deutsche Arbeit*). Moving quickly to ally the new order with the new art, Weidemann invited Walter Gropius and Herbert Bayer, the renowned Bauhaus graphic artist, to participate. To head the architectural organization of the exhibition, he wanted Mies. And, in a similar development, Robert Ley, head of the German Worker's Front (Deutsche Arbeitsfront), assessing Goebbels's new status as signaling a new Nazi line, asked the Propaganda Minister to name someone to head the KdF, the cultural division of his group. Delighted to have the opportunity to infiltrate a potential rival's organization with one of his trusted lieutenants, Goebbels named Weidemann. To head the fine arts section of his cultural division of the KdF, Weidemann appointed Otto Andreas-Schreiber. The two youthful Nazi leaders planned a series of competitions for the KdF in painting, music, literature, and architecture. For their jurors, they invited many of Germany's most renowned artistic figures, including Strauss, Hindemith, Nolde, Heckel, Barlach, and Mies.

These promising developments effectively ended whatever thoughts Mies may have entertained of staying in Switzerland. Despite the agitated, frenzied atmosphere of Germany— which from the sweet distance of Lugano seemed little more than a lunatic asylum for the criminally insane—it was still there that the greatest opportunities existed for him to build. He returned to Berlin in early November, in time to vote in the plebescite scheduled for the eleventh of that month, when the electorate was called upon to approve Hitler's decision to withdraw from the League of Nations.[33] Still in debt and delighted at the prospect of working again, Mies accepted Weidemann's proposals at once, undeterred by the fact that his architecture, initiated and praised for its commitment to universal ideals, was now being hailed for its "nationalistic" qualities. Given Weidemann's public announcement "that he expected Mies to someday build a palace of culture for Hitler"[34] and the Führer's recent assertion of his desire "to set the German economy in motion again ... by grand, monumental works,"[35] it seemed indelicate to argue over what appeared to be merely a question of semantics. "The first law of architecture," remarked Philip Johnson, "is to 'get the job'!"[36] Mies undoubtedly would have agreed. In his eyes, he was neither a judge nor a poet. He dealt with bricks, not words; and his task, as he saw it, was to build, not to measure clients or words.

In the face of events which seemed to reflect as much the power of human resolve, as its perversity, the Nazis—once scorned and derided—now looked forward to celebrating their first anniversary with their power more entrenched than ever. Modernism, whose denunciation had earlier served the Nazis so well, now seemed on its way toward becoming the official art of the Third Reich. And Mies, besieged for years by the Nazis, now anticipated their patronage. As Weidemann awaited Goebbels's final approval of his recommendations, Mies—his faith in his aesthetic incorruptibility and the primacy of reason undiminished—proudly awaited the call of his country.

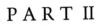

HITLER

CHAPTER 10

"NEAREST MY HEART"

[A]RCHITECTURE WAS THE ONLY FIELD IN WHICH HITLER HAD
A REAL INTEREST IN SOMETHING OUTSIDE OF HIMSELF, THE
ONLY AREA IN WHICH HE WAS ALIVE.

(**Erich Fromm,** *The Anatomy of Human Destructiveness*)

It was music, not architecture, that August Kubizek[1] loved, a
fact that did little to dissuade his fifteen-year-old-friend Adolf
Hitler from engaging him in his architectural fantasies in their
hometown of Linz. "He dragged me along wherever there was a
building going up," recalled Kubizek, who thirty years later
wrote of his friendship with the young Adolf between 1904 and
1908. What kept Kubizek at his friend's side was not the architecture, to which the young music student was noticeably
indifferent, but the inspiring flame of Hitler's intensity. For
Kubizek, Adolf seemed the very model of the dedicated soul.

> He [Adolf] was completely carried away by it . . . like one
> possessed. Nothing else existed for him . . . he was obliv-
> ious to time, sleep, and hunger.[2]

Hitler—growing bored with excursions to buildings under construction—soon turned toward more ambitious tasks. Having taught himself the art of drafting from books at the town library, he began to plan nothing less than the total rebuilding of Linz, a city second in size only to the imperial capital, Vienna.

Undaunted by the scope of his scheme—in fact, nurtured by its very impossibility—Hitler threw himself into this endeavor with even more than his usual fervor. Indeed, the rebuilding of Linz remained a lifelong obsession. When in 1938 Hitler announced his plans to make the Austrian city a rival to Budapest—"Ten years after the end of the war," he said, "Linz must have become the new metropolis on the Danube"[3]— Kubizek was amazed to discover that the new plan was "identical to the last detail" with the one from Hitler's youth.[4] In fact no circumstance was too grim nor mood too depressed to be relieved by Hitler's reviewing his plans for his beloved city. Shortly after the assassination attempt in 1944, when Albert Speer and Hermann Giessler (the architect in charge of the Linz project) came to visit Hitler at his headquarters, Martin Bormann commented, with obvious relief, that the Führer was bound to be diverted by the plans for Linz.[5] In the final hours of his life, with Russian tanks at the doorstep of Berlin and his plans for the thousand-year Reich crumbling in fetid ruin, a withered and red-eyed Führer sat silent within his bunker before the tiny models of his "new" Linz.

Through the Linz project, Kubizek came to understand a strange aspect of his friend: that the more remote the possibility for realization of his schemes, the more committed to them Hitler became. It was as though he was attempting to compensate for their lack of actuality through the sheer force of his will.

> To him these projects were in every detail as actual as though they were already executed and the whole town rebuilt according to his design. I often got confused, and could not distinguish whether he was talking about a building that existed or one that was to be created. But to him it did not make any difference; the actual construction was a matter of only secondary importance.[6]

Hitler seems to have suffered from a defective sense of reality. "It made no difference," noted Kubizek, "whether he was talking about something finished or something planned."[7] His observation was later corroborated by Erich Fromm, who wrote that "Hitler's fantasy world was much more real to him than the real world."[8]

Although Kubizek had long since learned not to judge his friend by ordinary measure—Hitler's ideas, he had noted, "always moved, more or less, on a plane above normal comprehension"—he was nonetheless filled with grave misgivings about his friend's apparent inability to distinguish between reality and the world of his imagination.[9] However, he said nothing to Hitler about his apprehensions. Having borne the brunt of Hitler's white-lipped fury, he was only too familiar with his friend's intolerance for dissent. "[H]e seemed to be very sensitive about questions that did not [please] him," noted Kubizek; "that much I had already discovered."[10]

There was nothing in Hitler's family background or the circumstances of his birth that pointed toward his later architectural propensities. As a matter of fact, his early history appears in a distinctly inverse relationship to these manifestations, as well as to his championship of the doctrines of racial purity and Germanic supremacy, as though—as in the case of his vast dreams of Linz—he was motivated by their very absence. Hitler was born of peasant stock in 1889 in Braunau am Inn, a small town on the Austro-German border. His father, Alois, was an illegitimate child who bore the name of his mother—Schicklgruber—until he was nearly forty years old, when his paternity was claimed by the brother of his putative father, Johann Georg Hitler, who had since died. Nevertheless, doubts remained over who Alois's father really was; some evidence even suggested that Alois's father had been a Jewish lawyer in whose home his mother had worked. Although this evidence was subsequently discredited, it did point up—as Fest has observed—"that Adolf Hitler did not know who his grandfather was."[11]

Alois, a low-level member of the Austrian Civil Service, changed residences frequently (some moves were due to his work) and married three times—each wife except the first already pregnant. His last wife, Hitler's mother Klara Pölzl, had entered his household as a maid. She had come from Spital, where the Hitler family had long lived, and with the changing of Alois's name to "Hitler" she became—at least, legally—his second cousin; a special dispensation from the church was required before they could marry.

Adolf Hitler was their fourth child. The three older children died in infancy, and a younger sister, Paula, survived. In addition, the Hitler household included two children of Alois's second marriage, Alois and Angela. Hitler's stepbrother Alois spent years in trouble with the law: he was arrested twice for theft and also for bigamy. He established a family in England, then deserted them, returning to Germany, where he opened a small beerhouse in a Berlin suburb. Angela worked as a housekeeper for Hitler and for others. Her daughter, Geli Raubel, became—in the words of William Shirer—"the only truly deep love affair of [Hitler's] life."[12] It was an undistinguished lineage, and to someone of Hitler's hypersensitivity, loathsome. No wonder Hitler flew into a rage at any mention of his family and background. In the same way that his architectural fantasies intensified the more removed from reality they were, so too did his racial theories compensate for his deep-seated sense of inferiority. Throughout his life, Hitler worked "to conceal" himself, his reputation as a "poseur" stemming, in part, from his effort to "cover his tracks."[13] As a young politician, Hitler considered any inquiry into his background to be "insulting"; as chancellor, he forbade it. Thus his Austrian birth seems to have spurred him toward claims of German consanguinity and superiority. His assertions in *Mein Kampf* that "[o]ne blood demands one Reich" echo the superpatriotism common to leaders, from Alexander to Napoleon, who were actually foreigners among their adopted countrymen.

Because of the family's frequent moves, Hitler attended several different primary schools. For two years, he attended a Catholic school at the Benedictine monastery at Lambach, where he seemed quite happy singing in the choir and, as he wrote in *Mein Kampf*, "intoxicat[ed] . . . with the solemn splendor of the brilliant church festivals," dreamt of taking holy orders.[14] When he was eleven, his father, who harbored ambitions for his son to follow him into civil service, sent him to the Realschule in Linz. However, artistically talented and prone to daydreaming, the boy rebelled. He wrote in *Mein Kampf*,

> I yawned, and grew sick to my stomach at the thought of sitting in an office, deprived of my liberty; ceasing to be master of my own time and being [confronted with] blanks that had to be filled out.[15]

The more his father insisted, the more the strong-willed Adolf resisted. Although he had done well in primary school, his career at the Realschule was abysmal. Not only was he battling with his father, but the move from a small village to the more sophisticated Linz, then as now a provincial center, put Hitler at a social disadvantage. Among the sons of "academics, businessmen, and persons of quality," he seemed but a "rough-hewn rustic, a despised outsider."[16] For the first time Hitler became aware of (and humiliated by) his own social inadequacies. He handled this by "keeping his distance," addressing his classmates with the formal *"Sie,"* rather than the more commonplace and familiar *"du."* It was here, claims Fest, that the young Adolf acquired a sense of class consciousness and a fierce determination to rise above what to him seemed humiliating origins.[17]

In 1903 his father died and his doting mother was unable to hold out against her son's determination to end his education. In the autumn of 1905, she consented to her sixteen-year-old son leaving school. Whether propelled by a vivid fantasy world, a "repugnance and hatred" for desk work, or a lazy nature that rebelled at regular work of any sort, or influenced by the high social esteem accorded the artist in Austria as in Germany, Hitler resolved to devote himself—accompanied by his friend Kubizek—to "art." In 1907 the two went to Vienna to further their education—Kubizek at the Conservatory of Music and Hitler at the Academy of Art. Now the reluctant and glum Kubizek found himself being dragged to the imposing buildings of the Ringstrasse—the Hof Opera, the House of Parliament, the Burg Theater, the university, the Stock Exchange, Karl's Church, the museums, the Town Hall, and so on—where

Hitler, "forgetting not only the time, but all that went on around him," deluged his morose friend with the pearls of information gleaned from the library.[18] For hours, the hapless Kubizek listened to details of origin, measurements, ornamentation, elevation, sections, ground plans, the location of side doors, back doors, and stairways, no matter too trivial or too obscure for his friend's fevered brain. Occasionally, Kubizek's patience wore thin.

> I could not understand the reason for these long drawn out and complicated inspections; after all, he had seen everything before, and already knew more about it than most of the inhabitants of the city.[19]

Unable to bear it any longer, Kubizek expressed his bewilderment to Hitler.

"Are you my real friend or not?" Hitler responded angrily. "If you are, you should share my interests!"[20] In the future, Kubizek kept his uneasiness to himself. The architectural monologue often continued back in their tiny room, where Hitler—forcing Kubizek to sit and listen for hours more—would continue his eulogy of the buildings they had just visited. Exhausting the Ringstrasse, the tireless Hitler would turn to his handbook of architecture, attempting to impress his weary friend with his "astounding" ability to distinguish Chartres Cathedral from the Pitti Palace.

Despite this enraptured interest, it appears that in 1907, when he applied to the Vienna Academy's School of Painting, Hitler considered himself more an artist than an architect. Only when the rector of the academy casually suggested that his talents lay more with architecture did he resolve "to become an architect."[21] He failed, however, to gain entrance into the Academy's School of Architecture—an experience so humiliating that he could not bring himself to tell his friend. Instead he suffered in silent rage Kubizek's strict schedule of classes at the conservatory mounted on the wall opposite his bed. Only when Kubizek, suspicious of Hitler's ability to sleep late in the morning while he had to race off to classes, confronted his friend, did Hitler—in an outburst so violent that

Kubizek could recall it vividly thirty years later—admit to the rejection. Cursing "the old-fashioned fossilized bureaucracy," Hitler referred "to 'trip-wires . . . cunningly laid'—I remember his very words!—for the sole purpose of ruining his career," wrote Kubizek.[22] "Those stupid lumps of officials," he screamed, his face white with rage and mouth compressed. "I'll show those incompetent senile fools that I can go ahead without them!" Turning to Kubizek, Hitler said, "The whole Academy ought to be blown up!"[23]

Again the scope of his ambitions enlarged in embittered counterpoint to their diminished prospect for realization, and Hitler pursued his studies with redoubled fervor. He now began plans for the rebuilding of Vienna—a daunting task for even the most experienced urban planner, but simply ridiculous for an inexperienced eighteen year old. Day and night he labored, planning railway lines and roads, industrial and residential centers, concert halls, museums, exhibition halls, and palaces. He agonized over whether or not such and such a building should be torn down and another erected in its place. His plans covered the walls and tables of their cramped quarters; an enormous map of Vienna hid the piano.

Kubizek soon realized that something was gravely amiss in his friend's pursuits. While Hitler's determination and intensity were undeniable, his studies seemed to lack utility and focus.

> [They were] not directed towards any practical goal. On the contrary, every now and again he got lost in vast plans and speculations.[24]

A seeker Hitler certainly was, but only for his own predetermined objectives. He tolerated no questioning; new ideas and experiences appeared to disturb and disorient him. He shared his ideas with no one, seeking from Kubizek not an exchange of ideas, but confirmation of his own genius. Contact with other architectural students or anyone remotely involved in the profession was notably avoided. He never sought employment in an architectural office, nor did he try to acquire practical experience in the field. In a city burgeoning with architectural activity, he never attended any of the numerous architectural lectures, nor did he seem aware of such path-breaking Viennese architectural figures as Otto Wagner, Josef Hoffmann, or Adolf Loos. Although Kubizek admired Hitler's dedication and commitment, it seemed clear to him that how-ever precise and thorough his performance, Hitler—in the final analysis—was merely engaging in playacting in a world of his own making, in Kubizek's words, "an interesting, but idle past-time." Indeed, this propensity was not limited to his architectural activities, but pervaded his entire personality. By virtue of an astonishing memory, which enabled him to weave in myriads of data from the real world, giving the appearance of legitimacy to what was ultimately a display of narcissistic self-indulgence, Hitler managed to convince himself, and others, that the tapestries he created were something more than an illusion. It was as though the emperor's imaginary clothes were held together with real thread. Through the ostentatious dis-play of this convincing "thread," Hitler would come to fool his colleagues, his nation, and eventually, much of the world.

In addition to inspiring unrealistic schemes, Hitler's rejec-tion by the academy also nurtured a seething vindictiveness that remained with him the rest of his life. "Adolf, homeless, rejected by the Academy, without any chance of changing his miserable position, developed during this period an ever-grow-ing sense of rebellion," wrote Kubizek.[25] Fulminating resent-ment and the burning desire for revenge became an inseparable characteristic of Hitler's mentality, architectural and other-wise. When Kubizek asked how Hitler intended to become an architect, lacking as he did both academy training and practi-cal experience, Hitler answered that this would happen through "the Storm of the Revolution," which would eliminate the necessity of "merely" formal qualifications; "only actual ability" would matter.

Hitler's cataclysmic rage seared its imprint on his architec-tural aspirations, linking not only the creative aims of build-ing, but also what Erich Fromm later characterized as "the only genuine interest in his life . . . the one constructive element in his character—perhaps the one bridge that linked him with life"—with his equally compelling urge to destroy.[26] The architectural drawings of gigantic triumphal arches and domed halls that he made while in jail in 1924–25 (which later served as prototypes for his building plans for Berlin) alternate across the pages with drawings of weapons and other armaments, revealing both the persistence of his architectural urges when realization of his political hopes appeared most unlikely, and the continued simultaneity of his constructive and destructive urges—an impression heightened by the later appointment of his favorite architect Albert Speer as armaments minister, and illustrated by the following anecdote that Speer recounted to Fromm:

> After his visit to recently conquered Paris, Hitler remarked ... that he often in the past considered destroying the French capital because it was so beautiful.[27]

Hitler's political inclinations stemmed from the same motivations as his architectural ones, and reveal many of the same characteristics.[28] Once formulated, neither his architectural nor his political views substantially changed throughout his life. His political involvement, according to his own account, emerged around 1909 in Vienna; it reflected much of the disquietude that permeated the city at the time.

Capital of the Dual Monarchy and bearing the especially weighty burden of the empire's multinational and multiethnic constituency, Vienna exuded an "ideologically seething atmosphere" that bordered on the schizophrenic.[29] It was a viciously anti-Semitic city, many of whose leading citizens—such as Freud, Mahler, and Wittgenstein—were Jews. Cradle of the avant-garde, it nurtured equally outspoken conservatives. Otto Wagner, Adolf Loos, and the Wiener Werkstätte (where Lilly Reich had studied) sowed the early seeds of modernism amidst the frenetically historicist styles of the Ringstrasse.

By 1909 Kubizek appears to have disappeared from Hitler's life; perhaps he found work or became deeply involved in his studies. In any case, Hitler, having no future in his chosen profession, found himself unemployed, penniless, and alone. Living in men's shelters, a dirty, unkempt vagrant, he was plunged into a political and social maelstrom. The

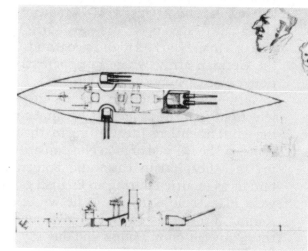

Adolf Hitler, sketchbook drawings, 1924–25; buildings, including an arch of triumph and domed halls, tanks, battleships, and a set for Richard Wagner's "Tristan" (Reprinted, by permission, of Verlag Ullstein GmbH, from Joachim C. Fest, *Hitler*)

Austro-Hungarian empire pulsed with outbursts of nationalism and socialism, anti-Semitism and pan-Germanism that
would shortly erupt into war. As much an outsider here as he
had been in Linz, restless and seeking simple solutions,
Hitler—indifferent as ever to the limitations of reality—now
turned his feverish attention to these sociopolitical issues that
seemed to mirror his own discontents.

Only with the outbreak of the war and its opportunity of
identifying himself with "true" Germans, did Hitler—now living in Munich—seem to find himself.[30] Hitler's face is clearly
visible in a photograph taken of a crowd gathered on the
Odeonsplatz on August 1, 1914 to hear the declaration of war.
His mouth gapes open, his eyes burn; in Fest's view, it is the
face of a man who had found a goal and a future.[31] Hitler joined
the German army, where he apparently served with distinc-
tion, twice earning the Iron Cross.

Germany's capitulation, like its entry into the war (and his
rejection from the academy), became a major emotional turning point in Hitler's life. Calling it "the greatest villainy of the
century," he learned of it on November 10, 1918, while recovering in a hospital in Pasewalk, Pomerania, from temporary
blindness incurred during an English gas attack. "[E]verything
went black before my eyes," he wrote of this event in Mein
Kampf. "I tottered and groped my way back to the dormitory,
threw myself on my bunk and dug my burning head into my
blanket and pillow [and wept]." This event, too, provoked a
primal cry for revenge.

> Would not the graves of all the hundreds of thousands
> open, the graves of those who with faith in the fatherland
> had marched forth never to return. Would they not open
> and send the silent mud- and blood-covered heroes back as
> spirits of vengeance to the homeland which had cheated
> them with such mockery of the highest sacrifice which a
> man can make to his people in this world?[32]

Where it had earlier inspired his architectural pursuits, his cry
for vengeance now inaugurated his political career. In the
tumultuous postwar days in Munich, to which Hitler
returned, his compulsion to remold society transferred itself
from architecture to politics. Peripherally involved with right-

wing, army-related groups that were working to quell the communist uprising that had taken place there, Hitler discovered his extraordinary oratorical gifts almost accidentally. His blazing articulation of pent-up rage and seething discontent evoked a sympathetic response among the confused and frightened populace that had—according to Stern—collectively experienced his injuries and resentments.[33] This revelation persuaded Hitler that the realization of his innermost aspirations—his drive to power and his desire to impose his will on others—lay now in politics, a career that would be unimpeded by his lack of educational, social, and professional resources. As he had transformed his own personal opinions and grievances into incontrovertible statements of "fact" before the submissive Kubizek, Hitler now—through the gift of his flaming oratory—touched the soul of a disillusioned and defeated people, bringing forth his vision of a proud and renewed Germany, as he had earlier brought forth his schemes of a renewed Linz and Vienna. As he had withdrawn from the struggles of his architectural contemporaries, so too did he now retreat into the shadowy mists of racial illusions. Begot as fortuitously as his earlier "career," Hitler's political mission was pursued with the same grim determination, intransigence, and zealousness. But his "earlier career" was never forgotten; politics, he claimed on many occasions to Speer, was merely a temporary diversion from his "true" vocation, architecture. "The finest day of my life," Hitler often said, "will be the day I quit politics."[34] And to Speer countless times he lamented, "How I wish I had been an architect."[35] In a speech of 1935, he publicly declared his sentiments.

> If I continually put architectural problems into the foreground, . . . that is because they lie nearest my heart.[36]

In the early 1920s, Hitler put aside his architectural interests as he set about establishing and consolidating the NSDAP. These interests reemerge in 1924, during his brief incarceration in the Landsberg prison, where he occupied himself by writing *Mein Kampf* and making his architectural sketches interspersed with drawings of armaments.[37] The imposing, overscaled buildings to which the lonely, angry, and puny youth had been attracted in Linz and Vienna reappear in these sketches, now metamorphosed into assertive symbols of a great state, of political power and invincibility, into what he called "the expression in stone of a German strength and German greatness in a new German Reich."[38] In later years, Hitler spoke often and with pride of the vast dimensions of architectural projects "such as the world had not seen . . . [which would make] men into ants."[39] *Lebensraum* and architectural gigantism were but dual expressions of his megalomania.

Along with his search for revenge, Hitler was obsessed with destruction—the purpose, after all, of weaponry. War, in his mind, initiated greatness; greatness was the goal of war—an insurance policy, so to speak, of aesthetic immortality—and its dénouement, in art as well as politics (although its precise connection remained undefined, like so much else in Hitler's thought). "Greek art," he noted, in a speech at the Hofbräuhaus on August 13, 1920, achieved its heights only "when the young state victoriously triumphed over the Persian army, [while Rome] became a city of art [only after the Punic wars]." He was inordinately preoccupied with architectural ruins; his speeches are replete with references to these "melancholy statement[s] of . . . destruction"[40] that bear "the critical scrutiny of millennia."[41] He feared that future generations might come upon a ruined Berlin and find only the remains of "the department stores of a few Jews as the mightiest works of our era."[42] He spoke of architects as "fighters . . . who [would assure] the success of [the] battle."[43]

Sharing a nearly incomprehensible magnitude of scope and scale, Hitler's architectural and political schemes may be viewed as essentially escapist. His gargantuan buildings were as unrealistic as the blond Aryan fighting race that was to inhabit them. Where fantasies of building had flourished earlier, now arose images of pan-Germanism: both constituted a pathological response to disappointment—the desire to seek revenge, to punish, rather than the more difficult task of submitting one's expectations to reappraisal. Those, such as Speer, who knew Hitler best, well understood the inseparability of "his sense of political mission and his passion for architecture."[44] "We know today," said Hitler in his August 1920 speech at the Hofbräuhaus, "that reciprocity exists between state, nature, culture, [and] art ... and that it would be crazy to believe that one could exist independent of the other." And indeed, his architectural images—with their pastiche of south German *Gemütlichkeit* (cozy contentment), echoes of the Wagnerian *Heldenleben* (heroic) tradition, and overblown neo-classicism—faithfully mirrored his vision of the Reich. Despite his own assertion that "to be German is to be logical," Hitler apparently saw no inconsistency in advocating the most nationalistic of values, while lauding their genesis in the pan-Hellenic, the most universal and internationalist style of all. "There is only one eternal art," Hitler claimed,

> the Greek Nordic art [sic]. ... When this ... Nordic layer disappeared—as, for example, with the Manchus—the art in those countries came to an end.[45]

To Hitler's half-educated mind, proof of Germany's greatness lay in its connection to ancient Greece, that most indisputably admired civilization. Contrary to common sense and history, not to mention his party's identification with indigenous traditions, the Hun became the golden heir of the Hellene, the Doric style the expression of the Germanic New Order. Those who did not share in this imagined "tradition"—the Jews, the church, the blacks, the gypsies, the Slavs, and the Bolsheviks, along with their art and architecture, "those cubist monstrosities ... [that mirrored Germany's] declining culture and ... general collapse"—would find no place in the new Reich.[46]

Architecture was to be the crown of Hitler's new Germany. The structures he was planning for the Third Reich would

> bear powerful witness to the strength of the new German phenomenon, help to unite and strengthen the people and fill the citizens of the German community with an everlasting self-consciousness of what it meant to be a German. At the same time, recognizing that it was not enough to be a power without culture, a strength without beauty, these buildings, as bearers and guardians of a higher culture, would also represent the highest justification for the political strength of the German nation, the moral justification for the raw realm of power.[47]

For Hitler—no less than for his contemporaries, Mies and Gropius—architecture was an expression of the central spirit of an epoch, possessing some eternal magical power that could lead men from confusion and chaos into the serene realm of Order. Their differences lay not in their perception of the power of architecture, nor in their understanding of its capabilities or limitations, but in their visions of the ideal world to which it led. For them all, architecture both waged the war and assured the victory.[48] In their visions of society, it was both cannon and crown, sword and halo; and, with the exception of Gropius (who was more open-minded), each was convinced that his vision alone mirrored the footsteps of God.

In 1933, Hitler's passion for architecture was unknown to all but his closest associates; even they believed it was simply a hobby. For most Germans, supporters as well as detractors, assertions of the Führer's "interest" in architecture seemed little more than attempts to enhance his image and strengthen his claims for legitimacy within a long-standing German tradition. They aroused as much interest as his purported weakness for cream puffs.

CHAPTER 11

"UNMISTAKABLY CLEAR"

ONE TALKS, IF MY EARS
STILL BEHAVE,
NOT OF A GROVE, BUT
OF A GRAVE.

(**Goethe**, *Faust*)

"I imagine the Professor's redone the ground-floor plans of the
House of Art," said Hitler to Albert Speer, who was seated by .
his side.[1] His voice, strident and harsh in public speech, was
now pleasant, seductive even, in its incisiveness—its broad
south German accent less obtrusive in private conversation
than in public oration. They were traveling by train to Munich
on one of the Führer's frequent trips to supervise the design of
the House of Art, the first official building of the Third Reich.
Tall, handsome, and only twenty-eight years old, Speer could
hardly believe his good fortune. Barely a year before he had
been an unemployed architect without a commission to his
credit, grateful to be earning a living managing his family's
buildings in Mannheim. Now, swaying easily from side to side
on the speeding train, he sat alongside the Führer himself,

Hitler making an architectural drawing (*Die Kunst im Dritten Reich*, July/August 1937)

sheets of architectural plans strewn on the table before them. As on the Führer's desk in Berlin, freshly sharpened pencils and neat stacks of drawing paper lay waiting.

Reaching for a pencil now, Hitler sketched some architectural details. Whatever he described—ornamental details, cross sections, perspective studies, or renderings to scale—his pencil revealed fluently, rapidly, and with ease. "An architect," observed the impressed Speer, "could not have done better."[2] It was clear that Hitler was very much at home with architecture, his skill and knowledge going far beyond those of the ordinary layman. "Some improvements are needed there," he said, studying the plans intently, his eyes glistening with delight. "I wonder whether the details for the dining room have been drafted yet?"[3]

Once he was satisfied with his review of the plans before him, Hitler began to speak of some of his favorite buildings—Garnier's Opera House in Paris, Poelart's gigantic House of Justice in Brussels, and the buildings of the Ringstrasse in Vienna—revealing throughout his monologue an intimate acquaintance with even the most insignificant aspect of these fussy and pretentious buildings. "Architecture relaxes me, Speer," he said, in his curiously panting enunciation. "Before going to bed I spend some time on architecture. I look at pictures. . . . Otherwise I wouldn't be able to sleep."[4] He was silent for a moment, his eyes held by the plans in front of them, then turned to the young architect. "I tell you, Speer, these buildings are more important than anything else. You must do everything you can to complete them in my lifetime."[5]

"For the first time," recalled Speer, "I had an intimation of what the magic word 'architecture' meant under Hitler."[6] Nowhere in evidence was the stridency or the vague stiffness and awkwardness, which provoked suspicions of affectation and quackery, that marked Hitler's public appearances. Speer wished his father could see Hitler as he himself saw him. The senior Speer, a retired second-generation architect and staunch liberal, had broken with his son when Albert joined the Nazi party in 1931. Surely, thought Speer, his father's attitude would soften if he realized that the Führer was but an "artiste man-

Paul Troost (Bundesarchiv)

qué," who, except for the lack of "a small commission at the beginning of the 1920s," might have made a competent—perhaps even talented—architect.[7]

From the railroad station, Hitler, accompanied by his aides and Speer, went at once to the studio of the architect Paul Ludwig Troost on Theriesenstrasse, near the Institute of Technology. Standing tall and imposing with his white surgeon's coat and close-shaven head, the "Professor" (as Hitler always called him) greeted the Führer, in his usual calm and restrained manner, not—to Speer's astonishment—at the front door as custom demanded but in the anteroom at the top of the stairs.

The Führer, normally draconian in his insistence on protocol, seemed not to notice and bounded enthusiastically up the stairs two at a time. He and Troost moved at once toward the plans and scale models of the House of German Art laid out meticulously before them.

Hitler's plans for the House of German Art, being built to replace the Glass Palace, which had burned down in 1931, had certainly been formulated before 1933; he claimed, moreover, to have initially thought of a new museum for Munich before 1918.[8] "The Führer has all his plans finished," noted Goebbels in his diary in February 1932, when Hitler was deciding whether or not to run for the presidency. These included not only his plans for new buildings in Munich but also those for what Goebbels described as the "spectacular rebuilding of Berlin," both of which Hitler mentioned at a meeting with Troost, his favorite architect, at that time. Designed by Troost, with Hitler's collaboration, the plans for the House of German Art were virtually complete by the time Hitler assumed the chancellorship in early 1933.

Hitler and District Leader Adolf Wagner inspect a model of the House of German Art (*Die Kunst im Dritten Reich*, July/August 1937)

Troost, although a respected name among the numerous German proponents of a stripped and severe neoclassicism that remained well within tradition, had never been considered a leading German architect until his affiliation with Hitler. Introduced in the late 1920s by the Bruckmanns—a highly cultivated publishing family who were early supporters of Hitler—Troost had collaborated with Hitler on several party buildings in Munich. By now—as Speer could see, watching them bent over the House of Art plans—the relationship between the two was well established. Although in a state of high excitement, Hitler, normally arrogant and argumentative, was never less than humble and deferential—timid even— before the towering professorial figure of Troost, and trans- formed himself, before the astonished Speer, from the iron- willed chancellor of the German Reich into an eager, ever- respectful student of architecture.[9]

Throughout the session, which lasted several hours, Hitler's attention was unflagging, his comments unceasing: "I think, Herr Professor, that it might look better this way, the improve- ment in the vista being the decisive point."[10] Where words proved inadequate, he would pick up a pencil to quickly illus- trate an idea. When the session was over, Troost once again flouted custom by bidding farewell to Hitler at the top of the stairs, and again Hitler paid no heed, content to permit this gesture of respect toward the architect.

"I can hardly wait to see it," said Hitler to Speer, as soon as they had left Troost's studio. His architectural appetite not yet sated, Hitler ordered his car to proceed immediately to the Führer House. Apparently no architectural detail was too minor to claim his attention, and he wanted to observe the installation of the stairway paneling. Paces ahead of his tiring entourage, Hitler stepped gingerly over the construction debris, demonstrating to his duly impressed companions that their Führer was as much at ease with the problems of con- struction as with the abstruse principles of architectural the- ory. Almost imperceptibly and in spite of himself, Speer began to think of his Führer as a professional colleague whom destiny had cruelly cast, against his will and inclinations, into the sordid world of politics.

After a brief respite, the group reassembled for lunch at the Ostaria Bavaria, an artists' hangout and Hitler's favorite restaurant. Once again, the apparently indefatigable Hitler spoke of architecture, principally the morning's visit to Professor Troost. "Hitler would be full of praise for what he had seen," recalled Speer of these visits; "he effortlessly remembered all the details."[11] He now launched almost without pause into a panegyric of the Ringstrasse buildings of Vienna, demonstrating—as he had done earlier on the train from Berlin—a Baedekerlike familiarity with every detail of these elaborate buildings, from their ground plans, measurements, and elevations, to every excrescence of ornamental detail. Unsatisfied with this virtuosic display of his phenomenal memory, he picked up a pencil and proceeded to sketch details of their heavy cornices, stone casings, enormous piers, and gigantic arches. In his enthusiasm for the Ringstrasse ("He went wild over its architectural richness," recalled Speer), Hitler managed to disregard the aesthetic distance between its florid buildings and Troost's style—which was no less the object of his extravagant praise.[12]

Speer, himself the protégé of an architectural mentor, Heinrich Tessenow, who like Troost preached the doctrine of architectural simplicity, suffered—as did countless others—a lapse in his discriminating judgment when in Hitler's presence. So heady and exhilarating was Hitler's pitch of excitement, so seductive and overwhelming the amazing fantasies he wove before the eyes of his listeners, that whatever reservations may have lingered in the mind of the young and ambitious architect regarding his architectural discernment were instantly swept away before the electrifying impact of Hitler's enthusiasm—much as a cultivated and intelligent citizenry had abandoned its better judgment before the galvanic persuasiveness of Hitler's zealous and overwrought aspirations.

On October 15, 1933, less than a year after his assumption of the chancellorship and a scant seven months after the national socialists had achieved their legislative majority, Hitler came to Munich to celebrate the laying of the cornerstone for the House of German Art. As would become customary with major party events, the occasion was celebrated with dazzling festivities, calculated to seduce the observer and make him, for the moment at least, forget the senselessness of what he was seeing.[13] To the stern beat of kettledrums, the sumptuous procession wended its way along the Marienplatz, toward the Prinzregentenstrasse, the site of the ceremonies. The drummers—dressed in red, silver, and gray—led the parade, followed by knights in black armor and maidens in gowns of red and green silk, their flaxen braids entwined with flowery wreaths. Between the groups, massive floats glided effortlessly. Horses with feathery headpieces and tasseled coverings pulled the first float, on which baroque winged "putti" fluttered above and about a gilded and pale, shell-shaped rococo fountain. Some distance back appeared the second float. On it, encaged within intertwining Gothic arches, a young woman sat upon a rearing unicorn, her lyre falling artfully across her lap. Gigantic images hovered above the heads of the assembled figures: the first, an eagle, symbol of the Nazi party, was followed by copies of an enormous Ionic capital, an old mural painting, and colossal models of a Greek torso and a gilded figure of Pallas Athena. The last and largest float—its importance heralded by eighteen green and gold robed, trumpet-playing youths on horseback—looked for all the world like a gigantic birthday cake. It bore an enormous model of the sternly neoclassical House of German Art.

Few who were present at the ceremonies that sunny fall afternoon appreciated the significance of the moment for Hitler. For the citizens of Munich, it was an occasion for a holiday. For the modernists, it seemed a particularly apt moment for the Nazis to reveal their artistic plans. "The Nazi policy on art remains undefined," Oskar Schlemmer had written on October 9, noting that he anticipated clarification of these "very important matters" at the House of German Art festivities the following week.[14] For Hitler, the pastiche of Tyrolian *Gemütlichkeit*, imagined Nibelungen reveries, and stern Hellenism that paraded before him reflected the essence and aspirations of the Third Reich—just as would his architecture, the "stone documents of the new ideology and of [his] political will to power," of which the House of German Art was just the beginning.

Whether they sought simply to wallow in communal discontent, or, like the modernists, wished to discern some meager sign of how they should order their lives and professions, Germans listened with uncommon attentiveness to Hitler's speech that October 15. All they heard, however, were their Führer's characteristic allusions to despair, suffering, and destruction as well as a reminder that the new building—this "treasure of German feelings . . . and art"—was to rise on the ashes of the old. Of his plans for architecture, or the significance of the moment for him, there was not a word. Until the "Storm of the Revolution" was completed and his regime secure, the depth and dimension of Hitler's passion for architecture would be a private matter. His decision to remain silent on matters of art and architecture did not mean—as Gropius, Mies, Schlemmer, and thousands of others were led to believe—that he cared little, but that—in fact—he cared too much.

Nevertheless, hints of Hitler's artistic intentions were beginning to appear. One of these resulted from his becoming involved in the Reichsbank competition. Hans Luther, president of the Reichsbank, had grown concerned over the large deficit facing the Reich and proposed a reduction in the reichsmark allocation for rearmament requested by Hitler. Infuriated, the Führer had Luther appointed ambassador to Washington, a post where his sense of fiscal responsibility would not be tested, and replaced him with Hjalmar Schacht, the financial wizard behind Germany's economic recovery in the 1920s, who was more appreciative of the importance of Hitler's rearmament program to the economic well-being of the country.

This unexpected involvement in the Reichsbank drew Hitler's attention to the competition, as yet undecided and normally beyond the concerns of the government in power or its chancellor. Hitler liked none of the designs, which generally lacked the grandiosity and impressiveness he deemed essential for buildings of state, and complained that they all looked like normal office buildings.[15] While there seems to be no record of Hitler's particular opinion of Mies's design, of the final entries, only his achieved the monumentality and impressiveness of scale that Hitler demanded, although at serious formal cost. In order to gain the requisite monumentality, Mies had placed the massive, unbroken facade along the narrow street, facing the old Reichsbank, its overwhelming bulk lightened by a line of ribbon windows that ran along its entire length. To allow for the eventual widening of the street on the north, as well as to permit the greatest amount of northern light into the building as requested by the program, Mies had set back the building's northern perimeter, requiring the addition of several stories in height to accommodate the necessary square footage. The resulting ten-story height considerably exceeded the height limitation of 25 meters. Probably because an unbroken mass of such height along so narrow a segment of the Spree River would have been visually disturbing, Mies had also disregarded the directive requiring maintenance of the riverbank wall and broke the mass into three consecutive wings lying at right angles to the river.

With Hitler's displeasure noted—he did not need to interfere directly—the Reichsbank expansion was quietly returned to the bank's own technical division from whose offices it had originated.[16] The Reichsbank competition—the most heralded architectural event of the year and the source of so many of Mies's hopes—was over.

Another hint of Hitler's artistic intentions appeared with Hans Weidemann's effort to gain the regime's acceptance of expressionist art and modern architecture. Weidemann, pursuing his goal, was arranging a private exhibition of expressionist paintings in the reception rooms of the Propaganda Ministry in the hope of educating the artistically unsophisticated Goebbels.[17] Wary of the shallowness of Goebbels's support—his purported artistic liberalism stemmed from a commitment to power more than to art—Weidemann was proceeding cautiously. Much as he had chosen the participants in the KdF jury, he was picking artists whose styles might have been controversial, but whose integrity and world renown were beyond dispute.

Weidemann, who had been trained as a painter, pursued his architectural appointments with even more discretion. Aware of Hitler's architectural interests and sensing Goebbels's possible reluctance to grant approval for Mies's architectural directorship of the German People–German Work exhibition without Hitler's blessing, Weidemann decided to go directly to the Führer, taking care not to convey the impression of undermining Goebbels's authority.[18] He chose to work through Walter Funk, the state secretary in the Propaganda Ministry, who held daily press briefings with Hitler and shared Weidemann's opinion of Mies. Explaining to Funk his belief that Mies was the only architect capable of handling an exhibition of such scale and significance, and his belief that a decision of such magnitude belonged only to Hitler, Weidemann persuaded Funk to show Hitler some photographs of the Barcelona Pavilion that Mies had given him for this purpose. Weidemann understood his boss well enough to know that what his Führer had approved, Goebbels would not dare to refuse.[19]

Hitler's reaction was hardly what Weidemann had hoped. Fortunately, for Funk, Hitler thought of him as a "financial," not an "artistic" man and, not taking his artistic judgments seriously, was able to disregard his impudent gesture.[20] Even so, he could hardly believe that Funk could be so insensitive as to suggest that the architect of the overdressed factory building whose photographs lay before him could possibly be considered for affiliation with his regime. It was not necessary to see such architecture in ideological terms, as "Bolshevik," or symptomatic of "cultural decadence" or of "international viruses" that had infected the purity of the German cause, to realize—in Hitler's view—that this bastard temple to technology, with its handcrafted chromes and luxuriously hand-polished marbles, was nothing more than a whorish mockery of the misguided worship of mass production.[21] Declaring his opposition with such firmness that even a "financial" man could understand, Hitler sternly brushed aside the offensive photographs.[22] A mortified Funk hastened to report to Weidemann. "For the time being," he said, his hand quivering and voice subdued, "Mies van der Rohe is dead as an architect in Germany."[23]

On January 21, 1934, Paul Ludwig Troost died and Hitler's brief, happy stint as an architectural student was over.

Although he initially entertained the notion of completing Troost's unfinished plans on his own, with the assistance of Troost's wife, Gerdy, Hitler soon realized that the pressing nature of matters of state precluded such thoughts. Hitler turned instead to Speer, who had impressed him with his charm and efficient supervision of Troost's design for the remodeling of the Chancellery in Berlin, and before whose inexperience and youth he could assume the professorial role of Troost.

Three days later, on January 24, 1934, in a move that further hinted at his artistic intentions, Hitler created a new party department responsible for supervising the entire intellectual and philosophical training of the party, as well as the KdF, known as the Office for the Supervision of Ideological Training and Education of the NSDAP. At its head, Hitler placed Alfred Rosenberg. While it remained unclear whether this new division superseded or even conflicted with Goebbels's Propaganda Ministry or his RKK, the move served to institutionalize the bickering between the two Nazi officials and, in effect, cancel it out. Although Goebbels possessed a clear advantage over this new group by virtue of his considerable head start, he was now forced to tread more cautiously. No longer willing to countenance the association of his organization with expressionism, Goebbels ordered Weidemann to remove at once the compromising paintings that he had just installed in the ministry's premises. Weidemann, as committed to modernism as to the party, refused, and Goebbels was forced to demote his lieutenant to a less prominent post within the Propaganda Ministry.

With Rosenberg now in charge of the KdF, Weidemann's days within that organization were numbered. In early February, he was discharged, along with the distinguished artists he had chosen for the jury. (Mies's name had already been removed from the list of participants after Hitler's rejection of him became known, although his participation in the German People–German Work exhibition had not been canceled.) While the news of Weidemann's demotion spread like wildfire throughout the beleaguered artistic community, there was little alarm. Not even Weidemann himself saw his dismissal as a signal of future artistic direction; it seemed but one more instance of the chancellor's poor artistic judgment.[24] In fact, contrary to what was perceived at the time, the disgrace of Hans Weidemann, Nazi idealist and outspoken party advocate for modernism (and Mies), meant that modernism would never be the "official" art of the Third Reich.

PART III

CONFRONTATION

CHAPTER 12

MOMENTARY EXAGGERATIONS

BE SENSIBLE, WHAT DOES THIS BIT OF "HEIL HITLER" MATTER!
DO AS WE DO, WITH YOUR TONGUE IN YOUR CHEEK.

(**Wolfgang Langhoff,** *Rubber Truncheon*)

Berlin, in the spring of 1934, was a city of contrasts. A large exhibition of the paintings of Max Liebermann opened to official commendation, while the music of Mendelssohn, the long-deceased Jewish composer, was banned by the Reich Cultural Chamber. Quiet-looking youths in SS uniforms strolled peacefully among the paintings in the Kaiser Friedrich Museum, as Erich Mühsam, anarchist poet and writer of some of the most beautiful German lyric verse in recent memory, lay tortured and broken in the Oranienburg camp.

Amidst such senseless events, it is understandable that one's expectations diminished. Perhaps this—along with his normally phlegmatic nature—explains Mies's impassive reaction when Weidemann told him of Hitler's rejection and that he could no longer be the architectural director of the German

People–German Work exhibition. Although a year of his efforts had come to naught—with the demise of his Reichsbank hopes and now this—Mies showed no emotion as Weidemann relayed the bad news, sitting before the Nazi official like an immense stony Buddha, calm, silent, and remote.[1] Both men were disappointed, but hardly devastated, seeing in Hitler's categorical rejection nothing more than personal capriciousness.[2] Gripping his hand firmly as he left, Weidemann assured Mies that he would indeed participate in the forthcoming exhibition, if not as overall architectural director, then in some important, if more discreet role. Adversity seemed only to fire the two men's resolve. With Mies's ambition bolstered by Weidemann's unwavering commitment, they parted, undaunted in the face of events that might have shattered less confident men. Convinced that his vision of heaven on earth was no less generous or worthy for its rejection, Mies's faith in himself remained unshaken. He would simply rest content with lesser goals.

Their confidence did not seem misplaced. In early June, Mies received invitations to participate in two major government-sponsored competitions.[3] One, coming from the Propaganda Ministry, was for a national pavilion to be built for the upcoming World's Fair in Brussels in 1935—the drawings and models for which were submitted to this ministry on July 3—and the other—whose source and inception date remain unknown— was for a prototype design for service stations to be built along the *autobahnen*, one of Hitler's favorite projects.[4] The German People–German Work exhibition, which opened in Berlin on April 21, 1934, also appeared to justify their optimism.[5] For a regime notorious for its mastery of propaganda, it displayed itself in a remarkably subdued manner; the swastika—for example—was restricted to the parking plaza. Both in style and ideological content, this first exposition of the new regime bore little evidence of its political sponsor. The slogan of the exhibition—"The only nobility in the future will be the nobility of work!"[6]—offered an awkward reminder of national socialism's debt to the left; while, among the most banal and ordinary designs, was displayed the work (uncredited) of Gropius, Herbert Bayer, Lilly Reich, and Mies.

Mies's section proved the highlight of the show, standing

out—as Henry-Russell Hitchcock had earlier commented with regard to his contribution to the 1931 Berlin Building Exhibition—amidst much "dull and bad work . . . like that of Schinkel in old Berlin."[7] Part of his original commission, the Hall of the History of the German Reich and that of the History of the German *Volk*—sections that might be considered to contain political overtones—were credited to Sergius Ruegenberg and Erni Walther, two of Mies's young associates whose names were unlikely to raise Nazi eyebrows. Photographs of

Gropius and Joost Schmidt, Nonferrous Metals exhibit, German People– German Work exhibition, Berlin, 1934; copper and brass section; each plate of the spiral is made of a different metal; the whole spiral slowly revolves (Photo courtesy of the Museum of Modern Art, New York)

these two "Miesian" rooms appeared in several architectural journals and considerably enhanced the Nazi regime's claim to artistic liberality.[8] Although uncredited, Mies's contribution to the German Mining Exhibition was unmistakably his, remaining vivid in Speer's and other's recollections forty years later.[9] Three towering walls—one of rock salt and two of coal—formed the centerpiece of this design, their startling material, clarity, and uncompromising simplicity offering graphic demonstration of his belief that the creation of "order out of the desperate confusion of our time" remained the single most significant goal of creative work.[10] The smallest and most delicate of the three structures was the wall of rock salt, whose rusticated face of pale stone contrasted with the precision of its horizontal coursework. Directly behind it hovered the tallest wall, a meticulously hewn structure of the blackest anthracite coal. The intensity and purity of its color, as well as the jewellike precision of its alternately polished and

Mies van der Rohe, German Mining exhibit, German People–German Work exhibition, Berlin, 1934 (Photo courtesy of Mies van der Rohe Archive, the Museum of Modern Art, New York)

unpolished surfaces contrasted brilliantly with the striated pale pink and beige tones of the rock-salt wall before it. Opposite the two stood a wall of bituminous coal, its brownish-black color less intense and consistent than the anthracite, while its overall rough treatment, with its more square-cut blocks and precisely laid courses, contrasted with the wall of salt.

Expressing his belief that the value of a material lay in its use, not in the material itself, Mies had treated rock salt and coal, two of the most commonplace and banal materials, in a manner more often reserved for precious marbles and stone. By opening people's eyes to the potentialities of the "new" (here salt and coal; but usually steel and plate glass), he was seeking to affirm the possibilities of the technological age; while his treatment of the materials—the finesse of masonry technique, the structural honesty, refinement of detail, proportional relationships, and expression of material—paid homage to the past. The design expressed his view—unlike that of many of his fellow modernists, who denigrated tradition, or that of the Nazis, who extolled it—of architecture as a unity of past and present, indebted equally to technology and the principles of industrialization and to the teachings of antiquity.

To a regime dedicated to both the restoration of German tradition and the expansion of German technology, Mies's striking architectural concepts, expressed here with such poetry and force, presented both challenge and rebuke. By revealing the unity of past and present, of German craft and German technology, Mies was offering a notable, elegant, and reasonable course to a regime that had yet to express its artistic direction. However, Hitler, locked like Mies into his own certainties, was not interested in lessons. For him, questions of significance were limited to a narrow range of criteria; he measured worth in terms of ostentation and intimidation, and perceived modernism as necessarily and intrinsically opposed to tradition. What, for Mies, appeared a logical and reasonable solution, to Hitler seemed simply an affront. "He didn't like the exhibition," Speer recalled. "He thought it was bad: it angered him."[11] Only Speer and his closest aides knew this; publicly, Hitler kept his reaction to himself. But he neither forgave Mies nor forgot.[12]

* * *

In April 1934, Hitler had more pressing concerns on his mind. Spurred by the fading health of the eighty-six-year-old President Hindenburg, long-smouldering issues with regard to the succession and the Reichswehr's continuing support of his government were coming to a head and threatening the future of his regime. Like every postwar German government, his, too, was dependent on the support of the Reichswehr, now being jeopardized by the president's weakening condition and the army's well-known antipathy to the SA. With its membership numbering over two and a half million—more, in fact, than the army itself—and its leader, Ernst Röhm, pushing to incorporate his group into the army (with himself as head), the SA had long been a source of concern for the Reichswehr. Indebted to both the SA and the Reichswehr, Hitler had—up to now—successfully placated both. In early April with Hindenburg's health rapidly failing, the delicate situation altered considerably.[13]

However senile and faded he had become, Hindenburg remained a revered and magisterial symbol of authority to ordinary citizens and government leaders alike. His benign tolerance of the most abusive Nazi acts did much to encourage among the German people the indifference that foreigners found so infuriating; his ability, as president, to declare martial law and to turn the control of the state over to the Reichswehr inhibited Hitler's more malevolent instincts. With Hindenburg's displeasure over the course of the Nazi government and his well-known preference for the reestablishment of the monarchy upon his death (now apparently imminent), along with the army's increasing nervousness over the SA, Hitler was suddenly forced to choose between the two. Unless he suppressed the SA—the conditions for securing the backing of the Reichswehr—Hitler realized that his government was finished.

On June 30, after a week of tense military maneuvers, Hitler—his decision reached—moved swiftly to eliminate the SA. All over Germany, rampant killings took place. In Munich, Hitler personally confronted Röhm, one of his closest friends and earliest supporters, and "allowed" him to commit suicide. The precise number murdered during this episode remains unknown. Figures ranged from seventy-seven to more than a thousand and included SA leaders; past and present enemies of the regime and acquaintances of enemies, as well as their wives; targets of personal revenge; and outright mistakes.[14] By Sunday, July 1, with most of the killings over, Hitler—having flown back to Berlin from Munich the night before—hosted a tea party that afternoon in the gardens of the Chancellery.[15]

The events of June 30 struck Germany like a thunderbolt. It was not the shocking suddenness or even the brutality of the attack that appeared to disturb people the most—after all, a clash between the Reichswehr and the SA had long been anticipated—but that it had been carried out by the Nazis themselves, rather than the army. The fact that a massacre without precedent in modern European history had taken place did not seem as dreadful as the fact that it had occurred in a country and by a leader whose moral superiority had been affirmed with a resoluteness and pride that had transfixed his people and shaken the world. Outside Germany, the events were seen quite differently. Virtually unanimously, the foreign press saw the horrifying event as marking "the beginning of the end for the Nazis. . . . Their prestige is tremendously shaken," observed *The Nation*, echoing sentiment around the world.[16]

> [The Nazis] can no longer pose as supermen with a united Germany behind them. At their doors lie . . . not pacifists or Communists or Social Democrats or Jews this time, but men of their own crowd, comrades in uniform murdered in a St. Bartholomew's night as unexpected as it was horrifying.

What had outraged the world, within Germany seemed to be a source of pride. On Monday, July 2, telegraphing Hitler and Göring from his sickbed at his family home in Neudeck, President Hindenburg thanked them for their "determined action and gallant personal intervention which have nipped treason in the bud and rescued the German people from great danger."[17] On Tuesday, July 3, signaling the unconditional backing of the Reichswehr, General Blomberg congratulated Hitler on behalf of the cabinet and issued an order to the army expressing the satisfaction of the high command with the turn of events and promising to establish "cordial relations with the new SA."[18] For countless Germans, these expressions of approval by the country's most venerated symbols of incorruptibility served to assuage discomforting reflection, much as these same individuals' quiet acquiescence had done in the months before.

Yet, without the deep and broad support enjoyed by Hitler, such approbation, even coming from such impeccable sources, would have fallen on deaf ears. Whatever his limitations, excesses, or failures, Hitler remained the symbol of the "new Germany." In many German eyes, he had accomplished much that seemed praiseworthy. He had pulled the country together; he had lifted Germany out of the valley of humiliation and had made the world respect her again. But, most important, he had achieved what many in Germany had ceased to expect from their politicians: he had remained in power for more than a year; he had removed the burden of political responsibility from a people for whom politics was an onerous obstacle to their daily pursuits; and he had restored the most treasured of German virtues—order, civic obedience, and national pride.

Germans therefore remained silent. Dismissing this latest outrage as but another "momentary exaggeration" on the part of the Nazis, they returned to their private preoccupations. Albert Speer, beginning to fancy himself a second Schinkel, "like most Berlin architects with government commissions,"[19] occupied himself with his latest commission from Hitler, the renovation of the Borsig Palace, now occupied by Papen's offices but intended by Hitler to house the new leadership of the SA, which he was anxious to transfer quickly from Munich to Berlin. Coming upon a large pool of dried blood on the floor of the room where Herbert von Bose, one of Papen's assistants, had been shot on June 30, Speer turned away and thereafter avoided the room.[20]

Mies, having submitted his Brussels and service-station projects, occupied himself with the design of flower stands, furniture (whose patents formed most of his current income),[21] and "court-houses"—simple rectilinear dwellings entirely enclosed within masonry walls. Where, ten years earlier, he had explored the possibilities of outward-flowing space (in his country house projects of 1923 and 1924), he now understood, like so many of his fellow countrymen, that respite—in architecture, as in life—came only from turning within.

Then, on August 2, 1934, the comforting mantle that had

shielded the German people from the grim realities of the Third Reich was lifted, along with the shackles of restraint that had bound Hitler: President Hindenburg was dead.

At twelve noon, three hours after Hindenburg's death, a stunned Germany learned that Hitler had assumed the power of head of state, as well as commander-in-chief of the armed forces. The title of president was abolished and the offices of the presidency and chancellorship were combined. From now on, Hitler was to be known as "the Führer and Reichs Chancellor" and members of the government and armed forces were ordered to swear an oath of loyalty to him personally; all of these were illegal and outrageous actions that caught Germany by surprise. In a characteristically bold move, Hitler then offered the German people the illusion of legitimacy, if not the fact, calling upon them to legitimize his unlawful acts in a national referendum on August 19.

Serious impediments, however, lay before him, most notably the plight of the economy, whose dismal state not even the Nazi-controlled press could conceal. With little foreign exchange or credit, its gold reserve exhausted and exports dwindling, Germany seemed fast advancing toward another crash. A potato famine in July had fired alarming rumors of impending food restrictions. Rationing was widely anticipated with the coming of winter. Affairs were no better on the foreign front. England's support of France and Russia—clearly signaled by Stanley Baldwin's blunt announcement that England's frontier lay on the Rhine—revealed Germany's isolation in Europe and the collapse of Nazi foreign policy. Nazi Germany was swaying perilously close to the edge of extinction. It was no wonder that the Nazis approached the campaign with the ardor of political desperadoes.

Shaken by the loss of Hindenburg, anxious and preoccupied with hoarding clothes, food, and other necessities against the imminent hardships of the winter ahead, Germans paid little heed to the high-pitched Nazi rhetoric. Nowhere was this lack of support more apparent than in Berlin, never a Nazi stronghold. The change in the city's atmosphere was palpable during the summer of 1934. Berliners seemed more relaxed, conversation more open. Fewer Brown Shirts were on the streets: one no longer had to duck into a store to keep from saluting the standard of some passing SA or SS battalion or else risk a beating. There were fewer Hitler salutes and "German Greetings." It was difficult to pinpoint the cause of this new freer attitude. Was it the hot summer sun or merely the insouciant Berlin spirit that rebelled against taking anything seriously for too long? It might also have been the realization that the concentration camps could not possibly hold the entire population, or that the police—the wildly suspicious gestapo, Göring's special police, the SA, and the SS—since June 30 seemed more interested in watching each other, than ordinary, nonpolitical folk.

This general withdrawal from political concerns—especially marked in Berlin but pervasive throughout the country—was no joking matter to the Nazis, engaged in what they saw as their final and most important campaign. The circumstances clearly demanded extraordinary efforts. On August 13, less than a week before the referendum, the Nazis appealed to some of the country's most renowned cultural leaders, some of whom, in more confident days, they had pilloried as "cultural bolshevists," to sign a proclamation in support of the Führer. Party ideologues were outraged by such groveling. "[I]t is very depressing," wrote Rosenberg to Goebbels,

> to have to beg each one individually for their signature for the Führer, when we have fought their cultural politics to the utmost for years.[22]

One of the recipients of this perplexing "request" was Mies.

> From the President of the
> Reichs Chamber of Literature
> August 13, 1934
>
> Dear Professor van der Rohe:
>
> In cooperation with the Reichsminister for National Enlightenment and Propaganda and the Presidents of the National Chambers of Music and the Creative Arts, the president Dr. Blunck [Hans Friedrich Blunck was President of the Chamber of Literature] wishes to bring the enclosed proclamation to a popular vote. He is asking you

through me to declare your immediate agreement, so that your name may also be placed under the proclamation. In view of the haste which is necessary for the publication of this proclamation, I would be extremely obliged to you if you would let me know your agreement by telegram, for which I have taken the liberty of enclosing the required postage in the form of stamps.

I thank you for your endeavors and am, with sincere greetings and Heil Hitler!

Signed: For Dr. Haupt

[Gunther Haupt was Managing Director of the Reich Chamber of Literature][23]

Stunning his contemporaries and apparently embarrassing even himself, Mies would ultimately acquiesce to this demand. He "immediately apologized to his friends," complained Rosenberg to Goebbels, revealing that Mies was under Nazi surveillance.

[T]he particulars come from the circle around Barlach and Nolde and one of your government counsellors.[24]

"Is it necessity or ambition?" asked Ivo Panaggi, commenting on Mies's participation from Florence in a letter of August 25 to Gropius.

I can imagine [what his motives are] because, ever since the Nazis came to power, Mies always feared becoming a "second class German". Now he's guaranteed to remain in the "first class".[25]

In 1964, citing his signing of this document, Sibyl Moholy-Nagy, the wife of László, derided Mies's "desperate attempts to play up to National Socialism."[26] It is worth noting that neither Panaggi nor Moholy-Nagy were living in Germany at this time. Panaggi wrote from Florence and the Moholy-Nagys—rightfully frightened by László's Red-tainted past—had fled Germany that January. Did they realize what refusal would have meant? Did they know that Mies had two important projects under consideration by government offices? Did they know that since January 10, Mies (along with Gropius, who had been interrogated on December 29, 1933) was under criminal investigation for charges stemming from the ongoing proceedings against Fritz Hesse in Dessau?[27] Mies had been charged with politicizing the Bauhaus, as well as the embezzlement of Bauhaus license fees, both of which he refuted at his interrogation in January.[28] Although the charges were flagrantly fictitious and eventually (in 1935) dropped, Mies could not have been unaware that the gestapo jails and internment camps were filled with individuals convicted of far more spurious charges.[29] Under circumstances which "concentrated the mind wonderfully,"[30] it would have been surprising if Mies had turned down the Nazi request. Yet, in spite of these compelling circumstances, Mies apparently did not agree at once, as Rosenberg indicated to Goebbels.

> Professor Mies van der Rohe, the creator of a memorial for Liebknecht and Rosa Luxemburg, *finally* [italics mine] conceded.[31]

How much Mies's "gesture" of political accommodation was a response to the particular circumstances of the moment or consistent with long-held beliefs—in lieu of his silence—can only remain a matter of conjecture. It is worth pointing out that Gropius—with far stronger political convictions than Mies and like him under criminal investigation—was also making gestures, and these uninvited, to the Nazis. "Shall this strong new architectural movement [i.e., modernism] which began in Germany be lost to Germany?" he wrote in March 1934 to Eugen Hönig, president of the Reich Chamber of Fine Arts.

> Can Germany afford to throw overboard the new architecture and its spiritual leaders, when there is nothing to replace them?[32]

Under the bewildering circumstances of the day, the struggle to reconcile ideals with the equally compelling instinct for survival was difficult, even for those free from Nazi charges. "I vacillate constantly between secret hopes and total despair," complained Friedrich Meinecke, the noted historian, that August.[33]

Yet, forgetting for the moment the peculiar exigencies of the day, Mies's political "gesture" of allowing his name to appear in support of Hitler certainly falls within his framework of "apoliticism" and is consistent with his behavior with regard to the Bauhaus, his most immediate prior confrontation with the regime. Since his goal was the creation of art—which, in his mind, was "above" mere politics—he seemed to be amenable to any gesture, however political, to accomplish this. In his mind, the means justified the end. Prone to differentiate between the "real," what truly mattered—in his case, his art—as opposed to the "insignificant," such as the realm of politics, Mies, undoubtedly under the prodding of Lilly Reich, would do almost anything to be left alone to pursue his art. He had made this clear in his 1930 speech in Vienna.

> [W]hat is right and significant for any era . . . is . . . to give the spirit the opportunity to exist. Let us accept changed economic and social conditions as a fact. All these take their blind and fateful course.[34]

Being apolitical, in Mies's view, meant to stand above and aside from politics: his ability to remove himself from the factionalism that had marked German modernism had been a significant factor in his professional success. His colleagues had learned to expect from him a measured and reasoned view that was devoid of political bias. While opinions varied on his architectural style, none doubted his seriousness, integrity, and commitment to his art, save for the far right (Rosenberg-KDK) wing of the Nazis. The party's permission to reopen the long-despised Bauhaus indicates that even they—at least the more "liberal" faction—recognized his apoliticism, in spite of their rhetoric. But Mies's apolitical convictions had been spawned in calmer, more "normal" times, when the circumstances of life did not contradict those of dreams, when apoliticism was believed to be the mark of a "higher" mind and politics seen as inconsequential and inevitable.

But the times had changed: what seemed simple and right in calmer times, no longer mattered. The world had turned upside-down. Now the government claimed that "he who is not for us is against us!"[35] The apoliticism that had earlier been so admired was now reviled, and—especially for an architect seeking government commissions—downright dangerous. Mies's fate, if not his heart, was very much linked to the political world.

Apoliticism, in the best of times, is an ambiguous concept. The "pure" artist, unconcerned with all but aesthetic issues, is not always distinguishable from the opportunist, who utilizes his political neutrality much like a moral umbrella, protecting him from the vagaries of all political claims. While the sincerity of Mies's aesthetic convictions is beyond doubt, so is his universal availability. And when does a "gesture"—with its intimations of insignificance, of lack of weight—become something more? When does the "appearance" of support become support itself? What motivates an act frequently differs from its perception by others—one man's traitor is another's patriot! As unpleasant as it may be to contemplate, apoliticism under the Nazis seems to have been a luxury available only to the common folk—the invisible ones—individuals whose names were barely known to their neighbors, those whose shoulders never felt the heavy Nazi tap.

The proclamation appeared in the *Völkischer Beobachter* on August 18, 1934, the day before the referendum. Alone among the prominent figures associated with the Bauhaus, and right next to that of Paul Schultze-Naumburg, appeared the name of Mies van der Rohe.[36]

> A Call by Cultural Leaders!
> Fellow countrymen! Friends!
>
> We have buried one of the greatest men in German history. At his casket, the young Führer of the land spoke for us all and gave an avowal for himself and the future of the nation. He pledged his word and life for the renewal of our people, to live in unity and honor, secure, free and as one. We believe in this Führer, who has fulfilled our fervent wish for unity.
>
> We trust his work, which asks sacrifice beyond all carping sophistry;
>
> We place our hope in the man who, beyond man and things, believes in God's providence.
>
> Because the writer and artist create for the people with

Aufruf der Kulturschaffenden

Berlin, 17. August.

Die unterzeichneten Persönlichkeiten richten folgenden Aufruf an die Öffentlichkeit:

Volksgenossen, Freunde!

Wir haben einen der Größten deutscher Geschichte zu Grabe geleitet. An seinem Sarge sprach der junge Führer des Reiches für uns alle, und legte Bekenntnis ab für sich und den Zukunftswillen der Nation.

Wort und Leben setzte er zum Pfand für die Wiederaufrichtung unseres Volkes, das in Einheit und Ehre leben und Bürge des Friedens sein will, der die Völker verbindet. Wir glauben an diesen Führer, der unsern heißen Wunsch nach Eintracht erfüllt hat.

Wir vertrauen seinem Werk, das Hingabe fordert jenseits aller krittelnden Vernünftelei, wir setzen unsere Hoffnung auf den Mann, der über Mensch und Dinge hinaus in Gottes Vorsehung gläubig ist.

Weil der Dichter und Künstler nur in gleicher Treue zum Volk zu schaffen vermag, und weil er von der gleichen und tiefsten Überzeugung kündet, daß das heiligste Recht der Völker in der eigenen Schicksalsbestimmung besteht, gehören wir zu des Führers Gefolgschaft.

Wir fordern nichts anderes für uns, als was wir anderen Völkern ohne Vorbehalte zugestehen, wir müssen es für dieses Volk, das deutsche Volk, fordern, weil seine Einheit, Freiheit und Ehre unser aller Not und Wille ist.

Der Führer hat uns wiederum aufgefordert, in Vertrauen und Treue zu ihm zu stehen. Niemand von uns wird fehlen, wenn es gilt, das zu bekunden.

Werner Beumelburg, Ernst Barlach, Rudolf G. Binding, Hans Friedrich Blunck, Verleger Alfred Bruckmann, Richard Euringer, Professor Emil Fahrenkamp, Erich Feyerabend, Gustav

Frenssen, Wilhelm Furtwängler, Professor Dr. Eberhard Hanfstaengl, Gustav Havemann, Erich Heckel, Professor Eugen Hönig, Heinz Ihlert, Hanns Johst, Georg Kolbe, Erwin Kolbenheyer, Werner Krauß, Franz Lenk, Heinrich Lersch, Professor Karl Lörcher, Architekt Walter March, Agnes Miegel, Börries Freiherr von Münch

hausen, Emil Nolde, Paul Pfund, Hans Pfitzner, Professor Dr. Wilhelm Pinder, Mies van der Rohe, Professor Dr. h. c. Paul Schultze-Naumburg, Hermann Stehr, Richard Strauß, Joseph Thorak, Generalintendant Heinz Tietjen, Oberbürgermeister Dr. Weidemann, Arnold Weinmüller.

Proclamation by German cultural leaders urging support for Hitler that appeared in the *Völkischer Beobachter* on August 18, 1934 (Bauhaus-Archiv)

> equal devotion, and because he brings the same deep devotion . . . we thus belong to the Führer's followers. . . .
>
> . . . The Führer has called upon us to stand by him in trust and faith. None of us will be missing when an affirmation of trust is needed. The nation will never dissolve when it remains united and true.
>
> Unanimously say "Yes!"

On August 19—the day after the publication of the proclamation—Germany voted overwhelmingly in favor of Hitler's usurpation of power. Ninety-five percent of those registered went to the polls, 90 percent of whom—more than 38 million people—voted for Hitler.[37] How much the vote was an expression of support and how much of fear remained unknown: the result spoke for itself. Counseled by many of their most respected countrymen, the German people—whatever their qualms of conscience, whatever their gnawing doubts—had given a jubilant Hitler unchallenged mastery of the Third Reich.

CHAPTER 13

"NOISY, BOTHERSOME AND SLIGHTLY CRAZY"

HITLER DOESN'T EXIST; HE IS ONLY THE NOISE HE MAKES.

(Kurt Tucholsky)

With Hitler's victory, it was no longer possible for someone seeking participation in "official" projects to appear apolitical. In August, Mies applied for membership in the NS Volkswohl-fahrt,[1] a Nazi-sponsored social welfare organization dedicated to the needs of the poor that offered an attractive and "harmless" way of declaring to the authorities that one supported—or, at least, did not reject—the regime.[2] Given Mies's demeaning view of politics, it is unlikely that his gestures altered his view of himself as apolitical. In his mind, the road to Calvary was only important because of where it led. While others might pay heed to the signposts; he noted only their destination.

But, after Hitler's success in 1934, more was involved in government-sponsored architectural projects than these expressions of good will. The prospectus, for example, of the Brussels Pavilion competition dictated a sternly political course.

> The exhibition building must express the will of National
> Socialist Germany through an imposing form; it must act
> as the symbol of . . . National-Socialist fighting strength
> and heroic will.[3]

Translation of these programmatic ideals involved hard-core
artistic decisions, such as the inclusion of the swastika and the
German eagle, especially troublesome for someone like Mies,
who was known for refusing to compromise his design integrity for anything or anyone. In 1929 he had refused to employ
the German eagle insignia of the Reich in his Barcelona Pavilion. Although only five years separated these two projects, the
circumstances could not have differed more. As the prospectus
for the Brussels Pavilion indicates, the free hand permitted him
in the earlier work was now denied. Yet Mies was hardly
known for following the dictates of any program! The presence
of the swastika and German eagle in the Brussels Pavilion
reveals his accommodation to the Nazis, as does the awkward
nationalism of the letter that appears to have accompanied the
drawings and model he sent to the Propaganda Ministry (the
evident source of the invitation) on July 3:

> During the last years, Germany has developed a form for
> its expositions that more and more . . . progressed from
> exterior embellishment to the essential . . . to a real pic-
> ture of German achievements. . . .
> This clear and striking language corresponds to the
> essence of German work. . . .
> Upon entering the German section, one reaches the hall
> of honor through a forecourt. This hall of honor . . . serves
> to accommodate the national emblems and the representa-
> tion of the Reich.[4]

Aside from the requisite political symbols, however, Mies's
design—two sections, one for machinery and heavy industry,
and the other for culture—a long, low building, built partly of
brick, with reflecting pools—appears to be little affected by its
political context. The service station was also composed of two
main elements—a large cantilevered roof, supported by steel
pillars, that extended over the gas pumps, and a service building, which, in accordance with the requirements of the

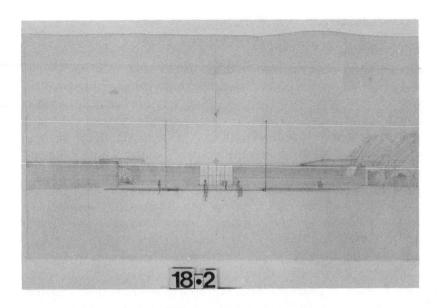

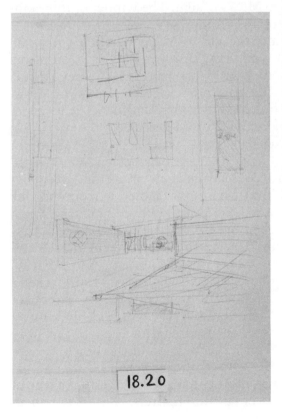

Mies van der Rohe, Brussels Pavilion project, 1934: TOP, exterior perspective; BOTTOM, two plans, three exterior elevations, and one perspective (Collection, Mies van der Rohe Archive, the Museum of Modern Art, New York. Gift of Ludwig Mies van der Rohe)

program was to be built from local, indigenous materials, such as brick in the north and white-painted stucco in the south.[5]

Hitler chose to judge these competitions himself. The models and drawings of the Brussels Pavilion were brought to his office in the Chancellery, while the service station models went to the exhibition hall at the Prussian Academy of Arts. Hitler's reaction to the pavilion entries is unknown. However, the state in which they were found—lying in a heap behind his desk—suggests that his response was violent. "Hitler had sealed his decision with his foot," recalled Sergius Ruegenberg, Mies's young assistant, who was sent to retrieve the models and found them there.[6] Speer recalls that Hitler was dissatisfied with all the proposals and decided, because of this, not to participate in the Brussels Exposition.[7] The design for the service station appears to have suffered a similar, if less brutal, fate. According to Ruegenberg, it was rumored that Hitler returned repeatedly to Mies's design. The winner of this competition, however, remains unknown.

That Hitler's violent reaction to Mies's pavilion entry had little to do with political considerations may be seen in his similarly bad behavior toward his partisans. When he was asked to prepare a preliminary proposal for a "Party Forum" in Nuremberg, Paul Schultze-Naumburg considered it just recompense for his long and dedicated service to the party. But Hitler disliked his design, and—with as little regard for Schultze-Naumburg's reputation as he had given Mies's, without even allowing the "courageous pioneer" (as the *Völkischer Beobachter* called him) the opportunity to defend his scheme—Hitler discarded the plans with an abruptness and callousness that shocked Speer.[8] Hitler then ordered a new competition: this time, he selected the architects himself.

The Nazi regime was now a year and a half old and still lacked a single spokesman articulating a clear artistic direction. Muted, but no less acrimonious, the Goebbels-Rosenberg struggle continued. Five months after Hitler's appointment of him to supervise the cultural education of the Reich, Rosenberg's influence still lagged significantly behind that of his rival. On June 6, after confiding in his diary that "a real tug of war is now beginning over cultural matters," Rosenberg, in an effort to counter Goebbels's RKK, merged the KDK and its theatrical affiliate, the Reich Association of the German Stage (Reichsverbandes Deutsche Bühne) into his cultural office under his leadership.[9]

The confusion of the artistic situation was apparent everywhere. Writing in *Bauwelt,* a leading architectural journal, Alfons Leitl predicted that "[t]he architecture of the Third Reich . . . will be a mixture of Schmitthenner and Mies van der Rohe."[10] Schmitthenner's architecture had been described as "a refined imitation of what was the international style of about a hundred and twenty years ago."[11] Walter Gropius, one of the first to describe the "internationalism" of the new architectural style—in his *Internationale Architektur,* published in 1925—now argued for the style's inherent nationalism in impassioned pleas to Nazi leaders.

> [A]bove all, I myself see this new style as the way in which we in our country can finally achieve a valid union of the two great spiritual heritages of the classical and the Gothic tradition. Schinkel sought this union, but in vain. Shall Germany deny itself this great opportunity?[12]

Frustrated by the vague and procrastinating replies he received, and sensitive to the dangers of his leftist reputation, Gropius began making plans to leave Germany. Obtaining permission to attend an international theater conference in Rome, he and his wife went from there into exile in London.[13] Of the country's leading modernist architects with broad international repute, only Mies now remained in Germany.

Hitler's "Cultural Address" on September 5, replete with his usual metaphors of destruction, did nothing to clear things up. Certain phrases appeared to support Goebbels and the "Berlin" faction.

> We cannot rape modern times in favor of the Middle Ages when it comes to art. Your presumably Gothic medication fits poorly into the age of steel and iron, glass and concrete. . . . Just as the crossbow is unacceptable as a modern weapon, so too are railroad stations in original German Renaissance style. . . . New tasks demand new materials [in order to keep pace with] the contemporary discoveries that interest the period.

But Hitler continued,

> All this stammering about art and culture by cubists, futurists, dadaists, and others is neither racially founded nor sufferable by the people. . . . [Such modern art] is nothing less than the cultural complement [of] political destruction. . . . Once and for all, it must be clearly expressed, the development of the Third Reich—cultural as well as political—will be determined by those who have created it and not by those who do not even grasp and comprehend its scope. . . . Our soul will resound in the music and our spirit will be eternalized in the stones.[14]

The vagueness of these terms ensured that no definite understanding could be extracted from them. Therefore, as 1934 drew to a close, the cultural cast of the regime remained as uncertain as ever, even to those like Goebbels and Rosenberg who were widely believed to be in charge of it. Mies van der Rohe and Schultze-Naumburg, representing two antithetical poles of German art, both rejected and humiliated by those who had earnestly sought their favor—and both able to claim strong supporters among the Nazi leadership—found themselves in unexpected and unhappy accord. Affirming a creed of singularity—"my way and no other"—to which the Germanic nature seemed so prone, they had envisioned heaven; instead, they found only hell.

By 1935 Mies's deteriorating financial situation had begun to take its toll. His household staff—the chauffeur-butler, who accompanied him everywhere, and the cook—were let go. His daughter Georgia recalled visiting and seeing him standing at the stove cooking some eggs and spinach for his dinner. He could no longer afford to pay for his daughters' education. Said Georgia,

> I remember how happy we were when my sister got married. It meant one less mouth to feed. It was very sad![15]

Mies had to borrow money almost constantly, "mostly from Frau Reich," recalled Hirche, Mies's assistant, but from others as well. He even had to borrow a few "pfennigs" from me. Things were very bad![16]

Mies never spoke of the hardships of these years; it is from others that one learns of them. "[F]or Mies, it is especially difficult," complained Lilly Reich in a letter to J. J. P. Oud, the Dutch architect.[17] To those ignorant of his circumstances, Mies appeared as self-confident, haughty, and optimistic as ever. George Nelson, a young American designer who came to interview Mies in 1935, wrote:

> At the present time, oddly enough, Miës is on the upgrade. Hitler and his aides have condemned modern architecture repeatedly, evincing a preference to a kind of bombproof Nuremberg style. But Miës, who has never shown much love for pitched roofs, has been made head of the architects in the German Academy. [Considering that he had been asked to resign a short time before, his assertion seems unlikely. That he was unwilling—or unable—to convey the truth of his situation is apparent.] And only a short while ago his competition drawing for a new Reichs-bank won first prize, although his design will not be built. Whatever it is that accounts for his enviable position, it is to be hoped that he will get some jobs out of it. With Mendelsohn, the Tauts, and Gropius out of the country, there surely ought to be a commission or two for those who remain, and it would be interesting to see what Miës would do on an important building.... He is brilliant, slow, affable, and vain. Impractical, utterly uninterested in politics, the social or economic aspect of architecture, he is paradoxically the only one among Germany's great modern architects who has anything like a sure position in the country at this time.[18]

Even allowing for the circumspection that marked conversation at this time—especially with foreigners—Mies appeared genuinely unaffected by the difficulties of the hour.[19] No doubt this was because in general the affairs of life—family no less than politics, its delights as well as its pain—left him essentially untouched. Although he enjoyed having money and, when he could afford to, lived like a prince, enjoying the finest of wines and food, such pleasures were as incidental to him as onyx and marble were to his architecture. He could just as easily do without. Despite the lack of commissions (the Hubbe House, a small home that he worked on in 1935, was never built), his routine remained unchanged.[20] For hours on end, alone and in total concentration, he worked on problems of the "court-house"; new types of automobile seating; new furniture designs, in plastic and in bentwood; new methods of photographing wallpaper; ingenious devices of spiral locomotion—struggling, with every fiber of his mind, to extract the essence of the problem at hand and bring it to a state of glowing perfection. Sketches were developed, models made, and patents applied for. Impervious to circumstances that were bringing his family, colleagues, and countrymen to the edge of despair, Mies—true to the German tradition of the man of *Kultur*—remained in the clear, cool realm of art and the sublime—challenged, inspired, and unbent.

Bolstering Mies's normal political distance was a realization that he shared with a broad segment of the German population in 1935, that a vast chasm lay between the Nazis' actual programs and the noisy rantings of their press. This realization, along with the continuing existence of isolated pockets of liberality, allowed many individuals—native as well as foreign—to regard the Nazis as little more than "a noisy, bothersome and slightly crazy phenomenon in noisy and slightly crazy times."[21]

This immense divergency between reality and the claptrap of the press was particularly apparent in the world of art. In 1935 Hitler delivered his most stinging denunciation of modern art, at the same time that the Abstract Cabinet in the Hannover Museum, undoubtedly the world's most distinguished public collection of modern abstract art, remained open and unmolested. In his Cultural Address of September 11, Hitler referred to the creators of modernism as "criminals of the world," "destroyers of our art," with whom "scores" would have to be settled, "imbecile degenerates interested in the destruction of the nation" who belonged in "prison or the madhouse." Given this speech, not to mention the extent of Nazi persecution of comparable art in other areas of Germany, the continuing ability of the Abstract Cabinet to stay open was nothing less than astonishing.

The collection, which included the works of such first-generation abstract artists as Léger, Gleizes, Baumeister, Moholy-Nagy, Mondrian, Malevich, Gabo, El Lissitzky, and Picasso, was revolutionary, not simply in its devotion to abstract works of art, but also in the architecturally harmonious manner in which the art was displayed. In the ten years since its opening in 1925 by Alexander Dorner, with the assistance of El Lissitzky, the Abstract Cabinet had become the most famous room of twentieth-century art, drawing visitors from all over Europe and America, and was an important progenitor for the Museum of Modern Art in New York, established shortly thereafter. Alfred Barr, the director of the Museum of Modern Art and witness, in 1933, to many of the regime's early artistic excesses, was amazed to find it open and accessible.

> The first thing I asked to see after being welcomed by Dr. Dorner was the gallery of abstract art. Elsewhere in Germany modern painting had disappeared from museum walls, so I half expected to find the famous room dismantled. Yet it was still there and accessible to the public, though to visit it may have been risky for a German since there were spies even in the museums. Dr. Dorner showed me the abstract gallery proudly.[22]

But it was in architecture that the difference between Nazi fact and fiction, between ideology and reality, was most pronounced. From private homes[23] to party-sponsored buildings, from Adolf Hitler housing developments to modernist factories, the actual architectural production of the Third Reich in fact differed little from that of its Weimar predecessor—despite the party's loud claims of a new "national socialist style, the departure of many of the modernist leaders, Hitler's attacks on modernism, and Mies's personal travails. In the architectural journals of 1935, one could read about Bauhaus-inspired lamps,[24] a glass and steel skyscraper designed by Holabird and Root, the Chicago architects,[25] and homes whose unabashed use of such modernist devices as plate glass and ribbon windows, simple, white, unornamented cubic forms, and ships' railings seemed—except for their slightly sloping or pointed roofs—not unlike residences of pre-Nazi times.[26] Such stylistic continuity with Weimar trends is even evident within

Diversity of architecture during the Third Reich, TOP TO BOTTOM: Herbert Rimpl, Airplane factory (Photo by Heinrich Heidersberger, courtesy of Herbert Rimpl)
Housing development (Bilderdienst Süddeutscher Verlag)
Albert Speer, the New Chancellery, Berlin. Vossstrasse portal (*Die Künst im Dritten Reich*, 1939. Photo from Avery Architectural and Fine Arts Library, Columbia University in the City of New York)

Ernst Sagebiel, the Reich Air Force Ministry Building, Berlin, 1935 (Ullstein Bilderdienst)

Nazi-sponsored architecture—for example, the folksy style of the Adolf Hitler housing projects; the neoromanesque of some minor party and government projects; and the overripe neo-classicism of the major party buildings, already visible in the House of German Art and Speer's mammoth Nuremberg complex, both currently under construction and whose severe, disciplined, and unornamented style revealed their common heritage with many of the neoclassical principles that underlay German modernism. This striking disparity between actual building construction and party ideology also appeared in the major public commissions awarded by the top party leaders. Looking for an architect to design the new Air Force Ministry building, which opened in October 1935, Hermann Göring, who fancied himself an aesthete, turned to the head of the building division of his own ministry, the forty-three-year-old Ernst Sagebiel, whose architectural credentials of having worked as field supervisor for Eric Mendelsohn, the famed Jewish modernist, hardly qualified him as a Nazi ideologue, but whose overscaled and simplified architecture fit him comfortably within the Nazi public building style. But it was in industrial construction—accelerated by the regime's rearmament priorities—that modernism actually flourished, uncompromised and at a standard consistent with those established by the great German pioneers and honored by Hitchcock and Johnson in their epochal exhibition of "The International Style" at the Museum of Modern Art in 1931.[27] Indeed through industrial construction, the modernist style would come to far exceed all other styles of building in the Third Reich, with the possible exception of workers' housing—a fact notably and pointedly omitted in Nazi literature.

According to Speer, Hitler not only expected and approved—but actually enjoyed—modern architecture in industrial construction, where it was devoid of ideological demands. "Do you see this facade?" he said to Speer, while reviewing a new steel plant.

> How fine the proportions are. What you have here are different requirements from those governing a Party forum. There our Doric style is the expression of the New Order; here, the technical solution is the appropriate thing. But if one of these so-called modern architects comes along and wants to build housing projects or town halls in the factory style, then I say: he doesn't understand a thing. That isn't modern, it's tasteless, and violates the eternal laws of architecture besides. Light, air, and efficiency belong to a place of work; in a town hall I require dignity, and in a residence a sense of shelter that arms me for the harshness of life's struggle. Just imagine, Speer, a Christmas tree in front of a wall of glass. Impossible! Here, as elsewhere, we must consider the variety of life.[28]

It was modernism's assertion of one style's suitability for every place and every purpose to which Hitler objected. "He realized full well," wrote Speer,

> that an autobahn restaurant or a Hitler Youth home in the country should not look like an urban building. Nor would it have occurred to him to build a factory in his public-display style.[29]

For whatever reasons then—Hitler's basic disregard of architecture outside buildings of state; the disparity of impulses

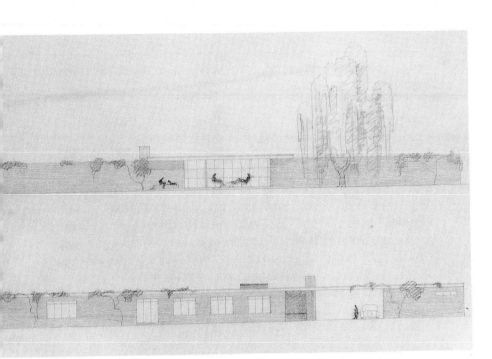

Mies van der Rohe, two elevations of the Ulrich Lange House, second project, Krefeld, 1935 (Collection, Mies van der Rohe Archive, the Museum of Modern Art, New York. Gift of Ludwig Mies van der Rohe)

within Nazism (rooted as it was in controversies of the Weimar period, of which architecture was but a single manifestation); or the inability of any governing power, no matter how authoritarian, to totally control every aspect of building activity—the architectural production of the Third Reich exhibited much of the stylistic diversity of the Weimar period, despite the massive attempts of Nazi propaganda to make it seem otherwise. Much as the worldwide attention paid the German modernists made their actual production within the overall building picture of the Weimar period appear larger than it was, so too did Nazi propaganda distort the actual building output of the Third Reich.[30]

It is this reality, rather than the myth, that explains Mies's attitude with respect to the next important opportunity that he received. Learning of his financial difficulties, the Lange family, his long-standing patrons, asked him to design a home for their son Ulrich in Krefeld. Now that private commissions appeared to be his sole remaining architectural opportunity, this project offered far more than involvement in a building type long of interest to him;[31] at stake was his continuing survival in Nazi Germany.

If ever there was a moment in Mies's career that called for compromise, it was now. An ever-so-artfully sloped roof to hide the "un-German" flatness, some vague historicist reminiscences to ally the building with an "ennobled" past were typical devices of the day. Yet, his proposed design,[32] set far back on its large, wooded site, its facade hidden from the street by trees, was an uncompromisingly modernist structure, with typical Miesian features such as a forthright plan, simple elevations, flowing space, elegant detailing, and, of course, a flat roof. This building bore little resemblance to either the architecture depicted in the Nazi propaganda journals, or the subtly disguised modernist residences with sloping or slightly pointed roofs that appeared in the professional journals. Mies's Lange House design was either a pugnacious testament to one man's faith in the integrity of his vision before a world apparently gone mad, or else an act of unparalleled stubbornness, ignorance, or naïveté.

Claiming that it was "un-German," the local building commission rejected his design for the Lange House; its action, according to Speer, was "insulting" to an architect of Mies's stature.[33] Autonomous and powerful, these *Baupolizei*, as the local building commissions were called, were responsible, to a large degree, for much of the heterogeneity that characterized German building production during the Third Reich. Functioning as quasi-autonomous governing bodies, like building commissions everywhere, the *Baupolizei* were authorized not only to determine if the proposed construction adhered to local building and zoning codes—their traditional task—but whether or not the proposed structure was properly "German." A nebulous and subjective judgment at best, it often resulted in a building that was banned in one town being built in the next.

Mies moved at once to defend his plans before the town council, which had the power to overrule the decision of the *Baupolizei*. This request, while legal, was highly unusual and the council's acceptance of Mies's appeal reflected not only the importance of the Lange family within the community, but also that of the architect.[34]

It was more than the Lange House, however, about which

Mies spoke before the town council; it was really the issue of modernism that he addressed. Clearly and simply, he explained how the design of the Lange House evolved out of the aesthetic tenets of modernism, the functional demands of the client, and considerations of the site, and not out of political instinct. He apparently argued well, for to both his and the Lange family's astonishment, the town council agreed and decided that except for one "minor" change—the construction of an earthen wall to hide the house from the street—the house could be built exactly as designed by Mies. Impressed by the scope of his architect's triumph and interpreting the restriction as a mere face-saving device by the council, Lange agreed immediately. Mies, however, did not. He was enraged and offended that his architecture could be thought of as some shameful, idolatrous image, a dreaded virus from which the *Volk* had to be shielded.[35] To the Langes' regret, he refused to allow the house to be built.

Mies returned by train to Berlin, empty-handed, his future seriously in doubt, an outcast in his own land. How had it come to this? What had brought him to such a foul and pathetic fate that he must choose between his country and his art? How could it be that loyalty to his art meant betrayal of his country? The train slowed its pace as it approached the river. Flowing gray and broad, the silvery Rhine reflected the lush velvet of the sky. It was a docile grayness—one that Mies knew well. He loved this land of the Rhine—incubus of German myth and womb of the Reich, the source and sustenance of the fatherland. He had been born here; the land's vigor and strength, spires and wines, ancient stones and fertility had formed him as they had his country. And now, the disciples of an alien outcast and purveyors of national purity had branded him "un-German."

Deprived by this episode of the certainties of his art, that luminous vision that obscured as much as it revealed, Mies now stood exposed and vulnerable before the brutal reality of the Third Reich. Reluctantly and against his will, he was coming to share the anguish that for so many had already become an inescapable fact of life and which he had so earnestly and persistently sought to ignore.

CHAPTER 14

"A SHAMEFUL, DISHONOURABLE FATE"

HAPPY ARE THOSE WHO QUIETLY ROT IN THE JAILS OF THEIR
FATHERLAND . . . FOR GERMAN AIR BLOWS THROUGH THEM
AND THE JAILER SPEAKS GERMAN.

(Heinrich Heine)

The repudiation of his design for the Lange House appeared to
shut the door on Mies's architectural fate in Germany; and
long after the rage had spent itself, the pain remained. "[The]
situation is distressing," wrote Lilly Reich to J. J. P. Oud,

> but we do not know how we can change it. How sad . . .
> that we had to be born into such hard times.[1]

The arrival in mid-December 1935 of an offer to teach in
California the following July presented Mies with an alternative to his dismal state. The offer to teach at Mills College had
come in the form of a telegram from Alfred Neumeyer,[2] a
former university lecturer in the History of Art in Berlin and
student of Heinrich Wölfflin and Adolf Goldschmidt, who had
emigrated to California in 1934. Not a close acquaintance of
Mies, he felt compelled—in the explanatory letter that arrived

240

about two weeks later—to remind him in whose homes in Berlin they had met.[3] Currently a visiting lecturer at Mills, Neumeyer had suggested Mies's name as someone who might be interested in teaching a summer course for prospective artists and architects. The pay was good and included travel expenses; the only requirement was that he speak English, a skill that Mies did not possess.

For the first time since the Nazis had come to power, Mies was compelled to face the possibility of emigration. He was only too aware of how "temporary visits" were turning into permanent exile, and his response—after an agonizing interlude of procrastination and uncertainty—was as much an expression of personal temperament and national character as of universal feelings oblivious to political bounds. Lazy by instinct, with a massive frame that seemed to impede rapid thought, gesture, and movement, Mies naturally tended toward immobility. A man who drew well, but preferred to let others do his drafting; who kept his bed in his bathroom to avoid traveling too far for his morning bath; who did not dress until two o'clock in the afternoon, having spent the entire morning drinking countless cups of coffee and thinking, could not be expected to view such a physical and emotional upheaval with favor. "Me? Leave Berlin?" he exclaimed, as amused as he was dismayed by the notion. "And what would *I* do in America?"[4]

Like most cultured Europeans of the day, Mies entertained a rather fanciful image of America as a freewheeling place, where *"Kultur"*—in the refined European sense—did not exist, and the "quick buck" and glitzy, meaningless pleasures obscured more profound aspirations. He could not imagine himself living among cowboys and Al Capone, Hollywood and Benny Goodman. Aside from the work of Frank Lloyd Wright, the legendary skyscrapers, and perhaps the silos out West, there was no architecture in America he longed to see. While in Germany he was recognized and enjoyed the prestige and social status of a "Herr Professor," in America he was nobody. Here, he lived among friends, family, and familiar surroundings; there he knew no one. He did not speak English and with his "tin ear"[5] he could not imagine learning a new language a few weeks short of his fiftieth birthday. Moreover, even if he had been inclined to leave, the restrictions on doing so had now become formidable. Except for "professional purposes" approved beforehand by the Ministry of the Exterior, since August 19, members of the Prussian Academy of Arts had been forbidden to travel abroad.[6] Even if he had been able to gain such permission, only ten silver marks could legally be taken out of the country.

Leaving one's homeland is never easy. In Germany, "so false and unnatural a turn" (as emigration was described by Thomas Mann) was an especially wrenching issue, involving far more profound considerations than language deficiencies or inability to find a job. However threatened they may have been, most German cultural figures left reluctantly, according to Laura Fermi: many of those who wound up going to America had initially refused invitations.[7] Upbringing, images of self-identity and self-respect, and what Thomas Mann called the sense of "happy accord with the temper of [the] nation ... and its intellectual traditions" tended to bind its citizens to the homeland. Known as *Heimatgebund,* it was how Hirche spoke of Mies.[8] Germanness implied a profoundly intimate connection to the soil of the fatherland—"a mutually nourishing bond" in Mann's words, so obscenely distorted by the Nazi ideology of "blood and soil" (*"Blut und Boden"*).

Even among those forced to flee, leaving Germany provoked enormous resistance. "Emigration is a false way," wrote Kurt Tucholsky from exile in Sweden; slightly less than a year later he committed suicide.[9] "One doesn't change one's country like an old shirt," said Ludwig Grote, the former curator of the Dessau Municipal Gallery and a close friend of Mies and the Bauhaus, who turned down repeated requests by his wife's English mother to leave the country.[10] For his patriotism, this eminent art historian would find himself a foot soldier in Russia at the age of fifty. Ernst Cassirer, in exile, described himself as "[a] German philosopher torn from the German earth." To most Germans, life as an émigré "expropriated [and] outlawed," as Mann wrote, was unthinkable. "I am too good a German, too closely involved with the cultural traditions and language of my country for the prospect of a year-long or perhaps life-long exile not to have a hard, ominous meaning for me," Mann had written in February 1933, while out of the country on a lecture tour.[11] He was unaware as he wrote these words, that his "life-long" exile had already begun, for while still abroad he was warned not to return.

Most cultivated Germans therefore clung "with every thread to Germany," as René Schickele wrote of Mann; even Bertolt Brecht, forced to flee early in the Nazi regime, wrote, "There is no greater crime than leaving."[12] People taught since early youth to value "spiritual strength" over the easy way out, perceived running away as a failure of "character." "How unjust, how shabby, how pitiful it is to run away from here to seek one's personal safety," commented Alfred Döblin.

> How awful, to be forced into the expedient of having to escape! A shameful, dishonourable fate. Who has brought me to this?[13]

Despite continuing threats and harassments by the Nazis, Käthe Kollwitz chose to remain in Germany. "I must live by the rules," she declared.[14]

Even German Jews, humiliated, and since December 15, with the promulgation of the Nuremberg Laws, deprived of their citizenship, felt the same. As Goebbels, on November 5, 1935, boasted that "the RKK is today pure of all Jewish elements"[15] and German schoolchildren lined up to be "scientifically" measured in the government's attempt to discover pronounced Aryan types, the Jewish poet Gertrud Kolmar declared, "I do not want to flee from that to which I am inwardly committed,"[16] and Adolf Goldschmidt, the famed Ordinarius Professor of Art History in Berlin, refused to heed the urgings of his friends to leave. "He saw no reason to leave," said Philip Johnson, who met with him in 1935.[17] "Who are these stupid and limited Nazis," declared Goldschmidt,

> to tell me that I don't belong in a land where my forebears have lived for over six hundred years?[18]

But he did leave Germany in 1938, forcibly placed aboard a train to Switzerland by his friends. Gertrud Kolmar, picked up in one of the final roundups of Jews in Berlin, died in March 1943.

There seemed in fact to be none who left out of choice, out of some deep moral outrage, without financial or political impetus. Emigration was almost accidental for Albert Einstein, who was visiting the California Institute of Technology in Pasadena when Hitler became chancellor, and for Thomas Mann, who took three years to bring himself to accept the fact of his exile and make his final break with Germany; his subsequent role as an outspoken opponent of fascism often obscures his initial resistance and hesitation. George Grosz, one of Germany's most socially and artistically radical artists, was teaching in the United States in 1932 and had decided, two weeks before Hitler came to power, to settle there.[19] Paul Tillich, dismissed from his professorship in philosophy at the University of Frankfurt-am-Main when Hitler came to power because of his categorical rejection of national socialism, was invited to the Union Theological Seminary by Reinhold Niebuhr, who happened to be visiting Germany that summer.[20] Erwin Panofsky, the famed art historian, teaching at Princeton University at the time of the 1933 Enabling Act, revealed a further psychological impediment to emigration. "I had the good fortune of coming to the United States as a guest rather than a refugee," he wrote.[21]

It seemed far more preferable to those unburdened by prominence or specific Nazi persecution to seek actively to remain apolitical, to "pull one's hat down over one's eyes" and "disappear" into benign anonymity. Artists turned to advertising, photography, theatrical design, monument repair, magazine illustration, exhibition and display design, house painting, typography, color research, and art history, and spoke privately, and among trusted friends, of "painting for the drawer." Architects, even those who had studied at the Bauhaus, found employment as construction supervisors, marble salesmen, exhibition designers, and most commonly, in the busy architectural firms, such as that of Herbert Rimpl, designing and supervising the factories, aircraft hangars, and hydroelectric plants that Germany was beginning to turn out at a record pace. Of the thirty-seven German nationals associated with the Bauhaus who appeared in Eckhard Neumann's book *Bauhaus and Bauhaus People*, twenty-three remained in Germany, two were jailed, and only twelve left, one of whom left before 1930.[22]

Despite what many have come to believe, the decision to leave or to remain in Germany is no barometer of Nazi sympathy. Whether they were forced out or chose to remain, most German intellectuals (in a perplexingly schizoid manner) lauded Hitler's brilliant political achievements as they decried the more repugnant aspects of the regime, particularly the government's unprecedented interference in the cultural life of the nation. If the prominence of those who left has made their number seem larger than it was, so too has it diminished the number and personal standing of those who remained behind, often in the face of grave personal risk. For them the maxim that "opposition takes many forms,"[23] simply and absolutely did not include the option of flight from the beloved homeland.

By the summer of 1935 the rapidly rising office buildings, sports and party arenas, factories, government buildings, public housing, renovations, airfields, barracks, laboratories, industrial buildings, and *autobahnen* had turned Germany into one vast construction site. Nowhere were the building priorities of the Nazi regime more apparent than in Berlin, where Werner March's massive sports complex (for the 1936 Olympic Games), the autobahn ring around Berlin, Ernst Sagebiel's Tempelhof airport and his austere and imposing Air Force Ministry building were currently under construction. That this massive building program represented something more than the urgent need to stimulate a still-moribund economy, preparation for the upcoming Olympic Games, a specific Berlin building tradition, or the instinct of a totalitarian government to impress with stony symbols of its might became clear when Hitler revealed in his Cultural Address of September 11 that architecture "lies nearest my heart."[24] Two years after achieving national office, with his power now firm and unchallenged and the opposition destroyed, Hitler could at last reveal his architectural priorities.

There was much in his speech that was expected by now. His hostility toward modern art seemed boundless; he called it both imbecilic and criminal. Under no circumstances, Hitler declared, would the "dadaist-cubists and futurists" have any part in his "cultural renascence." Once again, apocalyptic imagery intruded on his architectural reflections. Speaking of such long-dead civilizations as Egypt, Greece, Rome, along with the Mayans, Hitler declared that

> even if the last living witnesses of such an unfortunate people have closed their mouths in death, then the stones will begin to speak.... No people lives longer than the evidence of its culture!

But, according to Hirche, it was Hitler's seemingly boundless enthusiasm for architecture that most interested Mies.[25]

> The National Socialist Movement ... is bound to strive by every means to transform its ... view into ... creative achievements ... especially ... in the field of architecture.... He who would educate a people to be proud of itself must give it visible ground for pride....
>
> [I have only] one wish and one alone ... that Providence may grant to us the great masters who shall echo in music the emotions of our soul, [and] immortalize them in stone.... [W]e need great buildings and their erection cannot be postponed. Our purposes demand their fulfillment....
>
> We realize that the cultural creations of our day, especially in the field of architecture, must be as immortal in the feeling for beauty of their proportions and relations as they are fitted to our materials employed in their construction.... [T]he artist should give to the main purpose which, as a whole the building is to serve, a form which corresponds with that purpose and brings it into clear expression.... The architect will not hesitate to use modern building materials or to employ them for artistic effect.... [T]here remain a number of modern tasks for which the past provides no examples and no models. It is precisely in these tasks that an opportunity is offered to the really gifted genius to enlarge art's form-language.[26]

To Mies it was clear that Hitler had a convincing understanding of architectural principles. Like Mies, he saw architecture as civilization's highest art form, the most significant barometer of the zeitgeist. However objectionable Hitler's other remarks might have been, Mies could find nothing to fault in the Führer's assertion that architecture brought to the people

> a conviction of [their] general and ... special high mission. ... Our cathedrals are witness to the greatness of the past; the greatness of the present will ... be measured by those creations of eternal value which it leaves as its legacy. ... [Architecture is] the imperishable creative force ... [that] raises the suffering and anxious human spirit ... above the weakness of the moment. ... [From its] flowering ... [is gained] the consciousness of a higher destiny!

However, it was difficult to reconcile this public commitment to architectural excellence with the limited experience of the youngster Speer or the pompous incompetence of a Sagebiel, whose titanic, Schinkelesque and vaguely modernist Air Force Ministry building possessed the singular virtue of minimizing the huge bulk of its director, Field Marshal Göring. To whom, then, was Hitler appealing when he issued his call to greatness; when he urged the sons of Goethe, Beethoven, and Hegel toward "supreme cultural achievements"; when he challenged "the really gifted genius to enlarge art's form-language"; and summoned "German art to new great tasks ... in the spirit of a millennial inheritance?"

With Hitler's announcement of his architectural priorities—and given the already highly visible Nazi building program—it seemed inconceivable that someone of Mies's stature could long be ignored. Although their standing had lately been diminished, Mies still had supporters within the Prussian Ministry of the Interior, as well as the RKK—as his participation at the beginning of the year in a program presented by the film section (headed by Hans Weidemann) attests.[27] As for Hitler's personal animus toward Mies's style, it no longer seemed so disturbing since the Furtwängler affair, the artistic "cause célèbre" of 1935.

Like most German intellectuals, Wilhelm Furtwängler had taken Goebbels's assurances of artistic freedom at face value, and, in a concert given in December 1934, had conducted the avant-garde German composer Paul Hindemith's "Matthis der Maler," infuriating the Nazi leadership and leading to a party outcry against him. Shaken and humiliated, Furtwängler resigned his post as director of the Berlin Philharmonic in protest, an action that was quickly picked up by the foreign press. Acutely sensitive to its accusations of cultural harassment, Rosenberg and Hitler moved quickly to reinstate the renowned conductor, who was rumored to have accepted the directorship of the Philadelphia Orchestra. Hitler's appearance at a Beethoven concert conducted by Furtwängler in Munich in June 1935, and Furtwängler's appointment as director of the 1936 Bayreuth season signaled the conductor's resurrection.

The Furtwängler incident was widely reported and discussed, both at home and abroad. According to Hirche, Mies saw himself as being much like Furtwängler. "They were the same rank," said Hirche, "and in much the same situation."[28] The lessons of the Furtwängler affair seemed clear. Not only were the Nazis intensely sensitive to anything that might blemish Germany's cultural image; they intended to use the international prestige of its cultural figures to enhance their own. Surely it appeared that they did not wish to lose any more of them—a Mies van der Rohe no less than a Wilhelm Furtwängler. Most significantly, it seemed clear that despite the occasional and undeniable forays into abominable stupidities, the Nazis would ultimately—by the sheer weight of public pressure—be forced to pursue a course of moderation, culturally as well as artistically.

On January 27, 1936 Mies wrote to Mills College declining its invitation.[29] Berlin was his home, Germany his country, and here—like Furtwängler—he intended to stay.

CHAPTER 15

"IT IS TIME . . ."

I DO NOT GO TO CHURCH TO HEAR THE SERVICE. I ONLY LOOK
AT THE BEAUTY OF THE BUILDING.

(Adolf Hitler)

In 1936 the peculiar connection between construction and
destruction that existed in Hitler's mind began to reveal itself,
as his architectural programs began to appear, so too emerged
his plans for war. The first manifestation of this phenomenon
was the 1936 Olympic Games, which Germany was hosting,
an event that, with its husbanding of resources and massive
coordination of the population, Hitler seems to have viewed as
practice and metaphor for war, as his New Year's Eve address to
the nation makes clear.

> How much good-will, how much time, hard work, and
> personal sacrifice on the part of thousands of Germans . . .
> have been necessary in the past year to—yes—to right the
> battle that we now have behind us and to prepare for the
> coming decisive warfare of the new year.[1]

249

The Olympiad was to be, in Goebbels's words, "the year's greatest national undertaking," and the nation's entire resources, financial as well as propagandistic, were unleashed on its behalf.[2] An unremitting radio and press campaign exhorted everyone to "do his part to make it a success": every citizen was made to see himself as a soldier for the Reich.[3] In a display of Teutonic thoroughness, the entire country was mobilized to play the perfect host for the Winter Games, scheduled for February in Garmisch-Partenkirchen, and the summer events in August in Berlin.

No detail seemed to be overlooked. Bands were provided with rubber sheet music that could not be washed away by rain or wet snowfall; glass coverings were provided over typewriters to keep correspondents' fingers warm. In an effort to spare foreign sensibilities, spectators were urged to wear civilian clothes and leave the military uniforms at home. Signs announcing "Aryan wool" and "Aryan cheese" and "Jews Not Wanted Here" were removed; and copies of Julius Streicher's viciously anti-Semitic paper *Der Stürmer* were nowhere to be seen.

On February 6, with six loudspeakers booming his words to the 50,000 spectators and nearly 1,600 athletes, Hitler declared the games open. The stunning spectacle of the opening had pleased him—the playing of "Deutschland über Alles," the national anthem, before the respectful silence of the crowds; the brightly garbed athletes parading smartly, country by country, to the vigorous strains of his favorite tune "The Badenweiler March"; the sight of the swastika flying briskly next to the Olympic banner and the flags of the twenty-eight participating nations; the flame of the Olympic torch appearing, at the sound of his words, high above the stadium; the ringing of the Olympic bell, answered by all the church bells of Garmisch; the boom of the cannon that had been lugged into the arena by oxen; the dirgelike solemnity of the Olympic hymn; Willi Bogner, the German skier, high on the steps of the fir-bedecked rostrum, taking the Olympic oath on behalf of the athletes, his right arm raised high in the Olympic salute that bore so striking a resemblance to that of the Nazis'; the cheers, yelling, clapping, and "Heils" of the crowd that echoed down from the mountains. As the athletes paraded out of the stadium, it did not go unnoticed that Herr Reichsführer Hitler, his tiny mustache white with snow, was smiling.[4] The rest of the world seemed equally entranced. Gustavus Town Kirby, the treasurer of the American Olympic Committee, "almost waxed poetic" when he returned from Germany. Calling the facilities "the best he ever saw," he also said that he found

> no sign of anti-Semitism. . . . I saw no discrimination whatsoever, but I am willing to let the others tell what they saw. I am confident that not a single person at Garmisch will bring back a report other than I have.[5]

One month later, Hitler opened his war on a more literal front. At dawn on the morning of March 7, over the objections of his high command and with a grave risk of war, he ordered German troops to occupy the Rhineland, which had been declared a neutral zone by the 1925 Locarno Treaty (based on the Versailles Treaty's prohibition of German fortification and military force in the area). Although he faced French troops that greatly outnumbered the small German force that crossed the Rhine, as well as the possibility of British intervention, Hitler was encouraged to take this bold course by France's failure to act upon his announcement on March 16, 1935 of German conscription, a violation of Article V of the Versailles Treaty. Contrary to the opinion of his general staff, Hitler was convinced that France would once again refrain from calling Germany to task. At ten o'clock that morning the ambassadors of Britain, France, Belgium, and Italy, the four Locarno powers, were notified that the Reich considered French ratification of a pact with the Soviet Union on February 29 a violation of the letter and spirit of the Locarno Treaty and that henceforth Germany no longer felt bound by it. Disguising his provocative actions behind aggrieved and conciliatory phrases—a technique he had brought to perfection—Hitler audaciously proposed a new nonaggression treaty. At high noon, with German and French troops facing each other for the third time in less than a century, Hitler, who did not yet know the outcome of his risky venture, announced to a hysterically cheering Reichstag that German troops were already in the Rhineland. Unlike the pale and obviously agitated members of the Reichswehr high command, Hitler betrayed no sign that these were, as he later said, "the most nerve-wracking [hours] in my life."[6]

Three French divisions moved near the German frontier; but Hitler, convinced that the French would not march, rejected the recommendations of his nervous and wavering high command to pull back. And indeed, responding to British as well as domestic pressures, France did not march. The four Locarno powers, citing the German remilitarization of the Rhineland as a "clear violation" of the Locarno and Versailles treaties, appealed instead to the League of Nations. With this single, bold, and undeniably brilliant stroke, Hitler clearly demonstrated the lack of resolve on the part of both France and Britain to impede his schemes. Militarily, as well as politically, he proved the superiority of his judgment over that of the hallowed Reichswehr. He had raised a triumphantly resurgent Germany from the ashes of defeat to resume its role as a sovereign nation, an equal among the continental powers, its wretched humiliation avenged; and in so doing, he had united a wavering, disillusioned, and discontented nation. It was indeed—as he was later to claim—"the most daring of all his undertakings."[7]

Immediately after the success of his Rhineland venture was apparent, and ostensibly seeking the approval of the German people for his party's performance over the past three years, but actually wishing to secure approbation of his new, aggressive foreign policy, as well as affirmation of his right to say that he alone spoke for the nation, Hitler ordered a plebiscite for March 29. With only one legal party (the formation of any party outside national socialism, as well as criticism of the party or any of its representatives was illegal), one ticket, and one way to vote, the results, offering little more than an expression of faith in Hitler, were assured. In this demonstration of what the Nazis called "ennobled democracy," the outcome mattered less than the margin of victory. Nothing less than a 90 percent majority would satisfy Hitler: warnings of the Führer's "wish" were passed to Nazi officials in charge of the campaign.

With these officials' own careers at stake and with the entire propaganda apparatus of the state at their disposal, the campaign assumed an intensity and dimension that dwarfed all previous Nazi electoral efforts. Local party officials worked

ceaselessly to get out the vote in their districts, not hesitating
to use intimidation and harassment.[8] Slogans blanketed the
country. "Germany is Free!" proclaimed huge posters. "In a
world of burning convents, rebellions, and war, only Germany
is an island of peace!" "The Führer asks you," declared enormous streamers, "Do you know what it means to see your
dearest ones starving and cold?" Huge signs appeared wherever
a new road was being built. "Thanks to the Führer, we are
building here!" Loudspeakers roared in railroad stations everywhere. "The Führer is Freedom, Honor, Peace, and Bread!" It
was more than being pressured: one felt inundated, over-
whelmed, as before some cataclysmic force of nature. Even
foreigners spoke of feeling intimidated and undermined.[9]

Mies's own circumstances were as disheartening as those
around him as he approached his fiftieth birthday on March 27.
Correctly anticipating that this important milestone would be
ignored within Germany, Lilly Reich, in a letter of February 12
to J. J. P. Oud in Holland, asked for his help.

> Mies has his fiftieth birthday on March 27, and for all sorts
> of reasons it would be desirable and nice if in one or
> another of the foreign professional journals some notice of
> it could be made. . . . [Things are] not easy for us.[10]

On the 27th, Mies and Lilly Reich celebrated his birthday with
a small group of friends that included Ludwig Grote and the
painter Max Beckmann along with their wives, Ludwig
Hilbersheimer, and Herbert Hirche. All were "politically suspect" owing to their association with modernism—unable to
stay and unwilling to leave, their precarious lives hovering
between insensate inertia and profoundest gloom—and what
should have been a festive occasion proved somber and
depressed.[11]

Grote—art historian, befriender of the Bauhaus, and of
Mies—had a young family to support and was desperately
seeking work. In order to secure museum (and hence state-
supported) work in Berlin, he had begun to think of ways to
make himself politically acceptable. Before making such a
commitment, he had asked a friend with access to party

records to look up his file to see if there was anything that might prove damaging to his efforts. After doing so, his friend reported,

> Forget it! Forget about ever doing anything as long as this government's in power![12]

No longer content to pursue only those who opposed them, the Nazis were now turning against those who simply wished to stand aside. Beckmann too was beginning to find the pressure intolerable. He had been out of work for three years—having lost his teaching position at the Städel Academy in Frankfurt in 1933—and his wife was urging him to leave for Holland, where her sister was married to a Dutchman. Like Mies and Grote (whose mother-in-law was still urging him to come to England), Beckmann was reluctant to leave. But how much longer he could hold out, he did not know.

The main topic of discussion that evening as it passed from hand to hand was a letter Mies had recently received from Armour Institute of Technology in Chicago, inviting him to consider becoming head of its architecture school.[13] As with the earlier offer from Mills College, neither Mies nor his friends had heard of the school or of the writer of the letter, John A. Holabird, Sr.

Holabird was, in fact, a partner in the Chicago architectural firm of Holabird and Root. Along with Jerome Loebl, a young Chicago architect, and other prominent local architectural figures, he had been appointed by Henry Heald, President of Armour Institute, to an advisory committee to find a new director for the department of architecture—an individual who, they hoped, would revive the rather down-at-the-heels, traditional school. The committee had considered several American prospects, none of whom—for one reason or another—had worked out.[14] Mies's name had appeared frequently on the lists of potential candidates submitted by architects across the country. He was not known to anyone on the committee personally, however, nor were any of them familiar with his work. One day, Loebl and Holabird spotted David Adler coming down the steps of the Art Institute and decided to stop and ask this well-known residential architect what he knew of Mies van der Rohe.[15] Adler was "exceedingly enthusiastic" about Mies, referring to him, according to Loebl, as a "truly great architect."[16] Without a moment's hesitation, Adler took the two men into the Burnham Library, where he showed them photographs of the Barcelona Pavilion—the very building that had ended Mies's career in Germany. Loebl and Holabird now became as enthusiastic as Adler and upon further inquiry and discussions with some Americans who had studied with Mies, they decided to explore his availability.[17]

March 20, 1936

Dear Sir:

We have in Chicago an Architectural School forming a part of the Armour Institute of Technology. The School is housed by itself in the Art Institute of Chicago, has 100 to 120 students and is, by reason of its location, more or less independent of Armour Institute.

The Trustees and President of Armour Institute are very anxious to secure the best available head for the Architectural School with the idea of making it the finest school in this country. . . .

. . . In talking the matter over with the Advisory Committee, I thought that as we were considering the possibility of a European heading this school that I would like to ask if you would, under any conditions, consider such an appointment. I am, of course, a great admirer of your work and if we are to consider the best I would naturally turn to you first.

The School itself can be made anything that the proper man might wish; he would have a free hand with the authorities of the Institution. He could organize the School in such a manner that he could establish his private practice. . . .

. . . Please pardon me if I seem presumptuous in even suggesting such a position to you. It may be that you could recommend someone who might consider coming to this country.

Yours truly,
John A. Holabird (signed)[18]

Characteristically—with an indifference that had struck Weidemann as it had infuriated his Bauhaus students—Mies exhibited no reaction to the offer. Considering the precipitous decline he had suffered—a tobogganlike slide that had brought individuals such as Grote and Beckmann to the point of collapse—Mies retained an astonishing, if only slightly saddened, tranquillity—like some invincible seer locked into his own golden dreams who gazed distractedly at the travail of a pitifully distressed humanity from the distant and exhilarating heights of paradise. Like his immutable architecture that so disdainfully ignored the vagaries of place and clime, Mies—as committed as ever to his certainties—remained remarkably insulated from the melancholia of the day. Requiring little more than solitude, wine, and good cigars, he had settled into a disconsolate immobility, content to sustain himself on those meager wisps of reality of which enough remained even in the worst of times to justify continued hope.

Extraordinary building activity was turning 1936 into a surprisingly good time for architects. While most of the work was government-sponsored and hence unprocurable for Mies, ideological consistency seemed to be counting for less and less each day.[19] Ernst Sagebiel, Mendelsohn's mediocre associate, continued to receive lavish commissions from Göring. Baldur von Schirach, head of the Nazi Jugend (who, because of his American mother and aristocratic background, considered himself more "advanced" than most of his party compatriots) had recently gone on public record as favoring the more "youthful" style of glass, steel, and concrete for his organization's buildings.[20] A letter to Mies from Gustav Stotz, secretary of the German Werkbund in Baden-Württenberg and a friend of his since about 1927, referring to the publication of this speech in the *Frankfurter Zeitung*, indicates that Mies was aware of his comments.[21] It was not too farfetched to believe that with his deeper involvement in foreign affairs, Hitler would have to participate less in architectural matters, no matter how close they were to his heart. Given the regime's much-touted desire for German supremacy in all areas, it seemed to Mies only a question of time before the country had to turn to him.[22] His cautious optimism is perhaps reflected in the comments of

Sergius Ruegenberg, Mies's young assistant, which appeared in a letter to the editors of *Bauwelt*.

> Today, at a time when stylistic forms are the object of renewed interest . . . I would like to remind you of Mies van der Rohe.[23]

However, Lilly Reich, far shrewder in her appraisal than Mies, rejected such speculation as wishful thinking.[24] Strong-willed and totally dedicated to Mies, certain that her purpose in life was to guide, inspire, goad, and support him, she was more determined than ever that he had to get out of Germany. Of stoical disposition, she had long ago accepted his irritability and periodic need to escape from his dependency on her.[25] Demanding neither notice nor appreciation, she had learned to ignore the pain caused her by the often resentful way in which Mies acquiesced to their relationship.[26] Alone, she was but one designer among many: with Mies, she had, in more ways than one, touched eternity. More than anyone, she understood his need for the "stuff" of building—the bricks, the grit, the sheen of steel and glass—and his discomfort in the role of theoretician. As others needed to breathe, Mies needed to build. In her eyes, the offer from Chicago seemed both generous and timely. She was determined that neither Mies's indolent nature nor his endless rationalizations be allowed to impede what she clearly saw as being in his best interest.[27] Three months earlier he had turned down Mills; she would not let him act so unwisely again.

While the more than 98 percent majority for Hitler announced by the Propaganda Ministry as a result of the March 29 plebiscite was dismissed by most Western observers as little more than an elaborate and costly farce, to Hitler (his inability to distinguish between fact and fiction as marked as ever) it could hardly have been more satisfying. In his mind public approbation, no matter how falsely secured, vindicated his acts, no matter how illegal. But the plebiscite results offered more than proof of German solidarity behind him; they transformed him into a Christlike embodiment of the spirit, the will, the very soul of Germany. "Adolf Hitler *is* Germany!" declared Goebbels;[28] while Göring spoke of Hitler's rise as being nothing less than a "national miracle" through which a "resurrected" nation found itself again and for whom

> [p]rophets went up and down the land and awakened the people.[29]

The deification of Hitler had begun, and the National Socialist party itself receded into the background. To oppose Hitler had become more than an act of almost superhuman moral assurance, more than simply an unpatriotic deed, or one even of blundering stupidity. It had become a moral sin, a heresy; and the nation of Kant and Hegel became a nation not of reason but of unquestioning faith and eager martyrdom.

While for some, Hitler's apocalyptic vision bore the unequivocal imprint of the most demonic and depraved sort of orthodoxy, others saw in it the unmistakable, and no less frightening, specter of war. For Hitler himself, as had been true since his youth in Linz, the blurring of fantasy and reality, the threats of brimstone and fire, of redemption through vengeance and suffering, of death and transfiguration evoked nothing less than a splendid and chilling prologue to architecture. "It is time to build," he said to an astonished and mystified Speer sometime in April, his sapphire-blue eyes sparkling brightly. He did not mean the roads, the factories, the workers' housing, the government and party buildings that were turning Germany into a single, vast building site, but—in his words— "the greatest of all" plans,[30] the expression and culmination of his now supreme and indestructible Third Reich: the rebuilding of Berlin.

Although it eventually came to be known as *his* Berlin project, the city's need for major renewal long preceded Hitler's coming to power. It was based as much on the frenetic pace of Berlin's growth, its rapid industrialization and need for housing at the turn of the century, as on the circumlocutions of its difficult site, located along the broadly meandering Spree River. With its basic street pattern laid out in 1862, when it was a provincial capital, Berlin's urbanization had not kept pace with the needs of a modern twentieth-century metropolis

that had become an industrial, cultural, and national administrative center. Huge railroad stations, built in the midst of the
city, linked Berlin with the rest of the country, while commu-
nication within the city—most notably between its northern
and southern sectors—was virtually nonexistent. Recognition
of Berlin's need for urban reorganization began as early as
1910. In 1917, in an effort to solve what had already become a
near strangulation of circulation, Martin Mächler proposed a
reorganization of Berlin along its north-south axis, the thor-
oughfare thus created to be lined with administrative and commercial buildings; a plan shown in a Berlin exposition in 1927.
Seen by Hitler at that time, it formed the basis for his own
plans. Although the various schemes for urban renewal formed
a major concern of Berlin architects and civic authorities
throughout the 1920s and involved many of Germany's most
renowned architects, including Mies (see his 1928 proposal for
the renewal of Alexanderplatz),[31] most of them never got off
the ground, but for various workers' housing projects, one of
which was Mies's Afrikanischestrasse apartment house built
in 1926–27.

Hitler initially became involved in the plans for Berlin eight
months after coming to power, when he attended a meeting on
September 19, 1933 between the representatives of the Reichs-
bahn and the Berlin municipal authorities. They had convened
to discuss the creation of a north-south railroad line and
attempt to resolve the conflict between the needs and demands
of the railroad and those of the city planners.[32] At this meeting,
Hitler instructed the authorities to come up with a plan to
create a north-south road to be situated west of the Branden-
berg Gate and to make certain that their plans for the recon-
struction of Berlin were appropriate to

> the creation of a capital city of hitherto undreamed-of
> display [and to give it the appearance] . . . of a sublime
> metropolis.[33]

Although he did not yet reveal the scope of his intentions,
Hitler envisioned his "Great Development Plan" for Berlin as
an opportunity to express architecturally the might and
worldly ambitions of the Reich. "What is ugly in Berlin," he
later told Speer,

we shall suppress. Nothing will be too good for the beau-
tification of Berlin. When one enters the Reich Chancellery, one should have the feeling that one is visiting the
master of the world. One will arrive there along wide
avenues containing the Triumphal Arch, the Pantheon [the
domed hall], the Square of the People—things to take your
breath away. Our only rival in the world is Rome and we
shall succeed in eclipsing it. It will be built on such a scale
that St. Peter's and its square will seem like toys in comparison. . . . Berlin must change its face for its great new
mission. . . . It will be the capital of the world—comparable only to ancient Egypt, Babylon or Rome. . . . Paris will
be nothing compared to this![34]

Ignoring the city's critical urban problems, much as he had
done in his youthful architectural schemes, Hitler's plans for
Berlin consisted of the construction of two monumental structures, an overscaled arch of triumph and an equally megalithic
domed assembly hall—preliminary versions of which he had
designed ten years earlier during his Landsberg imprisonment.
"I've always saved them," Hitler later told Speer.

I never doubted that some day I would build these two
edifices.[35]

These two gargantuan structures were to be linked by a vast
"via triumphalis," modeled after Paris's Champs Élysées.[36]
Six months later, in March 1934, the plan, which included
the north-south road that he had demanded and which would
form his "via triumphalis"—essentially an elaboration of
Mächler's earlier design—was presented to Hitler and
accepted. It was not until a later series of meetings that Hitler
gradually revealed the staggering scale of his intentions. His
north-south avenue was to be three miles long and 130 yards
wide—"[W]e'll make ours seventy-odd feet wider [than the
Champs Élysées]," declared Hitler[37]—capped at its north by
the great domed Assembly Hall, the city's dominant structure
(into whose vast space of about 410,000 square feet, St. Peter's
cathedral could fit several times over and which could hold
more than 150,000 people), and at the south by the enormous

Arch of Triumph, 386 feet high, 550 feet wide, and 392 feet deep. Dedicated to "the unvanquished army of the world war," the Arch of Triumph—into whose granite flanks were to be inscribed the names of all the 1,800,000 Germans who had perished in World War I—offered a graphic demonstration of Hitler's compulsive need to unite death with the creative act of building. To carry out these monstrous plans, as well as to create a new municipal supervisory authority, Hitler, at a meeting with the city authorities in July 1934, requested a yearly allocation of 60 million reichsmarks for each of twenty years. Even Julius Lippert, mayor of Berlin and an old party member, could not bring himself to accept such a monstrous scheme that not only trampled over the city's very real and urgent needs, but whose megalomaniacal scale was unsuited to the city, of questionable artistic merit, and whose costs, even under the best of circumstances, were astronomical. Although meetings continued to take place over the course of the next two years, neither side would budge.[38] By April 1936, invigorated by his flirtations with war and political triumphs and fed up with the resistance displayed by the city authorities, Hitler had begun to toy with the notion of removing the plans from their control and proceeding independently. His remarks to Speer that "it is time to build" indicate that he no longer intended to be thwarted.

While it is highly unlikely that someone as distant from Hitler's immediate circle as Mies would have known of his intentions—neither Weidemann, Mies, nor anyone close to Mies, such as Hirche, the Grotes, or members of his family, ever gave any indication that he knew of Hitler's intentions at this time—it is not unreasonable to assume that the impasse between Hitler and the city authorities over the renewal plans for Berlin would have been known within professional circles, especially by someone as prominent as Mies, who had participated in its projects before. Despite the Führer's professed interest in architecture, it seemed unlikely—given the circumstances of the day—that he could devote much attention to urban renewal or to the architects involved in it. But the effect of any possible knowledge that Mies might have had of Hitler's plans, as well as his own personal inclinations, seems to have been outweighed by Frau Reich's determination that he should leave; and on April 20 (coincidentally, Hitler's birthday) he responded by wire to John Holabird:

> Thanks for letter. Am interested. Letter to follow.
> Mies van der Rohe.[39]

Except perhaps in his own architecture, never had so little hidden so much. Crafted with the same painstaking intensity that marked Mies's architecture, its lack of definite commitment spoke of a lingering ambivalence, while its taut spareness revealed nothing of Mies's desperate plight, the agonizing deliberation, nor the searing personal consequences that now confronted the determined, but weary Lilly Reich.

And so, in April 1936, three years into his regime, as Germany's leader focused a renewed attention on architecture, the country's leading architect—the one individual capable of successfully realizing his vast architectural schemes—was forced, by circumstances that defied both logic and imagination and against his will and inclination, to turn away.

CHAPTER 16

THE OLYMPIC SPIRIT

ONLY A DETERMINED DEAF-AND-BLIND VISITOR TO ANY COR-
NER OF THIS LAND COULD FAIL TO SEE AND HEAR THE SIGHT,
THE SOUND OF GERMANY'S FORWARD MARCH.

(Janet Flanner)

It was not until May 20, six weeks after he had received the
offer, that Mies sent a letter to Holabird. Concisely written, the
letter simply, but firmly, detailed his demands.

Dear Sir:

My answer to your letter of March 20 is thus delayed
through the circumstances of my having been away from
Berlin.[1] On April 20 I sent you a cable to let you at least
know of my interest in your proposal. Today I wish to
thank you sincerely for the confidence you have shown
in me.

I was interested to learn of your plans for reorganization
of your Institute's architectural school and of its promise. I
welcome your intentions, as I am certain of their justness
and worth. They have led me to follow up your suggestions
and earnestly to deliberate the thought of guiding such a
school.

Since by reasons of my experience, I have certain definite conceptions about the organization of a school of architecture, I would like to know more particulars about the present structure of the school, so that I might gain a wider view of possible supplements and changes in the course of instruction. Would you therefore be kind enough to let me have such particulars, together with a prospectus and the curriculum hitherto followed. I would also like to know whether additions and reorganization of the teaching staff may be possible, the extent of the present budget of the school, whether practical workshops for training purposes can be found and finally, the relation, if any, of the architectural school to the Art Institute.

... I also consider it definitely in the interest of the school that I carry on my private practice. Would you let me know something of the possibilities and outlook on this point.

Again I want to express sincere thanks for your confidence in wishing to entrust the school to me. I should like to take over the work, however, only if the possibility is there to find a basically new form for such a school, in keeping with the spirit of the times.

Yours truly,
Mies van der Rohe (Signed)[2]

Sober and reasonable, the letter was hardly the anxious response of someone with his back against the wall, grasping at any opportunity to leave Germany. In fact, the pressure to leave had probably lessened thanks to an important commission Mies had recently received from his long-standing patron Hermann Lange, president of the Association of German Silk and Velvet Manufacturers and of the Verseidag group,[3] who had invited Mies to participate in a major textile exhibition that the association was planning for the spring of 1937.[4]

For the languishing and dejected architect, this offer came as a godsend. Not only was it an important commission, both challenging and financially rewarding, but it gave him an almost unique opportunity to work beyond the constraints of what had become a maddeningly harassing bureaucracy—no mean achievement in Germany in 1936. For as part of the Nazis' ceaseless efforts to bring all cultural activities under their control, the Reich Chamber of Fine Arts (the RBK) was proposing legislation (that would be enacted on July 29) requiring the approval by one of their local representatives of all building plans submitted to the *Baupolizei;* an architect's refusal to heed the demands of the building authorities could entail loss of professional membership, and hence the ability to practice architecture. Mies thus brought to this commission not only his usual diligent attention and meticulous concentration, but a very special joy. It opened significant new possibilities for him in his homeland, and perhaps made him more willful and independent in negotiations with Armour than he might otherwise have been.

Autocratic by nature, and unfamiliar with the more collegial practices of American institutions, Mies had been taken aback by the letter of May 12 that he had received from Armour's president, Willard E. Hotchkiss, confirming Holabird's offer, but advising him that a final offer could only be made by the Board of Trustees.[5] Although Hotchkiss's comments were assuredly pro forma, Mies appears to have been offended. In an undated letter—its tone markedly different from his earlier one—Mies, somewhat testily, notes that the changes that he has in mind for the curriculum

> would have to be so fundamental as to extend beyond the present setup of [your] architecture department.[6]

Although Hotchkiss was quick to reassure the skittish architect, Mies appears to have lost his taste for Armour and turned the focus of his attention to offers from the Museum of Modern Art in New York and Harvard University.

On June 20, 1936, Mies received a visit from Alfred Barr, director of the Museum of Modern Art, who had come to Berlin to see if he was interested in designing the museum's proposed new building.[7] In Europe that summer to collect material for the museum's upcoming surrealist exhibition, Barr had also been entrusted by the Board of Trustees to speak to several architects, including J. J. P. Oud in Holland, Gropius in London, and Mies. In addition, Barr was also entrusted with another task while in Europe—a mission shrouded in secrecy, according to Henry-Russell Hitchcock, who was with him in London at the time.[8] He was supposed to inquire whether any of these men were interested in heading Harvard University's new Graduate School of Design, in preparation for a more formal interview being planned by Dean Joseph Hudnut for later that summer.[9] Mies seems to have been genuinely excited by the prospect of designing the new building. "Your museum plans interest me," he wrote to Barr, "it could be a rare and wonderful assignment."[10]

Always more comfortable in his role of craftsman-builder than as "Herr Professor," there is a feeling of spontaneity and simple delight in Mies's note to Barr that is notably missing in his correspondence with Armour and subsequently with Harvard, as well as in his often strained and vague theoretical statements.

With regard to his mission from the museum, Barr felt strongly that the institution that had literally introduced modern architecture to America and made modernism's cause its own should commission one of the great modernist architects when the time came to build for itself. Having had difficulties with Frank Lloyd Wright and Le Corbusier over the International Style show, Barr had, from the start, excluded them as being too hard to work with.[11] That left Oud, Gropius, and Mies, whom the museum's building committee authorized Barr to contact. Barr's own personal choice was Mies, to whom he referred as "possibly the world's finest architect"[12] in a letter written in July to Abby Aldrich Rockefeller, one of the museum's founders and one of the board members who wanted to hire an American architect.[13] Other members of the board also seriously questioned his choice.

"Why do you prefer foreign architects, Mr. Barr?" asked one.

"No," he replied, "not foreign, distinguished."[14]

Unable to reconcile himself to the thought of a foreign architect designing the facade of a leading American institution, Nelson Rockefeller, a member of the building committee and son of Abby Aldrich Rockefeller, remained unconvinced. With Barr in Europe and unavailable to argue his case, Rockefeller took it upon himself to find another architect and turned to Philip Lipincott Goodwin, an architect and fellow board member, whose affiliation with modernism stemmed more from his taste in art than his architectural style.[15] Apparently suffering second thoughts, Rockefeller, at the suggestion of Wallace K. Harrison, a longtime friend and codesigner with Raymond Hood of Rockefeller Center, induced the board to hire as his associate Edward D. Stone, a thirty-four-year-old architect who had worked with him as principal designer of the Radio City Music Hall and had won some renown as the designer of a 1933 home known as the first International Style residence in the East.[16]

On July 17, a wire was sent to Barr in Paris, advising him of the board's decision. In a letter of July 19—five days after Mies had expressed his pleasure over the possible commission—Barr had to withdraw his offer. "I have tried very hard to have our museum bring you to America as collaborating architect on our new building," wrote Barr,

> but I am afraid I shall not succeed. Believe me, I am very disappointed in my defeat. It has been a hard battle.[17]

Barr encouraged him to continue with his plans to come to America, and expressed hope

> for a favorable outcome to your conversation with Dean Hudnut.

Involved at the moment in the Textile Exhibition, and reluctant, in his heart, to leave Germany in any case, Mies—rather characteristically—appears to have taken the loss of the museum commission in his stride. But, another reason for his lack of response—far more speculative—may have been his being offered an opportunity to participate in the massive Berlin renewal project, which had reached an exasperating impasse between Hitler and the city authorities in the spring of 1936. While the evidence for Mies's possible involvement is scanty and circumstantial, several individuals who knew Mies well but did not know each other, and whose versions vary only slightly, frequently asserted that he was, suggesting that he may indeed have been offered a role in this major architectural project. His daughter Georgia mentioned this offer in a personal interview[18] and again in a biographical film that she prepared with Mies's assistance and participation.[19] It was also mentioned by officials at Verseidag in Krefeld[20] and in a letter from Jerome Loebl, the Chicago architect instrumental in inviting Mies to Armour, who wrote

> [A]s I understand it, [the Berlin job] was offered to Mies before Speer got the assignment.[21]

Given Hitler's distaste for modernistic public buildings, and his special antagonism toward Mies, as well as his intense involvement in this project, on the surface the possibility of such an offer appears little short of ludicrous: one is inclined to ascribe the suggestion of Mies's involvement to the bitter imaginings of a disillusioned and proud artist forever unable to come to terms with his country's rejection. Yet, one can also imagine the reprobation to which the normally reticent Mies would have exposed himself had he admitted his willingness to participate in so morally questionable an affair. "It would have been the kiss of death," commented Speer, not without a touch of irony, when advised of Mies's potential involvement.[22] Thus, despite the absence of objective corroborative evidence, the persistence of these comments invites consideration.

Although Hitler undoubtedly believed himself capable of redesigning Berlin (as he had done earlier with Linz and Vienna), even he understood that limitations of time precluded his doing so. Also, he was not much interested in the project beyond his avenue and two major structures;[23] and he was more than willing to leave the details to someone else—with, of course, his supervision. As early as 1934, when Lippert had first suggested the establishment of a separate planning office to handle the Berlin reurbanization program, Hitler—still believing he would be working with the city administration—had been trying to come up with the name of an appropriate architect to head it. Had Troost been alive, he would have been his first choice, Hitler told Lippert.[24] Schultze-Naumburg was out of the question; and he needed someone more malleable than either German Bestelmeyer or Paul Schmitthenner, two architects whose severe and sternly monumental public style was in keeping with the national socialist image. Speer was young and unproven; and Hitler was unsure if he had the experience and ability to handle so vast a project.[25] Before considering Speer, he wanted to see how he handled the design of the party's buildings in Nuremberg, a commission that Hitler had assigned to him in 1934. By June 1936, his mind was still not made up; at this time he showed Speer his plans for the city with no mention of giving him the commission (although he did mention the difficulties he was having with the city government).[26] Several weeks later—the exact date is unknown—Hitler, apparently fed up with Lippert's recalcitrance, "tersely" sent for Speer and gave him the assignment, telling the startled young architect

> There's nothing to be done with the city government. From now on you make the plans. . . . When you have something ready, show it to me.[27]

At this time no one—neither Lippert, the city officials, nor even Speer—appeared to realize that Hitler was removing the plans from municipal authority. In their eyes, he was simply appointing Speer to head a department that had been proposed two years before. During the fall of 1936, the various parties—city officials, ministry heads, and the chancellery—were still arguing over the nature and jurisdiction of this Office of Urban Renewal.[28] How independent from the city government Hitler intended this department to be was not made clear until January 30, 1937, with his public announcement of Speer's appointment. In addition, several members of the city council were concerned over Speer's competence to handle a project whose nature and scope could only be compared to those of Friedrich Wilhelm III and Schinkel 119 years earlier.

It is possible that others involved in the negotiations were as frustrated as Hitler. By the end of June, when Hitler turned over the plans to Speer, numerous individuals—party, municipal, and cultural—had come in contact with the proposal. In a city so much of whose scale and character had been determined by Friedrich Wilhelm III and Schinkel, it was understandable that Hitler's scheme should bring to mind the historic collaboration between a Prussian ruler and the leading architect of the day. While Hitler doubtlessly envisioned himself as both generous patron and inspired architect—seeing in the young Speer little more than a willing and eager instrument of his own architectural genius—others, ignorant of the Führer's architectural obsessions, might understandably have thought otherwise. And to those neither dependent on party favor, nor seduced by party rhetoric, possessing a modicum of aesthetic discernment, only one German architect—a true "Schinkelschüler"—possessed talent, skill, experience, and stature equal to the magnitude of such a project—Mies van der Rohe.

Who Mies's "sponsor" was remains unknown. Given Hitler's distaste for modernism in general, and for Mies in particular, it seems unlikely that such an offer would come from any party official close to him, or—given Goebbels's awareness of Hitler's disposition—from within the Propaganda Ministry. Neither Weidemann nor Speer knew anything about the offer. However unaware of Hitler's personal architectural predilections such a sponsor may have been, he was certainly in a high enough bureaucratic position to know of the plans, and a person of sophisticated architectural discernment, relatively independent of Nazi dogma. Speer has speculated that the offer might have come from Finance Minister Popitz, later condemned for the July 20 assassination attempt of Hitler, who—even in these early years—"stood in a kind of opposition to Hitler."[29] Perhaps the offer came from someone within the Prussian Ministry of Culture, under whose aegis the Berlin Building Commission functioned and where, according to Weidemann, Mies had many "friends."[30] Or, in an effort to temper Hitler's overzealous and unrealistic plans, someone within the city bureaucracy may have approached Mies. The timing of the offer remains as speculative as its sponsor. It seems likely to have occurred around June or July of 1936, when the deadlock between the city and Hitler seemed at its height and concerned city (or perhaps even party) authorities desperately sought an alternative to the unofficially appointed and inexperienced Speer. The total absence of documentation or drawings, either from Mies or government sources, suggests that the offer did not advance very far.

By now, according to Georgia, Mies was aware of how the Nazis operated. He well understood that his association with so significant an official project might prove embarrassing to the government and was prepared to allow a less controversial architect to "sign off" the design.[31] Such matters were unimportant to him: his name was not what made his architecture. What he was not prepared to do, however, was compromise his style ... which was precisely what was demanded. According to Georgia, Mies's unknown sponsor demanded that Mies "not use so much glass and steel," restrictions which Mies found totally unacceptable.

Hungry for work, financially troubled, excited by the monumental scope of the project, and indifferent to the moral credentials of its sponsors, Mies felt honored to have been considered, but dishonored by the terms. The man whose slowness of action and thought was legendary, turned the offer down at once—"[a]nything less than perfection is unacceptable," he would later say[32]—and Mies's latest association with the replanning of Berlin did not extend beyond the preliminary stage. If he could not follow the "Geheimer Oberbaurath," as Schinkel was known, in the glory of his country's praises, Mies would be content to follow simply in the glory of his art. In the face of defeat, the beckonings of a distant and foreign America were transformed into a seductive siren's song.

A mood of collective euphoria gripped Berlin during the summer of 1936, as the city eagerly awaited the opening of the Summer Olympic Games on August 1. If anything, German preparations had exceeded those of the previous winter. A civic cleanup—described by *The New York Times* as unparalleled in history—had been going on for the past two years. The city was scoured, scrubbed, decked out with new buntings and flower beds; new linden trees were planted along the broad center pathway of the Unter den Linden. Even German domination of the number of medals was assured. The night before the opening—in a perverted expression of the "Olympic Spirit"—it was announced that Germany had already won several medals in an arts competition that took place prior to the opening and in which few other nations participated.[33]

Among the thousands who poured into Berlin that summer were Egon Hüttmann, an ex-Bauhaus student and young architect from Itzehoe in north Germany, and Joseph Hudnut, the newly appointed dean of the Faculty of Design at Harvard University.[34] Both had come to see Mies: Hüttmann had been asked by him to supervise the construction of the Textile Exhibition, and Hudnut was there to pursue Mies's expression of interest in heading Harvard's Graduate School of Design.

According to Hüttmann, the plans for the Textile Exhibition were already completed when he arrived, and the young architect was astonished by the amount of work that Mies and Lilly Reich had put into an exhibition scheduled to last a mere eighteen days, from March 25 to April 11, 1937.[35] Mies was notorious for his intense involvement in his projects. "I do not believe in talent," he had said.

Everyone can have that. . . . I believe in work.[36]

As with the memorable salt and coal walls of the 1934 exhibition, which functioned as both space-defining elements and virtuosic expression of materials, Mies had designed a nine-meter-long, sinuously curved S-shaped wall of dark-colored glass, illuminated like the interior-lit onyx wall in the Barcelona Pavilion, over which a rainbow-hued display of silks was to be luxuriantly draped, similar to what had been done in the 1927 Exposition de la Môde and, more recently, in the S-shaped, aluminum-foil-covered wall that he had designed as the centerpiece of a room for a fund-raising festival held at the Berlin Bauhaus in February 1933.[37] Characteristically, even the custom-crafted showcases that Mies had designed for the Textile Exhibition displayed meticulous preparation, their surfaces and dimensions as finely calibrated and finished as the columns and roofs of his villas.[38]

The subject of the exhibition was no less studied than its mode of display. No aspect of silk was ignored—from its broad range of colors and textural variety, including lush velvets, sumptuous brocades, shiny taffetas, and the most diaphanous chiffons to the wide variety of techniques for manufacturing it, including the most advanced use of printing on fabric by photography. The entire project demonstrated Mies's concern with balance, order, and clarity. As always, arch symmetry was avoided. Yet, the brilliant colors, the delicate balance between opacity and light, curvilinear and rectilinear forms, the variety of textures, the exquisite proportions and finish spoke of his poetic, well-nigh voluptuous sensibility, so often ignored by his critics.[39]

The plans were ready to go out for bidding to the various craftsmen. Hüttmann was told to return to Berlin at the beginning of the new year. His work would begin only with the final selection of contractors.

On July 21, Hudnut had written to Mies telling him of his pleasure in learning from Barr of his interest in the Harvard position and that he was looking forward to meeting with him in Berlin in mid-August.[40] On August 14, two days before the closing of the Olympics, Dean Hudnut met with Mies, informing him of his earlier meeting in London with Gropius, who had also expressed to Barr his interest in the Harvard opening.[41] According to Hirche, Mies did not take Harvard's offer to Gropius very seriously, considering his rival a far inferior architect and refusing to believe that so famed and supposedly judicious an institution could possibly prefer Gropius over himself.[42] The meeting with Hudnut seems to have gone well. Seeing himself as the sole contender for the Harvard post, Mies—in a letter of September 2—broke off his negotiations with Armour and asked to have his name removed from consideration.

> I must advise you that ... I have received an offer from another American university, which I intend to accept.
>
> Because of this, I can no longer pursue your proposition. However, in all probability, I will be in America in the spring of the coming year. I hope that it will be feasible at that time to have a meeting to discuss personally and privately our interesting problems.
>
> I was and am also now obviously pleased to make available to your institute my counsel and my experience.
>
> Mies van der Rohe[43] (Signed)

Considering the exasperating delay to which they had been subjected, Armour's response could not have been more gracious. Acknowledging that they knew of Mies's negotiations with "one of the institutions in the East," Armour, in a letter of September 21, invited him to come to Chicago during his spring visit, when Mies apparently anticipated being at Harvard.[44]

Mies's letter to Armour of September 2 indicates that he

gravely overestimated the nature and degree of Harvard's commitment to him: a misjudgment that Hudnut's letter, written to Mies from London on September 3, makes abundantly clear.

> I should like as soon as I reach Cambridge, to make a final request to the President of the University in respect to the appointment of a Professor of Design. I hope that I may receive from you a letter telling me that you are able to consider favourably the acceptance of a chair should this be offered you by the President.

Not only did Hudnut make clear that his "offer" was simply preliminary—the final offer having to come from the university's president—but he also mentioned anticipating "opposition to the appointment of a modern architect" to this post. Although he noted that the president was sympathetic with his plans and that "I have every reason to suppose that I can successfully carry them out," he did make clear the necessity of presenting more than Mies's name for the position.

> The President suggests that my chance of success may be improved if he is able to present to the Senate at least two names, each of which is acceptable to me. This is a customary procedure at Harvard, where the Board of Overseers expects always the privilege of considering an alternate.... I should like, therefore, to propose not only your name but also that of Mr. Gropius. If for any reason this does not meet with your approval, I hope that you will tell me so frankly.[45]

Mies—whose apprehension over the cultural level of America seemed confirmed by the behavior of the museum and now the university—exploded in anger. "If they don't know the difference between me and Gropius, let them keep him!"[46]

His response to Hudnut on September 15 barely conceals his fury.

> Your letter from London has taken me aback. It forces me to the unpleasant decision of having to qualify the agreements I made to you....
> I am willing to accept an appointment, but not to make

myself a candidate for a chair. If you stand by your intention to submit several names to the President of the University, kindly omit mine.

I trust I am not adding a burden to your efforts.

I would be grateful if you were to advise of further
plans.[47]

For whatever reasons—his own insecurity in his new position,
an uncommon sensitivity to the prickliness of a proud German
unaccustomed to a position of humiliating dependency, or a
genuine predilection toward Mies's appointment—Hudnut
responded to Mies, in his letter of October 26, in an amazingly
conciliatory manner. He promised not to declare Mies a "candidate," and that he would endeavor to secure the position for
him on his merits alone.[48]

Mies was also kept informed about the Harvard situation—
whose indecisive status and desultory pace were beginning to
unnerve him—by Michael van Beuren, one of his former Bauhaus students, who was championing Mies's cause while in the
United States looking for work. Hudnut, wrote van Beuren,
was having difficulties "with his bosses on the Board."
Although van Beuren had yet to meet with Hudnut—a meeting was planned for around November 1—he had the impression that Gropius's name had been put forward "merely for
tactical reasons." "Hudnut," he wrote

knew [Gropius] was not the right person for Harvard.

While it was clear to van Beuren that Hudnut was "out for
something big . . . something positively stellar," it seemed that
he was "unclear" himself about exactly what and whom he
wanted.[49] But these assurances did little to raise Mies's dampened spirits.[50] Shaken by the grave insults that he believed he
had suffered at the hands of two of America's most prestigious
institutions, Mies's resoluteness, equivocal at best with regard
to leaving, began to falter. The persistent rejection by his country, coupled by what appeared to be the same abroad—or, at the
very least, the absence of the high regard that he had anticipated in America—seemed to shake the illusion of certainty
that formed the bedrock of the man and his ideology. With the

distractions of the Olympics over, Mies was forced to take stock of Germany's—and his own—lamentable state of affairs.

The high-handedness that Mies exhibited in his negotiations with Harvard—perhaps instigated by the aggressive posturing of Lilly Reich[51]—is all the more remarkable in light of the foreboding implications contained in Hitler's Cultural Address of September 1936.

> May the bearers of our people's cultural life understand that . . . the development of human society is only conceivable by means of overcoming . . . unrestrained personal . . . freedom, the unchecked randomness of purely private conceptions . . . in favor of a greater common bond.

Hitler denounced criticism as

> a gnawing, nagging, and weakening sin against the German community, that had crippled its common will . . . [and brought about] anarchist tendencies of collapse, destructive sedition, and general decay. . . .
>
> The reestablishment of a blind authority . . . unshakeable and self-assured . . . is the most important work which could ever be assigned to people. . . .
>
> [The] victory of National Socialism has ended the play of free powers introduced by democracy. . . . Democracy only demolishes . . . [We will wage an] unyielding war of purification [against its] last elements. . . .
>
> The art of a Christian epoch can only be Christian : . . . the art of a National Socialist period can only be National Socialist.[52]

Events that fall of 1936 only too accurately reflected his words. On October 30, the Crown Prince's Palace, which under the direction of Dr. Eberhard Hanfstaengl, had continued to display contemporary art, was closed on orders from Reichsminister Rust; on November 26, Goebbels announced the "final and irrevocable" banning of all art criticism throughout the Reich. From now on, only descriptions of art were to be allowed and these only where the writer signed the article with his full name.

Such depressing developments were forcing many of those who had earlier dismissed thoughts of emigration to reconsider. However painful and difficult this decision may have been, it was a relative privilege that many in Germany no longer enjoyed. Holland was beginning to look more and more appealing to Max Beckmann. In Paris on a visit that fall, he told friends that he was thinking of leaving Germany.[53] Alexander Dorner, who had been struggling to support himself and his wife as an art critic in Berlin, began to make his plans to leave.[54] And Mies, too, was uncharacteristically unsure and anxious, as he revealed in a conversation with Otto Andreas-Schreiber, the discredited young Nazi leader whom he unexpectedly met on a crowded Berlin bus.[55]

Custom and habit, as well as the architect's well-known reserve, led Andreas-Schreiber to anticipate merely the briefest of nods, a distracted and distant smile of recognition from the famed architect. Thus, the confidential nature of the conversation that ensued both startled and honored the young Nazi leader, whose sympathies for modernism had cost him so dearly within the party.[56] Given the hazardous times and perilous place—anyone on the bus who overheard them might have reported their conversation to the authorities—this indiscretion spoke as much of Mies's despair as of his innocence. He told Andreas-Schreiber of his offer from Harvard and his discouragement at its desultory pace; of his difficulties with the Lange House, and the impossibility of his building even a private house. Proposed legislation requiring architects to design buildings that expressed "proper architectural views" had made him fear not being able to build at all.[57] He spoke of not wanting to leave Germany and his attachment to the land, and of how leaving, in his eyes, seemed a cowardly act. But, most of all, he confided, he was afraid of not being allowed to return once he had left. He could not cope, he said, with the thought of a final, irrevocable severance with his country.

"We discussed the problem back and forth," recalled Andreas-Schreiber, who—like Lilly Reich—argued that the possibility of building without any obstructions outweighed all other considerations, even what seemed to be a dishonorable act. "I advised him strongly, absolutely to go to the United

States," Andreas-Schreiber recalled. "Surely," he said, recalling his advice to Mies,

> if you're careful not to make any political or anti-German statements to the press or radio in America that might expose you to possible retributional actions on your return, I can envision no impediment to your eventual return as an internationally renowned architect ... after five or ten years, even if only for a visit.

Mies, however, remained unconvinced. "When we parted," said Andreas-Schreiber, "he was still undecided."

On November 6, van Beuren wrote again to Mies, bringing him up-to-date on the stalled Harvard situation.

> [T]he difficulties are absurd ... grave and great.

In addition to the usual prejudices against "foreigners," everyone who had any influence, it seemed, had their own favored candidate. Both Hudnut and the president of Harvard were relatively new to their jobs, and unable to cope with the "politics" of the situation. "Up to now," wrote van Beuren,

> only Hudnut, the President and Barr know that you are the one Hudnut wants. . . . Concerning Gropius, Hudnut says he likes him, that he has many ideas ... but first and foremost he's for you. He only mentioned Gropius because the president had so many other suggestions. Since you wrote to him he handed in only your name and intends to leave it like that. But he did say, in all honesty, that Gropius's name is great and that the opposition has something.[58]

Van Beuren also mentioned that he had met with the Armour people, who, considering their rejection by Mies, were being uncommonly solicitous with regard to his interests.

> Holabird and the temporary director asked me whether you were definitely headed for Harvard or still undecided [and] still considering the great possibilities of ... Armour. . . . They were forthcoming and even named some architects who would attend the school provided you would be teaching there. Above all, they wanted to know if

you would not perhaps like to go on a lecture tour before deciding on a definite job. Holabird asked me to talk to you about this again: whether you wouldn't like to lecture at ten different schools. He'd make the arrangements. . . . They were enthusiastic and stressed the absolute liberty of a director [of Armour] and that he would be given an assistant to do the organizing, so he'd have more time for himself. They made offer after offer with overflowing hearts.

On November 16, Hudnut wrote to Mies informing him that he was no longer being considered for the Harvard post.

> I am sorry . . . that I have not been successful in my plans . . . it will be impracticable to invite you at the present time to accept a Chair at Harvard. . . . [I]t will be necessary for me to consider now what other men may be available for appointment as Professor of Design. . . . I am very greatly disappointed . . . [P]lease be assured of my continued esteem.[59]

Clearly embarrassed by Harvard's delay in coming to this decision, Hudnut attempted to assuage Mies's disappointment by implying that the difficulty lay in the equally high qualifications of the candidates—a statement that Mies found as humiliating as he believed untrue. Hudnut's implication that he had "applied" for the position further enraged him. But it was not only the outcome that upset Mies. As someone who saw his preeminent task as "creat[ing] order out of the desperate confusion of our time,"[60] he was equally aggrieved by the discord and indecision that had surrounded the Harvard affair from the start. "It certainly was not handled well," Henry-Russell Hitchcock later commented.[61]

Gropius was offered and accepted the Harvard post. On December 14, Hudnut wrote to Barr informing him of this. Thanking Barr for all his help, Hudnut noted that Gropius was expected there in early February.[62] Mies, as contemptuous over Harvard's unhappy vacillation as that of his own, and sickened by the crushing weight of his impotence, returned—not without relief and a certain joy—to the exhilarating clarity, sureness, and peace of his art.

*   *   *

Hermann Göring announcing Hitler's Four Year Plan at the Sportpalast in Berlin, October 28, 1936 (Landesbildstelle Berlin)

Meanwhile, the German economy was in desperate shape. Although its industrial production had experienced an impressive increase—an increase, in fact, which led the world—the Third Reich was hovering on the edge of economic collapse. In an address given at the Party Day ceremonies on September 9, Hitler announced a new program of economic development. Known as the Four Year Plan, it was designed to make Germany economically self-sufficient within four years, mostly through technical innovation. Although it was ostensibly meant to stimulate the economy and was presented by Nazi publicists as yet another act of liberation from "the tentacles of Jewish finances,"[63] it was, in reality, nothing more than a feverish acceleration of rearmament. In a path "scarcely to be contemplated by sane men," the Führer, it was clear, was preparing for war.[64] In October, in an appointment that underscored not only his personal commitment, but the seriousness with which it was to be pursued by the regime, Hitler named Reichsminister Göring to head the plan. At a secret meeting in Berlin on December 17, Göring, addressing a group of prominent industrialists and high officials in a critical effort to gain support for the plan, was more forthright as to its real intentions. Speaking of the "approaching battle . . . [that demanded] a colossal measure of production capacity," Göring declared that Germany was

> already on the threshold of mobilization and . . . already at war. All that is lacking is the actual shooting.[65]

Weary and hungry, most segments of the population remained indifferent—if not antagonistic—to a program that demanded even more sacrifices. With the arousing of support an obviously formidable undertaking, Göring turned to a technique that the Nazis had successfully utilized in the past in initiating their programs. A massive propaganda campaign was organized and an exhibition entitled "Give Me Four More Years" (*"Gebt mir 4 Jahre Zeit"*) was planned, scheduled to open in Berlin on April 29, 1937—one month after the opening of Mies's Textile Exhibition.

In an otherwise artistically bleak Berlin, Mies's forthcoming exhibition was arousing even more excited anticipation than usual; and it did not go unnoticed by Göring. Worried that Mies's show might upstage the government's own efforts, and realizing the advantages of advancing the Nazis' propaganda efforts by a whole month, as well as of allying so prominent a segment of German industry as the textile manufacturers behind the government's controversial new economic program, Göring, as head of the Four Year Plan, appropriated the patronage of the Textile Exhibition.[66]

Thus Mies van der Rohe, whose destiny had so tantalizingly and so often converged with that of the Nazis over the course of the past three years, found himself the designer of an event that promoted the highest and most urgent priorities of the Third Reich. For Mies, this turn of events was a vindication of his faith in himself and his principles, his apoliticism, his government, and his country. For Reichsminister Göring, however, this circumstance represented a shocking and insupportable state of affairs.

CHAPTER 17

A KIND OF SUICIDE

LET MAN BESTIR HIMSELF WHILE IT IS YET DAY. THE NIGHT IS COMING WHEN NONE SHALL MAKE HIS MARK.

(**Goethe,** quoted by Oskar Schlemmer, diary entry, January 1937)

Hirche, Mies's young assistant, had always marveled at Mies's ability to remain calm while those about him trembled. But Mies's cool disinterest in the implications of Göring's patronage, his continuing indifference to the association of his name and repute with the Nazi cause, even as so many of his friends and colleagues had left or were preparing to leave or were suffering under Nazi oppression—not to mention Mies's own difficulties—deeply troubled the young man, who timorously questioned him about it.

"Doesn't Göring's patronage bother you?" he asked.

"Of course not," Mies responded. "What's there to be concerned about? It's only a lousy silk show, after all! What's so political about chiffons? Anyway," Mies went on, between languorous puffs on his cigar, "everything's finished; it's too late for the Nazis to make any changes, even if they wanted to.

There's nothing ... absolutely nothing ... in the show to which the Nazis could possibly object. At the very worst, they might forbid the use of my name, as they did in thirty-four. And that bothers me now about as much as it did then! Perhaps we might have to put in a few swastikas or other party emblems. But that's no real problem. So forget about it!"[1]

Normally, Mies's comments would have ended the conversation. Yet, while custom and his submissive nature inclined Hirche to silence, his conscience propelled him to speak. "Herr Professor," he said, the tremor in his voice poorly disguised, "now that the Textile Exhibition is sponsored by the Nazis, ..." he stopped short to catch his breath, "how can you justify your continued participation when you so little share their views?"

But this presumptuousness and uncharacteristic bluntness did not seem to offend Mies, who normally would have exploded at such lèse majesté. For a long while he said nothing. According to Georgia, he did not think too highly of Hirche's talents, regarding him as little more than a "sandwich boy," as she put it,[2] and it is likely therefore that he found it difficult to explain to him the ardor of commitment that obliterated all else; the unquenchable lust for perfection; the raw compelling need to create that would allow nothing, not even the most abhorrent client, to get in its way. It could not be explained: one either understood or not. It did not matter to Mies who gave him the commission, it only mattered that he could do with it as he pleased.[3] "Nazis, schmatzis," said Philip Johnson, "Mies would have built for anyone."[4]

Finally, after an interminable silence, Mies replied to Hirche. "Michelangelo was not a religious man," he said in his deep mahogany voice. "Yet he worked for the pope!"

It was one of those simplistic statements of his that was as apt to reflect astonishing insight as cloudy reasoning, or, as in this case, an outright error.[5] The simple fact was that Mies sought only to create Beauty: the circumstances of the commission—the client, budget, and program—were only important as means by which he could achieve his goal. "Whoever commissions buildings, buys me," said Johnson, whose own philosophy was very similar to that of Mies. "I'm for sale. I'm a whore. I'm an artist."[6]

*   *   *

Events, however, were moving away from the direction Mies had anticipated. Several weeks before the scheduled opening of the Textile Exhibition, a summons was issued ordering Mies to appear before the Berlin city council. He welcomed this call as an opportunity to gain "clarification," as he put it, of the new circumstances surrounding the exhibit. How exactly would Nazi sponsorship affect his design? Would they demand the usual party decorations—flags, swastikas, and so on? But Lilly Reich was alarmed; and as usual, her instincts proved correct.[7]

The chairman of the council wasted no time. "Herr Professor, let us come quickly to the point. As you know, Reichsminister Göring has now become the protector of the Textile Exhibition and he finds your participation offensive."[8]

Mies had not anticipated this. "Herr Chairman, I am sorry to hear that. I have brought the plans with me. Please look them over. There is nothing political about the exhibition. There is nothing to which Herr Reichsminister Göring could possibly object."

His calm manner belying his rising agitation, he moved to unroll the plans. "That will not be necessary, Herr Professor. We are not interested in seeing them."

"What exactly do you want?" Mies asked. "I'll be happy to do whatever you want."

He had come prepared to compromise, to have his name omitted, to add a few flags perhaps. Less than eight weeks remained until the opening. All the work was finished; the colors, textures, and finishes were chosen. As was his custom, he had left nothing unexamined, unmeasured, or unchecked. Soon, Hüttmann would be arriving to assure that his meticulous instructions were executed to the letter. "You must resign the commission at once," said the chairman.

His words hit Mies like a cannon shot. "He was furious," said Maude Grote, recalling that he seemed more upset by the Nazis' poor timing than by the action itself. "They are impossible," Grote said Mies complained later, "they take the glass of water right out of your hand!"[9]

"I have a contract," he said now, slowly and precisely, as though law and reason still mattered. "I will not resign. You are exceeding your bounds in ordering me to do so."

"Herr Professor, if I may, it is you who are exceeding . . ."

"I will not resign!" said Mies.

"You must . . ."

"I will not!"

Reaching across the table to the manila folder that lay before him, the chairman took another tack. "Herr Professor, he said, as the room grew silent. "For your own sake, sir," he went on slowly, presumably trusting that his implication would not be lost in the heat of Mies's anger, "I think you should reconsider. There seems to be some incriminating evidence on you. . . ."[10]

"I . . . will . . . not . . . resign!" Mies repeated, his bass voice firm and unwavering before what in fact constituted a none too discreetly veiled threat on his life.

Turning as rapidly as his thickset frame would allow, he stormed out of the room, a "criminal" ignorant of his crime, a patriot accused of treason, and an artist stripped of his ideals— or, some might claim, his delusions.

Shortly after this confrontation, he received a summons ordering his removal from the Textile Exhibition and commanding him to turn over all his plans to Ernst Sagebiel, Göring's apparent favorite, who had designed the Air Force Ministry building and the recently completed Tempelhof airport. Mies knew him from his earlier days as construction supervisor in the office of Eric Mendelsohn. Undistinguished in manner as in accomplishment, the forty-five-year-old Sagebiel seemed a man marked for anonymity; but like so many others of his type in these hours, he had come to the forefront of his profession, not because of ability or special talent, but due to the adversity of others. Less a committed Nazi than a grateful pragmatist, Sagebiel was only too aware of his indebtedness to policies that, if often repugnant, had enabled him to achieve a measure of prominence not otherwise imaginable for him.[11] Arrogant, dull, pompous, and without finesse—"much like his building," commented Speer[12]— Sagebiel, in the normal course of events, might have been able to forget this unsavory genesis of the honor he now enjoyed. However, his unanticipated involvement with Mies's project not only revived an association with modernism that he would now have preferred to forget, but undoubtedly brought home the reprehensible shallowness of his own new-found fame.

Ernst Sagebiel, 1937 (Ullstein Bilderdienst)

The first meeting between the two men, which took place in Mies's office, went "reasonably well," according to Hirche, who was not present, but heard about it from Mies. "Their manner was cool, but businesslike," he said.[13] Transferring plans so close to completion was an enormously complex undertaking; extensive explanations were necessary to familiarize a new staff with all the details. Ready for the contractors, the plans had literally to be redone in order to provide additional clarification. Precise positioning had to be indicated and explained in such a way that it could be understood by those unfamiliar with the project. A deadline of two weeks was agreed upon. At that time, the two architects agreed to meet in Sagebiel's office, when the actual transfer would take place.

At this second meeting, Sagebiel's behavior changed noticeably: his diffidence, apparent at the earlier session, had disappeared. Mies attempted to ignore his arrogant manner, as he carefully and patiently went over every aspect of the project. "That, of course, will have to be changed," said Sagebiel gruffly at one point, with a curt wave of his hand.

"He spoke to Mies like a stern general berating a subservient and disgraced lackey. No one ever spoke to Mies like that," recalled Hirche, still concerned, forty years after the event, that he had been unable to hide his mortification as well as had Mies. "I knew he was boiling, but he showed nothing. He acted very matter-of-factly."[14]

But Sagebiel was not finished. He turned to Hirche and asked if he would like to work for him and continue supervising the exhibition. "It was the final blow," said Hirche, who managed to retain his composure and turned Sagebiel down.[15]

The Textile Exhibition opened on the afternoon of March 24, 1937, with a glittering assemblage of officials that included Ministerpräsident Göring, members of the diplomatic community, and representatives of the clothing and textile industries—some six hundred invited guests in all—in attendance. Göring used this highly publicized occasion to exhort German industry to meet the goals of Hitler's Four Year Plan; his address, along with those of other officials, made clear the exhibition's political purpose. As for its artistic content, virtually nothing remained of Mies's efforts.[16] Ernst Sagebiel received sole credit; and, while time constraints had prevented a total transformation of Mies's work, Sagebiel's leaden touch was evident in the stifling symmetry, heavy "moderne" floor lamps, and a jagged nine-meter-long mirrored wall broken into three-meter flat segments—a graceless transformation of Mies's sensuously curved surface.

For Mies, the attempt to stay in Germany and view himself as a German architect was now finally and irrevocably over. He

The Textile Exhibition, Berlin, 1937 (Photos from the *Monatshefte für Baukunst und Stadtbau*, v. 21, 1937, courtesy of Avery Architectural and Fine Arts Library, Columbia University, New York)

was as humiliated by the means of his disgrace, as by the "cowardly act" (as mentioned to Andreas-Schreiber) that it imposed upon him. For the remaining three decades of his life, he could never bring himself to speak of this event again.

"Beinahe nichts" ("almost nothing") were words that Mies frequently used to express his architectural goals: now they could just as accurately describe his life. Stripped of his vocation, he stood rebuked, rejected, and shamed by his country. Thwarted in all his efforts to work, he was clearly unable to stay. Yet, lacking a formal job offer from abroad that would enable him to obtain an exit visa, and given the currency and countless other restrictions, he was equally unable to leave. A man of thought and procrastination, a ponderer and proselytizer of the rule of reason, he was reduced to that which he most despised—anger and impetuosity.

The fiery, headstrong, and explosive sensibility that lurked so uneasily beneath Mies's cool, phlegmatic facade was never more apparent than on those occasions when he felt thwarted, whether by Behrens, the Bauhaus students, Harvard, an obstreperous craftsman attempting to alter a detail of his design, or an interrogator questioning his verities. Spurred now by frustration and disgrace, this volatile side of his nature once more asserted itself. After years of clearheaded debate over the pros and cons of emigration, an enraged Mies, in one of the most momentous decisions of his life, acted precipitously. He simply ran away.

His act was not entirely without forethought. Officially, as a member of the Prussian Academy of Arts, he could not leave without a "bona fide" excuse, and then only with permission from the Ministry of Culture. The property of anyone even suspected of wanting to leave could now be confiscated, while secret transfer of funds abroad was punishable by death. There was simply no practical way for Mies to leave legally. Nor was he ready yet psychologically to permanently sever his ties with his homeland. His idea was to leave without appearing to do so, leaving open the possibility of returning.

He thus looked to his brother Ewald for help. The two bore a notable resemblance to each other, and it was on this which Mies counted now. Wishing neither to alert the authorities nor

endanger his brother, Mies decided to "borrow" Ewald's passport from his Vaalser Strasse apartment in Aachen without
informing him. Afterwards, from the safety of Holland, he
would phone Ewald to tell him what he had done.[17] Aside from
its accessibility to the border and his brother's passport being
there, there was something impeccably right about his returning to Aachen to reaffirm his patrimony before abandoning it.

The scene along Vaalser Strasse was familiar to him: the
settling in of the late winter dusk, the mist that had begun
the day now ending it.[18] Across the flat, fertile countryside, the
cold, gray fog rolled in, wrapping him, the sturdy houses and
church steeples, the herds of cows and grazing horses, and
neatly planted rows of bare trees in its gauzy embrace. The
slight upgrade of Vaalser Strasse made Mies's efforts to reach
the border more difficult: the arthritis that would later cripple
him had already begun its affliction. Large-boned, red-cheeked
peasants rode silently by on their bicycles, briefly obscuring
the signs that read "Niederland." Ahead, past the concrete
posts of the customs house, the black-and-white striped
levered gates, the steel-helmeted guards, the swastika flags
hanging limply in the cold dampness, could be seen the lights
from Wilhelmina Platz, just over the border in the Dutch town
of Lemiers. Well-acquainted with the residents on both sides,
the border guards—wary and suspicious with strangers—casually waved on the familiar travelers, their bicycles and carts
laden with goods. The chill winter dampness was bone pierc-
ing; even the guards stayed in their tiny concrete booths. The
steel arm of the gate lifted slowly, creaking in the dampness.
Mies walked on. Holland lay only a few paces ahead. Behind
him, growing distant and faint, lay everything: his land, his
art, his friends, Berlin—his *Heimatstadt*, with its "dreadful
tastelessness" (as Brecht had called it) that he had come to love;
its tumult and sly humor, its challenge and caustic edge, its
comforting familiarity.

With a dreadful crunch, the steel lever slammed down
behind Mies.

> "I felt," he later said, "like a flower plucked from its
> plant."[19]

*   *   *

Something in him also snapped shut. Although he had no way of knowing it at the time, this departure turned into permanent exile: despite two brief return visits to Berlin, his life in Germany was essentially over. He would go on to build elsewhere, but there was a change in his later work—a new coldness, a relentless austerity that many found offensive and that contributed toward discrediting the modern movement that he had earlier helped to found on gentler principles. Arthur Drexler spoke of Mies's "freezing down" in America, likening it, "in a way, to suicide."[20] Philip Johnson agreed.

> "An architecture of sensibility seemed more than he could bear," he said of Mies's later work.[21]

Except for perhaps two buildings out of the many that he built after leaving Germany—the Farnsworth House of 1951 and the 1958 Seagram Building—the exquisite sensibility, the breathtaking poetry, was gone. Mies went to America and honor and fame, but his heart remained behind.

Although Mies's departure in 1937 appeared on the surface to be a precipitous event, its genesis lay within the framework of the recent Nazi past. The same may be said of the resolution of the Nazi artistic direction, which also took place in 1937. In a speech before the Reichstag on January 30, 1937, on the fourth anniversary of his attainment of national power, Hitler made two important announcements that appeared unrelated but actually reflected the persistent leitmotiv of his regime. Announcing Germany's withdrawal from the Versailles Treaty—an arrogant, belligerent gesture that would soon lead to war—he also made public his plans for the renovation of Berlin and his appointment of Albert Speer as Inspector General of Buildings for the Renovation of the Federal Capital, a title as daunting as the task it described.

Yet despite its heralded public debut, Hitler's massive renewal scheme for Berlin, now under Speer's aegis, was going nowhere. Young, inexperienced, and of low party rank, Speer was making as little headway in imposing the proposals, with their terrifying scope, on the Berlin building authorities as had Hitler before him. Since the penchant of the local *Baupolizei* for obstructionism was as marked, if not more so, in Berlin as elsewhere, some way had to be found to circumvent the authorities if the Führer's architectural dreams were to be realized. Hitler therefore ordered State Secretary Lammers to issue a directive granting Speer extensive powers and making him directly subordinate to Lammers. Speer would thereby escape the jurisdiction of both party and civic authorities. He noted,

> Hitler explicitly exempted me from having to inform the city government or the party of my plans.[22]

He was now responsible only to Hitler. To match his exalted position, he was given new quarters—the elegant Arnim Palace, which for thirty years had housed the Prussian Academy of Arts. Despite the academy's rigorous attempts to remain above politics—including the "cleansing" of its ranks and an admissions policy of admitting no one to whom the Nazis might object—the worst was not yet over. Looking for suitable quarters for his new Generalbauinspektor Speer, Hitler was attracted by the palace's generous space, accessibility to his own office, and ministerial gardens where he could avoid being seen by the public during the frequent visits he gleefully anticipated.

His architectural penchant was, by now, becoming well known. Among those invited to dine at his table, an invitation to view the architectural models of the planned Berlin renovation became a very special mark of favor. With flashlights beaming and keys jangling, Hitler—like some proud and mischievous Pied Piper—would lead his guests through the special doors and corridors he had ordered installed to link his office with those of Speer in the Arnim Palace. There, Hitler's guests were astonished to see their usually stiff and formal Führer drop to his knees, his eyes sparkling, his manner vivacious, before the vast model of the grand boulevard which stretched one hundred feet down the darkened hall, where spotlights illuminated models of the "new Berlin." Although much of the display was still only roughly blocked out, "his" buildings—the gigantic Hall of the Reich and the Arch of Triumph, as well as the grand boulevard—were reproduced down to the smallest detail, with the wood painted to simulate

Speer (based on Hitler's drawings), the Great Hall of the Reich, Berlin, model
(Bundesarchiv)

the materials that would actually be used. Here, peering an
inch or so above the level of the models to gain the right
perspective, Hitler would extol the perfection of his architectural vision; there, he would call for an adjustment of the
brilliant illumination to simulate a different hour of the day.[23]

Now that Hitler was released from his student posture before
Troost, his much-vaunted allegiance to Troost's austere and
restrained classicism was disappearing. Contrary to Speer's
expectations, Hitler reverted to the Habsburgian affinities of
his youth. Curvilinear flourishes and impulses toward gigantism and historical fantasy had begun to dominate his own
architectural proposals and with them the work of his young,
impressionable, and grateful protégé.

The House of German Art was to open on July 18 with an
exhibition of contemporary German art, many of whose works
had been personally selected by Hitler. These so-called "re-
spectable" paintings and sculptures, which according to the
Nazis, symbolized the "restoration and rebirth of German

Speer (based on Hitler's concept), the Grand North–South Boulevard with the Arch of Triumph and the Great Hall of the Reich, planned renovation of Berlin, model (Ullstein Bilderdienst)

culture,"[24] were finally and conclusively to define the nature of "Nazi" art—a demonstration awaited by the Nazi leadership no less anxiously than by the nervous artistic community. And Hitler, in addition to his roles as political visionary, prophet, messiah, racial purifier, conscience of the nation, and voice of the *Volk*, could now reveal himself as master builder and artistic connoisseur. Once again, he was not content merely to show what he was for and what he opposed. Now four years into power, fully and firmly in control, he could implement the reprisals that he had anticipated in *Mein Kampf* a decade before.

> And side by side with the coming resurrection I sensed that the goddess of inexorable vengeance . . . was striding forth.[25]

The "enemy" was now German modernist art and its beleaguered creators. Thus on June 30, acting "[o]n the basis of an expressed desire of the Führer," Minister Goebbels ordered the impounding and placing into custody of all "suspect" paintings and sculptures created since 1918, declaring them "degenerate" along with their creators, some 1,400 artists. Twelve thousand graphic works of art, five thousand paintings and sculptures—works of such non-German artists as van Gogh, Derain, Chagall, Cézanne, Matisse, Braque, Modigliani, Vlaminck, Archipenko, Léger, and Rouault—were confiscated in 101 German museums, including Hanfstaengl's Crown Prince's Palace in Berlin and Dorner's Hannover Museum, which provided the greatest single source of art. The art was condemned as "bolshevistic": the fact that most of it was equally unacceptable to the Soviet regime seems to have passed unnoticed. So that the German people might have the opportunity of comparing this art with that approved by the regime, Goebbels ordered Adolf Ziegler, President of the Reichs Chamber of Fine Arts (RBK), to set up a second exhibition, to be held concurrently in Munich with that scheduled for the House of German Art two weeks hence.

The malevolent compulsions that accompanied Hitler's "creative" instincts also appeared in another action that took place at this time. In a memorandum of June 24, labeled "Top

Secret," and signed by Field Marshal Blomberg, but (according to William Shirer) undoubtedly initiated by "his master in the Reich Chancellery"[26]—the commanders-in-chief of Germany's armed forces were ordered to mobilize their troops in preparation "for a possible war."[27]

The sudden emergence of the regime's cultural disposition— however long it had been intimated, however long feared— threw the artistic community into stunned disarray. "This is only the beginning of the avalanche," said Eberhard Hanfstaengl, the director of the now-closed Crown Prince's Palace, to Max Beckmann.[28] Himself threatened with imminent dismissal (he was ousted from his post on August 4, 1937), he urged the renowned painter to leave as soon as possible. Others also were disturbed. "I see the situation as dangerous," wrote Oskar Schlemmer,

> although I am unable to picture precisely what might happen. . . . Does this mean one will be forced to emigrate?[29]

Schlemmer remained in Germany and was forced to earn his living as a house painter until 1940, when Dr. Kurt Herberts, who was already providing employment for Georg Muche, Gerhard Marcks, Willi Baumeister, and other artists, invited him to work in the color laboratory of his lacquer factory in Wuppertal. Exhausted by the conflict between his artistic interests and commercial necessities, Schlemmer died in 1943, at the age of fifty-five. On the other hand, Alexander Dorner, who thanks to his prominent association with avant-garde art had been living a "haunted existence" in Berlin, with the help of an anti-Nazi publisher who provided him with a written assignment to cover the Paris World's Fair, obtained exit permits for himself and his wife, escaping by one week arrest by the gestapo for "political unreliability."[30]

Cultural institutions were also caught unawares by this startling revelation of the Nazi cultural program. The Prussian Academy of Arts again found itself the target of Nazi attack, as the result of the continuing inclusion among its membership of so many individuals associated with the now officially discredited modernism. Since the academy was still by reputation, if not in fact, the country's most prestigious cultural institution, the regime found this—along with the exclusion of artists it praised—no longer merely embarrassing, but intolerable. With the Munich exhibitions imminent, it was imperative that a new system be devised at once that would permit immediate admission of those individuals desired by the regime. Therefore, acting in his capacity as Prussian Ministerpräsident and curator of the academy, on July 1, Göring abolished the existing charter of the academy and ordered Minister Rust to work out a new "timely [charter] as soon as possible." Until then, Göring, "in accordance with his duties," would direct the "rejuvenated academy."[31]

On July 8, Alexander Amersdorffer—first standing secretary of the academy since 1910—was summoned to the office of Dr. Schwarz, one of Rust's deputies, where he was advised of the changes—all illegal and without precedent—to be imposed on the academy. He was handed a list of "proposed" new members, fifty-nine in all, that included the names of artists such as Arno Breker and Josef Thorak, whose works were to be featured in the forthcoming German Art exhibit, and architects such as Ernst Sagebiel and Albert Speer. With membership numerically limited, an ingenious means was devised to accommodate these new "members." Persons found by the party to be neither particularly desirable nor objectionable were placed in a new "inactive" category of membership. Into this rank were put, among others, Peter Behrens; Theodor Fischer, whose students had included prominent modernists;[32] Speer's teacher, Heinrich Tessenow; Heinrich Wolff, the architect of the Reichsbank; and Paul Schultze-Naumburg. Nine other members, Amersdorffer was told, were to resign at once—the painters Ernst Nolde, Max Pechstein, Ernst Ludwig Kirchner, Emil Rudolf Weiss; the sculptors Rudolf Belling, Ludwig Gies, Ernst Barlach; and the architects Bruno Paul and Mies van der Rohe. An identical letter, stamped "confidential," was sent at once, by registered mail, to all nine.

> The reorganization of the academy, which has been planned for some time, also encompasses a revision of the membership of the academy. Since, according to my information, it is not expected that you will continue to be a

member of the academy in the future, I would like to advise you, in your own interests, to declare your resignation from the academy as soon as possible.

The President (Signed)[33]

Ten days later, Hitler stood before an adoring throng of 30,000 that filled Munich's Prinzregentenplatz. Behind him, dazzling white in the July sun, stood the completed House of German Art. For Hitler—hailed now in a speech by Adolf Wagner, Bavarian minister of the interior, as "the greatest of living German artists . . . the greatest builder of all time . . . not only the patron of German art, but its greatest master"—this dedication was a moment of supreme and joyous personal fulfillment, and typically, a moment as well for retribution.[34] "Let no one have illusions," he declared, no longer constrained to cloak his intentions in deliberate obscurities,

> National Socialism has set out to purge the German Reich and our people of all those influences threatening its existence and character. . . . While this purge cannot occur in one day, all those taking part in such pollution do not want to forget that sooner or later the hour will strike for their disappearance.

Hitler's address on this occasion exposed the startling depth of his destructive tendencies. "With the opening of this exhibition," he declared,

> has come the end of artistic lunacy and with it the artistic pollution of our people. . . . From now on we will wage an unyielding cleanup war against the last elements of our cultural destruction. . . . My comrades and I have struggled and built [this state today] against a world of enemies.

Art that did not fall within the prescribed parameters was not simply to be excluded from the exhibition and labeled "decadent" and "degenerate," it was to be excoriated, condemned, disgraced, and destroyed, and its creators threatened with criminal prosecution or worse. "The new age of today is at work on a new human type," continued Hitler.

Men and women are to be more healthy, stronger: there is new feeling of life, a new joy in life. Never was humanity in its external appearance and in its frame of mind nearer to the ancient world than it is today. . . . This, my good prehistoric art-stutterers, is the type of the new age: and what do you manufacture? Misformed cripples and cretins, women who inspire only disgust, men who are most like wild beasts; children who, were they alive, must be regarded as cursed of God. . . .

And let no one say to me that it is how these artists see things. From the pictures sent in for exhibition, it is clear that the eyes of some men show them things otherwise than as they are—that there really are men who on principle feel meadows to be blue, the heavens green, clouds sulphur-yellow—or as they perhaps prefer to say "experience" them thus.

I need not ask whether they really do see or feel things in this way, but in the name of the German people, I have only to prevent these pitiable unfortunates who clearly suffer from defects of vision from attempting to violently persuade contemporaries by their chatter that these faults of observation are indeed realities, or from presenting them as "Art."

Here only two possibilities are open: either these "artists" really do see things in this way and believe in that which they represent—then one has but to ask how the defect in vision arose, and if it is hereditary, *the Minister for the Interior will have to see to it that so ghastly a defect . . . shall not be allowed to perpetuate itself* [italics mine]—or if they do *not* believe in the reality of such impressions, but seek on other grounds to impose upon the nation by this humbug, then it is a matter for a criminal court.[35]

The exhibition of modern German art, entitled Degenerate Art, opened on Monday, July 19. Aside from its defamatory name and manner of installation, it bore a striking resemblance to the Museum of Modern Art show entitled German Painting and Sculpture that had been held in New York in 1931. The participating artists in the Munich exhibition, some 112 in all, included Max Beckmann, Otto Dix, George Grosz, Erich Heckel, Karl Hofer, Ernst Ludwig Kirchner, Paul Klee,

Nazi parody of expressionist style in poster advertising the Degenerate Art exhibition held in Berlin at the end of 1937, after its initial showing in July in Munich (Bundesarchiv)

Oskar Kokoschka, Franz Marc, Emil Nolde, Max Pechstein, Christian Rohlfs, Oskar Schlemmer, Karl Schmidt-Rottluff, Gerhard Marcks, Ernst Barlach, and Rudolf Belling. Honored abroad, these artists were now declared in the exhibit's catalogue, to be

> cripples and mental defectives . . . cliques of gossips, dilettantes, and artistic cheats [who] will be sought out and suppressed.

The 730 works—all produced in Germany between 1918 and 1933, the period referred to by the Nazis as "diseased . . . the era of national shame"—were hung in poorly lit halls, unframed and helter-skelter, as though by deranged children. The art was grouped by "foreign" influence, such as cubism, futurism, and surrealism; or by subject matter, such as "Insults to the Honor of German War Heroes," "The Mocking of Christianity," "The Manifestation of the Soul of the Jewish Race," and "The Derision of German Women." The catalog of the exhibition offered a litany of attacks against modern art, concluding with Hitler's chilling threats of sterilization and euthanasia.

Hitler's "shocked" reaction to "degenerate art." On wall and deliberately mishung is Erich Heckel's "Seated Man" of 1913 (Ullstein Bilderdienst)

Modernist architecture had escaped this abuse, but barely. Konrad Nonn, a former associate of Alfred Rosenberg now in the Prussian Ministry of Finance, had pressed Ziegler to include architecture. But Ziegler, who was short of time and also—like so many within the party hierarchy—wary of relinquishing a shred of authority, had refused.[36]

The Führer's surrogates followed his lead. "Come and see art by 'mentally sick' artists," declared Ziegler at the opening of the Degenerate Art exhibition

> who dared to depict whores and degenerates while ridiculing German mothers and German soldiers—indeed everything that the nation reveres. . . . Come to see this incomprehensible and disgusting art purchased for public museums out of the hard-earned savings of German workers.

Goebbels, undoubtedly hoping that the virulence of his words might erase memories of his earlier, and now embarrassing, support of modernism, also picked up the motif. "Come," he declared,

> so that you may realize how low German art had fallen under the influence of these filthy molders of artistic taste.[37]

Whether curious or simply obedient, Germans flocked to the Degenerate Art exhibition. More than two million visitors went there, more than three times the number that went to the House of German Art just down the street. It was the most well-attended artistic event in German history.

German art was at last subject to the regimentation and control that pervaded all aspects of German life: the number of regulating decrees was estimated to have amounted to more than a thousand a week. Constraints existed everywhere. No construction was possible without a special government permit. No factory could be built to produce a product deemed "unnecessary," that is, anything not useful to the armaments industry. The price for every agricultural product was fixed by the government, which controlled the entire financial resources of the nation—from production to distribution. The Reichsbank directed and controlled the financing of all private business; without its consent virtually no major business transaction could be negotiated or concluded. Strikes and lockouts were no longer permitted. Trade unions, along with the instruments of collective bargaining, had been dissolved. Despite the rapidly rising cost of living and the shortage of labor, wages were held at the level of 1933.[38] *Gleichschaltung*—the policy of bringing all realms of life under party control, to which the entire thrust of the Nazi regime had been directed—was now virtually complete.

It was in this context that the members of the Prussian Academy of Arts had to decide what to do. Most of those who remained as members were Aryan; conservative in their politics, if not their art; comfortable with many of the tenets of national socialism, if not openly sympathetic to it; and quiet. Now, however, after having been silent when others were threatened, some academy members found a voice for themselves. "In all innocence," wrote Ernst Ludwig Kirchner, protesting the request for his resignation from the academy,

> I am neither a Jew nor a Social Democrat. . . . I am not an enemy. If I were in good health, I would be so happy to work with you in creating a new German art.[39]

Already pushed to the limit of his endurance by the strains of the First World War, the fifty-five-year-old Kirchner was unable to tolerate any further abuse. The following July, with more than six hundred of his paintings removed from public collections, he committed suicide in Davos, Switzerland. "I would still like to emphasize," wrote sixty-three-year-old Bruno Paul, a member of the academy for thirty years, protesting his forced resignation,

> how much I have regretted, and still regret, that I was not able to use my extensive experience and knowledge in the area . . . of art . . . in the service of national socialistic principles.[40]

Sixty-seven-year-old Ernst Barlach, who considered himself the most German of sculptors, found the Nazi accusation of his being "alien to the *Volk*" particularly galling. Declaring his intention of staying at his "post whatever the consequences," he retired to his home in Mecklenburg, where he was kept a virtual prisoner. The following year, his condition undoubtedly aggravated by ceaseless harassment, he died of a heart ailment.[41]

However pale and withered it had become, this last vestige of national esteem seems to have been difficult to shed. Rudolf

Belling did not resign until August, while Max Pechstein simply refused to; he was forced out by Rust in September. Ernst Nolde, a member of the NSDAP, was understandably irate over his rejection from the academy. Retiring in humiliation to his home in Seebüll, near the Danish border, Nolde, who was eventually forbidden to paint, spent his days proclaiming his loyalty to his country and his party, reaffirming the "Germanness" of his art, and reminding Nazi leaders, in a ceaseless outpouring of correspondence, that

> even before the National Socialist movement I, virtually alone among German artists, fought publicly against the foreign domination of German art.[42]

From Holland, Mies had gone to Paris. There he had met with Alfred Barr, who, still chagrined over the difficulties Mies had encountered with his American prospects, was delighted to be able to recommend Mies to Mrs. Stanley Resor, a prominent collector of modern art and the wife of the director of the J. Walter Thompson advertising agency, who was looking for an architect to design a country house in Jackson Hole, Wyoming.[43] Barr arranged a meeting between the two in Paris, where Mrs. Resor offered Mies the commission to design the house, and also to pay his transportation expenses to America. With this job in hand, Mies returned to Berlin to obtain a proper exit visa and thus leave legally. While there, he received a telephone call from Secretary Amersdorffer on July 13, requesting his resignation from the academy.[44] According to Amersdorffer's memorandum of the conversation, Mies requested "an hour's time to reflect." There is no known record as to why Mies asked for this delay. Was it pride, or his characteristic slowness of nature that urged Mies to carefully weigh his course? As Philip Johnson noted, Mies's membership in the academy meant a great deal to him; it was the single remaining tribute that he bore from his country.[45] Since at this time Mies believed his departure from Germany to be temporary, he apparently wished to minimize as much as possible any impediments to his ultimate return. From this perspective, suggested Albert Speer, the difference on his record between

PROFESSOR L. MIËS VAN DER ROHE · BERLIN W 35 · AM KARLSBAD 24 · FERNRUF B 2 LÜTZOW 4567

An die

Preußische Akademie der Künste

B e r l i n   W 8

Pariser Platz 4

Akademie d. Künste Berlin

№ 0696 * 21. JUL 19

19.Juli 1937

Ich habe Ihnen noch Ihr Schreiben vom 8.Juli 1937

und die mit Herrn Professor Amersdorfer geführte

Unterredung am 13.Juli 1937, worin ich der Akademie

meinen Sitz in der Akademie zur Verfügung stellte,

zu bestätigen.

Heil Hitler!

Ludwig Mies v.d. Rohe

Mies van der Rohe's letter of resignation to the Prussian Academy of Arts, July 19, 1937 (Photo courtesy of the Archiv der Preussischen Akademie der Künste, Akademie der Künste, Berlin)

"expelled" ("*ausgeschlossen*") and "resigned" ("*ausgetreten*") would have been considerable.[46] Mies's behavior here brings to mind his elaborate negotiations to create the impression that *he* ordered the closing of the Bauhaus, rather than the Nazis, as well as his dealings with Harvard. He seems to have had the need to see himself—and be seen by others—as being in control of what otherwise might be perceived as a demeaning situation. At the end of his hour's grace period, then, Mies returned Amersdorffer's call and informed the secretary of *his* decision to resign from the academy.

On July 19, the opening day of the Degenerate Art exhibition, Max Beckmann, apparently heeding Hanfstaengl's advice, left Germany; 509 of his paintings would be seized by the regime. That same day—almost exactly four years since he had announced his decision to close the Bauhaus before an astonished faculty—Mies confirmed his resignation from the academy in writing. In leaving, as in his attempts to remain, he offered no apologies.

I still have to confirm your letter of July 8, 1937 and the discussion with Professor Amersdorffer on July 13, 1937, in which I put my seat in the academy at the disposal of the academy.

> Heil Hitler!
> Ludwig Mies van der Rohe[47]

Mies left Germany a few days later. He arrived in New York on August 20 and departed immediately to inspect the Resor building site in Wyoming. During his travels between New York and Wyoming, he met with Armour officials in Chicago, and after prolonged negotiations, an agreement was finally reached in December 1937. The announcement of his appointment as head of Armour Institute's architectural school was made on April 2, 1938. With his arrangements in America settled, he left three days later, on April 5, for Berlin, to put his affairs there in order and also to properly reenter the United States on an immigrant visa.

With the antimodernist cultural policy now firmly established and ruthlessly implemented with the full force of the government, Mies was far more personally imperiled upon his brief return to Germany in 1938 than he had been before, a situation about which he had been warned in America before he left. His vulnerability became frighteningly clear in August, when he was supposed to go to the local police authorities to pick up his immigration visa—for whose completion the police had retained Mies's passport. Fearing detention if he went personally to pick up the documents, he sent Karl Otto, a former assistant, in his place. His worries appeared justified: for when Otto returned, he found a pale and shaken Mies being "roughly interrogated" by two gestapo officers who had come by without notice and found Mies with no passport.[48] With Otto's arrival, he was able to placate the officers and they left. Frightened by this episode, Mies quickly changed his departure schedule and, packing whatever he could throw into a single suitcase, slipped out of Berlin at once. Only Hirche was at the train station when he left. "Hirche," said Mies, "come soon yourself!"[49] Hirche never did, but later, Hilbersheimer and Peterhans, former associates of his from the Bauhaus, joined him in Chicago.

Mies's wife and daughters, however, remained in Germany and his departure cost them dearly. As the family of a declared "enemy emigrant," as Mies was termed after his more formal, "official" departure, they fell into disrepute. Their bank accounts were confiscated and none of the money was ever made available to them; after the war, it simply disappeared. Ostracized and blackballed, Georgia, an actress, found it difficult to obtain work.[50] Like most Germans, Mies's family suffered greatly during the war, and for many years afterward gratefully received the "Care" packages that he arranged to have sent to them. After the war his daughter Marianne and her three children were trapped in what became the Russian zone, and only with the assistance of Walter Päncke, who later became the leader of East Germany, and whom Mies had known during the 1920s, were they able to get to the West. In 1948, after several years of trying to obtain visas, two of his daughters visited Mies in the United States. Years after last seeing him, they still felt apologetic over any inconvenience a visit might impose on their astonishingly self-absorbed father. "I hope it won't scare you too much," wrote Waldtraut, the third daughter, in 1946,

> if one or two daughters pop in one day. We won't intrude too much on your life.[51]

When they arrived, his Chicago office did not know who they were: Mies had never mentioned his family![52] His wife, Ada, who had remained unwell, died of cancer in 1951.

Lilly Reich also stayed behind, as devoted to Mies after he left as she had been before. It was she who took care of his office, his correspondence, and the endless legal disputes regarding his patents in which he was perpetually involved. She packed his files, and whatever drawings and documents survived the war did so because of her efforts. She attempted to ease the lot of his family, helping them financially when she could, and advising Mies, before the war and afterward, about their condition and needs. In July 1939, she visited him in Chicago, and for a few brief weeks, part of which was spent working and relaxing in the Wisconsin countryside, their partnership was restored. As the war clouds gathered over Europe, the decision had to be made as to whether or not she should stay. But Mies never asked her; and she, proud and independent, would not remain unasked. Given his character, his not asking her was predictable, although he never spoke of his reasons for not doing so. By the time the German army invaded Poland on September 1, she was gone: her boat, the North German passenger liner *Bremen*, was intercepted on its journey home. There were stories about her having to return to care for an invalid brother in Berlin and business matters that needed attention, but they were excuses only. Although no one better understood Mies's need for freedom and solitude—and, as a letter she sent him on June 12, 1940 reveals, she seems to have half-expected his rebuff—she was deeply hurt. According to Philip Johnson, Mies knew he had hurt her.[53] Her letters, which maintained a scrupulously businesslike tone, after her visit became even more *sachlich* (matter-of-fact). Only the letter of June 1940 hints at her sadness. "I am powerfully reminded of the last days and hours in Chicago," she wrote. Referring to her intuition at the time that she would not see him again, she continued,

> I fear my instincts did not deceive me, despite the fact that I wished nothing more, both then and now, than to be proved wrong. I am sad that I have received only the slightest word from you in the last weeks, and that, pertaining solely to business affairs. Perhaps you have no time, perhaps you have sent more letters than I know. That the mail connections stop now makes it all the harder to bear.... Will you try to find a way to be in touch?[54]

She was more open in her correspondence with her friend, Maude Grote. "I am often a little sad," she wrote on February 11, 1938, of Mies's new life abroad,

> when I hear now about how many beautiful things are over there.

Returning from her visit to Mies in Chicago, she wrote on September 9, 1939, while at sea.

> I am on my way back from America where I was with Mies a few weeks and was then upset by the news of the war. It

was not at all easy for me. I realized ahead of time that returning from there would be very, very difficult for me. . . . But I don't want to talk about it. You will understand somehow.[55]

Lilly Reich never saw Mies again. She died in Berlin in 1947.

Mies, meanwhile, adjusted slowly and with difficulty to his new life. The language proved a formidable obstacle; it was four years before he felt confident enough to speak English in public. He lived in the United States for the remaining three decades of his life, virtually the same span of time that he had lived in Berlin, becoming a citizen in 1944. He changed remarkably little over the years in America; if anything, traits notable in Germany—his solitary nature, his phenomenal concentration, his disdain for commonplace practicalities, his powerful personality, his willfulness and single-mindedness of purpose that continued to attract worshipful acolytes— became even more pronounced over the years.

Nearly two decades would pass before Mies spoke about his Bauhaus years and his commentary with regard to the Nazis remained negligible. Despite the grave difficulties of packing his German files, keeping them intact and unharmed during the war, and negotiating their release from the German Democratic Republic (they had been stored in Mülhausen, now East Germany), Mies ignored them—five cartons that constituted the sole remaining documentation of his German years—when they arrived in Chicago. Only after several weeks, to the "exasperation of his staff," were they opened.[56]

Neither his experience with the Nazis, nor living in pluralistic America, nor even the growing dissatisfaction with the tenets of modernism that marked the architectural world during Mies's final years caused him to give any thought to the relationship between his ideals and their disabuse. His ideology, in fact—like most everything else about him—became more rigid. "You don't do a thing because you like to do it," Mies commented toward the end of his life, "but because it is right."[57]

Numerous honors were bestowed on him during his last years. He was ultimately the grateful recipient of seven honorary doctorates, memberships in numerous professional so-cieties, and scores of gold medals. In 1963 he was awarded the Presidential Medal of Freedom of the United States, and he died in 1969, at the age of eighty-three, an American hero.

AFTERWORD

WHEN TIMELESS DOGMAS ARE ALLOWED TO RUN UNCON-
NECTED TO TIME, THAT IS, TO THE ACCUMULATED EXPERI-
ENCE AND CONTENDING CURRENTS OF HUMANITY, AN
IDEOLOGY CAN ENCOURAGE PEOPLE TO MURDER AS EASILY AS
IT CAN ENCOURAGE THEM TO CLAIM NOBILITY. NOT EVERY
BLOODLESS ABSTRACTION WILL NECESSARILY SPILL SOMEONE
ELSE'S BLOOD, BUT EVERY BLOODLESS ABSTRACTION, OF LEFT
OR RIGHT, WILL NECESSARILY SWELL TOWARDS AUTHORI-
TARIANISM, AND FROM THE URGE TO CONTROL TO THE SELF-
RIGHTEOUS JUSTIFICATION TO KILL IS BUT A SHORT STEP.

> (**A. Bartlett Giamatti,** Baccalaureate Address, Yale
> University, 1982)

But for Hitler's interest in architecture, Albert Speer believed,
modernism—as promulgated by the Weidemann–NS Students' Association faction—would have developed as the
"official" style of National Socialism. Although the stern,
megalithic neoclassicism that ultimately came to dominate
the public style of the Nazi regime is seen today as the artistic
embodiment of the antihumanistic, aggressive principles of
national socialism, historical evidence appears to support
Speer's view. The early efforts of the party's cultural "liberals"—the so-called Berlin wing—to establish a technologically advanced, modernistic aesthetic compatible with both
nationalism and the tenets of modernism, as exemplified by
Mies—whom they specifically cited—were ultimately sty-

311

mied by Hitler's unexpected intervention. Although Hitler allied his severe neoclassicism with Hellenism in an effort to racially link the Hellenes with the Aryans, a far stronger case could be made of the Schinkelesque (and hence Germanic) origins of modernism—a case which many modernist architects, from Mies to Gropius (in his urgent letters to party officials) argued.

Hitler's architectural proclivities not only came to determine the style that much of national socialistic public architecture eventually assumed, but contributed directly to Mies's inability to obtain work, whether public or private. Every official—from the local *Baupolizei* to Hitler's lieutenants themselves—eagerly scanned the Führer's pronouncements for a glimmer of cultural direction. Although the virulent racism and lurid accusations that eventually came to predominate Nazi cultural policy had long been evident in the statements of Rosenberg and the KDK, it was not until Hitler made his sentiments known that they became something more than one voice among many. Hitler's cultural voice grew bolder as his political position strengthened, and whatever hopes the party's cultural "liberals" may have harbored with regard to modernism quietly faded away.

Hitler's perverted artistic instincts were responsible not only for the regime's architectural aura, but—characteristically melded with his destructive urges—determined as well its antimodernist cultural voice, which also affected Mies. However long it had been simmering, the forceful emergence in mid-1937 of the vicious "degenerate art" program simultaneous with the first realization of Hitler's long-harbored architectural fantasies, the House of German Art, was no accident. Goebbels did not initiate this episode: ever sensitive to his Führer's wishes, he was merely its efficient expediter. However much it came to be perceived as such, the persecution of modernist art and artists was not necessarily intrinsic to fascism; only Hitler's particular artistic bent appeared to make it so. Mussolini, after all, one of Hitler's early mentors and no fascistic slouch, chose to utilize his close association with the futurists as symbolizing his regime's modernity and advanced technological orientation. This much-publicized relationship was very well known to the German modernists and their party supporters.

While Hitler's idiosyncrasies, rather than any innate opposition to Nazism, pushed Mies to leave, his own personal tendencies—most notably his astonishing inertia—pushed him to stay. Mies's notorious reluctance to move himself—a characteristic that astounded and infuriated both friend and foe— was intrinsic to his brooding, ruminative nature. This deep, speculative bent, combined with his prodigious ability to concentrate and hone his thoughts to their basic essentials—were intrinsic to his refined, abstracted "almost nothing" architectural style. His physical inertia then, which played so significant a role in his remaining in Germany as long as he did, was an essential element of both his personal and architectural aesthetic.

Yet, neither Mies's principles nor his actions during the Third Reich, however conditioned they may have been by his personal idiosyncrasies, were unique: whatever he did or attempted to do was done by others. His basic conceptual assumptions, such as his idealism—the belief that the validity of ideas exists outside experiential verification—and his aesthetic elitism; his perception of himself as an artist and intellectual, removed from the crass political machinations of the day (and consequent low view of politics and politicians); his efforts to gain official commissions, quietly and freely pursue his profession, and remain in the Prussian Academy of Arts; his deep reluctance to leave Germany and his viewing of such an act as both contemptible and cowardly were shared by most of his peers.

Not all of these tendencies were unique to his time: the notion that the demands of art are superior to those of humans extends far beyond Mies's milieu. Understanding that profundity of insight demands a singular concentration and dedication, society has long chosen to permit to "great men" what it denied to, even deplored, in ordinary mortals. In return for their beneficent wisdom and aesthetic enlightenment, society has traditionally chosen to exempt artists, philosophers, and poets from the common ethical standards by which ordinary individuals are judged. "Artists are children," we say. *"Künstler sind Kinder."* Similar sentiments abound. "[T]he true artist," wrote George Bernard Shaw in *Major Barbara*

> will let his wife starve, children go barefoot, his mother drudge for his living at seventy, sooner than work at anything but his art.

We smile in benign toleration to learn that Monet, fascinated by the changing colors of his wife's face as she lay on her deathbed, took out his paintbrushes to record them. Gregor Piatigorsky, the noted cellist, also commented on this.

> [E]very musician, every artist ... must really ... devote their lives to something larger in which they believe. We see that art is what matters.[1]

Surely, when viewed through the telescope of time, issues of morality fade as the art endures. While of undoubted concern to his contemporaries, the question of whether or not Justinian, the creator of the magnificent Hagia Sofia, was a "good" ruler now seems quite irrelevant. To the slave labor that built them, the Greek temples we now so admire surely did not seem so beautiful—nor do the Romanesque cathedrals seem today marred by having been built with the booty of the Crusades.

That Leonardo da Vinci was, to put it kindly, a "difficult" person; Degas, mean spirited; Beethoven, rude; that artists may be selfish, liars, cheats, braggarts, or wife beaters is not only generously overlooked, but half expected. Pursuit of the divine, it seems, renders the artist and his product immune from moral critique. The artist, after all, lives under a "higher" obligation—or, as Goethe wrote, more is permitted to poets than to ordinary mortals.

Nowhere did these ideas gain greater credence, pervasiveness, and acceptability than in Germany. To be "Herr Professor" marked the epitome of German aspirations: there the artist/intellectual was king. Within the rigid, stratified atmosphere of German society, no one else was permitted the same privileges. To him were accorded the honors and exceptions of a generally conservative and conformist society that worshiped erudition—or, at least, its appearance. Nowhere else was an artist/intellectual so encouraged to take the liberties he felt necessary to pursue his art. Friedrich Schlegel wrote in 1800,

> Do not waste faith and love on the political world, but offer up your innermost being to the divine world of scholarship and art.

Within this framework, no one, to the German mind, was lower than the politician. As opposed to the artist/intellectual, he was concerned with affairs of this world, with transient, ephemeral events that did not matter in the ultimate scheme of things. This disdain for politicians permeated all levels of German society, and few politicians referred to themselves as such. Hitler, for example, referred to himself as an "artist" and his politics an "art." This long-standing German tradition was one reason that people paid little heed to assertions of Hitler's "interest" in architecture. Even that most inartistic of monarchs, Wilhelm II, felt compelled to proclaim, "If I were not Kaiser, then I would wish to be a sculptor!"

But more than political disdain, simply feeling "above it all" or aesthetic elitism lay behind the propensity of Mies and his peers to turn a blind eye to the moral perversities of the Third Reich, which we today find as shameful as it is nearly incomprehensible. Time and time again during this inquiry into Mies's actions, we are confronted with the spectacle of individuals who have been lauded for creating what has generally come to be acknowledged as the unique twentieth-century contribution to world culture pursuing participation in what is undoubtedly one of the century's most despised manifestations. Perhaps, in Mies's case, the reason lies in the striking resemblance of the motivating and dynamic forces that underlay his style (and, by implication, all of architectural modernism)—its idealism, deprecation of empirical reality, absolutism, and arrogance—to the principles that supported the Third Reich.[2] Mies, like others of his generation, including the Nazis, perceived the existence of a singular meaning beyond the multifarious nature of daily life. They believed that beneath the seemingly chaotic variety, the inconsistencies and frequent absurdities that mark human existence lay something called "Truth," or "the Good," or, as Mies was fond of saying, "the spirit of the age." This alone was what mattered: this alone defined the age. The true seer discerned it, the true leader preached it, and the true architect built it. Life was perceived within a stern hierarchy of values in which all was sublimated toward this higher goal. For Mies, it was his architectural ideal; for the Nazis, it was the state. Within this framework the individual, with his multiplicity of interests, desires, and values, counted for little. In 1924 Mies declared,

> The individual is losing significance. His destiny is no longer what interests us.[3]

Goebbels, in 1933, expressed similar sentiments.

> The dethroning of the individual [is] the most essential principle of our now victoriously conquering movement.[4]

Concerned as they were with "higher" things and convinced that meaningfulness lay somewhere outside empirical reality, both Mies and the Nazis deprecated the values and constraints of the everyday world—the Nazis, its moral code; and Mies, the demands of context and client. That Mies's orientation resulted in an architecture of extraordinary beauty, that society was infinitely enriched and irrevocably changed by his vision, makes its price no less high. Shielded from the disorder of human reality by the steely certainties of his faith, Mies adhered to artistic ideals that, however noble their claims or glorious their achievement, themselves seem neither so noble nor so reasonable.

This confounding and disturbing similarity, along with Mies's generative influence on the development of modern architecture and the near-universal acceptance of the principles under which he operated, as well as the ubiquity of his actions among his peers, suggest that the problem of Mies and the Third Reich is more than *just* a German issue or even an architectural one. Those of Mies's generation believed that an individual could stand apart from and above the world. While we challenge this view and ruefully acknowledge our spiritual kinship with it, we must not ignore its bounty. If our humanistic priorities preclude another Third Reich, we must also recognize that it precludes as well another Mies.

NOTES

PREFACE

1. Sibyl Moholy-Nagy et al., "MAS [Modern Architecture Symposium] 1964: The Decade 1929–1939," *Journal of the Society of Architectural Historians* 24 (March 1965): 83–84.
2. Franz Schulze, *Mies van der Rohe: A Critical Biography* (Chicago: The University of Chicago Press, 1985), 198.
3. Ludwig Mies van der Rohe, "Architecture and the Times" (1924), quoted in Philip C. Johnson, *Mies van der Rohe* (New York: The Museum of Modern Art, 1947), 186.
4. "Modernism" is an elusive word whose meanings are as numerous as its practitioners. In the context of Mies, however, its meaning is very specific. He viewed himself—and was seen by others—as participating in a general outlook that manifested itself in many countries about the turn of the century in response to the pervasive feeling that tradition no longer satisfied the demands of the new century. Picasso, Stravinsky, Wright, Schoenberg, Sant'Elia, and Loos are some artists who manifested this tendency. Although the belief that art should relate to life was a recurring concern during the nineteenth century, along with the justification of art by linking it to something "beyond" itself (such as nature or "Truth"), the new century offered the impetus toward its realization. The particular manifestation varied from country to country, as well as from one individual to another. Within Germany, dominated as it was by Hegelian idealism, the need for justification of artistic goals by philosophical principles was particularly strong. Convinced that the defining element of the twentieth century was technology, with all its implications for new materials, patronage, and forms, the architectural modernists sought a means of integrating industrial forms, techniques, and principles into a radically new building style. Given their idealistic propensity, as well as their Beaux-Arts tradition, it is understandable that the German architects should look toward the neoclassicism of their recent past, most notably in the style of the great nineteenth-century architect Schinkel, to find both "meaning" and architectural vocabulary, such as the disposition in a harmonious, but not necessarily symmetrical manner, of white unembellished geometrical forms. This use of simple (white, for the most part)

317

cubic masses along with such evidence of technology as ships' railings and large panes of plate glass came to signify the new "modern" style in Germany. While most of the modernists, including Mies, saw themselves as continuers of their Schinkelesque tradition; others viewed them as antithetical to the German past. The mutual genesis of these two opposing branches of twentieth-century German architecture out of the neoclassical tradition helps to explain the endless disputes between the modernists and their opponents as well as their noteworthy similarities. Mies freely admitted his indebtedness to nineteenth-century German neoclassicism, a style that also influenced Albert Speer and Hitler, the latter implacably opposed to modernism. Transposed to foreign shores, where this stern, indigenous tradition did not exist, the notion of modernism became severed from its cultural, philosophical, and stylistic roots, and its most notable émigré proponents, such as Mies and Gropius, anxious to minimize their Germanic roots, came to assert the style's independence from tradition and context. Thus, the much-discussed "failure" of modernism pertains more to claims than style and belies our own ignorance of the circumstances of its birth, development, and unwanted transposition to alien shores.

CHAPTER 1–PRELUDE: HITLER'S WEATHER

1. Christopher Isherwood, *The Berlin Stories* (New York: New Directions, 1963), 179.
2. Ibid., 87.
3. Hans Keszler, Letters of a Bauhaus Student, The Last Two Years of the Bauhaus, unpublished, Bauhaus-Archiv.
4. Ludwig Mies van der Rohe, *Steglitzer Anzeiger*, 1932.
5. Stephen Lackner, *Max Beckmann: Memories of a Friendship* (Coral Gables: University of Miami Press, 1969), 18.

CHAPTER 2–A STRANGE DUALITY

1. Philip Johnson, comments at The Museum of Modern Art Symposium, Mies van der Rohe Centennial, 25 February 1986.
2. Henry-Russell Hitchcock and Philip Johnson, *The International Style* (New York: W. W. Norton, 1932, 1966), Appendix, 237.
3. Mies's most renowned projects, such as his Friedrichstrasse skyscraper and his villa designs of the early 1920s, were not meant to be built. His most important building, the Barcelona Pavilion, was dismantled after the closing of the International Exposition.
4. "Four Great Makers of Modern Architecture: Gropius, Le Corbusier, Mies van der Rohe, Wright," (New York: Columbia University, 1963), 112. The verbatim record of a symposium held at the School of Architecture, Columbia University, New York City from March to May 1961.
5. Georgia van der Rohe, personal conversation with author, 10 May 1973.
6. Mies, *Aachener Nachrichten*, 3 June 1959.

7. Mies, *Mies van der Rohe*, film sponsored by Knoll International and Zweites Deutsches Fernsehen, Mainz; directed by Georgia van der Rohe; produced by IFAGE-Filmproduktion, Wiesbaden; English version, 1979, German version, 1980.

8. Mies, from Peter Carter, "Mies van der Rohe: An Appreciation on the Occasion, This Month, of His 75th Birthday," *Architectural Design* 31 (March 1961): 97.

9. Mies, *Print* (February–March 1957): 39.

10. Friedrich Heer, *Charlemagne and His World* (London: Weidenfeld & Nicolson, 1975), 83.

11. Richard E. Sullivan, *Aix-La-Chapelle in the Age of Charlemagne* (Norman: University of Oklahoma Press, 1963), 31.

12. Heer, *Charlemagne*, 85.

13. Albert Speer, personal conversation with author, 24 July 1978. Speer has also written of Hitler's admiration of Charlemagne: "[Hitler] drifted off into lengthy expiations on the role of the individual in history. What had counted had always been the will of a single individual: Pericles, Alexander, Caesar Augustus, and then Prince Eugene, Frederick the Great, Napoleon. He drew all his heroes from two historical periods: antiquity and the eighteenth and nineteenth centuries. The only exception was Charlemagne, whose empire he occasionally called a prelude to his own plans for European power." Albert Speer, *Spandau: The Secret Diaries*, trans. Richard and Clara Winston (New York: Macmillan, 1976), 58.

14. Mies, "Mies Speaks," *Architectural Review* 144 (October–December 1968): 451.

15. Carter, "Mies: An Appreciation," *Architectural Design* 31: 96.

16. Schulze, *Mies*, 12.

17. Ibid., 13.

18. Ibid.

19. Mies, letter, on the occasion of the seventy-fifth anniversary of the Gewerbeschule, 1963, Library of Congress.

20. Schulze, *Mies*, 14.

21. Ibid.

22. Ibid., 15.

23. Mies, 1938 Inaugural address as director of Architecture at Armour Institute of Technology, quoted in Philip C. Johnson, *Mies van der Rohe* (New York: The Museum of Modern Art, 1947), 192–193.

24. Mies, "Mies Speaks," *Architectural Review* 144: 451.

25. Carter, "Mies: An Appreciation," *Architectural Design* 31: 97

26. Schulze, *Mies*, 16.

27. Ibid.

28. According to Schulze, Ewald Mies was famous among the stonemasons in Aachen for being able to detect a misalignment of a millimeter in the letters of a tombstone from the distance of 2 meters. Ibid., 16.

29. Doris Schmidt, personal conversation with author, 31 July 1974.

30. Schulze, *Mies*, 18.

31. Ibid.
32. Elaine Hochman, "The Politics of Mies van der Rohe," *Sites* 15 (1986): 47.
33. Carter, "Mies: An Appreciation," *Architectural Design* 31: 95.
34. Mies, interview with Anna Teut, *Die Welt*, 10 October 1964.
35. John W. Cook and Heinrich Klotz, *Conversations with Architects* (New York: Praeger, 1973), 73.
36. Schulze, *Mies*, 288.
37. Georgia van der Rohe, personal conversation with author, 10 May 1973.
38. Schulze, *Mies*, 281.
39. "Berlage's Exchange had impressed me enormously. . . . What interested me most in Berlage was his careful construction, honest to the bones." Mies, "Mies Speaks," *Architectural Review* 31: 451.
40. Schulze, *Mies*, 282.
41. For further discussion of the contents of Mies's libraries in Germany and America, see Fritz Neumeyer, *Mies van der Rohe: Das kunstlose Wort-Gedanken zur Baukunst* (Berlin: Siedler Verlag, 1986).
42. Werner Blaser, *After Mies: Mies van der Rohe—Teaching and Principles* (New York: Van Nostrand Reinhold, 1977), 283.
43. Philip Johnson, quoted in John W. Cook and Heinrich Klutz, "A Conversation with Philip Johnson," *Architecture Plus* 1:8 (September 1973): 80, a slightly abbreviated version from Cook and Klotz, Conversations with Architects (1973).
44. Carter, "Mies: An Appreciation," *Architectural Design* 31: 97.
45. Mies, speech on the occasion of his being awarded the Gold Medal of the American Institute of Architects, San Francisco, 1960. From Exhibition Catalog, Chicago Art Institute, 1968.
46. Mies, quoted by Peter Blake in, "Four Great Makers," 93.
47. Mies, quoted in Carter, "Mies: An Appreciation," *Architectural Design* 31: 115.
48. See Jeffrey Herf, *Reactionary Modernism: Technology, Culture and Politics in Weimar and the Third Reich* (Cambridge: Cambridge University Press, 1984), for an examination of the effort by some members of the reactionary right (the precursors of the Nazis, referred to by Herf as "reactionary modernists") to incorporate technology into *"Kultur"* in Germany.
49. Edward Edgeworth, *The Human German* (London: Methuen, 1915), 264.
50. Literally, "flicker boxes."
51. Schulze, *Mies*, 19.
52. Ibid., 3.

CHAPTER 3–A BLIND AND FATEFUL COURSE

1. Schulze, *Mies*, 21.
2. Whether or not Mies ever received certificates from these institutions remains unknown. In any case, being "technical," rather than the more highly regarded academic institutions of learning, such degrees counted

for little within the upper echelons of German society to which Mies aspired.

3. Schulze, *Mies*, 22.
4. Ibid., 24.
5. Ibid.
6. Johnson, *Mies van der Rohe*, 10.
7. Ibid.
8. Schulze, *Mies*, 23.
9. Members of the Riehl circle who later became Mies's clients included Professor Herbert Gericke, director of the German Academy in Rome; the painters Emil Nolde and Walter Dexel; the manufacturer Erich Wolf; and the banker Ernst Eliat. Neumeyer, *Mies*, 66.
10. Mies, "Mies Speaks," *Architectural Review* 144: 451.
11. Mies, quoted by Peter Blake in, "Four Great Makers," 93.
12. Mies, "Mies Speaks," *Architectural Review* 144: 452.
13. Mies, quoted in George Nelson, "Architects of Europe Today: 7—Van der Rohe, Germany," *Pencil Points* 16:9 (September 1935): 460.
14. Mies, quoted by Peter Blake in, "Four Great Makers," 94.
15. Schulze, *Mies*, 49.
16. Ibid., 41.
17. Ibid., 39.
18. Ibid.
19. It was this building, designed in partnership with Adolf Meyer in 1911, that initially brought Gropius international recognition. Going beyond Behrens, Gropius showed that modernism need not depend on neoclassicism, however stripped of ornament or severe its forms. The building, however, appeared far more innovative than it actually was. Despite the use of a thin sheathing of glass that hung from an external steel framework (anticipating the curtain wall), it utilized a traditional wall-bearing structural system.
20. Schulze, *Mies*, 61.
21. Ibid., 60.
22. Ibid., 69.
23. Doris Schmidt, personal conversation with author, 31 July 1974.
24. Egon H. Rakette, *Bauhausfest mit Truxa* (Munich and Berlin: A. Herbig Verlagsbuchhandlung, 1973), 104.
25. Schulze, *Mies*, 75.
26. Ibid.
27. Karl Jakob Hirsche, quoted in Paul Raabe, ed., *The Era of German Expressionism*, trans. J. M. Ritchie (Woodstock: Overlook Press, 1974), 230.
28. As might be expected within any group of highly individualistic artists, the degree of political involvement and persuasion varied enormously, not only from group to group, but within single groups. Membership in these organizations did not necessarily indicate political leanings. In fact, a questionnaire submitted to the membership of the November Group revealed unanimity of opinion only with regard to the issue of art reform. With few commissions during this period, members of the artis-

tic avant-garde felt almost compelled to join one or more of these groups. About 1922, when most of its political motivations had disappeared, Mies joined the November Group, apparently because of its exhibition opportunities. Emil Nolde, whose beliefs would later propel him to early membership in the Nazi party, was also a member.

29. Ulrich Conrads and Hans G. Sperlich, *The Architecture of Fantasy: Utopian Building and Planning in Modern Times*, trans. Christiane and George R. Collins (New York: Praeger, 1962), 25.

30. Ulrich Conrads, ed., *Programs and Manifestoes on 20th-century Architecture*, trans. Michael Bullock (Cambridge, MA: MIT Press, 1970), 49.

31. Tut Schlemmer, ed., *The Letters and Diaries of Oskar Schlemmer*, trans. Krishna Winston (Middletown: Wesleyan University Press, 1972), 65.

32. Scheerbart's slim volume *Glass Architecture* was published in 1914. Scheerbart died the following year, in 1915, at the age of fifty-two.

33. Paul Scheerbart, *Glass Architecture*, ed. Dennis Sharpe and trans. James Palmes (London: November Books, 1972).

> Our culture is to a certain extent the product of our architecture. If we want our culture to rise to a higher level, we are obliged, for better or for worse, to change our architecture. And this only becomes possible if we take away the closed character from the rooms in which we live. We can only do that by introducing glass architecture, which lets in the light of the sun, the moon, and the stars, not merely through a few windows, but through every possible wall, which will be made entirely of glass. (p. 41)
> ... The new glass environment will completely transform mankind. (p. 74)

34. Mies, 1938 Inaugural address as director of Architecture at Armour Institute of Technology, Johnson, *Mies van der Rohe*, 190.

35. Mies, Speech upon receiving the Golden Medal of the BDA, Berlin, 30 September 1966, Library of Congress.

36. Mies, "Architecture and the Times," Johnson, *Mies van der Rohe*, 186.

37. Mies, quoted in Carter, "Mies: An Appreciation," *Architectural Design* 31: 116.

38. Mies, quoted in Johnson, *Mies van der Rohe*, 188.

39. Philip Johnson, from "A Conversation with Philip Johnson," *Architecture Plus* 1: 75.

40. Mies, quoted in Johnson, *Mies van der Rohe*, 190.

41. Mies, quoted by Peter Blake in, "Four Great Makers," 100–102.

42. Mies, speech, San Francisco, 1960, printed in Exhibition Catalog, Chicago Art Institute, 1968, 9.

43. Philip Johnson, quoted in Charles Jencks, *Modern Movements in Architecture* (Garden City, NY: Anchor Press/Doubleday, 1973), 40.

44. Mies, quoted in *Interiors*, "The Word on Design by Wright, Mies, Gropius, Le Corbusier," (1952), 116.

45. The Perls House, 1910–11.

46. The Society of German Friends of the New Russia was founded in order to foster economic and cultural ties between the two countries through exhibitions, lectures, and slide shows. By mid-1926, with the German

economy beginning to flourish and the revolutionary days of the Weimar Republic over, the faded rhetoric of the communist revolution had evolved into a pan-European spirit. During this period, many private groups such as The Society of German Friends were founded to encourage and support this fragile new ecumenical spirit. The essentially conservative nature of this organization was evident not only in the benign and conciliatory rhetoric of its pamphlets, but in its leadership, which included such respected individuals as Albert Einstein, Max von Schillings (the president of the Prussian Academy of Arts), and Paul Loebe, the president of the Reichstag.

47. Mies, quoted in Donald Drew Egbert, *Social Radicalism and the Arts: Western Europe* (New York: Alfred A. Knopf, 1970), 661.

48. The Liebknecht-Luxemburg commission, along with his membership in the Society of German Friends, plagued Mies throughout his life. Not only did it get him into trouble with the Nazis; but, in 1947, during the "Red scare," when he underwent a security clearance in the United States in order to design the American Embassy in Havana, this affiliation raised questions about his loyalty, and he was denied the commission.

49. Mies van der Rohe Centennial Exhibition, The Museum of Modern Art, 1986.

50. Johnson, from Cook and Klotz, "A Conversation with Philip Johnson," *Architecture Plus* 1:69.

51. Blaser, *After Mies*, 30.

52. Ibid., 97.

53. "Mies Speaks," *Architectural Review* 144: 451.

54. Mies, quoted in H. T. Cadbury-Brown, "Ludwig Mies van der Rohe: An Address of Appreciation," *Architectural Association Journal* (July–August 1959): 29.

55. Bertram Goldberg, letter to author, 3 January 1973.

56. Mies, as told to Mildred Whitcomb, "Only the Patient Counts: Some Radical Ideas on Hospital Design," *Modern Hospital* 64:3 (1945): 65.

57. Neumeyer, *Mies*, 244.

58. Mies, quoted in H. T. Cadbury-Brown, "Ludwig Mies van der Rohe," 29.

59. Mies, "Six Students Talk with Mies," transcript of Recorded Conversation, *Student Publications of the School of Design* (North Carolina State College, Raleigh, N.C.) 2:3 (1952): 28.

60. Georgia van der Rohe, personal conversation with author, 10 May 1973.

61. Mies, "Talk with Mies," *School of Design* (N.C.) 2:25.

62. Schulze, *Mies*, 251.

63. Ibid., 321.

64. This was the popular name for the Vereinigte Seidenwebereien Aktiengesellschaft, that is, the United Silk Weaving Company.

65. In addition to several unbuilt projects, Mies was also involved, in 1931–1935, in the designing of a factory complex and two family homes.

66. See the Exposition de la Môde and the Tugendhat House of 1928–30.

CHAPTER 4—"THE IRON FIST"

1. Mies's work in 1930 appears to have consisted of participation in two competitions, neither entry of which was built—the Krefeld Golf Club and the remodeling of the interior of Schinkel's Neue Wache as a memorial honoring Germany's war dead; and the redesign of a mill and dyeing plant for Verseidag in Krefeld, a minor job that was not built as he intended and to which he never referred. Sergius Ruegenberg, an assistant in Mies's office at the time, believed that Lange, unhappy with the original design by the company's own Technical Division, turned the commission over to Mies because of his concern over the architect's poor financial situation (Sergius Ruegenberg, personal conversation with the author, 24 July 1974). For a more detailed study of this project, see Elaine S. Hochman, "A Study of Ludwig Mies van der Rohe's Factory Building for the Silk Industry, *Vereinigte Seidenwebereien AG*, Krefeld, Germany," unpublished paper, Mies van der Rohe Archive, The Museum of Modern Art, 1973.

2. Philip Johnson, quoted in Schulze, *Mies*, 179.

3. Mies, quoted in Johnson, *Mies van der Rohe*, 190.

4. Albert Einstein, quoted in Ronald W. Clark, *Einstein: The Life and Times* (New York: Avon, 1971), 520.

5. Mies directed "The Dwelling for Our Time" section and designed a critically acclaimed house as a temporary exhibit for the German Building Exposition that opened in Berlin on 9 May 1931 and closed on 2 August of that year.

6. Wolf Tegethoff, *Mies van der Rohe: The Villas and Country Houses* (New York and Cambridge, MA: The Museum of Modern Art; Cambridge and MIT Press, 1985), 114.

7. In the elections of 1928, the Nazis claimed 810,000 votes. By 1930, they were able to attract 6,409,600 votes and increase their seats in the Reichstag from 12 to 107.

8. Members of this "elite" Nazi organization took an oath of personal loyalty to Hitler.

9. William Shirer, *The Rise and Fall of the Third Reich: A History of Nazi Germany* (Greenwich: Fawcett Crest, 1959), 202.

10. In addition to the Reichswehr, those in the government who opposed Hitler at this time included Hindenburg's son Oskar, a major in the army and his father's liaison with the military; Oskar's close friend and another representative of the Reichswehr's powerful interests, the scheming general Kurt von Schleicher, chief of the political bureau of the Defense Department; Chancellor Franz von Papen, handpicked for his post by Schleicher in June 1932 in hopes of bolstering the rightist government, an ex-general staff officer and member of the Prussian Landtag (Senate); and the wily Otto von Meissner, secretary of state and chief of the presidential chancellory.

11. Count Harry Kessler, *The Diaries of a Cosmopolitan, 1918–1937*, trans. and ed. Charles Kessler (London: Weidenfeld & Nicolson, 1971), 425.

12. Shirer, *Rise and Fall*, 232.
13. Bismarck was both chancellor of the Reich and Prussian foreign minister for over two decades.
14. Fritz Stern, *Dreams and Delusions: The Drama of German History* (New York: Alfred A. Knopf, 1987), 126.
15. Harry Kessler, *Diaries*, 427.
16. A. J. P. Taylor, *The Course of German History* (New York: Capricorn, 1946), 210.
17. Isherwood, *Berlin Stories*, 86.
18. The Red Front, or, more accurately, the Red Front Fighters Association (Rotfrontkämpferbund) was formed in 1924 as more of a propaganda organization designed to attract workers to the party and to counter the Socialist party's Reichsbanner Schwarz-Rot-Gold. With the increase in political violence in Germany in the 1920s, its emphasis shifted to countering the violent tactics of the Nazis. Following fatal clashes between its fighters and those of other political street-fighting organizations, most notably the Nazis, the Red Front was banned in the spring of 1929, first in Prussia and then throughout Germany. With its membership greatly reduced, it continued to function underground.
19. Bertram Goldberg, letter to author, 3 January 1973.
20. As part of the agreement to make Hitler chancellor, the Nazi party was given the right to fill certain positions in the state governments.
21. Eric Mendelsohn, quoted in Dieter Schmidt, ed., *In Letzter Stunde: 1933 bis 1945, Künstlerschrift II* (Dresden: VEB Verlag der Kunst, 1964).
22. Harry Kessler, *Diaries*, 448.
23. *The Nation*, 29 March 1933, 332.
24. *The Nation*, 5 April 1933, 360.
25. Ibid.
26. Schlemmer, *Oskar Schlemmer*, 309.
27. For discussion of Germany's antidemocratic tendencies prior to Hitler, as well as its history of militarism within the government and impatience with the limitations of parliamentary democracy, see Taylor, *German History*, Chap. 4, n.16, 209–211; Gordon A. Craig, *The Germans* (New York: G.P. Putnam's Sons, 1982), 33; Fritz Stern, *The Failure of Illiberalism: Essays on the Political Culture of Modern Germany* (New York: Alfred A. Knopf, 1972), Introduction; Peter Gay, *Weimar Culture: The Outsider as Insider* (New York: Harper & Row, 1968).
28. Herbert Hirche, personal conversation with author, 10 August 1973.

CHAPTER 5 - SO DEADLY A BATTLE

1. Philip Johnson (15 March 1974), John Rodgers (23 May 1974), and Herbert Hirche (10 August 1973), personal conversations with author.
2. Herbert Hirche, personal conversation with author, 10 August 1973.
3. Hildegard Brenner, *Die Kunstpolitik des Nationalsozialismus* (Reinbek bei Hamburg: Rowohlt Taschenbuch Verlag, 1963), 16.
4. Barbara Miller Lane, *Architecture and Politics in Germany, 1918–1945* (Cambridge, MA: Harvard University Press, 1968), 137.

5. Mies, quoted in Conrads, *Programs and Manifestoes*, 81–82.

6. Brenner, *Kunstpolitik*, 17.

7. Miller Lane, *Architecture and Politics*, 135.

8. Ibid., 156.

9. Ibid., 134.

10. Around since the mid-nineteenth century (See Count Joseph Arthur de Gobineau's 1853 "Essai sur l'inequalité des races humaines"), racist theories reemerged in strength in 1926, the year that Hans F. K. Gunther published his book *Race and Style*, which further developed the racial formulations proposed in his 1922 book *Racial Understanding of the German People* (*Rassenkunde des Deutschen Volkes*).

11. Miller Lane, *Architecture and Politics*, 134.

12. Anna Teut, *Architektur im Dritten Reich: 1933–1945* (Frankfurt/M Wien: Verlag Ullstein Bauwelt Fundamente, 1967), 53.

13. Brenner, *Kunstpolitik*, 16.

14. Director of the Staatliche Schauspielhaus in Berlin since 1919, Leopold Jessner was called by Peter Gay "the most powerful man in the Weimar theatre." His use of expressionistic staging and free interpretation of the German classics, such as his conversion of the patriotic tones of Schiller's *William Tell* into "a call for revolution against tyranny" provoked much Nazi criticism. See Peter Gay, *Weimar Culture: The Outsider as Insider* (New York: Harper & Row, 1968), 110–112.

15. Miller Lane, *Architecture and Politics*, 157.

16. Schlemmer, *Oskar Schlemmer*, 307.

17. Ibid., 308.

18. Adolf Hitler, *The Speeches of Adolf Hitler, April 1922–August 1939*, trans. and ed. Norman H. Baynes, 2 vols. (London: Oxford University Press, 1942), 568.

19. For an examination of the relationship between expressionism and the Nazis, see Victor H. Miesel, *Voices of German Expressionism* (Englewood Cliffs, NJ: Prentice-Hall, 1970).

20. Brenner, *Kunstpolitik*, 66.

21. Albert Speer, *Inside the Third Reich: Memoirs*, trans. Richard and Clara Winston (New York: Macmillan, 1970), 22.

22. Mies, "Talk with Mies," *School of Design* (N.C.) 2:16.

23. Georgia van der Rohe, personal conversation with author, 10 May 1973.

24. Egon Hüttmann, personal conversation with author, 27 July 1974.

25. Howard Dearstyne, *Inside the Bauhaus*, ed. David Spaeth (New York: Rizzoli, 1986), 223.

26. Philip Johnson, personal conversation with author, 7 March 1973.

27. Dearstyne, *Inside*, 57.

28. Schulze, *Mies*, 39.

29. Conrad, *Programs and Manifestoes*, 44.

30. Frank Whitford, *Bauhaus* (London: Thames and Hudson, 1984), 37.

31. Hans M. Wingler, *The Bauhaus: Weimar, Dessau, Berlin, Chicago*, trans. Wolfgang Jabs and Basil Gilbert, ed. Joseph Stein (Cambridge, MA.: MIT Press, 1969), 65.

32. Whitford, *Bauhaus*, 30.
33. Ibid., 44.
34. Ibid., 38.
35. Ibid.
36. Disappointed over the Soviet government's reaction against experimental art, the fifty-six-year-old Kandinsky fled to Berlin in 1921. He had earlier worked in Germany, but returned to Russia during World War I after Germany had expelled him as an "enemy alien." During the Russian Revolution, he had been active in the reformation of art education and the establishment of art schools in much the same manner and spirit as Gropius, with whom he was in touch.
37. Dearstyne claims that Mies told him this personally in Chicago on 5 August 1957. Dearstyne, *Inside*, 43.
38. Wingler, *Bauhaus*, 136.
39. Ibid.
40. Claude Schnaidt, *Hannes Meyer: Buildings, Projects and Writings* (Stuttgart: Verlag Gerd Hatje, 1965), 105.
41. Lyonel Feininger, quoted in Dearstyne, *Inside*, 46.
42. Ibid., 198.
43. Whitford, *Bauhaus*, 124.
44. Speaking in Leipzig in 1919, Gropius condemned "the dangerous worship of might and the machine which had led us over the spiritual to the economic abyss." Whitford, *Bauhaus*, 38.
45. Ibid.
46. Miesel, *Voices*, 151.
47. Whitford, *Bauhaus*, 151.
48. As early as 1920, Schlemmer remarked, "They want to do much, but can do nothing for lack of funds. . . . It is incredible that there is scarcely a planing-bench, and that in an institution based on the crafts." Whitford, *Bauhaus*, 80.
49. Ibid., 128
50. Ibid., 132.
51. Mies, quoted in Schulze, *Mies*, 117.
52. Wingler, *Bauhaus*, 87.
53. Kurt Schwitters, quoted in Whitford, *Bauhaus*, 154.
54. Gropius, quoted in Schnaidt, *Meyer*, 121.
55. Lyonel Feininger, quoted in Dearstyne, *Inside*, 53.
56. Ibid.
57. Wingler, *Bauhaus*, 136.
58. Hannes Meyer, quoted in Schnaidt, *Meyer*, 105.
59. According to Philip Johnson, Mies believed that Meyer was "a bad architect." Personal conversation with author, 7 March 1973.
60. Hannes Meyer, quoted in Schnaidt, *Meyer*, 105.
61. Ibid., 123.
62. Georgia van der Rohe, personal conversation with author, 10 May 1973.
63. Gropius later admitted that his appointment of Meyer had been an "error of judgment." He claimed that he had spoken to Meyer before his

appointment about keeping politics out of the school and had received his assurances about this. "He was as emphatic as I in this," declared Gropius. Meyer's "mask" fell, claimed Gropius, only after his appointment. Schnaidt, *Meyer*, 122.

64. Gropius is rumored to have originally offered the post of director to Mies in 1928, before offering it to Meyer. "This is nonsense," wrote Ise Gropius. According to her, Gropius brought Meyer to the Bauhaus with the intention of turning over the directorship to him whenever Gropius wanted to retire. "When it turned out that Hannes Meyer was so left-oriented . . . the mayor dismissed . . . Meyer and asked Gropius to return and direct the school again. Gropius declined. . . . It was then and not earlier that he proposed to Mayor Hesse to ask whether Mies might want to take over" (Ise Gropius, letter to author, 7 April 1974). Mies never mentions being offered the position prior to 1930.

65. Schlemmer, *Oskar Schlemmer*, 267.

66. See Mies article "Die Entwicklung der heutigen Kunst: Architektur," *Berliner Tageblatt- Morgen-Ausgabe*, Berlin, 19 March 1927; also Mies's address at the opening of the Weissenhofsiedlung, the Werkbund's housing development in Stuttgart that Mies headed, quoted in *Staats-Anzeiger für Württenberg*, 23 July 1927.

67. Mies, quoted in Johnson, *Mies van der Rohe*, 190.

68. Wingler, *Bauhaus*, 170

69. Howard Dearstyne, quoted in *Bauhaus and Bauhaus People*, ed. Eckhard Neumann (New York: Van Nostrand Reinhold, 1970), 214.

70. Dearstyne, *Inside*, 220.

71. Ludwig Grote, letter to author, 4 February 1974.

72. Dearstyne, quoted in Neumann's *Bauhaus*, 214.

73. Ludwig Grote, letter to author (see n. 71). The exact date of this event is not known.

74. Dearstyne, quoted in Neumann's *Bauhaus*, 214.

75. Bauhaus-Archiv (1985), *Bauhaus Berlin: Auflošung Dessau 1932; Schliessung Berlin 1933; Bauhäusler und Drittes Reich: Eine Dokumentation* (Berlin: Kunstverlag Weingarten, 1985), 43.

76. Rakette, *Bauhausfest*, 256.

77. Teut, *Architektur*, 62.

78. Egon Hüttmann, personal conversation with author, 27 July 1974.

79. Bauhaus-Archiv, *Bauhaus Berlin*, 47–49.

80. Wingler, *Bauhaus*, 176.

81. Bauhaus-Archiv, *Bauhaus Berlin*, 72.

82. Wingler, *Bauhaus*, 175.

83. Bauhaus-Archiv, *Bauhaus Berlin*, 47–49.

84. Mies, "Talk with Mies," *School of Design* (N.C.) 2: 21–28.

85. Mies, "The End of the Bauhaus." Transcript of recorded conversation. *Student Publications of the School of Design* (North Carolina State College, Raleigh, N.C.) 3:3 (Spring 1953): 16.

86. Dearstyne, *Inside*, 233.

87. Neumeyer, *Mies*. See Chap. 2, n.41, 272.

88. Ibid.
89. Reich, Peterhans, Rudelt, Scheper, Albers, Kandinsky, Hilbersheimer, and Engemann remained; while Arndt and Schmidt resigned.
90. Bauhaus-Archiv, *Bauhaus Berlin*, 109.
91. Hans Keszler, letter to his mother, 1 December 1932, Bauhaus-Archiv.
92. Lothar Lang, *Das Bauhaus, 1919–1933: Idee und Wirklichkeit* (Berlin: Zentralinstitut für Formgestaltung, 1965), 139.
93. Bauhaus Archiv, *Bauhaus Berlin*, 112.
94. Dachau opened on 20 March 1933.
95. Neumeyer, *Mies*, 272–73.
96. In addition to the *Deutsche Allgemeine Zeitung*, Furtwängler's letter also appeared in the *Vossische Zeitung*; while Goebbels's was published in the *Berliner Lokal-Anzeiger* on the same day.
97. Herbert Hirche, personal conversation with author, 30 July 1974.
98. Brenner, *Kunstpolitik*, 177–81.

CHAPTER 6–BLACK LEATHER BOOTS AND BAYONETS

1. Mies, "The End of the Bauhaus," *School of Design* (N.C.) 3:16.
2. Mies, "Mies Speaks," *Architectural Review* 144: 452.
3. Mies, "The End of the Bauhaus," *School of Design* (N.C.) 3:17.
4. Ibid.
5. Mies, "Mies Speaks," *Architectural Review* 144: 452.
6. Mies, Conversation with Students at the School of Design, North Carolina State College, Original Text, Library of Congress.
7. Mies, "The End of the Bauhaus," *School of Design* (N.C.) 3:17.
8. Mies, "Mies Speaks," *Architectural Review* 144: 452.
9. Rudelt taught construction engineering and mathematics.
10. Dearstyne, *Inside*, 242.
11. Dearstyne was questioned a few evenings later in his apartment. His investigation ceased when they learned he was an American. Ibid.
12. Mies, "Mies Speaks," *Architectural Review* 144:452.
13. Eric Mendelsohn, *Letters of an Architect*, trans. Geoffrey Strachen, Intro. Nikolaus Pevsner (London, New York and Toronto: Abelard-Schumann, 1967), 126.
14. Mies, "Mies Speaks," *Architectural Review* 144:452.
15. "Mies keeps on laughing, but when didn't he ever laugh . . . in situations like these?" Helmut Heide, letter to Carl Bauer, 31 May 1933, quoted in Bauhaus-Archiv, *Bauhaus Berlin*, 134.
16. "Wettbewerb für den Erweiterungsbau der Reichshauptbank in Berlin," *Zentralblatt der Bauverwaltung vereinigt mit Zeitschrift für Bauwesen* 53:33 (2 August 1933): 386.
17. Ernst Hanfstaengel, quoted in Robert Cecil, *The Myth of the Master Race: Alfred Rosenberg and Nazi Ideology* (London: B.T. Batsford, 1972), 34.

18. *The Nation*, 31 May 1933, 607.
19. Tacitus defined the Germans as "propriam et sinceram et tantum sui gentem" ("a distinct, unmixed race, like none but themselves"); for a discussion of this (p.11) and the long German preoccupation with their uniqueness, see Gordon A. Craig, *The Germans*, Chap. 4, n.27.
20. Wilhelm Rüdiger, "Grundlagen deutscher Kunst," *NS Monatshefte* 4:43 (October 1933): 469.
21. Cecil, *Myth*, 21.
22. Throughout the Third Reich, the awesome churnings of Nazi propaganda contributed a misleading impression of consensus to both native and foreigner alike.
23. Wassily Luckhardt, "Vom Preussischen Stil zur neuen Baukunst," *Deutsche Allgemeine Zeitung*, 26 March 1933.
24. Herbert Hirche, personal conversation with author, 30 July 1974.
25. Andreas-Schreiber, deputy leader of District 10 (Berlin) of the NS Students' Association, had come to the party from the Jesuit New Germany society by way of the SA. At the time he made these statements during the spring of 1933, he represented four Berlin art schools in the Students' Association. Hildegard Brenner, "Art in the Political Power Struggle of 1933 and 1934," *Republic to Reich: The Making of the Nazi Revolution*, ed. Hajo Holborn (New York: Pantheon Books, 1972), 400.
26. Otto Andreas-Schreiber, quoted in Brenner, *Kunstpolitik*, 67.
27. Ibid.
28. Herbert Hirche, personal conversation with author, 30 July 1974.
29. Bauhaus-Archiv, *Bauhaus Berlin*, 131.
30. Albert Speer, personal conversation with author, 29 July 1974.
31. Albert Speer, personal conversation with author, 9 August 1973.
32. Hans Weidemann, letter to author, 14 February 1975.
33. Miller Lane, *Architecture and Politics*, 176.
34. Herbert Hirche, personal conversation with author, 30 July 1974.
35. Ibid.
36. Philip Johnson, personal conversation with author, 15 March 1974.
37. Mies, "The End of the Bauhaus," *School of Design* (N.C.) 3:17.
38. Herbert Hirche, personal conversation with author, 30 July 1974.
39. Mies, quoted in Wingler, *Bauhaus*, 187; unexpurgated text, Library of Congress.
40. Mies's frank language (see n. 39) was later expurgated from the printed text.
41. Helmut Heide, letter to Carl Bauer, 16 April 1933, quoted in Bauhaus-Archiv, *Bauhaus Berlin*, 131.
42. Bauhaus-Archiv.
43. Howard Dearstyne, letter to author, undated.
44. Egon Hüttmann, personal conversation with author, 27 July 1974.
45. George Orwell, "Reflections on Gandhi," *A Collection of Essays* (New York and London: Harcourt Brace Jovanovich, 1946), 177.

CHAPTER 7–A FEARSOME SILENCE

1. Mies, "Mies Speaks," *Architectural Review* 144:452.
2. Mies, "The End of the Bauhaus," *School of Design* (N.C.) 3:18.
3. Helmut Heide, letter to Carl Bauer, 5 May 1933, quoted in Bauhaus-Archiv, *Bauhaus Berlin*, 131.
4. Helmut Heide, letter to Carl Bauer, 17 May 1933, ibid., 132.
5. Ibid.
6. Helmut Heide, letter to Carl Bauer, 5 May 1933, ibid., 131.
7. Helmut Heide, letter to Carl Bauer, 17 May 1933, *Bauhaus Berlin*, 132.
8. Bauhaus-Archiv, *Bauhaus Berlin*, 131.
9. Hans Weidemann, letter to author, 14 February 1975.
10. Helmut Heide, letter to Carl Bauer, 5 May 1933, *Bauhaus Berlin*, 132.
11. Herbert Hirche, personal conversation with author, 30 July 1974.
12. Harry Kessler, *Diaries*, 453.
13. Herbert Hirche, personal conversation with author, 30 July 1974.
14. Founded in 1696 by Elector—later king of Prussia—Friedrich III, the academy had a twofold purpose: to ensure that the artistic and architectural standards of the then young capital city of Berlin were equal to the highest in Europe and to foster an appreciation of the arts among the general public.
15. Among its members were Ernst Barlach, Rudolf Billing, Otto Dix, Karl Hofer, Ernst Ludwig Kirchner, Oskar Kokoschka, Georg Kolbe, Emil Nolde, Max Pechstein, Christian Rohlfs, Karl Schmidt-Rottluff, Martin Wagner, Peter Behrens, German Bestelmeyer, Paul Bonatz, Wilhelm Kreis, Max Liebermann, Eric Mendelsohn, Hans Poelzig, Paul Schmitthenner, Paul Schultze-Naumburg, Bruno Taut, Heinrich Tessenow, Heinrich and Thomas Mann, Alfred Döblin, Walter von Molo, Franz Werfel, Frank Lloyd Wright, Edvard Munch, Alexander Glazunow, Jean Sibelius, and Igor Stravinsky.
16. Peter Paret, "The Enemy Within: Max Liebermann as President of the Prussian Academy of Arts," The Leo Baeck Memorial Lecture No. 28 (New York: Leo Baeck Institute, 1984): 17–18.
17. Egbert, *Social Radicalism*, 629.
18. The poster depicted working-class people singing, their hands joined in solidarity. "We protect the Soviet Unity," proclaimed the inscription.
19. Dieter Schmidt, *In Letzter Stunde*, 27.
20. *Deutsche Allgemeine Zeitung*, 14 February 1933.
21. Teut, *Architektur*, 137ff.
22. Käthe Kollwitz, quoted in Dieter Schmidt, *In Letzter Stunde*, 30.
23. The recounting of events is taken from the minutes of the various meetings of the Prussian Academy of Arts, Archiv, Akademie der Künste.
24. The notable lack of response to Kollwitz's ouster was probably due as much to her sex as to her outspokenly leftist beliefs.
25. Dieter Schmidt, *In Letzter Stunde*, 28.
26. Ibid.

27. In the 1920s Martin Wagner had been a member of the Ring, an avant-garde architectural group in Berlin to which Mies also belonged.

28. Hildegard Brenner, "Ende einer Bürgerlichen Kunst-Institution: Die politische Formierung der Preussischen Akademie der Künste ab 1933," *Der Vierteljahrshefte für Zeitgeschichte*, Schriftenreihe 24 (Stuttgart: Deutsche Verlags-Andstalt) : 31.

29. Oskar Schlemmer, quoted in Dieter Schmidt, *In Letzter Stunde*, 27.

30. Hans Poelzig, quoted in Brenner, "Ende," *Vierteljahrshefte* 24:31.

31. Although political meetings were banned, the Free Speech Congress—being ostensibly nonpolitical—was permitted to meet.

32. The meeting was disbanded when the police official on duty took offense at the juxtaposition of Christianity with Nazism made by a former minister of justice.

33. Harry Kessler, *Diaries*, 446.

34. Heinrich Mann, letter to Alfred Kantorowicz, 3 March 1942, quoted in André Banuels, *Heinrich Mann: Le poète et la politique* (Paris: Librairie C. Klincksieck, 1966), 620.

35. Ernst Barlach, letter to Max von Schillings, 23 February 1933, quoted in Dieter Schmidt, *In Letzter Stunde*, 31.

36. Max von Schillings, letter to Ernst Barlach, 28 February 1933, quoted in Dieter Schmidt, *In Letzter Stunde*, 32.

37. Ernst Barlach, Letter to Karl Barlach, 14 March 1933, quoted in Dieter Schmidt, *In Letzte Stunde*, 421.

38. Max Liebermann, quoted in *Die Bildenden Künste im Dritten Reich: Eine Dokumentation*, Joseph Wulf, ed. (Gütersloh: Sigbert Mohn Verlag, 1963), 36.

39. Max von Schillings, letter to academy members, 13 May 1933, quoted in Dieter Schmidt, *In Letzte Stunde*, 43.

> Dear Sir . . .
> Dear Madam,
>   The nomination of members to the division of fine arts by the former minister of culture, Dr. Grimme, which took place in August 1931 has, as you know, resulted in strong opposition and a regrettable schism within the department. Mr. Rudolf Belling informs us that a number of members nominated at that time are desirous of contributing to a solution of this unhappy conflict, and to take a position on the option according to the regulations of this statute, by declining the nomination. This would, in any case, be a respectable solution for the nominated artists, as well as for the academy itself.
>   I would be grateful if you would kindly inform me of your personal opinion about this suggestion and of your own decision as quickly as possible.
>
> > With friendly greetings,
> > The President

40. Philip Johnson, personal conversation with author, 15 March 1974.

41. Miller Lane, *Architecture and Politics*, 177.

42. Ibid.

43. Mies, letter to Max von Schillings, 18 May 1933, quoted in Wulf, *Die bildenden Künste*, 40.

44. Eric Mendelsohn (on the brink of leaving Germany), Emil Nolde, Renée Sintenis, Ludwig Gies, and Ludwig Kirchner turned down the resignation request. The response of Edwin Scharf remains unknown.
45. Craig, *The Germans* (New York: G. P. Putnam's Sons, 1982), 22.
46. Stern, *Dreams*, 177.

CHAPTER 8–TRIUMPH

1. Hans Keszler, letters, Bauhaus-Archiv.
2. Although its name was new—being a shortened version of Geheimstaatspolizei—and it had frequently been suppressed in the past, a secret political police force had long existed within the Prussian police.
3. For information regarding Diels and the early years of the gestapo, see Shlomo Aronson, *Reinhard Heydrich und die Frühgeschichte von Gestapo und SD*, Studien zur Zeitgeschichte Herausgegeben vom Institut für Zeitgeschichte (Stuttgart: Deutsche Verlags-Anstalt, 1971).
4. Hans Weidemann, letter to author, 14 February 1975.
5. There appears to be no evidence precisely dating this meeting. In a letter dated 26 May 1933, Hans Kessler (see n. 1) mentions Mies being informed by the police that the Bauhaus will be opened (quoted in Bauhaus-Archiv, *Bauhaus Berlin*, 178); while, in a letter dated 3 July to Carl Bauer (*Bauhaus Berlin*, 136), Mies speaks of his receiving such permission "three weeks ago," which would date it about the second week in June. It may reasonably be assumed that his meeting with Diels predated his receiving such permission. From Helmut Heide's complaint of 5 May, in his letter to Carl Bauer (*Bauhaus Berlin*, 131) that "as good as nothing had been done for fourteen days [following the closing of the school]," and that Heide, along with other rightist students, made the initial contacts with the police authorities, subsequently followed by Mies, it seems unlikely that the meeting between Mies and Diels could have occurred prior to mid-May. Mies's reference, twenty years later before the North Carolina students in 1952, to his going to gestapo headquarters "for three months every other day," which—starting from the date of the Bauhaus raid on 11 April would bring it up to mid-July—appears to have been incorrect.
6. See Chap. 5., n. 36.
7. Mies, "The End of the Bauhaus," *School of Design* (N.C.) 3:18; and Mies, "Mies Speaks," *Architectural Review* 144:452.
8. Helmut Heide, letter to Carl Bauer, 17 May 1933, *Bauhaus Berlin*, 132.
9. Ibid.
10. Ibid.
11. Helmut Heide, letter to Carl Bauer, 31 May 1933, *Bauhaus Berlin*, 134.
12. Wingler, *Bauhaus*, 188.
13. Letter from Mies to the mayor of Dessau, 17 June 1933:

> Die Zahl der Mitläufer wurde stetig geringer und die Führung ging allmählich an die nationalgesinnten Studierenden über, die die Unterstützung des Lehrkörpers fanden. . . . Die Wandlung innerhalb der Studierenden war im Herbst 1932 so weit vorgeschritten, dass die Schliessung

des Hauses fast nur national gesinnte junge Mensche traf. (Bauhaus-Archiv, *Bauhaus Berlin*, 139).

14. Herbert Hirche, personal conversation with author, 10 August 1973.
15. Bauhaus-Archiv, *Bauhaus Berlin*, 132–35.
16. Alcar Rudelt, letter to Carl Bauer, 20 June 1933, *Bauhaus Berlin*, 135.
17. Helmut Heide, letter to Carl Bauer, 31 May 1933, *Bauhaus Berlin*, 134.
18. Christian Wolsdorff, letter to author, 29 July 1986.
19. Brenner, "Ende" *Vierteljahrshefte* 24:128.
20. Ibid., 129–30.
21. Ibid., 130.
22. Herbert Hirche, personal conversation with author, 30 July 1974.
23. Ivo Panaggi, letter to Walter Gropius, 25 August 1934, Bauhaus-Archiv, *Bauhaus Berlin*, 226.
24. "Wettbewerb," *Zentralblatt*, 53:386.
25. Ibid., 385.
26. See Mies's Stuttgart bank building project of 1928; his project for the remodeling of the Alexanderplatz of the same year and the 1929 office building on the Friedrichstrasse.
27. Herbert Hirche, personal conversation with author, 30 July 1974.
28. Born in 1876, the historian and critic Arthur Moeller van den Bruck was a leader of the conservative revolutionaries during the Weimar era and an intellectual forerunner of Hitler and Nazism. Violently opposed to democracy, which he characterized as mad egalitarianism, he preached "the mystique of the national idea" and the formation of "a new German self-consciousness." He was contemptuous of international law and sympathetic to racial doctrine, supporting the notion of a superior Nordic race. He stressed the idea of *Volkstum*, a living national spirit, a "national rhythm," which he said was felt by all Germans. These ideas were expressed in his major work, *The Third Reich*, first published in 1923, two years before his death by suicide. His discussion of Prussian architecture may be found in his book *The Prussian Style*, originally published in 1916 and reprinted in 1931. He exerted a profound, though unacknowledged, influence on Hitler.
29. Philip Johnson, "Architecture in the Third Reich," *Hound and Horn* 7:1 (October–December 1933): 139.
30. The others were Fritz Becker, Kurt Frick, Mebes and Emmerich, Pfeifer and Grossman, and Pinno and Grund. See *Bauwelt* 33 (1933): 4.
31. Mies, "The End of the Bauhaus," *School of Design* (N.C.) 3:18.
32. Wingler, *Bauhaus*, 189.
33. Mies, letter to Diels, 20 July 1933, quoted in Wingler, *Bauhaus*, 188. Mies's letter predates by one day the gestapo letter of 21 July. It seems that Mies was alerted to the gestapo decision prior to receipt of their letter. For his plan to work, his announcement of the school's closure had to predate the gestapo letter, so that the police would have no excuse to withhold their permission to reopen that Mies so ardently sought. Letters quoted in Wingler, *Bauhaus*, 188.
34. The official announcement of the closing and dissolution of the Bau-

haus was made to the student body on this date. See Wingler, *Bauhaus*, 189.

CHAPTER 9–AN ASTONISHING TURN

1. Schlemmer, *Oskar Schlemmer*, 316.
2. Walter Gropius, Memorandum to Eugen Hönig, president of the Reich Chamber of Fine Arts, 18 January 1934, Bauhaus-Archiv, *Bauhaus Berlin*, 148.
3. Ibid.
4. Speaking before four thousand schoolteachers at Harzburg on 28 August 1933, Dr. Haupt, a Nazi leader, said that "[t]he reply to the Treaty of Versailles is that the German people have left the path of Western civilization." Quoted by Robert Dell in "The German Nightmare," *The Nation*, 18 October 1933, 434.
5. Henry Wyman Holmes, quoted in Richard Neuberger, "The New Germany," *The Nation*, 4 October 1933, 376.
6. Alfred H. Barr, Jr., "Art in the Third Reich—Preview, 1933," *The Magazine of Art* (October 1945): 211–30.
7. Ibid.
8. Schlemmer, along with Karl Hofer and Hans Poelzig, had been granted "vacations" from their teaching posts; while Dr. Max Friedländer, the Jewish director of the Kaiser Friedrich Museum and one of the foremost living authorities on Netherlandish and German painting of the fifteenth and sixteenth centuries, had been removed from his post.
9. Schlemmer, *Oskar Schlemmer*, 311.
10. Ibid.
11. Otto Andreas-Schreiber, letter to Hans Weidemann in response to author's queries, 10 January 1975. Andreas-Schreiber alludes to Mies's presence at this event. With the Bauhaus and Reichsbank issues as yet unresolved, and with his personal stake in supporting this so-called "liberal" wing, it seems unlikely that Mies would not lend his prestigious presence to this highly anticipated cultural event. Mies himself never spoke of this in later reminiscences; understandable in lieu of the fact that this was—after all—a Nazi-sponsored event.
12. Brenner, *Kunstpolitik*, 68.
13. Joseph Goebbels, Speech, 17 June 1933, quoted in *Der Angriff*, 18 June 1933.
14. Brenner, *Kunstpolitik*, 68.
15. Ibid.
16. Otto Andreas-Schreiber, letter, published in the *Deutsche Allgemeine Zeitung*, 12 July 1933, quoted in Miller Lane, *Architecture and Politics*, 178.
17. "Revolution is not a permanent condition: it cannot become a permanent state," said Hitler on 6 July 1933, quoted in Domarus, *Hitler: Reden und Proklamationen*, (Würzburg: Verlagsdruckerai Schmidt, Neustadt a.d. Aisch, 1962–63), I, 286.
18. Walter Hansen, quoted in Brenner, *Kunstpolitik*, 70.

19. Albert Flechtheim, quoted in Kessler, *Diaries*, 462.
20. Otto Andreas-Schreiber, quoted in Brenner, *Kunstpolitik*, 70.
21. Taking their cue from Hitler—the title of whose book *My Battle* (*Mein Kampf*) offers the most obvious example—party leaders constantly referred to the political arena as some sort of battleground: hence Hinkel's use of the term "the front" (Brenner, *Kunstpolitik*, 70).
22. Brenner, *Kunstpolitik*, 71.
23. Ibid.
24. Herbert Hirche, personal conversation with author, 30 July 1974.
25. Hitler, Culture Day address, 1 September 1933, quoted in Teut, *Architektur*, 90–91.
26. Hans Weidemann, letter to author, 12 April 1975.
27. Albert Speer, personal conversation with author, 24 July 1978.
28. In actual practice, however, Jews were not specifically forbidden to join the RKK until 1935, when membership applications began to include questions regarding the applicant's ancestry.
29. An invitation and program for the opening concert are in Mies's personal files at the Library of Congress.
30. Joseph Goebbels, Speech, 15 November 1933, quoted in *Völkischer Beobachter*, 16 November 1933; also quoted in Miller Lane, *Architecture and Politics*, 176.
31. Max Sauerlandt, 7 January 1934, quoted in Brenner, *Kunstpolitik*, 74.
32. The KdF, as it was popularly known, was based on the Italian fascist organization known as Dopolavoro (After-Work). Involving sports, travel, cultural activities, the aesthetic milieu of the factory, and adult education, it ensured party supervision during every hour of every worker's life.
33. John Rodgers, personal conversation with author, 23 May 1974.
34. Although Pius Pahl, a Bauhaus student, identified the speaker only as "the head of the Chamber of Arts and Culture" (quoted in Neumann, ed., *Bauhaus and Bauhaus People*, 231), according to Albert Speer, only Weidemann would have made such a public comment. Albert Speer, personal conversation with author, 29 July 1974.
35. Hitler, quoted in Joachim C. Fest, *Hitler*, trans. by Richard and Clara Winston (New York: Harcourt Brace Jovanovich, 1974), 429.
36. Philip Johnson, quoted by John Russell, *The New York Times*, 26 July 1985, Section 2, 29.

CHAPTER 10–"NEAREST MY HEART"

1. August Kubizek's recollection of his experiences with the young Hitler, entitled *Young Hitler: The Story of Our Friendship*, trans. by E. V. Anderson (London: Allan Wingate, 1954) is not without controversy. Some scholars, such as Joachim Fest, dismiss it as hagiographical; others, such as William Shirer, John Toland, and Werner Maser, view it more positively. The author thus approached it with grave reservations. Far from being an idolatrous portrait, it is replete with incisively drawn characterizations of some of Hitler's more repugnant qualities, such as his fear-

some temper, his intolerance for debate, and his delusional personality traits. Kubizek portrays him not as an incipient genius, but as a potential madman. His observations ring true, especially with regard to the early and pronounced manifestation of Hitler's architectural inclinations. Albert Speer concurred with the author's evaluation of the validity of Kubizek's observations.

2. Kubizek, *Young Hitler*, 51.
3. *Hitler's Secret Conversations, 1941–1944*, trans. by Norman Cameron and R. H. Stevens (New York: Farrar, Straus, and Young, 1953), 361.
4. Kubizek, *Young Hitler*, 53.
5. Robert R. Taylor, *The Word in Stone: The Role of Architecture in the National Socialist Ideology* (Berkeley and Los Angeles: University of California Press, 1974), 49.
6. Kubizek, *Young Hitler*, 53.
7. Ibid., 8.
8. Eric Fromm, *The Anatomy of Human Destructiveness* (New York: Holt, Rinehart & Winston, 1973), 428.
9. Kubizek, *Young Hitler*, 147.
10. Ibid., 8.
11. Fest, *Hitler*, 15.
12. Shirer, *Rise and Fall*, 26.
13. Fest, *Hitler*, 13.
14. Hitler, *Mein Kampf*, 6.
15. Ibid., 8.
16. Fest, *Hitler*, 18.
17. Ibid., 19.
18. Kubizek, *Young Hitler*, 119.
19. Ibid.
20. Ibid.
21. Ibid., 130.
22. Ibid., 129.
23. Ibid., 113.
24. Ibid., 130.
25. Ibid., 116.
26. Fromm, *Anatomy*, 421.
27. Ibid., 396.
28. This characteristic has been noted by most of Hitler's biographers, including Fest and Maser, as well as by Speer. For a specific examination of this subject, see Jochen Thies, *Architekt der Weltherrschaft: Die "Endziele" Hitlers* (Düsseldorf: Droste Verlag, 1976).
29. Fritz Stern, "Germany 1933: Fifty Years Later," The Leo Baeck Memorial Lecture No. 27 (New York: Leo Baeck Institute, 1983): 5.
30. Fest has speculated that Hitler, the impassioned advocate of war and the proselytizer of a race of warriors, was a draft-dodger, moving his residence several times to avoid induction into the Austrian army (p. 45). In 1913—again, in Fest's view—to avoid the Austrian draft, Hitler appeared in Munich, where—living still as a "loner"—he supported himself by

selling meticulously detailed architectural watercolors (p. 61). See *Hitler,* Chap. 9, n. 34.

31. Fest, *Hitler,* 64.
32. Hitler, *Mein Kampf,* 204–06.
33. Stern, "Germany 1933," Baeck Lecture No. 27:5.
34. Hitler, quoted in Werner Maser, *Hitler: Legend, Myth and Reality,* trans. by Peter and Betty Ross (New York: Harper & Row, 1973), 66.
35. Hitler, quoted in Speer, *Inside,* 80.
36. Hitler, Culture Day address, 11 September 1935, quoted in *The Speeches of Adolf Hitler April 1922–August 1939,* trans. and ed. by Norman H. Baynes, 2 vols. (London: Oxford University Press, 1942), 573.
37. Hitler spent slightly less than nine months there after his conviction for the ill-conceived and poorly executed "Beer Hall Putsch."
38. Hitler, Culture Day address, 6 September 1938, quoted in Baynes, *Speeches,* 610.
39. Hitler, quoted in Henry Picker, *Hitlers Tischgespräche im Führerhauptquartier: 1941–1942* (Stuttgart: Seewald Verlag, 1963), 90.
40. Hitler, Culture Day address, 11 September 1935, quoted in Baynes, *Speeches,* 573.
41. Hitler, Speech on 23 November 1938, opening the Exhibition of German Architecture, Arts and Crafts, quoted in *Völkischer Beobachter,* 24 November 1938; also quoted in Maser, *Hitler,* 58.
42. Hitler, *Mein Kampf,* 265.
43. Hitler, Culture Day address, 9 September 1937, quoted in Teut, *Architektur,* 188.
44. Speer, *Inside,* 80.
45. Hitler, purported conversation with Otto Strasser, 21 May 1930, quoted in Baynes, *Speeches,* 567.
46. Hitler, *Mein Kampf,* 266.
47. These phrases were compiled from several of Hitler's speeches of 1937 and 1939.
48. "We will win the war, but we will secure the victory through our buildings," said Hitler upon hearing of the capitulation of France in 1940, in an almost verbatim repetition of a statement made earlier by Wilhelm II. Quoted in Teut, *Architektur,* 13.

CHAPTER 11–"UNMISTAKABLY CLEAR"

1. Hitler, quoted in Speer, *Inside,* 39.
2. Speer, *Inside,* 143.
3. Hitler, quoted in Speer, *Inside,* 39.
4. Hitler, *Hitler's Secret Conversations,* 48.
5. Hitler, quoted in Albert Speer, *Secret Diaries,* 16.
6. Hitler, quoted in Speer, *Inside,* 28.
7. Albert Speer, "Die Bürde werde ich nicht mehr los," *Der Spiegel* 46: 20, 7 November 1966, 50.

8. Hitler Speech, 18 July 1937.
9. Fromm, *Anatomy*, 420.
10. Hitler, quoted in William Hamsher, *Albert Speer—Victim of Nuremberg?* (London: Leslie Frewin, 1970), 88.
11. Speer, *Inside*, 40. Hitler seems never to have wavered in his admiration for Troost. In January 1942, he said of Troost, "That man [has] revolutionized the art of building." *Hitler's Secret Conversations*, 107.
12. Speer, *Secret Diaries*, 112.
13. Photographs and description of this event appear in "Nachlang zum Fest des Deutsche Kunst," *Die Kunst*, (München, 1934): 79–81.
14. Schlemmer, *Oskar Schlemmer*, 316.
15. Albert Speer, personal conversation with author, 29 July 1974.
16. Albert Speer, personal conversation with author, 9 August 1973. According to Speer, the intuiting of Hitler's inclinations was a highly developed skill among his subordinates.
17. Hans Weidemann, letter to author, 12 April 1975. In this letter, Weidemann described Goebbels's attitude toward the arts as *"amüsisch"*—a devastatingly pejorative term, virtually untranslatable, meaning that a person is not only uncreative himself, but has absolutely no appreciation for the arts.
18. Hans Weidemann, letter to author, 15 February 1975.
19. Ibid.
20. Albert Speer, personal conversation with author, 24 July 1978. Speer said that Hitler tolerated judgments with which he disagreed from individuals who spoke outside their area of expertise. He was thus very forgiving with artists who spoke politically and politicians who spoke of art. Funk had been financial editor of the *Berliner Börsenzeitung* and worked mainly as a "contact man" between the party and important business leaders.
21. Albert Speer, personal conversation with author, 24 July 1978.
22. Hans Weidemann, letter to author, 15 February 1975. In describing his gesture, Weidemann wrote, *"Hitler jedoch lehnte entschieden ab."*
23. Ibid.
24. Hans Weidemann, letter to author, 12 April 1975.

CHAPTER 12–MOMENTARY EXAGGERATIONS

1. Hans Weidemann, letter to author, 12 April 1975.
2. Ibid.
3. See Schulze, *Mies*, 199, f. 47: also letter in the Mies Archives from Mathies, German general commissioner of the 1935 Brussels World's Fair, dated 11 June 1934, accompanied by a draft of the commission.
4. Hans Weidemann claimed to know nothing about this competition; letter to author, 12 April 1975.
5. The exhibit ran until 3 June 1934.
6. *"Es wird künftig nür einen Adel geben—den Adel der Arbeit!"*

7. Henry-Russell Hitchcock, "Architecture Chronicle," *The Hound and Horn* (October–December 1931): 94–96.

8. See *Monatschefte für Baukunst und Städtebau* (formerly *Wasmuth*) 6 (June 1934); and *Bauwelt* 22 (1934).

9. Albert Speer, personal conversation with author, 24 July 1978; also Gerhard Weber (Munich architect and former Bauhaus student), personal conversation with author, 25 July 1978.

10. Mies, quoted in Johnson, *Mies van der Rohe*, 194.

11. Albert Speer, personal conversation with author, 29 July 1974.

12. Ibid.

13. Shirer, *Rise and Fall*, 298.

14. Among the dead were Gregor Strasser; General Schleicher, his wife, and General Kurt von Bredow, his close friend; many of the staff of Franz von Papen, the vice-chancellor, who barely escaped with his own life; Erich Klausener, a prominent Catholic official; and a leading Munich music critic, Dr. Willi Schmid, who, sitting at home playing his cello, was mistaken for Willi Schmidt, a local SA leader. Shirer, *Rise and Fall*, 309–11.

15. Shirer, *Rise and Fall*, 312.

16. *The Nation*, 11 July 1934, 32.

17. Shirer, *Rise and Fall*, 312.

18. Shirer, *Rise and Fall*, 313.

19. Speer, *Secret Diaries*, 5.

20. Speer, *Inside*, 53.

21. See Ludwig Glaeser, *Ludwig Mies van der Rohe; Furniture and Furniture Drawings from the Design Collection and the Mies van der Rohe Archive*, The Museum of Modern Art, New York, Pl. 43, drawing dated 5 July 1934.

22. Alfred Rosenberg, letter to Joseph Goebbels, 20 October 1934, EAP (Einheits Akten Plan) 99/343, File of Rosenberg Chancellory, on National Archives Microfilm Publication, T.454, roll 74. (These records are generally described in Guide No. 28 of the *Guides to Captured German Records microfilmed at Alexandria, Va.*)

23. Gunther Haupt, letter to Mies, 13 August 1934, Library of Congress.

24. Alfred Rosenberg, letter to Joseph Goebbels, 20 October 1934, EAP:99/343.

25. Ivo Panaggi, letter to Walter Gropius, 25 August 1934, quoted in Bauhaus-Archiv, *Bauhaus Berlin*, 226.

26. Sibyl Moholy-Nagy et al., "MAS [Modern Architecture Symposium] 1964," *Journal of the Society of Architectural Historians*, 24:84.

27. Bauhaus-Archiv, *Bauhaus Berlin*, 149.

28. In turning the Bauhaus into a private institution (necessary in order to secure the school's assets from future government claim), Mies personally acquired all rights, including licensing fees and use of the Bauhaus name.

29. Christian Wolsdorff, letter to author, 19 August 1987. Dr. Wolsdorff

claims that there is no further information available regarding these criminal charges.

30. "[W]hen a man knows he is to be hanged in a fortnight, it concentrates his mind wonderfully." Boswell, *Life of Johnson*.
31. Alfred Rosenberg, letter to Joseph Goebbels, 20 October 1934, EAP:99/343.
32. Walter Gropius, letter to Eugen Hönig, 27 March 1934, quoted in Miller Lane, *Architecture and Politics*, 181.
33. Stern, *Dreams*, 177.
34. Mies, Johnson, *Mies van der Rohe*, 190.
35. *"Wer nicht für uns ist, ist wider uns!"*
36. Others whose names appeared on the proclamation were Werner Beumelburg, Ernst Barlach, Rudolf G. Binding, Hans Friedrich Blunck, Verleger Alfred Bruckmann, Richard Euringer, Prof. Emil Fahrenkamp, Erich Feyerabend, Gustav Frenssen, Wilhelm Furtwängler, Prof. Eberhard Hanfstaengl, Gustav Havenmann, Erich Heckel, Prof. Eugen Hönig, Hans Ehlert, Hanns Johst, Georg Kolbe, Erwin Kolbenheyer, Werner Krauss, Franz Lenk, Heinrich Lersch, Prof. Karl Lörcher, Architect Walter March, Agnes Miegel, Börries Freiherr von Münchhausen, Emil Nolde, Paul Pfund, Hans Pfitzner, Prof. Dr. Wilhelm Pinder, Hermann Stehr, Richard Strauss, Josef Thorak, Generalintendent Hans Tietjen, Oberbürgermeister Dr. Weidemann, Arnold Weinmüller.
37. In this election, 4,294,654 Germans voted against Hitler.

CHAPTER 13–"NOISY, BOTHERSOME AND SLIGHTLY CRAZY"

1. Mies, Copy of Letter to NS Volkswohlfahrt, 30 August 1934 (Library of Congress).

> We are still not in possession of the registration forms which we were promised verbally and we ask you to send them to us with your messenger. Thanking you in advance and Heil Hitler!
> Atelier Mies van der Rohe
> [Copy initialed by Mies]

2. Albert Speer, personal conversation with author, 24 July 1978.
3. Mies, "Concerning the Preliminary Draft of an Exposition Building for the 1935 Brussels Worlds Fair," quoted in Schulze, *Mies*, 199.
4. Ibid.
5. Herbert Hirche, personal conversation with author, 10 August 1973.
6. Sergius Ruegenberg, personal conversation with author, 24 July 1974.
7. Albert Speer, personal conversation with author, 24 July 1978.
8. Speer, *Inside*, 64.
9. Alfred Rosenberg, quoted in Brenner, *Kunstpolitik*, 78.
10. *Bauwelt* 1 (1934): 1–8.
11. Barr, "The Art of the Third Reich," *Magazine of Art*: 221.
12. Walter Gropius, letter to Eugen Hönig, president of the Reich Chamber of Fine Arts, 27 March 1934; quoted in Miller Lane, *Architecture and*

Politics, 181. According to Miller Lane (see f. 57, p. 181), Gropius also wrote another letter to Karl Lörcher, chairman of the BDA on 20 February 1934.

13. James Marston Fitch, *Architecture and the Esthetics of Plenty* (New York: Columbia University Press, 1961), 150.

14. Hitler, Culture Day address, 5 September 1934, quoted in *Völkischer Beobachter,* 7 September 1934.

15. Georgia van der Rohe, personal conversation with author, 10 May 1973.

16. Herbert Hirche, personal conversation with author, 10 August 1973.

17. Lilly Reich, letter to J. J. P. Oud, 12 February 1936, quoted in Tegethoff, *Mies: Villas,* 121.

18. George Nelson, "Architects of Europe Today: 7—Van der Rohe, Germany," *Pencil Points,* 16:9 (September 1935): 453–460.

19. Mies's caution is apparent in his refusal to allow publication of photographs of his buildings during this time. He was apparently fearful of the effect of foreign approbation within hypernationalistic Nazi circles. See Mies, letter to George Nelson, 20 July 1935:

     > As I already informed you . . . , I have no intention at the present time to publish my work in a foreign magazine. Please consider this decision as irrevocable. For this reason, photographs will probably no longer be needed (Library of Congress).

20. Tegethoff, *Mies: Villas,* 121.

21. Kurt Tucholsky, quoted in Fest, *Hitler,* 277.

22. Alfred Barr, quoted in Samuel Cauman, *The Living Museum: Experiences of an Art Historian and Museum Director—Alexander Dorner* (New York: New York University Press, 1958), 108.

23. See the private homes designed by Rudolf Schwarz that appeared in *Bauwelt* 52 (1934): 3, 8; and *Bauwelt* 26 (1935): 3.

24. *Die Kunst,* 74: 1 (October 1935): 23.

25. *Bauwelt* 5 (1935): 5.

26. Compare the homes illustrated in "Wohnbauten und Siedlungen," in the series *Deutsche Baukunst der Gegenwart,* ed. by Walter Müller-Wulckow, 1929 with house W. in Dahlem by Prof. F. A. Breuhaus, published in *Die Kunst* 37 (1935–36): 170; House of Dr. Heyne by J. Vassillière of Berlin in *Die Kunst* 74: 5 (February 1936): 97; Houses by Karl Wach and Heinrich Rosskotten in *Die Kunst,* 74: 2 (November 1935): 98; H. P. Schmohl in *Die Kunst* 74: 1 (October 1935): 5; and Hans Scharoun in *Bauwelt* 12 (1935): 4.

27. Compare Herbert Rimpl's Heinkelwerke in Marienehe bei Rostock, erected in 1934 with buildings from the exhibition, such as the Exposition Buildings by Zizler and Müller, Mannheim, 1930; Königsgrube Mine Works by Theodor Merril, Bochum, 1930; City Employment Office by Walter Gropius, Dessau, 1928.

28. Hitler, quoted in Speer, *Secret Diaries,* 174–75.

29. Speer, *Inside,* 142.

30. See *Architektur der Zwanziger Jahre in Deutschland* (1929); republished in 1975 (Konigstein im Taunus: Karl Robert Lanwiesche Nachfolger).

31. The "villa"—a single-story building extending horizontally across the landscape, most recently expressed in his "court-house" designs—was the model for many of Mies's most successful and renowned structures, including the Barcelona Pavilion and the Tugendhat House.
32. This was the second version of the design; the first was rejected by the family for reasons of cost and the unavailability of steel—restricted now to industrial purposes—for private construction. The substitution of cost-reducing elements and brick-supporting walls for the steel, as well as the modification of the inner courtyard and centrally placed view within the garden, did not compromise the integrity of the design.
33. Albert Speer, personal conversation with author, 24 July 1978.
34. Ibid.
35. Ulrich Lange, letter to Ludwig Glaeser, 25 March 1968,

> [H]e was so enraged ... and so offended that he relinquished the realization of this ... construction, to my regret. (Mies Archive)

CHAPTER 14—"A SHAMEFUL, DISHONOURABLE FATE"

1. Lilly Reich, letter to J. J. P. Oud, 1935, quoted in Neumeyer, *Mies*, 276–77, n. 72.
2. Alfred Neumeyer, telegram to Mies, 14 December 1935.

> Mills College offers six week summer course July 1936 with travel dollars 1,500—English necessary—More through Heise—Kamillenstrasse 2—Wire paid reply—letter follow—Neumeyer. (Library of Congress)

3. Alfred Neumeyer, letter to Mies, 13 December 1935, Library of Congress.
4. Maude Grote, letter to author, 9 September 1974.
5. Herbert Hirche, personal conversation with author, 30 July 1974.
6. Prussian Academy of Arts, Memorandum to members, 19 August 1935.

> The Ministry of the Exterior considers it imperative that all German members who will be concerned with preparation for a visit abroad, inform this department, in each case, beforehand. Therefore, I call upon all those who are intending to travel abroad, even when they have a purely professional purpose, to give me timely prior notification, so that I may report to the Minister, whose approval must be received prior to the commencement of the trip.
> Should members of the Academy be invited to a lecture or organization abroad, or wish to participate in foreign international congresses and meetings of similar sort, ... issuing invitations are to be accepted only with the permission of the Reichs and Prussian Minister for Science, Education and Culture. The execution of foreign travel, resulting from such useful purposes ... requires the consent of the Minister of Culture. (Library of Congress)

7. Laura Fermi, *Illustrious Immigrants: The Intellectual Migration from Europe, 1930–41* (Chicago: University of Chicago Press, 1968), 100.
8. Herbert Hirche, personal conversation with author, 30 July 1974.
9. Kurt Tucholsky, *Kurt Tucholsky in selbstzeugnissen und Bilddokumenten*, ed. by Klaus-Peter Schulz (Hamburg: Rowohlts Monographien, 1959), 166.
10. Maude Grote, letter to author, 1 September 1974.

11. Thomas Mann, *An Exchange of Letters*, trans. by H. T. Lowe-Porter (New York: Alfred A. Knopf, 1937), 110.

12. Bertolt Brecht, quoted in Frederic V. Grunfeld, *The Hitler File: A Social History of Germany and the Nazis, 1918–45* (New York: Random House, 1974), 253.

13. Alfred Döblin, quoted in Ibid.

14. Käthe Kollwitz, quoted in Dieter Schmidt, *In Letzter Stunde*, 33.

15. E. Wernert, *L'Art dans le IIIᵉ Reich: Une Tentative d'Esthétique Dirigée*. Publication No. 7 (Paris: Centre d'Études de Politique Étrangère, 1936): 63.

16. Frederic V. Grunfeld, *Prophets Without Honor: A Background to Freud, Kafka, Einstein and Their World* (New York: Holt, Rinehart, Winston, 1979): 259.

17. Philip Johnson, personal conversation with author, 7 May 1973.

18. Adolf Goldschmidt, quoted in Maude Grote, letter to author, 9 September 1974.

19. Egbert, *Social Radicalism*, 635.

20. Ibid., 628.

21. Erwin Panofsky, *Meaning in the Visual Arts* (New York: Doubleday/Anchor, 1957), 322.

22. The others who left went to Vienna in 1940. How many of those who left were Jewish, of leftist sympathies, or otherwise opposed by the Nazis is unknown.

23. "*Verschiedenartig ist diese Kunst des Widerstandes.*"

24. Hitler, speech, Baynes, *Speeches*, 569–584.

25. Herbert Hirche, personal conversation with author, 30 July 1974.

26. Hitler, Speech, Baynes, *Speeches*, 569–584.

27. President of the Reich Chamber of Fine Arts, letter to Mies, 3 December 1934, Library of Congress. In this document, Mies, along with other "prominent representatives from the creative arts," was invited to participate in an evening of film discussion planned for early 1934. Mies accepted the invitation. See Mies, letter to president of the Reich Chamber of Fine Arts, 18 December 1934, Library of Congress. Mies's involvement with the avant-garde filmmakers went back to the 1920s and his association with "G," as well as his longtime friendship with the Dadaist film creator, Hans Richter.

28. Herbert Hirche, personal conversation with author, 30 July 1974.

29. Mies, copy of letter to Alfred Neumeyer, 27 January 1936.

> Dear Mr. Neumeyer:
> For the invitation to teach at Mills College this summer, which you transmitted to me, I would like to thank the institute, and especially you, most sincerely.
> To my regret, I am unable to fulfill the provision which is connected with this offer, that is knowledge of the English language. Also I do not believe that I would succeed by this summer to adopt the language to an extent which would allow me to hold lectures.
> These reasons force me to ask you to give me up for this summer. I have talked with Dr. Heise and Miss Strauss in the same sense.

It is not easy for me to refuse you since it would have given me pleasure
to teach and at the same time to also get to know California.
Accept for yourself and for your wife my cordial and sincere greetings

Yours,

[Mies van der Rohe]

(Copy unsigned,

Library of Congress)

CHAPTER 15—"IT IS TIME . . ."

1. Hitler, quoted in *The New York Times*, 1 January 1936, 38.
2. Goebbels, quoted in Ibid.
3. Ibid.
4. *Time*, 5, 17 February 1936, 37.
5. Gustavus Town Kirby, quoted in *The New York Times*, 18 February 1936, 28.
6. Hitler, quoted in Shirer, *Rise and Fall*, 403.
7. Speer, *Inside*, 72.
8. Typical of the regimentation imposed upon the voting public was the manifesto that appeared in the Berlin suburb of Kleinmachnow and quoted in *The New York Times*, 29 March 1936, 1.

   > Voting begins at 9 in the morning and ends at 6 in the evening. No German comrade dare be absent, and I urge all voters most strongly to vote during the morning hours. By 1 o'clock in the afternoon the election must be over.
   > During the afternoon I will have all laggards dragged to the ballot box. None shall escape us. Kleinmachnow is surrounded and shut off. Kleinmachnow has stood in first place in all campaign events. This time we must have a 100 percent vote. We owe that to our Führer. Everyone shall go to the polls. . . . All those who support our Führer will display on their homes banners bearing slogans and the colors of the Third Reich. Each citizen shall show where he stands.

9. *The New Statesman and Nation*, 4 April 1936.
10. Lilly Reich, letter to J. J. P. Oud, 12 February 1936, quoted in Tegethoff, *Mies, Villas*, 121.
11. Maude Grote, personal conversation with author, 1 August 1974.
12. Ibid.
13. Herbert Hirche (30 July 1974) and Maude Grote (1 August 1974), personal conversations with author.
14. Henry Heald, letter to author, 2 October 1973. According to Heald, one of those architects who had accepted the post was Louis Skidmore. He withdrew after receiving some important commissions for the New York World's Fair, and established the architectural firm of Skidmore, Owings, and Merrill.
15. Jerrold Loebl, letter to author, 5 October 1973.
16. Ibid.
17. Most probably John Rodgers and Howard Dearstyne, who had studied with Mies at the Bauhaus and privately, after its closing.

18. John A. Holabird, letter to Mies, 20 March 1936, Library of Congress.
19. Sixty-seven and a half percent of German construction was government-sponsored in 1936, as opposed to 33 percent in 1933. Quoted in Teut, *Architektur*, 77.
20. Miller Lane, *Architecture and Politics*, 190.
21. Gustav Stotz, letter to Mies, 13 March 1936, Library of Congress.
22. Herbert Hirche, personal conversation with author, 30 July 1974.
23. Sergius Ruegenberg, quoted in Neumeyer, *Mies*, 24.
24. Herbert Hirche, personal conversation with author, 30 July 1974.
25. Philip Johnson, personal conversations with author. Johnson frequently spoke of Mies's ambivalent attitude toward Lilly Reich. On the one hand, he was completely dependent on her and within the context of his uncommunicative nature, grateful for her commitment to him. Yet, fiercely independent, he resented needing her as much as he did and considered the periods spent beyond her reach, moments of triumph.
26. Philip Johnson, Georgia van der Rohe, Herbert Hirche, and Maude Grote, personal conversations with author. These individuals have all made clear Lilly Reich's sternly self-disciplined nature. This quality, along with her attitude of self-denial, pervades her letters to Maude Grote, who was kind enough to share them with the author. In a letter to Mrs. Grote on 19 February 1938, with Mies in America, Reich admits to being "a little sad," but adds that she is "very happy" for him. Depressed over the lack of work, she hastens to admonish herself for admitting this. "I shouldn't even write that." In September 1945, with her life (and city) in shambles and going through a difficult series of radiation treatments for cancer, she speaks of getting "back to work and a somewhat normal life." Although she has lost almost everything, she is grateful for being alive and refuses to lose "faith." "[W]hen it's possible to work again, we will forget all the bad." (Personal files, Maude Grote).
27. Herbert Hirche, personal conversation with author, 30 July 1974.
28. Goebbels, quoted in *Newsweek*, 4 April 1936, 18.
29. Göring, quoted in *The New York Times*, 13 March 1936, 11.
30. Hitler, quoted in Speer, *Inside*, 73.
31. Architects involved at various moments in projects associated with the renewal of Berlin included the Luckhardt brothers, Hugo Häring, Martin Wagner, Hans Poelzig, Hans Scharoun, Emil Fahrenkamp, and Peter Behrens, among others.
32. Jochen Thies, *Architekt der Weltherrschaft: Die "Endziele" Hitlers* (Düsseldorf: Droste Verlag, 1976), 87. For more information on Hitler's involvement in the redevelopment plans of Berlin, see Jost Dülffer, Jochen Thies and Josef Henke, *Hitlers Städte: Baupolitik im Dritten Reich* (Köln, Wien: Böhlan Verlag, 1978).
33. Ibid.
34. Excerpts of Hitler's comments on his plans for Berlin are taken from Picker, *Table Talk*, 195; Picker, *Secret Conversations*, 67–68; Hitler's Speech, 2 August 1938, quoted in Speer, *Inside*, 138.

35. Hitler, quoted in Speer, *Inside*, 73.
36. Speer, *Inside*, 76.
37. Hitler, quoted in Ibid.
38. Lars Olof Larsson, *Albert Speer: Le Plan de Berlin, 1937–1943*, trans. Beatrice Loyer (Brussels: Aux Archives d'Architecture Moderne, 1978), 38.
39. Mies, wire to John Holabird, 20 April 1936. *"Dank für Brief. Bin interessiert. Brief folgt."* Library of Congress.

CHAPTER 16–THE OLYMPIC SPIRIT

1. Mies's frequent use of this excuse appears to indicate that he found it a convenient explanation for his chronically dilatory responses.
2. Mies, letter to John A. Holabird, Sr., 20 May 1936, Library of Congress.
3. See Chapter 3, p. 58.
4. "Reichsausstellung der Deutsche Textil-und Bekleidungswirtschaft" (National Exhibition of German Textile and Clothing Manufacturers).
5. Willard E. Hotchkiss, letter to Mies, 12 May 1936, Mies Archive.
6. Mies, letter to Willard E. Hotchkiss, undated, Mies Archive.
7. Margaret Scolari Barr, " 'Our Campaigns,' Alfred H. Barr, Jr., and the Museum of Modern Art: A Biographical Chronicle of the Years 1930–1944," *The New Criterion* (Summer 1987): 47.
8. Henry-Russell Hitchcock, personal conversation with author, 22 April 1975; see also comments by Barr, in "Four Great Makers," 93.
9. Margaret S. Barr, " 'Our Campaigns,' " *The New Criterion:* 47.
10. Mies, letter to Alfred H. Barr, Jr., 14 July 1936, Mies Archive.
11. Russell Lynes, *Good Old Modern: An Intimate Portrait of the Museum of Modern Art* (New York: Atheneum, 1973), 190.
12. Alfred H. Barr, Jr., letter to Abby Aldrich Rockefeller, quoted by Hilton Kramer, "MOMA reopened; the Museum of Modern Art in the Postmodern Era," *The New Criterion*, Special Issue (Summer 1984): 8.
13. Margaret S. Barr, " 'Our Campaigns,' " *The New Criterion:* 46.
14. Lynes, *Good Old Modern*, 190.
15. The critic Hilton Kramer described Goodwin as being "about as far from . . . a modernist as an architect could be in 1936," see Kramer, "MOMA reopened," *The New Criterion:* 8.
16. The Mandel House in Mount Kisco, New York.
17. Alfred H. Barr, Jr., letter to Mies, 19 July 1936, Library of Congress.
18. Georgia van der Rohe, personal conversation with author, 10 May 1973.
19. "Mies van der Rohe," film, see Chap. 2, n.7.
20. Verseidag officials, meeting and discussion with author, 26 July 1974.
21. Jerrold Loebl, letter to author, 14 October 1973.
22. Albert Speer, personal conversation with author, 9 August 1973.
23. Speer, *Inside*, 79.
24. Larsson, *Albert Speer*, 38.
25. Ibid.
26. According to Speer, while Lippert had difficulty in working up "any

enthusiasm for Hitler's architectural ideas," the issue—at this date—seemed to focus on the dimension of the grand avenue. Lippert would not agree to anything larger than 100 yards in width; Hitler insisted upon 130 yards. See Speer, *Inside*, 73.

27. Hitler, quoted in Speer, *Inside*, 74.
28. Larsson, *Albert Speer*, 39.
29. Albert Speer, letter to author, 9 November 1973.
30. Hans Weidemann, letter to author, 12 April 1975.
31. Georgia van der Rohe, personal conversation with author, 10 May 1973.
32. Mies, "Only the Patient Counts," *Modern Hospital* 64:65.
33. *The New York Times*, 1 August 1936, 6.
34. An architect and former professor of the history of architecture at Columbia University and subsequently head of Columbia's School of Architecture, Hudnut had just recently assumed his Harvard post.
35. Egon Hüttmann, letter to author, 8 November 1978.
36. Mies, address given on 30 September 1966 on the occasion of his receiving the Golden Medal from the Bund Deutsche Architektur, Library of Congress.
37. Dearstyne, *Inside*, 252.
38. Arthur Drexler, *Ludwig Mies van der Rohe* (New York: George Braziller 1960), 21.
39. What these critics seem to overlook is the fact that Mies's commitment to order was never perceived by him as an end in itself, as being anything more than "a means of achieving the successful relationship of the parts to each other and to the whole." Like them, Mies deplored the "overemphasis on the [idealistic principles of order that] satisfies neither our interest in simple reality nor our practical sense." See Mies's Inaugural address as Director of Architecture at Armour, quoted in Blaser, *After Mies*, 30.
40. Joseph Hudnut, letter to Mies, 21 July 1936, Mies Archive.
41. According to Mrs. Barr, Oud, not wanting to leave Holland, had "politely" turned down both the museum building and the Harvard position, see Margaret S. Barr, " 'Our Campaign,' " *New Criterion*: 47.
42. Herbert Hirche, personal conversation with author, 10 August 1973.
43. Mies, letter to Willard E. Hotchkiss, 2 September 1936, Library of Congress.
44. Willard E. Hotchkiss, letter to Mies, 21 September 1936, Library of Congress.
45. Joseph Hudnut, letter to Mies, 3 September 1936, Mies Archive.
46. Mies, as quoted by John Rodgers, personal conversation with author, 23 May 1974.
47. Mies, letter to Joseph Hudnut, 15 September 1936, Mies Archive.
48. Joseph Hudnut, letter to Mies, 26 October 1936, Mies Archive.
49. Michael van Beuren, letter to Mies, undated, Library of Congress.
50. Herbert Hirche, personal conversation with author, 10 August 1973.
51. Ibid.

52. Hitler, quoted in *Mitteilungsblatt der Reichskammer der bildenden Künste* 1: Berlin (1 November 1936).

53. Lackner, *Max Beckmann*, 23.

54. Cauman, *Living Museum*, 121.

55. Otto Andreas-Schreiber, letter to author, 10 January 1975.

56. Ibid.

57. The legislation that he is probably referring to is the Verordnung über Baugestaltung that was passed by the Reich Cultural Chamber on 19 November 1936. Without defining "proper architectural views," it passed on to the local building boards the broadest possible restrictive powers, see Miller Lane, *Architecture and Politics*, 193.

58. Michael van Beuren, letter to Mies, 6 November 1936, Library of Congress.

59. Joseph Hudnut, letter to Mies, 16 November 1936, quoted in Schulze, *Mies*, 208.

60. Mies, Inaugural speech, Armour Institute, 1938, quoted in Johnson, *Mies van der Rohe*, 190; and Blaser, *After Mies*, 30.

61. Henry-Russell Hitchcock, personal conversation with author, 22 April 1975.

62. Alfred Barr, in "Four Great Makers," 93.

63. Jeffrey Herf, *Reactionary Modernism: Technology, Culture and Politics in Weimar and the Third Reich* (Cambridge: Cambridge University Press, 1984, 1st paperback ed. 1986), 201.

64. William Woodside, "Germany's Hidden Crisis," *Harper's Monthly Magazine* (February 1937), 325.

65. Göring, quoted in Shirer, *The Rise and Fall*, 412.

66. Albert Speer, personal conversation with author, 24 July 1978. The author is indebted to Speer for his thoughts on Göring's possible motives for this action.

CHAPTER 17–A KIND OF SUICIDE

1. Herbert Hirche, personal conversation with author, 10 August 1973.

2. Georgia van der Rohe, personal conversation with author, 10 May 1973.

3. Herbert Hirche, personal conversation with author, 10 August 1973.

4. Philip Johnson, personal conversation with author, 7 March 1973.

5. Kathleen Weil-Garris Brandt, letter to author, 6 February 1973. Professor Weil-Garris Brandt claims that while the nature of Michelangelo's spirituality and religion appeared to change as he grew older—he came to feel that his earlier devotion to art might actually have stood in the way of genuine piety—he was certainly no "atheist." She also claims that Michelangelo's occasional anticlerical remarks were made in the name of authentic piety.

6. Johnson, *Architecture Plus* 1:69.

7. Herbert Hirche, personal conversation with author, 30 July 1974.

8. Egon Hüttmann, letter to author, 25 May 1973.

9. Maude Grote, personal conversation with author, 1 August 1974.

10. Egon Hüttmann, letter to author, 25 May 1973. The nature of this "incriminating evidence" was never made known. The criminal charges against Mies, stemming from Hesse's indictment in Dessau, had been dropped in 1935. However, as a leader of a movement labeled "cultural bolshevist" by the Nazis, and also as a former director of the Bauhaus and the creator of the Liebknecht-Luxemburg monument, Mies was highly vulnerable to Nazi attack. Lilly Reich was always concerned about this, although Mies could never think of himself as anything other than the committed apolitical artist.

11. Albert Speer, personal conversation with author, 24 July 1978.

12. Ibid.

13. Herbert Hirche, personal conversation with author, 30 July 1974.

14. Ibid.

15. Herbert Hirche, personal conversation with author, 10 August 1973.

16. Herbert Hirche (30 July 1974) and Maude Grote (1 August 1974), personal conversations with author. See also photographs in the *Monatsheft für Baukunst und Stadtbau*, 21 (1937): 195–196; and account of the opening of the Textile Exhibition, *Berliner Tageblatt*, 23 March 1937, 3. In view of the humiliation that the government had perpetrated on Mies, its most renowned architect, Göring's assertion that "[n]othing is impossible for the German people to accomplish" seems particularly ironical.

17. Georgia van der Rohe, personal conversation with author, 10 May 1973.

18. The exact date of Mies's departure remains unknown. However, Maude Grote's assertion, confirmed by Herbert Hirche, that the removal of Mies from the Textile Exhibition took place approximately eight weeks before its opening on 24 March, would place the date as approximately the end of January. Allowing for the two weeks to revise the plans, the date moves up to mid-February, if—in fact—Mies left immediately after this. According to Grote, Mies had already left by 24 March, the date of the opening.

19. Dearstyne, letter, *Journal of the Society of Architectural Historians* 24:254.

20. Arthur Drexler, comments made at symposium held in honor of the Mies Centennial, The Museum of Modern Art, 25 February 1986.

21. Philip Johnson, Ibid.

22. Speer, *Inside*, 76.

23. Speer, *Inside*, 133.

24. Miller Lane, *Architecture and Politics*, 213.

25. Hitler, *Mein Kampf*, 370.

26. Shirer, *The Rise and Fall*, 418.

27. Shirer, *The Rise and Fall*, 416.

28. Eberhard Hanfstaengl, quoted in Lackner, *Max Beckmann*, 26.

29. Schlemmer, *Oskar Schlemmer*, 368.

30. Cauman, *Living Museum*, 121.

31. Hermann Göring, Directive to Minister of Culture Rust, 1 July 1937, Archiv, Akademie der Künste.

32. Bruno Taut, Eric Mendelsohn, Hugo Häring, and the Dutch architect J. J. P. Oud were some of Fischer's students.
33. Alexander Amersdorffer, letter to nine members requesting resignation, 8 July 1937, Archiv, Akademie der Künste.
34. Adolf Wagner, quoted in *The New York Times*, 17 July 1937, 7.
35. Hitler, address, Opening of the House of German Art, 18 July 1937, *Völkischer Beobachter*, 19 July 1937.
36. Miller Lane, *Architecture and Politics*, 268.
37. Goebbels, quoted in *The New York Times*, 19 July 1937.
38. "V," "The Destruction of Capitalism in Germany," *Foreign Affairs*, 15:4 (July 1937): 595–607.
39. Ernst Ludwig Kirchner, quoted in Grunfeld, *Prophets*, 251.
40. Bruno Paul, quoted in Brenner, "Ende," *Vierteljahrshefte* 24:48.
41. Ernst Barlach, quoted in Grunfeld, *Hitler File*, 253.
42. Emil Nolde, letter to Joseph Goebbels, 2 July 1938, quoted in Miesel, *Voices*, 209.
43. Stanley Resor, Jr., letter to author, 27 July 1973.
44. Alexander Amersdorffer, Memorandum to Mies, 13 July 1937, Archiv, Akademie der Künste.
45. Philip Johnson, personal conversation with author, 6 April 1978.
46. Albert Speer, personal conversation with author, 24 July 1978.
47. Mies, letter to president, Prussian Academy of Arts, 19 July 1937, Archiv, Akademie der Künste.
48. Schulze, *Mies*, 217.
49. Herbert Hirche, personal conversation with author, 30 July 1974.
50. Georgia van der Rohe, personal conversation with author, 10 May 1973.
51. Waldtraut van der Rohe, letter to Mies, 16 August 1946, Library of Congress.
52. Georgia van der Rohe, personal conversation with author, 10 May 1973.
53. Philip Johnson, personal conversation with author, 6 April 1978.
54. Lilly Reich, letter to Mies, 12 June 1940, Library of Congress.
55. Lilly Reich, letter to Maude Grote, 9 September 1939, Grote files.
56. Schulze, *Mies*, 319.
57. Mies, quoted in Schulze, *Mies*, 313–14.

AFTERWORD

1. Gregor Piatigorsky, letter to the editor, *The New York Times*, 19 September 1976.
2. The peculiar similarities that exist between the elitism of the group and that of the individual—their mutual lack of a sense of reality, their disclaiming of this world, and preference toward focusing their aspirations on some future world that exists only in their minds—has long been noted. See Hannah Arendt, *The Origins of Totalitarianism* (New York: Meridian, 11th printing 1971), 335.

3. Mies, "Architecture and the Times," *Der Querschnitt* (bibl. 3) (1924), quoted in Johnson, *Mies van der Rohe*, 186.
4. Goebbels, quoted by Sibyl Moholy-Nagy, Letters, *Journal of the Society of Architectural Historians*, 24 (October 1965): 256.

SELECT
BIBLIOGRAPHY

This bibliography is by no means intended to be complete. It lists those writings that I have found useful in the course of this study, as well as those that I believe contain particular insight into their subject matter or may prove useful to readers in search of further information. While primary source material and contemporary accounts—here indicated with an asterisk—are normally preferred in historical studies, they must be approached with special wariness in research into the period of the Third Reich. Most contemporary accounts are highly biased, due to the extreme sentiments the regime tended to evoke in observers. The prodigious abundance of propaganda, the rigorous censorship, and the understandable reluctance of most Germans to express themselves without restraint further compound the difficulties. Later reminiscences of this period by its survivors are equally untrustworthy. After fifteen years of research into this period, I have come to the unhappy conclusion that its full dimensions will probably accompany its participants to their graves. With regard to those associates, friends, and students of Mies who knew him during those years, nearly all seemed reluctant to speak of him in anything other than the most heroic terms. Respect for his genius was universal; gratitude for being allowed to share in it inhibited nonpartisan dialogue. With regard to Mies, Philip Johnson's account remains unrivaled for its perspicacious insight and clarity of expression, despite being the first major study, written over forty years ago. (Its inaccurate chronology was revised in its later edition.) Franz Schulze's study offers the most

353

definitive biographical overview of Mies's entire career. Discussion of the events and personalities of the Third Reich leans heavily on Albert Speer's meticulous and detailed personal review.

*Adams, George. "Memories of a Bauhaus Student." *Architectural Review* 144, no. 859 (September 1968): 192–94.

Aquinas, Thomas. *The Pocket Aquinas: Selections from the Writings of St. Thomas.* Edited by Vernon J. Bourke. New York: Washington Square Press, 1969.

————.*Summa Theologiae.* Edited by Thomas Gilby. Garden City, N.Y.: Image, 1969.

Arendt, Hannah. *Men in Dark Times.* New York: Harcourt, Brace & World, 1968.

————. *The Origins of Totalitarianism.* New York: Meridian, 1971. Originally published in 1951.

————. "Home to Roost: A Bicentennial Address." *The New York Review of Books* 22, no. 11 (26 June 1975).

*Arnoux, Alexandre. "Tales from Two Cities: I. Berlin 1935." *Living Age* 348 (May 1935): 245–50.

Aronson, Shlomo. *Reinhard Heydrich und die Frühgeschichte von Gestapo und SD.* Stuttgart: Deutsche Verlags-Anstalt, 1971.

Banham, Reyner. *Theory and Design in the First Machine Age.* New York: Praeger, 1960.

Banuls, André. *Heinrich Mann: Le poète et la politique.* Paris: Librairie C. Klincksieck, 1966.

————. *Thomas Mann und sein Bruder Heinrich: Eine repräsentative Gegensätzlichkeit.* Stuttgart: W. Kohlhammer Verlag, 1968.

*Barr, Alfred H., Jr. "Art in the Third Reich-Preview, 1933." *The Magazine of Art* (October 1945): 211–30.

*Barr, Margaret Scolari. " 'Our Campaigns,' Alfred H. Barr, Jr., and the Museum of Modern Art: A Biographical Chronicle of the Years 1930–1944." *The New Criterion,* Special Issue (Summer 1987): 23–74.

Barraclough, Geoffrey. "What Albert Speer Didn't Say." *The New York Review of Books* 15, no. 12 (7 January 1971).

Barzun, Jacques. *Classic, Romantic, and Modern.* Chicago: University of Chicago Press, 2nd ed., rev. Originally published as *Romanticism and the Modern Ego,* 1943.

————. "Art in the Third Reich." *Magazine of Art* (October 1945): 211.

Bauhaus: 1919–1969. Catalog of the exhibition at the Musée National d'art moderne, Musée d'art moderne de la ville de Paris. 2 April–22 June 1969.

*Bauhaus-Archiv. *Bauhaus Berlin: Auflösung Dessau 1932, Schliessung Berlin 1933, Bauhäusler und Drittes Reich.* Berlin: Kunstverlag Weingarten, 1985.

Bauten der Arbeit und des Verkehrs aus Deutscher Gegenwart. Die Blauen

Bücher. Königstein im Taunus/Leipzig: Karl Robert Langewiesche Verlag, 1929.

*Baynes, Norman H. *The Speeches of Adolf Hitler, April 1922–August 1939*, 2 vols. London: Oxford University Press, 1942.

*Berger, Klaus, comp. *Exiles en France: Souvenirs d'antifascistes allemands émigrés, 1933–45*. Paris: François Maspero, 1982.

Blake, Peter *The Master Builders*. New York: Alfred A. Knopf, 1960.

———. *Mies van der Rohe, Architecture and Structure*. Baltimore: Penguin, 1960. Reprint 1966, 1968.

Blaser, Werner. *Mies van der Rohe: The Art of Structure*. New York: Praeger, 1965.

Bletter, Rosemarie Haag. "Paul Scheerbart's Architectural Fantasies." *Journal of the Society of Architectural Historians* 34, no. 2 (May 1975): 83–97.

———. "The Interpretation of the Glass Dream; Expressionist Architecture and the History of the Crystal Metaphor." *Journal of the Society of Architectural Historians* 40, no. 1 (March 1981): 20–43.

Böll, Heinrich. "Hymn to a New Homeland." *Saturday Review* 209 (3 May 1975): 12–15.

Brenner, Hildegard. *Die Kunstpolitik des Nationalsozialismus*. Reinbek bei Hamburg: Rowohlt Taschenbuch Verlag, 1963.

———. "Ende einer Bürgerlichen Kunst-Institution: Die politische Formierung der Preussischen Akademie der Künste ab 1933." *Der Vierteljahrshefte für Zeitgeschichte*, Schriftenreihe 24. Stuttgart: Deutsche Verlags-Anstalt, 1972.

———. "Art in the Political Power Struggle of 1933 and 1934." In *Republic to Reich: The Making of the Nazi Revolution*, Edited by Hajo Holborn, 395–434. New York: Pantheon, 1972.

Burckhardt, Jakob. *Force and Freedom: Reflections in History*. Edited by James Hastings Nichols. New York: Pantheon, 1943.

Bürgin, Hans and Hans-Otto Mayer. *Thomas Mann: A Chronicle of His Life*. Translated by Eugene Dobson. Alabama: University of Alabama Press, 1969. Originally published as *Thomas Mann: Eine Chronik seines Lebens* (1965).

Cadbury-Brown, H. T. "Ludwig Mies van der Rohe: An Address of Appreciation." *Architectural Association Journal* 75 (July–August 1959): 26–46.

Campbell, Joan. *The German Werkbund: The Politics of Reform in the Applied Arts*. Princeton: Princeton University Press, 1978.

Carter, Peter. "Mies van der Rohe." *Architectural Design* 31 (March 1961): 95–121.

*Cash, J. A. "Germany Today." *The Contemporary Review* 151, no. 854 (February 1937): 171–78.

Cauman, Samuel. *The Living Museum; Experiences of an Art Historian and Museum Director—Alexander Dorner*. New York: New York University Press, 1958.

*Causton, Bernard. "Art in Germany Under the Nazis." *The London Studio* 12, no. 68 (November 1936): 235–46.

Cecil, Robert. *The Myth of the Master Race: Alfred Rosenberg and Nazi Ideology.* London: B. T. Batsford, 1972.

Ciani, Plinio. *Graffiti del Ventennio: Guida al curioso, al comico, all'aneddotico nell'architettura e nell'arte mussoliniane.* Milan: Sugar Edizione, 1975.

Clark, Ronald W. *Einstein: The Life and Times.* New York: Avon, 1971.

Conrads, Ulrich and Hans. G. Sperlich. *The Architecture of Fantasy: Utopian Building and Planning in Modern Times.* New York: Praeger, 1962.

*———, ed. *Programs and Manifestoes on 20th-century Architecture.* Cambridge, MA.: MIT Press, 1970.

Cook, John W. and Heinrich Klotz. *Conversations with Architects.* New York: Praeger, 1973.

———. "A Conversation with Philip Johnson." *Architecture Plus* 1, no. 8 (September 1973). A slightly abbreviated version of *Conversations with Architects*: 62–81.

Craig, Gordon A. *The Germans.* New York: G. P. Putnam's Sons, 1982.

Dahrendorf, Ralf. *Society and Democracy in Germany.* Garden City, N.Y.: Doubleday/Anchor, 1969. Originally published in 1967.

Dearstyne, Howard. Reply (to Sibyl Moholy-Nagy, "The Diaspora," *Journal of the Society of Architectural Historians* 24, no. 1 [March 1965]: 24–26) and rejoinder (by Sibyl Moholy-Nagy), *Journal of the Society of Architectural Historians* 24, no. 3 (October 1965): 254–57.

———, *Inside the Bauhaus.* Edited by David Spaeth. New York: Rizzoli, 1986.

Delarue, Jacques. *Geschichte der Gestapo.* Düsseldorf: Droste Verlag, 1964.

1. Deutsche Architektur-und Kunsthandwerkaustellung im Haus der Deutschen Kunst zu München. Catalog of the exhibition at the House of German Art in Munich from 22 January to 18 April 1938. Munich: Verlag Knorr & Hirth, 1938.

*Domarus, Max. *Hitler: Reden und Proklamationen 1932–1945, kommentiert von einem deutschen Zeitgenossen,* 2 vols., Würzburg: Verlagsdruckerei Schmidt, Neustadt a.d. Aisch, 1962–63.

Drexler, Arthur. *Ludwig Mies van der Rohe.* New York: George Braziller, 1960.

Dülffer, Jost, Jochen Thies, and Josef Henke. *Hitlers Städte: Baupolitik im Dritten Reich.* Cologne and Vienna: Böhlan Verlag, 1978.

*Edgeworth, Edward. *The Human German.* London: Methuen, 1915.

Egbert, Donald Drew. *Social Radicalism and the Arts: Western Europe.* New York: Alfred A. Knopf, 1970.

Falkenhausen, Susanne von. *Der Zweite Futurismus und die Kunstpolitik des Faschismus in Italien vom 1922–1943.* Frankfurt am Main: Haag und Herchen Verlag, 1979.

Fermi, Laura. *Illustrious Immigrants: The Intellectual Migration from Europe, 1930–41.* Chicago: University of Chicago Press, 1968.

Fest, Joachim C. *Hitler.* Translated by Richard and Clara Winston. New York: Harcourt Brace Jovanovich, 1974. Originally published in 1973.

*Flanner, Janet. *Janet Flanner's World: Uncollected Writings, 1932–1975.* Edited by Irving Drutman. New York: Harcourt Brace Jovanovich, 1979.

Fosso, Mario and Enrico Mantero. *Guiseppe Terragni 1904–1943.* Como: Tipografia Editrice Cesare Nani, 1982.

"Four Great Makers of Modern Architecture: Gropius, Le Corbusier, Mies van der Rohe, Wright." New York: Columbia University, 1963. The verbatim record of a symposium held at the School of Architecture, Columbia University, New York City from March to May 1961. Reprint, 1970.

Franciscono, Marcel. *Walter Gropius and the Creation of the Bauhaus in Weimar: The Ideals and Artistic Theories of Its Founding Years.* Chicago: University of Chicago Press, 1971.

*Freund, Richard. "Germany Faces the Winter." *The Spectator* 158 (1 January 1937): 7–8.

Friedrich, Otto. *Before the Deluge: A Portrait of Berlin in the 1920's.* New York: Avon Books, 1972.

Fromm, Erich. *The Anatomy of Human Destructiveness.* New York: Holt, Rinehart & Winston, 1973.

Gay, Peter. *Weimar Culture: The Outsider as Insider.* New York: Harper & Row, 1968.

———. *Art and Act.* New York: Harper & Row, 1980. Originally published in 1976.

*German Library of Information. *A Nation Builds: Contemporary German Architecture.* New York: German Library of Information, 1940.

Ghirardo, Diane Yvonne. "Italian Architects and Fascist Politics." *Journal of the Society of Architectural Historians* 39, no. 2 (May 1980): 109–26.

*Gibbs, Philip. *European Journey: Being the Narrative of a Journey in France, Switzerland, Italy, Austria, Hungary, Germany, and the Saar, in the Spring and Summer of 1934 . . .* New York: Doubleday, Doran, 1934.

Gilbert, G. M. *Nuremberg Diary.* New York: Farrar, Straus and Cudahy, 1947. Reprint 1961.

Glaeser, Ludwig. *Ludwig Mies van der Rohe: Drawings in the Collection of the Museum of Modern Art.* New York: The Museum of Modern Art, 1969.

———. *Ludwig Mies van der Rohe: Furniture and Furniture Drawings from the Design Collection and the Mies van der Rohe Archive.* New York: The Museum of Modern Art, 1977.

Grass, Günther. *Cat and Mouse.* New York: New American Library, 1964. Originally published in 1961.

Grimm, Gerhard. *Der Nationalsozialismus: Programm und Verwirklichung.* Munich: G. Olzog, 1981.

Grosser, J. F. G., ed. *Die Grosse Kontroverse: Ein Briefwechsel um Deutschland.* Hamburg: Nagel Verlag, 1963.

Grosshans, Henry. *Hitler and the Artists.* New York: Holmes and Meier, 1983.

Grunfeld, Frederic V. *The Hitler File: A Social History of Germany and the Nazis, 1918–45.* New York: Random House, 1974.

————. *Prophets Without Honour: A Background to Freud, Kafka, Einstein and Their World.* New York: Holt, Rinehart & Winston, 1979.

Gusenberg, Richard M. and Dietmar Meyer. *Die Dreissiger Jahre.* Frankfurt/Main: Verlag Ullstein, 1970.

*Hahn, Lili. *White Flags of Surrender.* Translated by Sibyl Milton. Washington and New York: Robert B. Luce, 1974.

*Hajos, E.M. and I. Zahn. *Berliner Architektur der Nachkriegszeit.* Berlin: Albertus Verlag, 1928.

Hamilton, Nigel. *The Brothers Mann.* New Haven: Yale University Press, 1979. Originally published in 1978.

Hamilton, Richard F. *Adolf Hitler als Maler und Zeichner.* Catalog of oil paintings, watercolors, drawings, and architectural sketches. Zug, 1983.

Hamsher, William. *Albert Speer: Victim of Nuremberg?* London: Leslie Frewin, 1970.

*Harris, H. Wilson. "German Impressions." *The Spectator* 5, no. 525 (18 May 1934): 767–68.

*Hauser, Heinrich. "Casuals of Berlin." *Living Age* 344 (June 1933): 335–44.

Heer, Friedrich. *Charlemagne and His World.* London: Weidenfeld & Nicolson, 1975.

*Heidegger, Martin. "Die Selbstbehauptung der deutschen Universität." Paper read at inaugural address as rector of the University of Freiburg, 27 May 1933. Breslau: Wilh. Gottl. Korn Verlag, 1934.

Heilbut, Anthony. *Exiled in Paradise: German Refugee Artists and Intellectuals in America: From the 1930's to the Present.* New York: The Viking Press, 1983.

Hellman, Lillian. *Pentimento.* Boston: Little Brown, 1973.

Herf, Jeffrey. *Reactionary Modernism: Technology, Culture and Politics in Weimar and the Third Reich.* Cambridge: Cambridge University Press, 1984.

*Hilbersheimer, Ludwig. "Eine Würdigung des Projektes Mies van der Rohe für die Umbauung des Alexanderplatzes." *Das neue Berlin* 2 (February 1929): 39, 41.

————. *Mies van der Rohe.* Chicago: Paul Theobald, 1956.

Hinz, Berthold. *Art in the Third Reich.* Translated by Robert and Rita Kimber. New York: Pantheon, 1979.

*Hitchcock, Henry-Russell. "Architecture Chronicle: Berlin, Paris, 1931." *Hound and Horn* 5, no. 1 (October–December 1931): 94–97.

*————and Philip Johnson. *The International Style.* New York: W. W. Norton, 1932. Reprint 1966.

*————. *Modern Architecture: Romanticism and Reintegration.* New York: Hacker Art Books, 1929. Reprint 1970.

*Hitler, Adolf. *Mein Kampf.* Translated by Ralph Manheim. Boston: Sentry Edition, Houghton Mifflin, 1943. Originally published in 1925.

*————. *Hitler's Secret Conversations, 1941–1944.* Translated by Norman Cameron and R. H. Stevens. Foreword by H. R. Trevor-Roper on "The Mind of Adolf Hitler." New York: Farrar, Straus and Young, 1953.

Hochman, Elaine S. "Confrontation: 1933—Mies van der Rohe and the Third Reich." *Oppositions* 18 (Fall 1979): 49–59.

———. "The Politics of Mies van der Rohe." *Sites* 15 (1986): 44–49.

Holborn, Hajo. "German Idealism in the Light of Social History." In *Germany and Europe: Historical Essays.* Garden City, N.Y.: Doubleday, 1970.

———, ed. *Republic to Reich: The Making of the Nazi Revolution.* Translated by Ralph Manheim. New York: Pantheon, 1972.

Honey, Sandra. "Mies at the Bauhaus." *Architectural Association Quarterly* 10, no. 1 (1978): 52–59.

———, Adrian Gale, and James Gowan. "Mies van der Rohe: European Works," *Architectural Monographs* 2. London and New York: Academy Editions/ St. Martin's Press, 1986.

*Hürlimann, Martin, ed. *Deutschland: Landschaft und Baukunst.* Preface by Ricarda Huch. Berlin: Atlantis Verlag, 1934.

*Isherwood, Christopher. *The Berlin Stories.* New York: New Directions, 1935.

Jaffé, H. L. C. *De Stijl: 1917–1931. The Dutch Contribution to Modern Art.* Amsterdam: J. M. Meulenhoff, 1956.

Janik, Allan and Stephen Toulmin. *Wittgenstein's Vienna.* New York: Touchstone/Simon & Schuster, 1973.

Jencks, Charles. *Modern Movements in Architecture.* Garden City, N.Y.: Anchor Books/Doubleday, 1973.

*Johnson, Philip. "Architecture in the Third Reich." *Hound and Horn* 7, no. 1 (October–December 1933): 137–39.

*———. *Mies van der Rohe.* New York: The Museum of Modern Art, 1947. Reprint 1978.

Johnston, William M. *The Austrian Mind: An Intellectual and Social History 1848–1938.* Berkeley: University of California Press, 1972.

Kaiser, Kenneth. "From Typisierung to 'Tableau Vision' in German Political Architecture." Paper presented at symposium, Art and Architecture in Service of Politics, 8–9 December 1972, at Massachusetts Institute of Technology, Cambridge, MA.

*Kessler, Count Harry. *The Diaries of a Cosmopolitan, 1918–1937.* Edited and translated by Charles Kessler. London: Weidenfeld & Nicolson, 1971.

Kohn, Hans. *The Mind of Germany: The Education of a Nation.* New York: Harper Torchbooks/Academy Library/Harper & Row, 1960.

*Kubizek, August. *Young Hitler: The Story of Our Friendship.* Translated by E. V. Anderson. London: Allan Wingate, 1954. Originally published as *Adolf Hitler, mein Jugendfreund* (1953).

*Lackner, Stephan. *Max Beckmann: Memories of a Friendship.* Coral Gables: University of Miami Press, 1969. Originally published as *Ich erinnere gut an Max Beckmann* (1967).

Lang, Lothar. *Das Bauhaus 1919–1933: Idee und Wirklichkeit.* Berlin: Zentralinstitut für Formgestaltung, 1965.

Larsson, Lars Olof. *Albert Speer: Le Plan de Berlin, 1937–1943.* Translated by Beatrice Loyer. Brussels: Aux Archives d'Architecture Moderne, 1978.

Lehmann-Haupt, Hellmut. *Art Under a Dictatorship.* New York: Oxford University Press, 1954.

*Lindner, Werner. *Bauten der Technik: Ihre Form und Wirklung.* Berlin: Ernst Wasmuth Verlag, 1927.

Linn, Rolf. N. *Heinrich Mann.* New York: Twayne, 1967.

L'Oeuvre de Mies van der Rohe. Presented by Alexandre Persitz in collaboration with Danielle Valeix. Boulogne/Seine: Editions de L'Architecture d'Aujourd-Hui, 1958.

Lynes, Russell. *Good Old Modern: An Intimate Portrait of the Museum of Modern Art.* New York: Atheneum, 1973.

*Maier-Hartmann, Fritz. *Die Bauten der NSDAP in der Hauptstadt der Bewegnung.* Munich: Zentralverlag der NSDAP, Franz Eher Nachf.

Manchester, William. *The Arms of Krupp: 1587–1968.* New York: Bantam, 1970.

Mann, Thomas. *Buddenbrooks.* Berlin: S. Fischer Verlag, 1901. Reprint, 1961.

*———. *An Exchange of Letters.* Translated by H. T. Lowe-Porter. New York: Alfred A. Knopf, 1937.

*———. "That Man Is My Brother." *Esquire* 11, no. 3. (March 1939).

*———. "Germany and the Germans." An address presented at the Library of Congress, Washington, D.C., on 6 June 1945.

*———. *Thomas Mann: Diaries, 1918–1939.* Edited by Hermann Kesten. Translated by Richard and Clara Winston. New York: Harry N. Abrams, 1982.

Maser, Werner. *Hitler: Legend, Myth and Reality.* Translated by Peter and Betty Ross. New York: Harper & Row, 1973.

May, Arthur J. *Vienna in the Age of Franz Josef.* Norman: University of Oklahoma Press, 1966.

*Mencken, H. L., George Jean Nathan, and Willard Huntington Wright. *Europe after 8:15.* New York: John Lane, 1914.

*Mendelsohn, Eric. *Eric Mendelsohn: Letters of an Architect.* Edited by Oskar Beyer. Translated by Geoffrey Strachan. London, New York and Toronto: Abelard-Schumann, 1967. Originally published as *Briefes eines Architekten* (1961).

Merleau-Ponty, Maurice. *Sense and Non-Sense.* Translated by Hubert Dreyfus and Patricia Allen Dreyfus. Northwestern University Press, 1964. Originally published in 1948.

*"Mies in Berlin." Phonograph record of October 1964 interview of Mies by Horst Eifler and Ulrich Conrads, recorded by RIAS, Berlin. Bauwelt Archiv. Berlin. 1966.

Mies Reconsidered: His Career, Legacy, and Disciples. Catalog of exhibition at the Art Institute of Chicago. Chicago: The Art Institute of Chicago in association with Rizzoli, 1986.

*"Mies Speaks." Translated Transcription. *Architectural Review* 144, no. 862 (December 1968): 451–52.

"Mies van der Rohe." *Arts and Architecture* 72 (April 1955): 16–18.

Mies van der Rohe. Catalog of exhibition at the Art Institute of Chicago. Chicago, 1968.

* "Mies van der Rohe: The End of the Bauhaus." North Carolina State University College of Agriculture and Engineering School of Design *Student Publication 3*, no. 3 (Spring 1953): 16–18.

* Miesel, Victor H., ed. *Voices of German Expressionism*. Englewood Cliffs, N.J.: Prentice-Hall, 1970.

Miller Lane, Barbara. *Architecture and Politics in Germany, 1918–1945*. Cambridge, MA.: Harvard University Press, 1968.

Millon, Henry A. "Some New Towns in Italy in the 1930's." In *Arts and Architecture in the Service of Politics*, Edited by Henry A. Millon and Linda Nochlin, 326–341. Cambridge, MA.: MIT Press, 1978.

"Modern Architecture Symposium 1964: The Decade 1929–1939." *Journal of the Society of Architectural Historians* 24, no. 1 (March 1965): 24–93.

* *Moderne Architekturen: Ausgeführte Wohn-und Geschäftshäuser, Villen, Einfamilienhäuser* . . . Stuttgart: Architektur-Verlag Wilh. Kick, 1905.

* Moeller van der Bruck, Arthur. *Der Preussische Stil*. Munich: R. Piper & Co., Verlag, 1922.

* ———. *Germany's Third Empire*. Translated by E. O. Lorimer. London: George Allen & Unwin, 1934. Originally published as *Das Dritte Reich* (1923).

Mosse, George L. *The Crisis of German Ideology: Intellectual Origins of the Third Reich*. New York: Grosset & Dunlap, 1964.

———. *Germans and Jews*. New York: The Universal Library, Grosset & Dunlop, 1970.

* Müller-Wulkow, Walter. *Architektur der Zwanziger Jahre in Deutschland*. Konigstein im Taunus: Karl Robert Langewiesche Verlag, 1929. Reprint, Freiburg im Breisgau: Druckhaus Rombach & Co., 1975.

Müssener, Helmut. *Exil in Schweden; politische und kulturelle Emigration nach 1933*. Munich: Carl Hanser Verlag, 1974.

* Nelson, George. "Architects of Europe Today: 7—Van der Rohe, Germany." *Pencil Points* 16, no. 9 (September 1935): 453–60.

* *Die Neue Heimat: vom Werden der nationalsozialistischen kulturlandschaft*. Foreword by Fritz Wächtler. Munich: Deutscher Volksverlag, 1940.

* Neumann, Eckhard, ed. *Bauhaus and Bauhaus People: Personal Opinions and Recollections of Former Bauhaus Members and their Contemporaries*. New York: Van Nostrand Reinhold, 1970.

Neumeyer, Fritz. *Mies van der Rohe: Das kunstlose Wort-Gedanken zur Baukunst*. Berlin: Siedler Verlag, 1986.

Orwell, George. "Reflections on Gandhi." In *A Collection of Essays*, pp. 171–180. New York and London: Harcourt Brace Jovanovich, 1946.

Pachter, Henry. "Heidegger and Hitler—The Incompatibility of Geist and Politics." *Boston University Journal* 24, no. 3 (1976): 47–55.

Panofsky, Erwin. *Gothic Architecture and Scholasticism*. New York: Meridian, 1957. Originally published in 1951.

————. *Meaning in the Visual Arts*. New York: Anchor/Doubleday, 1957.

Paret, Peter. "The Enemy Within: Max Liebermann as President of the Prussian Academy of Arts." The Leo Baeck Memorial Lecture No. 28. New York: Leo Baeck Institute, 1984.

Passant, E. J. *A Short History of Germany: 1815–1945*. Cambridge: Cambridge University Press, 1966. Originally published in 1959.

Pehnt, Wolfgang. *Expressionist Architecture*. New York: Praeger, 1973.

*Picker, Henry. *Hitler's Tischgespräche im Führerhauptquartier: 1941–1942*. Stuttgart: Seewald Verlag, 1965.

*————and Heinrich Hoffman. *Hitler Close-up*. Jochen von Lang, comp. Translated by Nicholas Fry. New York: Macmillan, 1973. Originally published as *Hitler's Tischgespräche im Führerhauptquartier 1941–42* (1965).

*Platz, Gustav Adolf. *Die Baukunst der neuesten Zeit*. Berlin: Proplyläen-Verlag, 1930.

Pommer, Richard. "The Flat Roof: A Modernist Controversy in Germany." *Art Journal* 43 (1983): 158–69.

Popper, Karl R. *The Open Society and Its Enemies*. 2 vols. Princeton: Princeton University Press, 1962. Reprint, Princeton Paperback Edition, 1971. Originally published in 1945.

Posener, Julius. "From Schinkel to the Bauhaus." *Architectural Association Paper* 5 (1972).

Raabe, Paul, ed. *The Era of German Expressionism*. Translated by J. M. Ritchie. Woodstock: Overlook Press, 1974.

Rakette, Egon H. *Bauhausfest mit Truxa*. Munich and Berlin: F. A. Herbig Verlagsbuchhandlung, 1973.

*Rittich, Werner. *New German Architecture*. Berlin: Terramare Office, 1941.

*Rosenberg, Alfred. *Memoirs of Alfred Rosenberg*. Edited by Serge Lang and Ernst von Schenck. Translated by Eric Posselt. Chicago: Ziff Davis, 1949.

*————. *Das Politische Tabebuch Alfred Rosenbergs aus den Jahren 1934/35 und 1939/40*. Edited by Hans-Günther Seraphim. Göttingen: Musterschmidt-Verlag, 1956.

Rowe, Colin. *The Mathematics of the Ideal Villa and Other Essays*. Cambridge, MA.: MIT Press, 1976.

*Ruegenberg, Sergius. "Ludwig Mies van der Rohe, 1886–1969." *Deutsche Bauzeitung* 103 (1 September 1969): 660.

Schiavo, Alberto, ed. *Futurismo e Fascismo*. Rome: Giovanni Volpe Editore, 1981.

*Schlemmer, Oskar. *The Letters and Diaries of Oskar Schlemmer*. Edited by Tut Schlemmer. Translated by Krishna Winston. Middletown: Wesleyan University Press, 1972.

*Schmidt, Dieter, ed. *In Letzter Stunde: 1933 bis 1945*. Dresden: VEB Verlag der Kunst, 1964.

*————, ed. *Manifeste, Manifeste 1915–1933*. Dresden: VEB Verlag der Kunst, 1964.

*Schnaidt, Claude. *Hannes Meyer: Buildings, Projects and Writings.* Stuttgart: Verlag Gerd Hatje, 1965.

Schnitzler, Henry. " 'Gay Vienna'—Myth and Reality." *Journal of the History of Ideas* 15, no. 1 (January 1954): 94–118.

Schorske, Carl E. *Fin-de-Siècle Vienna: Politics and Culture.* New York: Vintage/Random House, 1981. Originally published in 1980.

———. *German Social Democracy, 1905–1917: The Development of the Great Schism.* Cambridge, MA.: Harvard Historical Studies, 1955. Reprint, 1983.

Schrader, Bärbel and Jürgen Schebera. *The "Golden" Twenties: Art and Literature in the Weimar Republic.* New Haven and London: Yale University Press, 1988. Originally published in 1987.

Schulz, Klaus Peter, ed. *Kurt Tucholsky in Selbstzeugnissen und Bilddokumenten.* Hamburg: Rowahlts Monographien, 1959.

Schulze, Franz. *Mies van der Rohe: A Critical Biography.* In association with the Mies van der Rohe Archive of the Museum of Modern Art. Chicago: University of Chicago Press, 1985.

*Schultze-Naumburg, Paul. "Rassengebundene Kunst." *Volk und Wissen* 13 (1934). Berlin: Brehm Verlag.

Sell, Friedrich C. *Die Tragödie des deutschen Liberalismus.* Stuttgart: Deutsche Verlags-Anstalt, 1953.

Serenyi, Peter. "Spinoza, Hegel and Mies: The Meaning of the New National Gallery in Berlin." *Journal of the Society of Architectural Historians* 30, no. 3 (19 October 1971): 240.

Sharpe, Dennis, comp. *Sources of Modern Architecture.* New York: George Wittenborn, 1967.

*Shirer, William L. *Berlin Diary: The Journal of a Foreign Correspondent, 1934–1941.* New York: Alfred A. Knopf, 1941.

———. *The Rise and Fall of the Third Reich. A History of Nazi Germany.* Greenwich: Fawcett Crest, 1959.

*Sidgwick, Christopher. *German Journey.* London: Hutchinson, 1936.

*"Six Students Talk with Mies." North Carolina State University College of Agriculture and Engineering School of Design *Student Publication* 2, no. 3 (Spring 1952): 21–28.

Smithson, Allison and Peter Smithson. "Mies van der Rohe." *Architectural Design* 39 (July 1969): 363–66.

Spaeth, David. *Mies van der Rohe.* New York: Rizzoli, 1985.

*"A Special Correspondent." "In Berlin: A Week Later." *The Spectator* 5 (13 July 1934): 44.

*Speer, Albert. "Die Bürde werde ich nicht mehr los." *Der Speigel* 20, no. 46 (7 November 1966): 48–62.

*———. *Inside the Third Reich.* Translated by Richard and Clara Winston. New York: Macmillan, 1970.

*———. *Spandau: The Secret Diaries.* Translated by Richard and Clara Winston. New York: Macmillan, 1976.

Stern, Fritz. *The Politics of Cultural Despair.* Garden City: Doubleday, 1965.

―――. *The Failure of Illiberalism: Essays on the Political Culture of Modern Germany.* New York: Alfred A. Knopf, 1972.

―――. "Einstein's Germany." In *Albert Einstein: Historical and Cultural Perspectives.* Princeton: Princeton University Press, 1982.

―――. "Germany 1933: Fifty Years Later." The Leo Baeck Memorial Lecture No. 27. New York: Leo Baeck Institute, 1983.

―――. *Dreams and Delusions: The Drama of German History.* New York: Alfred A. Knopf, 1987.

Sullivan, Richard E. *Aix-La-Chapelle in the Age of Charlemagne.* Norman: University of Oklahoma Press, 1963.

*Taut, Bruno. *The Crystal Chain Letters: Architectural Fantasies by Bruno Taut and His Circle.* Edited by Ian Boyd Whyte. Cambridge, MA.: MIT Press, 1985.

Taylor, A. J. P. *The Course of German History.* New York: Capricorn, 1946.

Taylor, Joshua C. *Futurism.* Garden City, N.Y.: The Museum of Modern Art/ Doubleday, 1961.

Taylor, Robert R. *The Word in Stone: The Role of Architecture in the National Socialist Ideology.* Berkeley and Los Angeles: University of California Press, 1974.

Tegethoff, Wolf. *Mies van der Rohe: The Villas and Country Houses.* Translated by Russell M. Stockman. New York and Cambridge, MA.: The Museum of Modern Art and MIT Press, 1985. Originally published as *Die Villen und Landhausprojekte von Mies van der Rohe* (1981).

Teut, Anna. *Architektur im Dritten Reich: 1933–1945.* Frankfurt/M: Verlag Ullstein Bauwelt, 1967.

Thies, Jochen. *Architekt der Weltherrschaft: Die 'Endziele' Hitlers.* Düsseldorf: Droste Verlag, 1976.

*Thompson, Dorothy. "Culture Under the Nazis: Aspects of German Life Today." *Foreign Affairs* 14, no. 3 (April 1936): 407–23.

*Troost, Gerdy, comp. *Das Bauen im Neuen Reich.* Bayreuth: vom Gauverlag Bayerische Ostmark, 1938.

*"V." "The Destruction of Capitalism in Germany." *Foreign Affairs* 15, no. 4 (July 1937): 595–607.

Weber, Helmut. *Walter Gropius und das Faguswerk.* Munich: Verlag Georg D. W. Callway, 1961.

Werner, Alfred. "The Fascist Mentality—Emil Nolde." *The Wiener Library Bulletin* 22, no. 2 (Spring 1968).

*Wernert, E. *L'Art dans le IIIe Reich: Une Tentative d'Esthétique Dirigée.* Centre d'Études de Politique Étrangère, Publication no. 7. Paris: P. Hartmann, 1936.

*Westheim, Paul "Mies van der Rohe: Entwicklung eines Architekten." *Das Kunstblatt* 11 (February 1927): 55–62.

*―――. *Helden und Abenteurer: Welt und Leben der Künstler.* Berlin: Verlag Hermann Reckendorf, 1931.

*Whitaker, J. T. "The New Germany." *Political Quarterly* 5 (October 1934): 480–90.

Whitford, Frank. *Bauhaus.* London: Thames and Hudson, 1984.

Whittick, Arnold. *Eric Mendelsohn*. New York: F. W. Dodge, 1956. Originally published in 1940.

Willett, John. *Art and Politics in the Weimar Period: The New Sobriety 1917–1933*. New York. Pantheon, 1978.

*Wingler, Hans M. *The Bauhaus: Weimar, Dessau, Berlin, Chicago*. Edited by Joseph Stein. Translated by Wolfgang Jabs and Basil Gilbert. Cambridge, MA.: MIT Press, 1969.

*Woodside, Willson. "Germany's Hidden Crisis." *Harper's Monthly Magazine* 174 (February 1937): 315–325.

*Wright, Frank Lloyd. "Frank Lloyd Wright Speaks Up." *House Beautiful* 95, no. 7 (July 1953).

*Wulf, Joseph, ed. *Die Bildenden Künste im Dritten Reich: Eine Dokumentation*. Gütersloh: Sigbert Mohn Verlag, 1963.

*Zentralblatt der Bauverwaltung vereinigt mit Zeitschrift für Bauwesen, "Wettbewerb für den Erweiterungsbau der Reichshauptbank in Berlin." *Zentralblatt der Bauverwaltung/Zeitschrift für Bauwesen* 53, no. 33 (2 August 1933).

INDEX

ABOUT THE AUTHOR

ELAINE S. HOCHMAN is a member of the faculty of The New School (History of Art) and the founder of Art Ventures International. She has written articles on Mies van der Rohe and the Third Reich that have appeared in *Oppositions* and *Sites*, and her research for this book has spanned more than a dozen years. She lives in New York City.